NATIONAL GEOGRAPHIC

T R A V E L E R

vienna

NATIONAL GEOGRAPHIC
TRAVELER

vienna

by Sarah Woods

National Geographic
Washington, D.C.

CONTENTS

Pages 2–3: A riverboat waits for passengers on the Donaukanal.
Opposite: A string quintet performing in a baroque palace

TRAVELING WITH EYES OPEN

Alert travelers go with a purpose and leave with a benefit. If you travel responsibly, you can help support wildlife conservation, historic preservation, and cultural enrichment in the places you visit. You can enrich your own travel experience as well.

To be a geo-savvy traveler:

- Recognize that your presence has an impact on the places you visit.

- Spend your time and money in ways that sustain local character. (Besides, it's more interesting that way.)

- Value the destination's natural and cultural heritage.

- Respect the local customs and traditions.

- Express appreciation to local people about things you find interesting and unique to the place: its nature and scenery, music and food, historic villages and buildings.

- Vote with your wallet: Support the people who support the place, patronizing businesses that make an effort to celebrate and protect what's special there. Seek out shops, local restaurants, inns, and tour operators who love their home—who love taking care of it and showing it off. Avoid businesses that detract from the character of the place.

- Enrich yourself, taking home memories and stories to tell, knowing that you have contributed to the preservation and enhancement of the destination.

That is the type of travel now called geotourism, defined as "tourism that sustains or enhances the geographical character of a place—its environment, culture, aesthetics, heritage, and the well-being of its residents." To learn more, visit National Geographic's Center for Sustainable Destinations at *www .nationalgeographic.com/travel/sustainable.*

NATIONAL GEOGRAPHIC TRAVELER

vienna

ABOUT THE AUTHOR

British-born travel writer **Sarah Woods** is a triple-award-winning author
with ten travel titles to her name. She has traveled extensively for almost two
decades, crisscrossing the world in several directions and clocking up more
than 62,000 miles (100,000 km) along the way. As part of her adventures,
Woods has spent extended periods journeying across Europe, during
which time she took the city of Vienna firmly to her heart. She has waltzed
with Austria's leading dance celebrity, cruised the waters of the Donau,
and enjoyed several pounds of Sacher torte. Woods also delved into the
lesser known inner reaches of Vienna's up-and-coming districts to discover
the city's funky, offbeat gems and best kept cultural secrets. A member of the
British Guild of Travel Writers and a Fellow of the Royal Geographic Society,
Woods is a regular on travel TV and radio worldwide. She also contributes
to the *Sunday Times, Independent, La Prensa,* and *Wanderlust,* and provides
high-quality online content for numerous Web-based travel publications.

Charting Your Trip

Vienna is a stately and dignified old city that has managed to resist the constantly rushing urgency of modern urban life. During your time in Vienna you'd be well advised to do as the locals do, and take the city at a gentle waltz rather than a galloping rush. In a city with as much to offer as Vienna, seeing everything is an impossibility, so the important thing is see what you want to see, and see it in style.

Getting Around

As the former center of a large empire, Vienna has excellent road and rail connections to other European cities. It also has one of the finest public transportation systems in Europe (www.wien.info/en/travel-info/to-and-around), with a far-reaching network of railroads (known as the S-Bahn), subways (the U-Bahn), streetcars (strassenbahn, trams), and buses. There are five lines in the U-Bahn system (note: there is no U5), and, with the exception of U6, they all serve the city's old core, the **Innere Stadt,** where most of the main tourist sights can be found. Travel on the public transport system is easy and relatively cheap (see sidebar p. 11). The strassenbahn is useful for reaching the slightly more out-of-the-way destinations, as well as providing an opportunity to see the city—strassenbahn route 1 is a great way to see the grand buildings of the Ringstrasse, the roughly circular road bounding the Innere Stadt.

Beyond the Ringstrasse are the inner suburbs, or vorstädte, which are also easily accessed by public transport. These areas—with plenty of attractions of their own—include Wieden, Neubau, Mariahilf, Josefstadt, Alsergrund, and Leopoldstadt. Visitors are unlikely to catch buses unless they are traveling to one of the attractions in the vororte, or outer suburbs (such as the church **Kirche am Steinhof**), but these are also cheap and surprisingly quick. The quality of the public transport is just as well when you consider how completely unsuited the city's streets are to heavy vehicle traffic. Large areas of the Innere Stadt are pedestrianized, and many more areas require special permits to drive through. The S-Bahn system also provides quick connections to many of the towns and villages around Vienna and beyond.

Coffee, cake, and the morning paper: café culture in Vienna

Visitor Information

The Viennese pride themselves on their efficiency and organization, and most major sites (as well as many minor ones) have detailed visitor information on their websites. For up-to-date listings for what's on in Vienna during your visit, as well as extra information you might need, the best place to look is the city tourist board website (www.wien.info). The tourist board also operates visitor information offices in several major subway stations and near notable landmarks, such as Karlsplatz and Stephansplatz.

If You Have Only a Few Days

Many people come to Vienna for a short stay. If you're going to be in town for only a few days, it's probably best if you restrict yourself mostly to the confines of the Innere Stadt. Here you're never more than a few hundred yards from a museum, gallery, or historic building, and the charming narrow streets are an attraction in themselves.

On **day one** get into the city early and head straight for the Hofburg, the former palace of the Habsburgs that dominates much of the Innere Stadt. It's a bit of a tourist trap, but few people will fail to find something enthralling in the palace's impressive facades and many museums and galleries. Even if you see nothing else of the Hofburg complex, no trip to Vienna is complete without a trip to the Schatzkammer (Treasury) and Spanish Riding School. After a morning looking around the Hofburg, head north, past the Roman ruins in Michaelerplatz, and along the exclusive, boutique-laden streets of the Golden U shopping district. Take the opportunity to do a little window shopping on the Kohlmarkt and fill yourself up with the delicious pastries on offer in the bakeries and confectioners on and around the Graben, one of the city's oldest streets. After lunch, head over to Stephansplatz to admire the masterpiece of medieval architecture that is St. Stephen's Cathedral. If you have time, it's worth touring the catacombs, where generations of Habsburg rulers (well, bits of them, at least) are laid out in a maze of eerie underground chambers. If you've still got the energy, head over to the Staatsoper opera house and join the queue for last-minute standing-room tickets.

Begin **day two** by visiting the Belvedere, Austria's national gallery and one of the city's finest palaces, just south of the Innere Stadt. There's a lot to see at the Belvedere, but it's worth taking the time to really explore the place. Make sure to check out both the upper and lower buildings of the palace—the lower for its historic interiors, and the upper for its world-class art collection. After leaving the Belvedere walk northwest for a few minutes to Karlsplatz, where you can see two of the city's finest architectural landmarks: the baroque Karlskirche and the Jugendstil Secession Building. If you have time, head down

NOT TO BE MISSED:

into the Karlsplatz U-Bahn Station and travel four stops north to Praterstern. From here it is just a short walk to the lush green oasis that is the Prater. You can either take a ride in the iconic Riesenrad (Ferris wheel) in the Prater's amusement park, or just relax in the park with a big wurstsemmel (hot dog) from a nearby würstelstand. In the evening, hungry visitors should head over to the open-air market and restaurants of Leopoldstadt's Karmelitermarkt (catch U-Bahn line U2 to Taborstrasse, one stop west of Praterstern) and fill themselves up with inventive ethnic cuisine.

On **day three,** it's worth making a sustained assault on the city's cavernous museums, many of which lie south of the Ringstrasse near the Hofburg. Head first to the Kunsthistorisches Museum, where the Habsburgs' centuries-old art collection is on display. Here you will see masterpieces by the great artists of the Renaissance, as well as exotic artworks and crafts from all over the world. Those with an interest in early human history will want to head across to the other side of Maria-Theresien-Platz, where the Naturhistorisches Museum houses its stunning collection of prehistoric artifacts. For a slightly more relaxed atmosphere, head to the southern side of

When to Visit

The climate in Vienna is considerably milder than that of the rest of Austria, thanks to its lowland location and sheltered microclimate. Visitors expecting to see picturesque snow-covered roofs in winter are likely to be disappointed, as while it does get very cold, snow is a rarity. The Viennese make up for this lackluster winter weather with an enthusiastic festive tradition that sees the city filled with holiday cheer from late November to Christmas. Some aspects of the city's tourist industry shut down in the winter months, however, so if you're not planning on doing any Christmas shopping it's best to put off your trip until spring. At the height of summer, Vienna can be stiflingly hot, and most of its historic buildings lack air-conditioning. As a result, many of the city's traditional cultural institutions and restaurants close during August so that their staff can flee to the cooler air of the mountains. The best time to visit is late spring and early summer, when the Viennese move their restaurant tables, cultural events, and social lives into the city's outdoor spaces.

Maria-Theresien-Platz, where the baroque facade of the old royal stables conceals the MuseumsQuartier, an innovative development that is equal parts cultural center and artists' colony. The must-see attraction in this area is the Leopold Museum, which is dedicated to the life and work of one of Vienna's most famous sons, the expressionist painter Egon Schiele. After a long day of artistic appreciation, it's a good idea to head around the back of the MuseumsQuartier to the relaxed historic streets of Spittelberg, where you can visit Café Sperl or one of Vienna's other famed coffeehouses and get something good to eat.

For **day four,** your last day in Vienna, it's worth venturing southwest out of the city center to the great summer palace of the Habsburgs at Schönbrunn, which is six stops from Karlsplatz on the U4 line. With its beautiful staterooms, massive formal gardens, and world-class zoo, the Schönbrunn Palace has more than enough to keep you occupied all day.

In the first few months of every year, thousands flock to Vienna for the ball season.

If You Have More Time

If you have more than just a few days in Vienna, it's worth expanding your horizons. In addition to its major museums and galleries, the city supports a constellation of small museums, historic properties, and galleries. For example, you may wish to explore the collections of medieval and Renaissance crafts at the **Dommuseum St. Stephan,** the **Deutschordenhaus,** and the **Schottenstift Museum** in the Innere Stadt.

The most distinctively Viennese of these many small museums are the numerous *musikerwohnungen* (musicians' houses). These are typically apartments that were once inhabited by famous composers. Many of them have been preserved in their historic condition and have their rooms populated with artifacts relating to the composers' life and work. The **Figarohaus** (just off Stephansplatz) is devoted to Mozart, the **Pasqualatihaus** (near the Platz Am Hof) focuses on Beethoven, and the **Johann Strauss Wohnung** explores the life and times of Vienna's Waltz King.

It's also well worth venturing beyond the city limits. To the west, public transportation can take you the 10 miles (16 km) to the hillside forests of the **Wienerwald** (Vienna Woods), a stunning area to explore at any time of year. And in summer there are few more beautiful areas than the Donau Valley, northwest of the city, especially between the towns of **Melk** and **Krems,** each about 50 miles (80 km) from central Vienna. ■

The Vienna Card

For just €18.50, the Vienna Card provides visitors to the city with unlimited access to the U-Bahn, Strassenbahn, and city bus services for 72 hours. Each Vienna Card also entitles a child under the age of 15 to travel with the cardholder for free. In addition, the Vienna Card also entitles the holder to significant ticket price discounts at most of the city's major tourist attractions and cut-price tickets for the airport shuttle.

The Vienna Card can be purchased from hotels citywide, as well as from the visitor information offices at Vienna International Airport, Albertinaplatz, and elsewhere on the U-Bahn.

History &
Culture

A traditional *fiaker* passes the grand entrance of the Hofburg Palace.

Vienna Today

Located at the center of Europe and the heart of modern Austria, Vienna is a vibrant metropolis where the handsome relics of the city's imperial past stand alongside glamorous shopping districts, exciting cultural venues, and offbeat modern architecture.

In the late 19th century, Austrian engineers crafted a great web of railways and roads that radiated out to the farthest corners of the empire. At its heart sat Vienna, the wellspring of imperial power and the final destination of those who wanted to make a mark on the world. In this era Vienna was a fairy-tale city, beautiful and stately while the other capitals of Europe disappeared beneath clouds of industrial smoke. This was the city of couples waltzing through glittering ballrooms, of writers and intellectuals talking among wreaths of cigar smoke in coffeehouses, and of the sensuous elegance of art nouveau.

The 20th century, however, saw the forces of the modern world catch up with Vienna, splitting it from its empire and forcing this waltzing city to stand, stock-still and sidelined, in the uncertain light of a new age. The city was forced to find a new identity and to rebuild its tarnished prestige.

Today, Vienna exists as two cities: One is a busy modern European capital, smaller than most, but growing; the other is the glamorous, candlelit city of the imperial golden age, still alive in the minds of the Viennese and preserved in the baroque fabric of their magnificent home.

These days Vienna (known to the locals as Wien) is Austria's economic powerhouse and main cultural center. It is both the capital city and the home of around one-fifth of the country's population. As a result, it exerts a powerful sway over Austrian society as a whole, acting as a progressive and creative influence on an otherwise fairly conservative country. Although it is many times larger than any other city in Austria, Vienna is not an overcrowded place; even with the strong growth of the past 20 years, its population is still significantly smaller than it was in its 1900s imperial heyday. With its excellent transport system, exciting cultural life, and beautiful public parks, Vienna is frequently rated as one of world's best places to live—an assessment that few of Vienna's inhabitants would disagree with.

Vienna has been continuously inhabited for thousands of years, and each era of its history has left some mark on the physical fabric of the city—whether it is the medieval-Gothic spires of St. Stephen's Cathedral, the grand baroque facade of the Hofburg Palace, or the socialist-built communal apartment buildings of Döbling or Landstrasse. While prone to nostalgia, Vienna is not stuck in the past, and even the vast edifices of its baroque golden age and 19th-century expansion are constantly being repurposed and reimagined by Vienna's creative civic leaders. The Hofburg complex, once the lavish home of the Habsburg royal family, now houses museums and exhibition spaces. The grand 19th-century gasometers in the south of the city house a shopping center, apartments, and offices. Even the six grim concrete *flaktürme*—Nazi antiaircraft defenses that are as ugly as they are indestructible—are being adapted into aquariums and design museums.

An "urban beach" and murals by the Donaukanal in Leopoldstadt

The Viennese

The Viennese themselves exemplify this combination of old-fashioned and modern. Vienna is very socially liberal by comparison to many cities in the United States, and most Viennese consider themselves to be a tolerant and modern people. They are particularly well known for their extremely relaxed attitude to nudity, which is fairly common in billboard advertisements and TV shows. Even within the city limits there are several nudist beaches (usually marked with the phrase Freikörperkultur, "free body culture," or FKK). They are also, for the most part, a scrupulously law-abiding bunch—it is still common to see newspapers left in bags near train stations, for example, that the Viennese happily pay for by dropping the correct change into a box next to the bag.

Any visitor to the city will be quick to notice though, that even the relaxed attitude of young Viennese urbanites carries a certain careful formality unusual in other cultures. Even in fairly casual settings people tend to shake hands (never hug) and use formal titles when introducing themselves (in Austria many academic qualifications allow you the use of a formal title, so someone with a Ph.D. becomes Herr or Frau Doktor, and someone with an M.A. becomes Herr or Frau Magister). Great importance is also placed on punctuality, even for social occasions—what might be considered "fashionably late" in the United States would be considered rude in Vienna.

The Viennese also have a reputation for being rather blunt, often to the point of

Population Decline

Vienna is the only major European city to have seen its population decline dramatically over the course of the 20th century. During the late 19th and early 20th centuries, the city's population grew rapidly, reaching a peak of around 2.1 million in 1910.

In the aftermath of the First World War (1914–1918), however, the population dropped sharply. The most obvious reason for this decline was the high number of Viennese men who died in the war (thought to be in the tens of thousands), but the majority of the population loss was due to other factors. The most significant of these was the departure of hundreds of thousands of Czechs, Hungarians, and other nationalities, who made up around 35 percent of the population. With the collapse of the Austro-Hungarian Empire, they found themselves living in a foreign country and, within about ten years, the majority of these immigrant groups had returned to their newly independent home countries. The other reason was the 1918–1920 influenza pandemic (often known as Spanish flu), which killed as much as 5 percent of the city's population.

In addition, during the 1930s and 1940s, the genocidal policies of the Nazis resulted in the city's entire Jewish population (which accounted for around 10 percent of the overall population) either fleeing the country or dying in the Nazis' concentration camps.

During the Cold War, Vienna's population continued to decline, although slowly, because of Vienna's stagnant economy (which was the result of it being surrounded on three sides by the closed borders of Soviet-controlled eastern Europe). Since the reopening of these borders in 1991, the population has been rebounding, although it is still a fair way short of pre-First World War levels.

appearing rude. Sometimes this is because they *are* rude (there's never a shortage of impolite people in big cities, after all), but more often this is simply due to a difference in American and Austrian ways of speaking. Viennese society doesn't place much importance on small talk or gentle conversational niceties—the Viennese tend to speak plainly and with little attempt to soften their statements or requests with polite adornments. Similarly, many of the polite phrases used in English are seen as confusingly insincere by German speakers.

The City in Its Context

Many people are surprised, when they look for Vienna on a globe, by just how far east this western European capital stands—farther east than Prague in the Czech Republic or Zagreb in Croatia. This location, beyond the edge of what is generally thought of as western Europe, has had a strong influence on the city's culture and economic development. During periods when the border between the two halves of the continent are closed to trade and travelers—such as during the period of Ottoman expansion (see pp. 25–26) or during the Cold War (see pp. 35–37)—Vienna suffers. When the borders are reopened, however, Vienna thrives.

Today, Vienna finds itself at the crossroads of eastern and western Europe, a position that brings not only economic

Vienna's fabulous Christmas markets attract shoppers from across Europe and beyond.

prosperity but also a constant flow of people and ideas from both sides of the continent. The opening up of markets on the other side of what was the Iron Curtain, along with the recent stabilization of the Balkan States, has seen Vienna go from strength to strength. Vienna's close links to both the east and west are symbolized by the slow-moving waters of the Donau (Danube) River, which winds its way down from the Black Forest in southern Germany before passing through Vienna and on to the eastern European capital cities of Bratislava, Budapest, and Belgrade.

Vienna stands on the edge of the Alps, with the foothills of the Wienerwald (Vienna Woods) rising to the west of the city. Its lowland location gives it a very different appearance from Austria's other cities, such as Salzburg or Innsbruck, which are perched high in the Austrian Alps. The city is politically distinct as well—due to its size, Vienna is an

Despite its unprepossessing name—which means "coal market"—Kolhmarkt is the glamorous home of Vienna's designer stores.

Austrian federal province (a *bundesland*—roughly similar to a U.S. state, although with less political autonomy), a separate governmental entity from the surrounding region of Lower Austria (Niederösterreich).

A City of Many Parts

Vienna is divided into 23 administrative districts (known as *bezirke*). Although each has a traditional name, it is not uncommon to see them referred to only by their number ("1st district" instead of Innere Stadt, for example). The Viennese are often very proud of their home district, believing it to be superior to all the others, and seem to regard other districts as mysterious foreign countries.

The Innere Stadt is the historic core of the city, comprising the narrow maze of medieval streets clustered around the Stephansdom Quarter and the Hofburg. The 2nd district (Leopoldstadt) is located on an island between the Donaukanal (Danube Canal—a narrow branch of the Donau that runs through the center of the city) and the main branch of the Donau to the east. Positioned just across the bridge from the Innere Stadt, Leopoldstadt is the second oldest part of Vienna.

Districts 3–9 are the city's inner suburbs, known as *vortstädte*. These were once the

settlements located between the inner and outer rings of defenses, which have now been replaced by the inner and outer ring roads (the Ringstrasse and Gürtel). They are numbered in a clockwise direction starting with Landstrasse (the 3rd district), which sits on the right bank of the Wienfluss (Vienna River, a small tributary of the Donau) southeast of the Innere Stadt. The other districts are Wieden (4th) and Margareten (5th) to the south of the city center, Mariahilf (6th) to the southwest, with Neubau (7th) and Josefstadt (8th) along the western side. The largest of these districts is Alsergrund (9th), located to the north of the city center.

Districts 10–20, as well as 23, are the city's outer suburbs, known as the *vororte* (outer suburbs). These include Meidling (12th), Hietzing (13th), Penzing (14th), Rudolfsheim-Fünfhaus (15th), Ottakring (16th), Hernals (17th), Währing (18th), Döbling (19th), and Liesing (23rd). These districts are much larger than the others, and are extremely varied in terms of urbanization. Floridsdorf (21st) and Donaustadt (22nd) are located on the other side of the Donau from the rest of the city, while Brigittenau (20th) shares the large river island with Leopoldstadt.

Only about one percent of the city's 1.7 million inhabitants live in the historic Innere Stadt. Around 370,000 live in the vorstädte, while the remainder live in the suburban developments and housing projects of the vororte. Although most Viennese don't consider them to be part of Vienna proper, the two eastern districts of Floridsdorf and Donaustadt are home to a significant proportion of the city's population (around 285,000 people).

Traditions

Although Vienna is a thoroughly modern city in most respects, Viennese culture is imbued with more than a hint of imperial nostalgia. This is, to a large extent, a show put on for visitors, but many Viennese do still look back fondly on the period when Vienna was the glittering capital of a vast empire. This nostalgia is often focused on the pomp and pageantry of the Habsburg royal family, whose glorious public personas have lingered in the public memory far longer than the political realities of their rule. Despite the fact that the royal family is long gone, many of the capital's traditional ceremonies, events, and institutions have been maintained.

To a large extent this is harmless fun, choreographed to amuse visitors, but it does have a darker side—even though the 20th century has seen Viennese society turned

Many Viennese do still look back fondly on the period when Vienna was the glittering capital of a vast empire.

Belying its reputation as a staid imperial city, Vienna boasts many modern boutiques.

upside down by wars, social upheavals, and a long period of military occupation, the rigid aristocratic class system has still managed to reassert itself. There are still plenty of establishments in the city where no amount of money will earn you acceptance if you don't know the difference between a dozen different types of fork, and the correct way to bow and scrape to a baroness.

Politics

As the city once known as Red Vienna (see pp. 31–33), it's hardly surprising to learn that Vienna's politics are typically much more liberal than those found elsewhere in the country. With the exception of the period between 1938 and 1945, when the city's mayors were chosen by fascist dictators, the Viennese have voted for the center-left Social Democratic Party (SPÖ) in every election since 1918. Their rivals, the center-right Austrian People's Party (ÖVP), have only limited influence over the city's politics, even during periods when the rest of the country is under their control.

Only once in the past few decades has the Social Democrats' hold on Vienna been threatened. That was in 1996, when Jörg Haider's (1950–2008) Austrian Freedom Party (FPÖ)—known for its far-right politics and perceived racism—won 28 percent of the vote. The FPÖ's surprising degree of success in Vienna is best understood as a reaction against the stagnant politics of the city's long-incumbent ruling party (akin to the success of the Tea Party movement in the United States), rather than a sign of Viennese politics swinging to the right. In the last few rounds of elections, Viennese politics has returned to business as usual.

The Viennese are largely insulated from the winds of international economics by a thick layer of government bureaucracy, which regulates everything from the sugar content of wine to rent levels. Curiously, for a city with such a large and all-encompassing bureaucracy, Vienna does not have any meaningful regulation of smoking in public areas, nor much in the way of government-sponsored public health campaigns. Recent studies have suggested that as many as 50 percent of the city's population are regular smokers, and this fact is immediately apparent the moment you step into a bar or restaurant.

An International City

Standing, as it does, on the crossroads of eastern and western Europe, Vienna has always had a cosmopolitan, international character, similar to that of Geneva or Zürich in neighboring Switzerland. Since the 1970s the United Nations has had a major base here—the UNO City/Vienna International Center in Donaustadt (see p. 169). This massive office complex is home to many of the UN's larger organizations and working groups. The UNO City, along with the presence of numerous international businesses and NGOs (nongovernmental organizations), means that Vienna has a very high population of resident foreigners (as many as 20 percent of the city's 1.7 million inhabitants).

> **Vienna has a very high population of resident foreigners (as many as 20 percent of the city's 1.7 million inhabitants).**

During the Cold War the city was also known for its large population of spies. Although the Cold War ended more than two decades ago, Vienna is still thought to be one of the world's major hubs for international espionage. Some sources have estimated that there are as many as 3,000 spies still active in the city. Surprisingly, most analysts believe that the spies come to Vienna for much the same reasons as the businessmen—it's a friendly, pleasant place to live, with excellent transport links to eastern and central Europe. The spies are generally tolerated by the Austrian authorities as long as they don't commit any violent crimes or turn their attentions to the Austrian government. ∎

Wienerisch

While few would use it when talking to a non-native speaker, in casual conversation many born-and-bred Viennese residents slip into a local dialect known as Wienerisch (Viennese). In the past there were several drastically different varieties of Wienerisch, unique to different areas of the city, but these local differences are now very minor.

Though it has many similarities to old High German (Hoch Deutsch), Wienerisch has a unique vocabulary and pronunciation that renders it practically unintelligible to German-speaking visitors, even those who are already familiar with the Austro-Bavarian dialect spoken elsewhere in Austria.

The most distinctive feature of this dialect is its slow, drawling pronunciation, which many Austrians find infuriatingly indistinct and lazy-sounding. The vocabulary of Wienerisch is characterized by an idiosyncratic combination of old-fashioned, formal German (derived from the now largely forgotten aristocratic dialect known as Schönbrunn German) and loanwords from Czech, Hungarian, and Yiddish.

History of Vienna

Amid the constantly shifting borders and empires of European history, Vienna has remained a fixed point, a prosperous city with a strong and distinctive culture. Although its circumstances have changed many times—going from a frontier fortress town to a shining imperial city to a modern international hub—its unique character has endured.

The Romans

Although Celtic tribes are thought to have inhabited the site since prehistory, it was the Romans who first put Vienna on the map: They established a military outpost, which they named Vindobona, in the early first century A.D. Forming the ancient foundations of the city of Vienna, this military base was built by

Roman Vienna is mostly invisible today, so the Habsburgs built their own "ruins" like this one at Schönbrunn Palace.

Roman engineers according to a standard square layout found throughout the empire. The quickly erected wooden walls of Vindobona were protected on one side by the Donau and had a deep, wide moat bordering the others. From this base, Roman legions marched out on campaigns in the area now covered by southern Germany, Hungary, and the Czech Republic. Several Roman emperors passed through on military campaigns, including the last great Roman emperor, Marcus Aurelius, who died in the city during the spring of A.D. 180.

Today, it is possible to see traces of Roman Vienna in the fabric of the modern city.

There was more to Vindobona than a military base, however. Excavations have unearthed evidence that it was a well-integrated Roman settlement, a thriving frontier town with a substantial civilian population alongside its military garrison. It had a sophisticated water supply system, busy marketplaces, and even an amphitheater that hosted gladiatorial combat. Vindobona housed as many as 30,000 residents at its peak in the third century A.D.

As the empire's power dwindled, Vindobona found itself on the dangerous frontier. In the fourth century, Vindobona was ransacked by warriors from local Germanic tribes. The blow that sealed the settlement's fate was dealt by a fire that devastated the town's granaries in the early fifth century. By A.D. 433 Emperor Theodosius had relinquished control of the entire region to Eurasian tribes.

Today, it is possible to see traces of Roman Vienna in the fabric of the modern city. Vindobona's major roads are now Vienna's Herrengasse and Augustinerstrasse, while the location of the Roman forum corresponds almost exactly with that of the present-day Hoher Markt. The Roman walls were rediscovered in the 19th century and excavated in the mid-20th century. Portions of two buildings dating back to the earliest period of Vindobona have been excavated in the Hoher Markt, while other sections of the Roman settlement can be seen near the entrance to the imperial palace.

Dark Ages

After the collapse of the Roman Empire, Vienna dropped into a dark age about which very little is known. The survival of the Roman road layout suggests that the settlement was inhabited during this period but was not big enough to warrant a mention in the chronicles of the time. Vienna doesn't reappear in the historical record until the late ninth century, when a Germanic chronicle mentions a battle fought between Germans and Hungarians near a town called Wenia. No buildings from this period survive, although the first Ruprechtskirche is thought to have been built at around this time.

Babenberg Rule

Vienna began to grow once again after the battle of Lechfield in A.D. 955, in which a Germanic army decisively defeated the Hungarian forces that had been raiding and terrorizing the area around Vienna for decades.

In the wake of the battle this newly pacified region—extending from Salzburg in the west to Vienna in the east—was granted to Leopold von Babenberg, the founder of the dynasty that would hold power in the area for the next two centuries. During this time, Vienna grew into a prosperous trade hub and river port. In 1160, the first phase of construction at St. Stephen's Cathedral (see pp. 68–71) was completed. The city's grand centerpiece was consecrated in the presence of many European noblemen, who had gathered to obtain a blessing before heading to the Crusades in the Holy Land.

The noblemen of Europe did not return from the Crusades with the same unity they had when they departed, however, and it was soon back to medieval business as usual. Returning alone from the Holy Land in 1192, English King Richard the Lion-Hearted was captured on the outskirts of Vienna by Babenberg duke Leopold V. The English were forced to pay an astronomical sum to secure Richard's return, reputed to have been as much as 23 tons (21 tonnes) of silver. Leopold V used his newfound wealth to fund the construction of Vienna's city walls and establish a royal mint. Building on his predecessor's work, Austria's next king, Leopold VI "the Glorious," expanded Vienna's power and influence and was the first to establish Vienna as a cultural center, attracting a community of poets and writers to his court. These included Walther von der Vogelwiede (?–1230) and Niedhart von Ruenthal, whose works inspired the 14th-century Niedhart Frescoes (see p. 89).

The crowning of a Habsburg descendant, Frederick III, as Holy Roman Emperor in 1453 brought even greater prestige to Vienna.

After the death of Leopold VI in 1230, the Babenberg dynasty went into decline. His son, who is known to historians by the apt name of Frederick "the Quarrelsome," had none of his father's diplomatic charm, and embroiled his kingdom in a succession of costly wars. After a few decades of chaotic infighting, during which Frederick was exiled, two candidates were left to battle for control of the city—Habsburg Duke Rudolf I (1218–1291) and King Ottokar II of Bohemia (1233–1278).

Early Habsburgs

Ottokar had the support of the Viennese people, but Rudolf had a more powerful army and the backing of many other European monarchs. Rudolf besieged Vienna and forced Ottokar to hand over his Austrian territories. Rudolf invested his sons with the Duchies of Austria and Styria (present-day southern Austria) and consolidated his control over the region. Vienna, however, remained largely outside Habsburg control for several decades, as many Viennese remained loyal to the kings of Bohemia. Vienna eventually accepted Habsburg rule, and in time the Habsburgs warmed to the city, lavishing it with special privileges and grand public projects like the grand Gothic nave of St. Stephen's and its first university.

The crowning of a Habsburg descendant, Frederick III, as Holy Roman Emperor in 1453 brought even greater prestige to Vienna. After almost losing the city to Hungarian king Matthias Corvinus, Frederick firmly established Vienna as the capital of his growing empire, and settled the imperial court in the Hofburg Palace—where it was to stay for almost 500 years.

Ottoman Sieges

Between the beginning of the 16th century and the end of the 17th century, Vienna was constantly under threat from the Ottoman Empire (an Islamic empire centered in present-day Turkey). Under Sultan Süleyman the Magnificent (r. 1520–1566), the Ottoman Empire had expanded rapidly northward, seizing control of Bulgaria, the Balkans, and Hungary. In the spring of 1529, the seemingly unstoppable Ottoman army set its sights on Vienna. The 120,000-strong force arrived on the outskirts of the city in the fall, and began battering the city with heavy cannon fire and explosives. With only outdated medieval defenses and a small garrison, the city appeared fated to fall. The weather, however, seemed to be on Vienna's side, and in the face of heavy rain, freezing temperatures, and the occasional snowstorm, the Ottoman army abandoned its siege and retreated back to Constantinople (present-day Istanbul).

The Habsburg Dynasty

The rise of Rudolf I in the late 13th century marked the founding of a royal dynasty that would dominate continental European politics for the next 600 years.

The Habsburgs spread their power, not through military might, but through an endless succession of dynastic marriages. Habsburg monarchs married young and had as many children as they could. With the exception of the oldest son, who was groomed for the throne, these children were used as diplomatic bargaining chips, traded for land and influence—often betrothed in childhood to people they'd never met. By the 17th century this practice had put Habsburgs on the thrones of Spain, Portugal, and the Netherlands.

Unfortunately, the power that would be gained from a marriage trumped all other considerations, including whether or not the prospective match was a close relative. This meant that as the generations passed, Habsburg monarchs grew increasingly deformed and struggled to produce heirs. This led to a constitutional crisis and the end of the Habsburg dynasty proper when future Empress Maria-Theresia was married to Franz I Stephan, Duke of Lorraine. All subsequent children were technically not Habsburgs but members of the Habsburg-Lorraine dynasty.

For the next 154 years, Vienna was right on the edge of Christian Europe, within a few days' travel of the Ottoman Empire's northern border. Its fortifications were completely rebuilt—destroying many old buildings in the process—and the garrison was increased to many times its former size. Very little was built in the city during this period that wasn't in some way related to defense. The decisive battle came in 1683, when Ottoman Grand Vizier Kara Mustafa Pasha (1634–1683) led an army of around 150,000 men to Vienna. The northward progress of his city-size army had not gone unnoticed by Emperor Leopold I, however, and a relief force was already being assembled by the time the Ottomans reached the city in July. Mustafa Pasha blockaded the city, but didn't make a serious effort to capture it, as he hoped that the defenders would surrender. Vienna held out, however, and the Ottoman army was trapped outside the city when the relief force led by Polish King Jan III Sobieski (1629–1696) arrived. What followed was the biggest battle Austria had ever seen, involving at least 160,000 men. It ended with a massed charge of Polish, Austrian, and German heavy cavalry that sent the Ottomans into a panicked retreat.

Baroque Vienna

Over the two decades that followed the 1683 siege, Austrian forces—led by Prince Eugene of Savoy (see p. 183)—pushed the Ottoman frontier farther and farther from Vienna. A few years after the siege, in 1686, the Austrians had control of Budapest (in Hungary), and by 1688 they had captured the city of Belgrade (in present-day Serbia). The war ended in 1699 with the Treaty of Karlowitz, which granted the Kingdom of Hungary and the large areas of the northern Balkans to the Habsburgs.

This geopolitical change had wide-reaching consequences for Vienna, ushering in a new period of security and relative peace. The Habsburgs named the city as their permanent residence—the Kaiserstadt or Imperial City—an act which encouraged the aristocrats of the Habsburg court to establish permanent homes in the city as well. The resulting boom in grand architectural projects (see pp. 48–51) has become the defining event of the baroque era in Vienna.

> **Maria-Theresia's public policies were always a strange mixture of highly conservative . . . attempts to control public morals . . . and Enlightenment-inspired . . . reforms.**

At the same time a process of less conspicuous, but arguably more important, change was sweeping the city. Freed from the nagging worry that the Ottomans would soon arrive and destroy everything, the city's newly formed commercial classes began expanding the city beyond its old fortified boundaries. As Vienna's first factories sprang up on the outskirts of town, the city began to grow rapidly—nearly doubling in population by the end of the 17th century.

In 1740 Emperor Charles VI died at the Palace Augarten. He left behind an empire mired in debt, a political system that had changed little since the Middle Ages, and an intricate network of diplomatic promises and peace treaties (in which the various states of Europe agreed not to contest his daughter's accession to the throne) that collapsed almost immediately after his death. His daughter, Maria-Theresia, faced an uphill struggle to maintain the empire and turn it into a modern state.

Maria-Theresia & Reform

The first decade of her reign was defined by constant warfare, as Austria's neighbors took advantage of its perceived weakness to try to break off chunks of the empire for themselves. Once these quarrels had been resolved, however, Maria-Theresia set about reforming the country's political system. Although most of her reforms were focused on the Austrian Empire's backward rural areas, they still had an effect on life in the city.

Maria-Theresia's public policies were always a strange mixture of highly conservative, prudish attempts to control public morals (usually triggered by her husband's philandering) and Enlightenment-inspired constitutional reforms. Thus she has the curious distinction of being the empress who abolished the death penalty and also the empress who made it illegal for a married man to spend any time in the company of an actress. On the death of her husband in 1765, she officially handed the throne to her son, Josef II, but remained the effective ruler of the country until her death in 1780.

Josef was an unusual ruler. He was a supporter of the libertarian ideals of the

Jewish Vienna

Vienna's Jewish community *(Israelitische Kultusgemeinde)* forms an intrinsic part of the city's history. It has played an important role in Vienna's economic and cultural development over the centuries. Many of the city's famous artists, intellectuals, and businessmen were either Jewish or had a Jewish family background.

Walking around the city today, it is hard to find evidence of Vienna's Jewish heritage outside the museums and exhibitions of the Judenplatz. At its height in the early 20th century, Vienna's Jewish community constituted around 10 percent of the city's two-million-strong population, yet so complete was its destruction that barely any physical tokens of its existence remain.

The first Jews to settle in Vienna arrived in medieval times. They formed a small but stable community, although they were excluded from civic life as a whole. The community was, however, driven from the city by a series of brutal attacks in 1420 and 1421. Many chose to commit collective suicide, immolating themselves together with their synagogue, rather than face the wrath of the mobs.

Jews were not allowed to return to Vienna until 1624, but had barely had time to put down roots before Emperor Leopold I banished them again, and named their former neighborhood after himself (Leopoldstadt). Economic hardships soon led Vienna to relax its prohibition on Jewish settlement, but it was not until Emperor Joseph II's Edict of Toleration that their place was secured. The reforms that followed the 1848 revolutions brought them more freedoms, and allowed some wealthier members of the community to move into the Viennese aristocracy.

From this point until the city's descent into anti-semitic violence in the 1930s, Vienna's Jewish community thrived. Jewish businessmen became prominent economic advisers to the monarchy, intellectuals and artists like Sigmund Freud and Arnold Schoenburg gained international renown for their revolutionary ideas, and the community produced many Nobel Prize–winning scientists.

However, this period was also characterized by increasing tension with the Christian majority. Although large-scale violence was rare, the popularity of political parties such as the openly anti-semitic Christian Social Party made it clear that Jews were still a long way from ever being socially accepted. It is no coincidence therefore, that Vienna was also home to the first organized Zionist movement, committed to the formation of a Jewish state. In the face of the growth of racist far-right parties, many Jews allied themselves with the socialist movement. As conditions worsened, however, this political grouping proved to be an indifferent and weak protector of the Jewish community.

Anti-Semitism & the Holocaust

Between the rise of fascism and the end of the Second World War, Vienna's Jewish community was almost completely wiped out. In the face of brutal and humiliating mistreatment, tens of thousands fled the country before the *Anschluss* (see pp. 33–34), while another wave fled in the early months of Nazi rule. By the early 1940s, only about 60,000 Jews were left in Austria, most of them in the ghettos of Vienna. By the war's end they had all been either shipped off to death camps or murdered in their homes. Only a few hundred Viennese Jews survived the camps, and, unsurprisingly, few had any desire to go back to their empty neighborhoods.

Today Vienna is home to a small Jewish community, around 8,000 people, mostly comprising Jews from the former Soviet Union who have arrived in the past 30 years.

Baroque extravagance lives on in Vienna. These incredibly elaborate cakes were made by the old imperial confectioner, Demel, whose creations once graced the royal banqueting table.

Enlightenment, but at the same time very attached to the power of his position. This resulted in a ten-year rule in which there were many reforms to the way things were done in the country, but very little change to the structures of power. Although he undoubtedly had noble intentions, his often intrusive public policies made him very unpopular with his subjects. The most important reform that Josef introduced, and one of the few that had any lasting effect, was the Edict of Toleration, which permitted freedom of religion (to an extent) in the Austrian Empire (see p. 27).

19th Century

The baroque era of reform was brought to an abrupt end in 1805, when Napoleon's advancing army forced the Habsburg court into an ignominious retreat to Hungary. Although the city was soon retaken, the ease with which Napoleon took Vienna was a humiliating demonstration of how little real power lay behind the ostentatious finery of the city's ruling elite.

After the threat of Napoleon was lifted, the first half of the 19th century was a quiet and peaceful period. The first emperor of the 19th century, Franz I (r. 1792–1835), was a very conservative man. He reversed a few of Josef II's more radical policies, but generally had little involvement in domestic politics. He was succeeded by his son, Ferdinand (r. 1835–1848), who was another product of the very small Habsburg gene pool. Ferdinand suffered from debilitating epilepsy, hydrocephalus (a genetic condition that gave him an abnormally large head and the mental ability of a child), and a severe speech impediment. Since the lumbering wheels of the Austrian civil service functioned perfectly well if left alone, however, his inability to make governmental decisions was not really a major problem for the empire.

This period of relative peace came to an end during the revolutions that swept Europe in 1848. Amid massive street protests in Vienna the long-serving chancellor (and de facto ruler of the empire) Klemens von Metternich (1773–1859) was forced to resign and flee the country. Without his long-time adviser, Ferdinand was at a loss as to what to do. A few months after the attempted revolution he abdicated in favor of his nephew, Franz-Josef, who would go on to rule the empire for the next 67 years.

Although the revolutionaries failed to overthrow the old system, the oppressive policies of the Habsburgs, which were stifling the city's economic and cultural growth, were greatly liberalized. One of Franz-Josef's first actions as emperor was to remove another factor that was inhibiting the city's development—its colossal 17th-century defenses. Their demolition opened up a huge swathe of land for the development of the *vorstädte* (inner suburbs) and initiated the construction of the grand buildings on the Ringstrasse.

In the second half of the 19th century, the diverse peoples of the Austrian Empire became increasingly resentful of Habsburg rule, and began pushing for independence. Hungary was grudgingly given equal status with Austria in 1867, creating the Austro-Hungarian Empire. The other regions of the empire were granted representation in the newly built Parliament on the Ringstrasse, where their delegates tried, largely in vain, to get Franz-Josef to recognize their demands for greater independence.

Fin-de-siècle Vienna

In the twilight years of the Austro-Hungarian Empire, the city of Vienna was a city of profound contradictions; the aristocratic elite paraded in the gilded finery

Maria-Theresia's Trusted Adviser & Vampire Hunter

In 1745, Empress Maria-Theresia hired the respected Dutch physician Gerard van Swieten (1700–1772) to attend to her health and that of her growing family. Maria-Theresia was impressed by his judgment and soon sought him out for advice on matters of public policy. Van Swieten was a strong supporter of the principles of the Enlightenment, and provided the impetus for many of Maria-Theresia's social reforms. For most of his career he controlled the censorship department, where he tried to loosen the restrictions on the press.

The most interesting of the many jobs he did for the empress took place in 1755, when Maria-Theresia asked him to investigate a wave of vampire attacks near a village in the Carpathian mountains. The local community of Austrian settlers had been panicked by reports of individuals rising from the grave to prey on the living, and were threatening to leave the frontier province.

Disappointingly, van Swieten found no mysterious castles or blood-drinking counts on his fact-finding mission. After a few weeks' research he laid the blame for the panic on the blind irrationality of the rural population, ascribing the reports of vampires to nothing more than mental illness and an ignorance of the process of decomposition. In his report on the trip, *Remarks on Vampirism*, he suggested that Maria-Theresia pass a bizarre-sounding law that forbade people from exhuming the dead and beheading them.

sometimes only streets away from the huge dormitory buildings where the city's young and underpaid workers slept in barrack-like halls. The population of Vienna had grown much faster than the physical fabric of the city could stand—going from just a few hundred thousand in 1850 to almost two million by the century's end.

There was, in addition to those who slept in dormitories, an underclass of chronically poor young men known as the *bettgeher,* or lodgers—individuals who worked night shifts and rented someone else's bed during the day. In many cases two or even three people would club together to afford the rent on one bed in a dormitory, and they would make sure that it was permanently occupied. During his youth, Adolf Hitler was one of the bettgeher, sleeping in the apartment of a local laborer while his family were out at work or school, paying most of his meager earnings for the privilege of doing so.

These problems bred a climate of simmering resentment, in which the city's poor quickly turned against foreigners and ethnic minorities that appeared to be doing better than they were. Their prime target, of course, was the city's Jewish population, which was becoming an increasingly visible part of Viennese public life. Viennese politicians like Georg von Schönerer and Karl Lueger (see sidebar below) fueled the flames of this anti-Semitism for their own political ends.

With this great increase in population and ethnic diversity, however, also came a dramatic and productive collision of cultures. In the ghettos of the city, Hungarian Jewish intellectuals sat in cafés with Czech artists and Serbian writers, discussing the ideas and issues of the day. Creative young people across the empire heard stories of the golden city and its vibrant cultural life, and were drawn in, forming an intellectual migration to parallel the great shift of labor.

Karl Lueger

There are few figures in Viennese history that divide opinion as sharply as Karl Lueger (1844–1910), who was mayor of the city from 1897 until his death. To some he was the architect of Vienna's Golden Age, a visionary who transformed the city and reformed the rotten political system. To others, however, he was a cynical populist who stirred up hatred against minorities for his own political ends.

Even Lueger's staunchest critics concede that he achieved a great deal during his time in office. Lueger instigated anticorruption reforms, created a social welfare system, and pushed for major improvements in the city's infrastructure. In just 13 years he made one of the most technologically and politically backward cities in Europe into a rapidly expanding modern metropolis.

These achievements, however, are always eclipsed by his public anti-Semitism. On the campaign trail Lueger would rail against the city's Jews, who, he assured audiences, were a malign influence on the city's politics, responsible for all its problems. He often called for them to be driven from the city, or worse, and continued his assaults when in office.

Despite the ferocity of his rhetoric, he rarely used his political power to make life difficult for the city's Jews, and by all accounts didn't dislike them personally. To him it was simply an effective campaign strategy. Whether or not his hatred was sincere, however, is irrelevant when you consider the broader influence his public persona had, especially on the young Adolf Hitler, who was one of his most enthusiastic supporters.

The ill-fated Archduke Franz-Ferdinand, whose death triggered the First World War

This era came to an end in 1914, when Archduke Franz-Ferdinand, along with his wife Sophie, were shot dead by Serbian nationalists while visiting Sarajevo (in present-day Bosnia-Herzegovina). Outrage at this event united the city for the first time in years, with even Vienna's Marxist papers supporting a military response. This surge of patriotic enthusiasm and political unity was thoroughly obliterated, however, as Austria's military response pulled the entire continent into a devastating world war. Vienna was a long way from the front line, but it felt the effects of the war as food supplies dwindled. Vienna was dealt another blow shortly after the war ended, when the 1918 influenza pandemic (often known as Spanish flu) swept through the city, killing tens of thousands. The end of the war also marked the end of the Austro-Hungarian Empire—the last emperor, Karl I, was forced to renounce his claim to the throne in 1918, and the empire was broken up into its constituent states. Vienna found itself the capital, not of a vast empire, but of a small central European country.

Red Vienna

On May 4, 1919, less than six months after the creation of the Republic of Austria, the country held its first democratic elections. In Vienna, these elections were marked by a landslide victory for the Marxist SDAPÖ (Social Democratic Workers' Party of Austria), which gave the SDAPÖ an absolute majority in the city parliament. For the generally conservative population of Austria, this result was a disturbing surprise. It marked the beginning of a period known as *Rotes Wien* (Red Vienna), during which the city's government tried to make Vienna into a socialist model city that would inspire workers all over Europe.

The local government funded major public projects to improve the lives of the city's poor. These included the creation of the massive Gemeindebau (community buildings), such as Karl-Marx-Hof (see p. 217), that greatly improved the available housing stock in the city. The socialists also instituted social programs that provided for children and the elderly, as well as a limited form of unemployment benefit. However, few of these new initiatives did anything for anyone outside the city limits. Vienna's tax revenue, which made up more than half of the country's total, was being spent almost entirely on projects within the city, a policy that generated considerable resentment elsewhere in Austria.

Adolf Hitler in a celebratory parade after the 1938 Anschluss

In a process that was mirrored in cities across continental Europe during the 1920s and 1930s, the political atmosphere within the city became increasingly polarized, with people's political affiliation (conservative or socialist) dictating almost every aspect of how they chose to live their lives. Tensions between the urban socialists and the rural conservatives reached a breaking point in the summer of 1934, when months of parliamentary deadlock spurred the fascist president to dissolve parliament and attempt to govern as a dictator. The socialists brought out their militias, who had been arming themselves over the preceding years, but this act of resistance spurred no greater revolutionary fervor in the people, and the socialist militias were defeated within a few days.

Tensions between the urban socialists and the rural conservatives reached a breaking point in the summer of 1934.

The Anschluss

Austria's 1938 Anschluss (union) with Nazi Germany came at a time when Austrian far-right groups had seized control of almost every public institution. After the assassination of Austrian Chancellor Engelbert Dollfuss by Austrian Nazis in 1934, successor Kurt von Schuschnigg faced increasing pressure from Nazi Germany to form an Austrian-German union. To let the people of Austria decide, Schuschnigg called a referendum in March 1938—a poll that Nazi Germany refused to recognize. Before the vote could be held, Hitler issued an ultimatum to Schuschnigg: Allow the Austrian National Socialists to take power or face invasion. Schuschnigg resigned after failing to get aid from Britain or France. Arthur Seyss-Inquart—the leader of the Austrian Nazi Party—was appointed Chancellor and invited the German army to occupy Austria (now renamed Ostmark) as part of the Third Reich.

When Hitler arrived in Vienna, he announced that Schuschnigg's planned referendum would be held anyway, to confirm his support. The results recorded that almost everyone in the city (99.73 percent, to be exact) voted for the Anschluss. This is hardly surprising when you consider that most of the Nazis' political opponents had been arrested, the Jewish population was barred from voting, and the intimidation tactics of the Nazi SS had made it clear to everyone else what would happen if they voted against union. None of this was shown in the propaganda reports, however, and with Austria seemingly a willing partner the Anschluss was signed and sealed.

In the next few months, thousands of Austrian Jews were arrested; some were immediately sent to concentration camps, while others were severely beaten before being released and instructed to leave the country immediately. The situation was at its worst in Vienna, where the racist policies of the Nazi government served to stoke the fires of the city's already violent anti-Semitism. The nights of November 9 and 10, 1938—better known as *Kristallnacht*—were largely uneventful in most of Austria, but in Vienna an armed mob descended on Leopoldstadt and the Jewish suburbs. Homes were ransacked, businesses trashed, and men, women, and children were attacked or even killed. By the end of this orgy of violence, almost every one of Vienna's nearly 100 synagogues had been burned to the ground.

Second World War

Vienna largely escaped the destruction of the Second World War. Before the Allies liberated France, the city stood a long way from the front line, comfortably beyond the range of Allied bombers. Toward the end of the war the city was bombed on a few occasions, killing many civilians and badly damaging a few major landmarks, but Vienna wasn't subjected to the devastating "area bombing" that flattened cities like Dresden. The target of the raids was usually the oil refineries in Floridsdorf. This was not the era of the precision air strike, however; the difference between hitting Floridsdorf and hitting the city center was a few seconds' hesitation.

To protect the city from aerial attacks, in 1944 the Nazis built a series of enormous reinforced concrete towers around the city, known as flaktürm. Although the top floors of these buildings once bristled with antiaircraft guns and searchlights, their placement close to the center of the city (chosen for propaganda purposes) meant they were of little use when the bombers came. All six flaktürm—two in Landstrasse, two in Leopoldstadt, and two in Mariahilf—are still standing (mostly because they're impossible to demolish).

During the war, Vienna was home to numerous satellite camps of the massive Mauthausen-Gusen concentration camp (located near Linz). These small camps housed several thousand slave-laborers who worked in the factories and rail yards of Vienna's suburbs. As they were brutally treated and chronically underfed, it is thought that hundreds if not thousands died during their time in the city. The majority of the inmates were Austrian, German, and Polish intellectuals—condemned for their political views. The death toll for the whole Mauthausen-Gusen system, with sites spread throughout Austria, is estimated to have been between 150,000 and 320,000.

> **The worst damage [during World War II] was done when a fire spread to St. Stephen's Cathedral, destroying the original roof and almost bringing down the spire.**

Were it not for the looming East–West conflict of the Cold War, the land war in Europe would have probably bypassed Vienna. The Soviets, however, saw the city as an important bargaining chip in the coming negotiations over the division of Europe, and so dispatched an army to liberate the city in April 1945. After slipping past Vienna's sparse outer defenses, the Soviet army was baffled to find themselves driving their tanks through pristine suburbs seemingly untouched by war. Once they got close to the Innere Stadt, however, the battle began. For the next four days German and Russian tanks clumsily smashed their way around the narrow streets of the Stephansdom Quarter, while infantry engaged in vicious house-to-house fighting. Surprisingly little

Occupation Zones in Vienna

The Allied Commission for Austria managed to reach a tentative agreement on the postwar administration of the country in July 1945. The plan it agreed on would see the country divided into four zones (controlled by the United States, Britain, France, and the Soviet Union) with Vienna (which was well inside the Soviet sector) divided along the same lines.

Under the four-power system, northern Vienna was administered by the United States, western Vienna by the French, southern Vienna by the British, and eastern Vienna, as well as the districts of Wieden and Favoriten, by the Soviets. In a slightly absurd compromise, the Innere Stadt was designated an international zone where power was shared between the four groups on a monthly rotation. It was this last detail that led to the Allied occupation being referred to as the "four in a Jeep" period, as each power required a representative of its forces be on every law-enforcement patrol in the Innere Stadt.

permanent damage was done to the city during the battle, although casualties on both sides were high. The worst damage was done when a fire spread to St. Stephen's Cathedral, destroying the original roof and almost bringing down the spire.

Four-power Vienna

In the aftermath of the Vienna Offensive, the city found itself a long way inside the Soviet-controlled half of Austria. Although a temporary plan of occupation was soon worked out (see sidebar above) the various treaties that had been negotiated among the Soviet Union and the other Allied powers were conspicuously quiet on the subject of what would happen to Austria as a nation.

This was a particularly grim period for the Viennese, especially those who had to live with the casual brutality of the battle-scarred Soviet occupying force. Between 1945 and 1948, when the Marshall Plan came into effect, the Viennese lived on a near-starvation diet, and food riots were common. Around a fifth of the city's buildings were partially or completely destroyed, and around 90,000 homes in the city were rendered uninhabitable. In Vienna's center, more than 3,000 bomb craters were counted while most bridges were destroyed and all major utilities (sewers, gas and water pipes, power stations and cabling, and phone lines) were severely damaged.

In the face of the results of the genocidal brutality with which the Nazis had wiped out their political opposition, the Western Allies were forced to largely abandon their de-Nazification process by 1948. Many former Nazis were allowed to take back their jobs as government officials and law-enforcement officers because there was simply no one to replace them. Attempts to maintain law and order in the city were crippled by the fuzzy legal status of the different zones and the unwillingness of the Soviets to allow the police force to be expanded or armed (they rightly suspected that the police were being trained as an anticommunist paramilitary force by the Western Allies). This meant that four-power Vienna was a black-marketeers' paradise, where gangsters, thugs, and opportunists cornered the market on everything from shoes to medicine (a situation that is chronicled in the 1949 movie The Third Man).

At the same time, the elected government of Austria, led by the moderate socialist

The Viennese take pride in their history as a grand imperial capital.

Karl Renner (1870–1950) and later by Theodor Körner (1873–1957), was shunned by the Western powers (who saw them as Soviet puppet regimes) and bullied by the Soviets (who responded to Renner acting against their orders by confiscating huge swathes of eastern Austria's economic output and industrial infrastructure). It took ten years for these politicians to win the cautious trust of the Western Allies, all the while fending off the Soviet Union's political intrigues and attempts to stir up unrest. The four-power era ended on May 15, 1955, with the signing of the Austrian State Treaty, which saw the occupying forces on all sides pull out on the condition that Austria remained neutral in the Cold War, joining neither NATO nor the Warsaw Pact.

Postwar Vienna

In 1943, while the Second World War was still raging, the three main Allied powers published a joint statement known as the Moscow Declaration. Among its various provisions, this document stated that Austria was to be considered "the first free country to fall a victim to Hitlerite aggression," rather than an enemy state. During the tense years of negotiations between Austria and the occupying powers, this assertion became a vitally important political distinction, one that protected Austria from being permanently divided or annexed by the Soviet Union.

In later years, however, this victim status meant that Austria was never forced to confront the extent of its involvement in Nazi war crimes. History lessons in schools often went no further than the First World War, and official publications compressed their overview of the events between 1938 and 1945 to just a few general phrases. However, student pressure in the late 1960s saw the beginnings of a change in thinking. Austrians were urged to come to terms—honestly—with what had happened. Slowly, people started to reevaluate the role their homeland had played in the Holocaust, a process referred to as *vergangenheitsbewältigung* (the struggle to come to terms with the past). During the 1980s, reports were conducted to establish the best way forward in righting some of the wrongs of World War II. These reports examined, in painstaking detail, the role of Austrian individuals and institutions in war crimes, as well as documented the historical ownership of various assets seized from the Jewish population. During the 1990s, a substantial government fund was established to compensate the families of Austrian Jews, and several major government initiatives were launched to encourage greater national introspection about Austria's role in the growth of Nazism. Nonetheless, the Austrian government is still widely criticized for what many perceive as a lack of frankness about the country's past.

This conflict with the ghosts of its past has defined Austrian politics for the past 50 years. Several national scandals have erupted as a result of revelations about a political candidate's past. The most severe of these controversies was that which surrounded Kurt Waldheim's (1918–2007) campaign for president in 1985. Waldheim, who was born in Vienna, served in the Wehrmacht (German army) during the Second World War, but always denied that he knew anything of Nazi war crimes. During the campaign it was revealed that this ignorance would have been nearly impossible, as his unit was involved in bloody reprisals against Bosnian civilians and that he had worked as an interpreter in Greece at a time when thousands of Greek Jews were being deported to concentration camps. Despite the U.S. government and several international organizations declaring Waldheim to be a war criminal, he still won the election. This left Austria in the awkward position of having a president that could not leave the country on state visits for fear of being arrested.

After the Cold War

Since the fall of the Soviet Union in 1991, Vienna has experienced steady growth, both in terms of population and economic performance. Although it is still neither as large nor as prosperous as it was before the First World War, Vienna has become an important center of interna-

> **Vienna has become an important center of international trade, as well as being frequently rated one of the world's most livable cities.**

tional trade, as well as being frequently rated one of the world's most livable cities. As one of the founding members of the European Free Trade Area, established by the Stockholm Convention in 1960, Austria had enjoyed close economic ties to the countries of the European Economic Community (later the European Union, EU). These links were strengthened in 1995 when the country joined the EU. During the late 1990s Vienna became an important base of operations for companies working in Eastern Europe, a role that has become increasingly lucrative as the nearby Balkan states have become more stable. In the 1990s and 2000s, while politics in the rest of Austria were dominated by the rise of Jörg Haider's extreme right-wing FPÖ (Austrian Freedom Party), Viennese politics remained the domain of the left-wing SPÖ (Austrian Socialist Party), preserving the city's liberal reputation at a time when the rest of Austria was facing something of a public relations disaster. ∎

Land & Environment

Green hills, flowery meadows, rugged mountains, thick forests, bird-filled wetlands, and the everchanging Donau (Danube) River all help shape the character of Vienna and the landscape surrounding the city.

Vienna stands at the meeting point of Austria's various different geographic regions. To the south and west lie the thickly forested hills of the Wienerwald (Vienna Woods), which stand on sandstone to the north and limestone to the south. The hills are the easternmost extension of the Alps. North of the city is the lower but older mountain range known as the Böhmerwald (Bohemian Forest). To the east stretches the low-lying fertile landscape of the Vienna Basin, a broad plain that extends into neighboring Slovakia and Hungary. The Austrian part of this flat sedimentary basin is known as Niederösterreich (Lower Austria—as opposed to Oberösterreich, or Upper Austria, the country's mountainous western half).

Much of the landscape of the Vienna Basin has been transformed over the centuries by agricultural development, becoming one of the country's most productive areas. Some parts, however, have been preserved in their natural state, particularly the Lobau floodplain (see pp. 222–224) that runs alongside the Donau from Vienna's outskirts to the border with Slovakia.

> **The countryside around Vienna is less threatened by urban expansion than the surroundings of many other European cities.**

Although Vienna's population has increased considerably in recent years (up 9.4 percent since 2000), the city still hasn't grown beyond its peak population in the early 20th century. The changing economic role of the city means that there is no shortage of former industrial sites that can be converted to new uses (such as the Gasometer complex; see pp. 177–178). As a result, the countryside around Vienna is less threatened by urban expansion than the surroundings of many other European cities. Most of the city's outward expansion is characterized by upscale residential developments in the lower Wienerwald.

A Green City

Vienna is proud of its role as a model environmental city and claims to be one of the "greenest" in the world. This was supported by a survey of urban quality of life in Europe (*www.urbanaudit.org*) conducted by the EU in 2006. It is also currently the fourth greenest of Europe's cities, according to the European Green City Index. This is due in no small part to its easy access to green space and dedicated leisure and recreation areas from inner city districts. An ongoing policy is focused on the promotion of public transportation and bicycles as favored mode of getting around the city. Coordinated and frequent services and the introduction of all-night buses, as well as an extensive network of cycle routes, provide a good alternative to private cars; the city has 390 cars per 1,000 inhabitants, compared with about 650 per 1,000 inhabitants in Washington, D.C.

The city authorities have long understood the positive impact that public transportation can have in reducing pollution and enhancing quality of life. Today, five underground lines, 30 tram lines, and 83 bus routes crisscross Vienna. What's more, this highly efficient public transport system links up with a dozen hiking trails and more than 35 cycle paths in the Wienerwald region—14 of which begin in central Vienna.

Spring sunshine in the Wienerwald

Deer graze in the Lainzer Tiergarten, southwest of the city.

More than half of Vienna is made up of green spaces of one description or another, from small local parks to the huge expanse of the Wienerwald; one-third of this open space is forested. In recent years the city's infrastructure projects have been conceived along ecological lines, and care has been taken to retain the balance between the built environment and its open spaces. Vienna contains eight nature reserves, covering about 37,000 acres (15,000 ha) of woodlands, parks, gardens, wetlands, plains, hills, vineyards, and meadows.

> **More than half of Vienna is made up of green spaces of one description or another, from small local parks to the huge expanse of the Wienerwald.**

Vienna's Waterways

The landscape of the Vienna Basin is dominated by the Donau River, which passes through the area on its winding 1,771-mile (2,850 km) journey from Donaue-schingen in Germany's Black Forest to the Black Sea on the Romanian-Ukrainian border. By the time the river reaches Vienna it has been enlarged by numerous tribu-taries from the Alps, and flows through the city at a rate of around 30 million gallons a minute. This massive river has burst its banks on many occasions, inundating the city. It was rerouted in the 1870s (see p. 157), however, and Vienna hasn't suffered a major flood since. There are several other rivers in Vienna, although today only one—the Wienfluss—is still visible aboveground. This usually small river originates in the rocky hills west of the city, where there is little soil to absorb rainfall; all it takes is a storm upriver and the water level can rise several feet in a matter of minutes. It is for this reason that the river passes through the city in a concrete channel that, most of the time, seems comically too large for the river itself.

Since 1994 the water quality of the Donau has been protected by the International Commission for the Protection of the Danube River, which now closely monitors all industrial activity and intensive agriculture near the river. As for drinking water, it is very clean: Since 1910 most of what comes out of the city's faucets has come from the mountains, brought by two mountain spring pipelines.

Flora & Fauna

Vienna has an enviable biodiversity. For example, it boasts 1,600 species of indigenous plants (with several hundred more introduced varieties), many of which are endangered; about 40 different kinds of mammals, ranging from tiny shrews to lumbering wild boars; many birds; and more than 130 species of butterflies and 70 different kinds of grasshoppers. The two most important areas for nature—both of which have public access—are the beech, oak, and hornbeam forests and meadows of the Wienerwald (see sidebar below) and the Donau wetlands, including the Donau-Auen National Park (see pp. 222–224). These wetlands, stretching 24 miles (38 km) east of the city, provide great habitat for 30 species of mammals, many birds (including white storks, black woodpeckers, nightingales, river warblers, collared flycatchers, and penduline tits), and reptiles, amphibians, and fish.

The main concern of the city planners is to position present-day Vienna in such a way that in 50 or 100 years it will offer living and environmental conditions that are at least as good as those its residents have now. ∎

City Wildlife

In the countryside surrounding Vienna, the once plentiful bears, wolves, and lynx were long ago wiped out by hunters and habitat changes. However, red deer, chamois, wild boars, marmots, and grouse can still be found within easy reach of the city. Spanning 334,000 acres (134,000 ha), the Wienerwald (Vienna Woods Tourism, www.weinerwald.info) forms the city's largest wildlife habitat. In addition to forest, this area also includes flower-filled meadows, lush pastures, and vineyards. Wild boar are plentiful, and resident birds such as northern goshawks, gray-headed and black woodpeckers, and crested tits are joined in summer by honey-buzzards, wrynecks, nightingales, hawfinches, golden orioles, and many more.

For a traveler with limited time, a few hours spent at Lainzer Tiergarten (see pp. 230–231; tel 1/4000 49 20-0, www.wien.gv.at/umwelt/wald/erholung/ lainzertiergarten) will be worthwhile. This is an area of forest and grassland on the edge of the Wienerwald just a few minutes from the Vienna suburbs. The history of this 6,054-acre (2,420 ha) wildlife preserve dates back to 1561 when Ferdinand I of Austria fenced off the area as a hunting ground. Since 1919, the land has been open to the public and is home to a wide variety of wildlife, including wild boar, fallow and red deer, and mouflons. Red-breasted and collared flycatchers can be seen here in summer, along with firecrests and more woodpeckers. The grassland areas have a fine selection of butterflies and other invertebrates in spring and summer.

Animals can be seen in a very different setting at Vienna's magnificent Schönbrunn Palace (see pp. 192–197), a baroque former menagerie that is now a zoological garden.

Food & Drink

Viennese cuisine, or *Wiener küche,* is every bit the cuisine of an imperial capital. It uses ingredients and techniques imported from all over Austria and the countries of what was once its empire, as well as unique combinations of these regional styles invented in the city's restaurants.

The Viennese adore their food, and today good meals can be easily found wherever you are in the city. The city has hundreds of high-class restaurants, sidewalk cafés *(schanigarten),* garden diners *(gastgärten),* coffeehouses *(kaffeehäuser),* and traditional inns *(beisln).* Viennese snack food tends to be of good quality (snacking is an important part of the Austrian diet) and are cooked fresh by vendors in and around the city's plazas. Today, the omnipresent sausage seller *(würstelstand)* and pretzel stall have been joined by many other fast-food options, particularly in the marketplaces of ethnically diverse districts like Leopoldstadt and Ottakring. In winter, Vienna's streets are laced with the thick, sweet smells of *lebkuchen* (gingerbread) and *gluhwein* (mulled wine) while shop window displays are filled with pastries, cakes, and richly decorated chocolates.

On a day-to-day basis, most Viennese breakfast at home; weekends are an exception to the rule when it is common to meet friends at a local *kaffeehause* (see pp. 140–141). A second snack breakfast *(gabelfrühstück)* is common at around 10 a.m., to bridge the void until lunchtime. In Vienna, lunch is usually the main meal of the day, catered to by the city's huge number of restaurants. However, like many busy modern cities, Vienna is fast becoming a place where lunch has been reduced to a hastily grabbed sandwich, meaning that the evening meal is growing in importance. Particularly hungry Viennese may head out for a mid-afternoon snack—typically an open-face sandwich, coffee, and a pastry—to tide them over until the evening.

> **Viennese cuisine is . . . unusually sweet, and it is often not entirely clear whether the dish on the menu is a very sweet main course or an extremely large dessert.**

Viennese cuisine is known for being unusually sweet, and it is often not entirely clear whether the dish on the menu is a very sweet main course or an extremely large dessert (if indeed, there is any difference). For example, it is not that unusual to see strudel (a long pastry with a sweet filling of fruit, pumpkin, or soft cheese), which is considered to be a dessert elsewhere in the world, served as a main course in Vienna. This strange aspect of the city's culinary tradition developed as a result of the famously indulgent tastes of the city's aristocracy, epitomized by Archduke Ferdinand I of Austria (r. 1830–1838), whose most famous saying was *"Ich bin der Kaiser und ich will marillenknödel!"*—I am the Emperor and I demand apricot dumplings!—which he shouted at a cook who suggested he eat something savory. In order to be distinguishable from the main course, Viennese desserts are very often extremely sweet and elaborate creations, crafted with large quantities of chocolate, cream, meringue, and pastry.

Traditionally, however, these dishes were the preserve of a small minority of the city's population who had enough money to have someone make them. For the rest of Vienna, the term Viennese cuisine meant something quite different. It is from the food of Vienna's working population that you get the other category of traditional Viennese dishes: filling, stodgy dishes with lots of potato dumplings, sausages, and big
(continued on p. 46)

The Hofburg Quarter's Café Hawelka (see p. 140), a traditional Viennese coffeehouse

Famous Viennese Dishes

Although there is no shortage of gastronomic innovation in Vienna's restaurants, most establishments reserve a place on their menus for a selection of traditional Viennese culinary standards. These hearty, usually meaty dishes become especially common in the winter, when the Viennese begin to feel the need for the heavy stews and soups of their traditional cuisine.

A slice of the famous Sacher torte from the Hotel Sacher Wien

Like any major city, Vienna is home to a wide variety of places to eat, from fancy nouvelle cuisine restaurants to street corner hot dog stands. The latter, known as *würstelstände,* sell fried and boiled sausages *(würste),* either in a bread roll or with mustard or ketchup, as well as *leberkässemmel,* a bread roll filled with a local specialty called *leberkäse.* Although its name translates as "liver-cheese," this bologna-like sandwich meat typically contains neither liver nor cheese. Its primary ingredients seem to vary but are usually listed as beef and pork—it's best not to inquire further.

The next level up in the city's culinary hierarchy are the hundreds of little bakeries, sandwich shops, and delis that sell open sandwiches, *jause* (cold cuts), and pastries.

For a sit-down meal, however, most visitors will want to head for Vienna's atmospheric *beisln* (inns), *gasthäuser* (inns), and *heurigen* (wine taverns). These traditional establishments serve a wide variety of hearty and filling old-fashioned cuisine, as well as delicious desserts. Although the menus vary considerably, the following dishes, or something very similar, usually have pride of place on these menus.

Apfelstrudel: A favorite with Austrians nationwide, this dessert is made from delicate layers of puff pastry filled with apples, sugar, cinnamon, ground cloves, raisins, and chopped walnuts sprinkled with icing sugar.

Beuschel: An old-style Jewish ragout made from veal lungs and heart, root vegetables, cream, herbs, and onions flavored with garlic, paprika, and peppercorns.

Bosna (or bosner): A hot dog made from a spicy bratwurst sausage sold at Vienna's *würstelstände* (sausage stands).

Erdapfelgulasch: A variant on the Hungarian *gulasch* (see below) made with potatoes instead of beef, many restaurants in Vienna make it with chopped sausage mixed in, seemingly to frustrate vegetarians.

Frittatensuppe: A combination of Austrian herb pancakes *(frittaten)* cut into strips and a typical plain bouillon *(suppe)*.

Gefüllte Paprika: This stuffed-pepper dish originates from the Balkans, once part of the Austro-Hungarian Empire. It is a roasted bell pepper with a filling of minced meat and rice, usually served with a tomato sauce and potatoes.

Germknödel: A dessert of yeast dough dumplings flavored with poppy seeds and sugar, filled with plum jam, and drizzled with melted butter. Typically served with cream.

Gulasch: This Hungarian beef stew is characterized by a spicy thick gravy flavored with paprika. It is traditionally served with dumplings or chunks of fresh bread.

Kaiserschmarrn: A fluffy, sweetened dumpling-pudding made from broken pieces of partially baked batter mix that is then cooked with butter and sugar in the oven.

Knödel: This Austrian dumpling made from bread or potato is a typical accompaniment to meat, fish, and poultry. Flavored sweet or sour, the most popular variations include spinach and cheese.

Leberknödelsuppe: Considered the best of Austrian's many soups, this fine clear beef broth is served piping hot with little liver dumplings.

Palatschinken: A thinner version of the common pancake that can be served sweet with preserves, sugar, and honey or savory with cheese or meat.

Punschkrapfen: A delicious cake soaked in rum and filled with pastry crumbs, nougat, apricot jam, and chocolate.

Sacher torte: This famous Viennese moist dark-chocolate tart is made to a secret recipe at the Hotel Sacher (see Travelwise p. 251). It has delicate layers of tangy apricot jam set between tiers of chocolate sponge made from ground hazelnuts and melted chocolate.

Schweinsbraten mit semmelknödel: Roast pork remains an important component of Viennese cuisine and is typically seasoned with fresh herbs, such as sweet, young garlic. This dish is accompanied by bread dumplings, salad, and gravy.

Selchfleisch: A traditional dish of smoked meats cooked with sauerkraut (shredded cabbage cooked in spiced brine with onion, salt, and white wine) and served with dumplings.

Suppentopf: A soup made with the same clear broth used in leberknodelsuppe, but with shredded beef and root vegetables.

Tafelspitz: Along with the *Wiener schnitzel,* this boiled beef dish is one of Vienna's signature dishes. It consists of a piece of boiled sirloin steak that is served with fried grated potato *(rösti),* horseradish, and apple sauce.

Wiener schnitzel: This distinctively Viennese dish consists of a thin, boneless cut of meat—traditionally veal *(kalb),* but today pork *(schwein)* or turkey *(puten)* is frequently used instead—covered in breadcrumbs and fried. The golden brown schnitzel is then usually served with Viennese potato salad *(erdapfel salat).*

Wurstsemmel: Served with cheese and a slice of pickle, this popular filled-roll snack is packed with *extrawurst,* a special thinly sliced smoked sausage.

Zwiebelrostbraten: This hearty meal of sliced roast beef topped with fried onion rings is served with a generous portion of mashed or roasted potatoes.

bread rolls called *semmel*. Many of these dishes can still be found in the city's traditional restaurants, where portions are always generous and accompanied by plenty of local beer and wine. Although traditionally these dishes would have been made with the weird and lumpy bits that the butcher had left over at the end of the day, most restaurants now use cuts of meat that visitors will have heard of.

Like many city dwellers, younger Viennese have been moving away from heavy traditional cuisine and toward lighter evening meals. A growing number of chefs across the city offer what has become known as *neue Wiener küche* (new Viennese cuisine) in a variety of eateries with decor and prices to match.

Although the situation is improving, the concept of vegetarianism is an unfamiliar one to many Viennese chefs, and veganism is almost unheard of. Aside from the city's small but growing number of vegetarian restaurants (see Travelwise), it's best to remember to ask *"Ist das mit fleisch?"* (Is that with meat?) when placing your order.

Drinks

The region that surrounds Vienna is the heart of Austrian wine country, home to the renowned vineyards of the Wachau valley and numerous other wine-growing regions. As with its food, however, Vienna's taste in beverages has always had a broader outlook. The most quintessentially Viennese drink is coffee, a beverage that the people of Vienna have consumed in vast quantities since the late 17th century. Viennese coffee comes in all shapes and sizes, and is best appreciated at one of the city's traditional *kaffeehäuser*.

Wine: The Viennese wine-growing tradition dates back more than two thousand years with over 1,729 acres (700 ha) of vineyards now cultivated within the city limits. A patchwork of small hillside vineyards provide Vienna's unique backdrop, and are testament to the healthy businesses of the 230 vintners located on the outskirts of the city.

Following a national scandal in the 1980s involving adulterated wine, the Austrian government has strictly regulated the labeling of wines, dividing them into categories according to the quality of the grapes and the techniques used to make them. The lowest category is *tafelwein* (table wine), which can include wine made by blending grapes from numerous different regions; the next is *landeswein* (country wine), which has to be from just one region. The next level up includes *qualitätsweine* (quality wine) and *kabinett*, which are typically more dry than the lower two types. The highest level is *prädikatswein* (special quality wine), which includes the dessert wines produced in the region around Vienna. The region's unique specialty is *eiswein* (ice wine), a very sweet wine produced by leaving the grapes on the vine until the first frost of the year, which concentrates their flavor. Austria's finest wines are grown in the

> **Viennese coffee comes in all shapes and sizes, and is best appreciated at one of the city's traditional *kaffeehäuser*.**

Vienna's restaurants benefit from the city's location in the heart of Austrian wine country.

Wachau Valley, about 50 miles (85 km) northwest of Vienna, using riesling and *grüner veltliner* grapes.

Beer: Surprisingly, for a city in the middle of Austria's wine country, beer is almost as popular here as it is in the nation's traditional "beer belt" around Salzburg. The types of beer on offer are mostly inspired by Bavarian and Czech brewing traditions, although international standards are usually still available. There are plenty of small breweries and brewpubs *(gasthausbrauerei)* in the city, as well as larger companies like Ottakringer. Types of beer commonly sold in the city include *dunkel,* a dark heavy lager originally from Bavaria; *weizenbier,* a light wheat beer; *kellerbier* (or *zwickelbier*), an unfiltered pale ale; *bock,* a very strong (12–15 proof) dark lager; and pilsner, a light pale lager traditionally brewed in the Czech Republic. Beer is commonly sold in three different measures: *pfiff* (200 ml/6.7 fl oz), *seiterl* (300 ml/10.1 fl oz), and *krügerl* (500 ml/17 fl oz), with larger 1-liter *(mass)* glasses available in some traditional bars and beer gardens. ■

The Arts

Vienna is one of Europe's major cultural destinations, with a long history of involvement in the arts, as well as a vibrant contemporary cultural scene. Although it is most often associated with the musical legacy of Mozart, Beethoven, and Brahms, Vienna has a distinguished history in many other areas of the arts, particularly painting and architecture.

For most of its history, there was only one real driving force behind the Viennese cultural scene—aristocratic patronage. Although the generous support of the imperial court attracted many great creative minds to Vienna, it meant that the city's cultural output was dictated by the relatively narrow tastes of the city's wealthy elite. For the most part, this meant that big spectacles—opera, ballet, and massive orchestral pieces—always received considerably more support than humbler forms of creative expression.

This began to change in the late 18th and early 19th centuries, as the city's rising middle class began to spend money on cultural events. This led to the growth of the city's theater scene (which had previously been largely confined to the Burgtheater, a venue open only to aristocrats) and the rise of popular music like lieder and waltzes. By the late 19th century, the Viennese aristocracy had become old-fashioned and stuck in its ways, and the role of cultural patron passed to the city's wealthy industrialists and businessmen. The bold new ideas of the Viennese Secession, while shunned by the aristocracy, were enthusiastically supported by industrialists like Margaret Wittgenstein, Ferdinand Bloch-Bauer, and August Lederer. During the Red Vienna era, great efforts were made to make high culture accessible to all—subsidizing many institutions and opening the formerly aristocratic institutions of the Burgtheater and Wiener Staatsoper (Vienna National Opera) to the general public.

> For most of its history, there was only one real driving force behind the Viennese cultural scene—aristocractic patronage.

Today, Vienna brings together its long history of high culture with a modern edginess that makes for a highly creative arts scene. World-class nonprofit art institutions, highly regarded galleries, and the finest art fairs in Europe work with Vienna's new design studios, independent filmmakers, writers, musicians, and artists to keep Vienna on the cultural map. The Viennese have a reputation for being discerning patrons of the arts. It is rare for new plays, operas, or concert seasons to struggle to find an audience. In addition to this popular support, Vienna's cultural institutions are financially supported, both at a local and national level, by the Austrian Ministry of Arts and Culture.

Architecture

Vienna is a city known for its spectacular architecture, which includes not only colossal landmarks like St. Stephen's Cathedral and the Hofburg Palace but also the

Gustav Klimt's "The Kiss" (1907), on display at the Belvedere

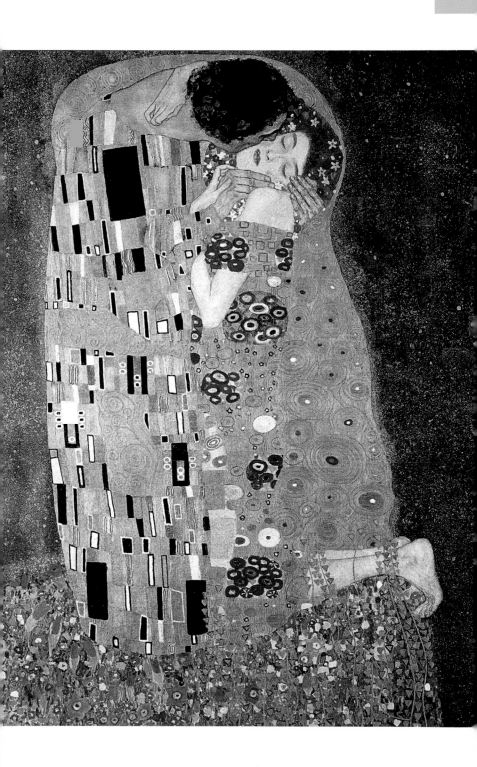

numerous, more modest masterpieces like the medieval Gothic Minoritenkirche or the elegant *Jugendstil* (see p. 51) commercial buildings on the Fleischmarkt. Although Vienna has seen its share of the wars and disasters that have swept through Europe over the centuries, its buildings are better preserved than those of many of its fellow European capitals, as it largely avoided the devastating area bombing of the Second World War.

Medieval Vienna was a compact walled city, not the imperial capital it would one day become, but certainly not a backwater. The oldest surviving building in the city is the Ruprechtskirche (see p. 86), which is a very simple church covered with ivy and topped by a squat stone tower. The city's first great architectural masterpieces were built between the 12th and 15th centuries, during which time the dukes of Babenberg and the early Habsburg emperors made Vienna into one of Europe's major cultural centers. Their generous patronage attracted a small army of highly skilled carpenters, masons, and sculptors to the city, who were put to work building the Gothic structures of St. Stephen's Cathedral and the Minoritenkirche.

Between the early 16th century and the late 17th century, the looming threat of Ottoman invasion meant that no major building projects were undertaken that weren't in some way related to defense. It was only after the Ottoman threat was lifted in the

The Masters of Viennese Baroque

Few individuals have had more of an influence over the appearance of Vienna than the two great architects of the baroque age: Johann Fischer von Erlach (1656–1723) and Johann Lukas von Hildebrandt (1668–1745). They arrived in the city, versed in the latest architectural ideas from Italy, just at the time when the Viennese aristocracy was realizing that more than a century had passed since their palaces had last been in fashion.

The older of the two architects, Johann Fischer von Erlach, was the first to establish himself in the city (in 1688). As a young man Fischer von Erlach studied in Rome under the Italian baroque architect Gian Lorenzo Bernini (1598–1680) and worked on projects in Venice. Almost as soon as he arrived in Vienna, his credentials got him commissions from the highest sources, including the emperor himself. His most notable buildings include the Karlskirche (see p. 187), the Winter Riding School (see p. 104), and the great hall of the Nationalbliotek (see pp. 111–112). He was made Court Archi-

tect in 1705, and held onto this position until his death.

His great rival was Johann Lukas von Hildebrandt, a German-Italian architect who arrived in the city in 1697. Lukas von Hildebrandt also trained in Italy, although with a less renowned mentor. He had followed his training with several years as a military engineer, during which time he served in the army of Prince Eugene of Savoy. In Vienna Prince Eugene was his most important early patron, putting him in charge of the construction of the prince's palaces (the Winter Palace and the Belvedere) after he quarreled with Fischer von Erlach.

Over the next 20 years, the two architects were locked in a bitter rivalry, constantly competing for work and prestige. Lukas von Hildebrandt was popular with the aristocracy but Fischer von Erlach was able to win royal commissions, thanks to his influence in court. Lukas von Hildebrandt was more prolific, however, and his many students continued his style after his death.

last two decades of the 17th century that the Viennese aristocracy felt comfortable sinking their money into grand residences and civic projects. In just a few decades, Vienna was transformed from a Renaissance fortress-town to a majestic baroque city. Flush with tribute and war booty, the vastly wealthy Austrian aristocracy went on a century-long spending spree. They were spurred on by notoriously extravagant Habsburg rulers like Leopold I (r. 1657–1705), Josef I (r. 1705–1711), Charles VI (r. 1711–1740), and Maria-Theresia (r. 1740–1780). Fashionable architects like Johann Lukas von Hilde-brandt and Johann Fischer von Erlach (see sidebar opposite) were inundated with work, and huge baroque palaces sprung up in the fields around the city.

The term baroque, at least as applied in Vienna, encompasses a broad range of 18th-century architectural styles from restrained neoclassical simplicity to nauseatingly ostentatious rococo. Elements of the style, such as ornate window surrounds and exterior stucco decoration, remained standard features of Viennese urban architecture until the early 20th century.

Otto Wagner's Jugendstil Kirche am Steinhof

During the 19th century, the unyielding conservatism of the last few Habsburg monarchs had a profound effect on the city's architectural tastes. Rather than go for something new, wealthy patrons increasingly chose designs that mimicked the styles of earlier generations. The numerous different architectural revival styles are typically grouped under the heading of historicism.

The style reached the peak of its popularity at around the same time that the city's planners were designing the Ringstrasse, meaning that many of the city's largest and grandest buildings were created using revival styles. Historicist architectural theory posited that some styles were ideally suited to particular types of buildings—neoclassical for institutions of government and finance; neo-Renaissance for cultural institutions; and neo-Gothic for churches. The historicist buildings of the Ringstrasse roughly follow these rules, with the Justizpalast and the Parliament built in the neoclassical style; the Burgtheater and the Staatsoper in the neo-Renaissance style; and the Votivkirche in the neo-Gothic style.

By the end of the 19th century, however, many architects had grown tired of the restrictive nature of historicism and wanted to branch out into something new. The most prominent figure among these experimental architects was Otto Wagner (1841–1918), whose style gradually drifted from academically correct historicism to a flowing, decorative style known as Jugendstil (youth style). A variation on French art nouveau, Jugendstil proved to be popular with the city's growing middle classes. Over the years the style became simpler as its proponents came under the influence of the proto-modernist architect Adolph Loos (1870–1933), who scorned exterior ornament and unnecessary architectural details.

Visual Arts

The area around Vienna has a long artistic history, one of the longest in the world, in fact. In 1908, a group of archaeologists from the Naturhistorisches Museum unearthed a roughly 24,000-year-old statuette in a village just upriver from Vienna. This 4.3-inch-high (10 cm) statuette, known as the "Venus of Willendorf" (see p. 115), is one of the oldest known examples of human artistic expression.

Vienna's ancient precursor, Vindobona, was too rugged a settlement to have any notable cultural life. Its population of soldiers and frontier traders were more concerned with practical matters like clean water, strong defenses, and good sewers than they were with art. However, some aspects of Roman artistic culture did make it this far north: Fragments of stone monuments have been found in a Roman graveyard near Herrengasse (once a Roman road named Limestrasse), and votive statues have been unearthed near Kärntner Strasse.

The art of the baroque era is known for its extravagance—its use of bold colors, dramatic subjects, and elaborate ornamentation.

Although it tends to be eclipsed somewhat by the city's baroque golden age, medieval Vienna was one of Europe's great cultural centers, attracting skilled craftsmen, writers, and artists from all over Europe. To a large extent the art of the time was an integral part of its architecture—the decoration of St. Stephen's Cathedral, for example, would have originally included colorful frescoes and wood-panel paintings in addition to the sculptures that you can see today. Similar religious art would have once adorned the interiors of almost every church and monastery in the city. What survives of this hoard of religious art is now kept in the city's great treasuries and museums. At the collections of the Dommuseum (see p. 71), the Deutschordenshaus (see p. 73), and the Schottenkirche (see pp. 137–138) visitors can see the beautiful illuminated manuscripts, altarpieces, and paintings that the city's religious institutions commissioned over a great many years.

Vienna's medieval art is not exclusively religious, however. The Niedhart Frescoes (see p. 89) are rare examples of medieval secular wall painting, commissioned by a Viennese merchant at the beginning of the 14th century. In the Middle Ages decorative artworks like this would have been a common feature in the homes of merchants and noblemen, but most have been lost to baroque renovations and general decay.

For most of the period typically associated with European Renaissance, Vienna was rarely visited by the Habsburg court. This meant that although Habsburg rulers were known as patrons of several Renaissance artists—most notably the German painter and engraver Albrecht Dürer (1471–1528), who created several of his most important works for Emperor Maximilian I—this had little impact on the cultural life of the city.

The art of the baroque era is known for its extravagance—its use of bold colors, dramatic subjects, and elaborate ornamentation. The most common format for painting in baroque Vienna was the fresco, a type of mural painting that required artists to paint directly onto the walls and ceilings of buildings. Baroque frescoes typically involved extensive use of trompe l'oeil painting techniques, which use tricks of perspective to create an illusion of depth and solidity. This is particularly striking in Andrea Pozzo's (1642–1709) ceiling fresco in the Jesuitenkirche (see p. 74), which features a trompe l'oeil dome painted onto a flat part of the ceiling. The technique was also used to striking effect by the Austrian painter Johann Michael Rottmayr (1656–1730), whose huge and complex frescoes can be seen in the Palais Liechtenstein and the Karlskirche.

During the 19th century, the visual arts in Vienna came to be dominated by the academic school of painting. This style emerged from Europe's academies of fine art (such as Vienna's Akademie der Bildenden Künste) in the late 18th century, and was characterized by a strong emphasis on technical skill. The Viennese had a particular liking for historicism—a variation on the academic style that placed an even greater emphasis on the imitation of past masters. The artists of the historicist period were known for their massive "history paintings." These were rigidly formulaic pieces that depicted scenes from ancient mythology and history.

After decades of creative stagnation, Vienna's visual arts scene exploded back into life in 1897 with the establishment of the Viennese Secession (see pp. 54–55). This self-consciously modern artistic movement laid the groundwork for a new generation of artists, whose highly stylized, roughly painted pieces were classified as expressionist. The most prominent exponent of this new style was Egon Schiele (1890–1918), a protege of Gustav Klimt whose paintings shocked Viennese society with their frank and often extremely unflattering depictions of the human form. Other prominent Viennese expressionists included Oskar Kokoshka (1886–1980) and Richard Gerstl (1883–1908).

This golden age of Viennese artistic culture ended rather abruptly at the end of the First World War. The interwar years were a lean period for Viennese art. During the 1920s, the city was dominated by the socialist SDAPÖ (see pp. 31–33), who had a rather utilitarian view of art, and the fascist takeover of the country in the 1930s forced many of the city's prominent cultural figures into exile.

The end of the Second World War saw the rebirth of the city's artistic community, centered on the recently reopened Akademie der Bildenden Künste, which was now staffed by former associates of Klimt and Schiele. The most prominent of the post-war artistic movements was the Viennese School of Fantastic Realism, led by Ernst Fuchs

(continued on p. 56)

Hans Makart

The most prominent painter from Vienna's historicist period was Hans Makart (1840–1884), whose highly decorative history paintings and carefully composed portraits made him a well known celebrity. He was enormously successful at just about everything he turned his hand to, whether it was furniture design, high fashion, or interior decoration. In 1879 he was entrusted with just about every aspect of Emperor Franz-Josef and Sisi's silver wedding anniversary parade. He designed the costumes, the coaches, and choreographed the whole event. In his later career, Makart's work became more stylized and began to display hints of the sensual ornamentation that would later become the hallmark of the Viennese Secession painter Gustav Klimt.

The Vienna Secession

In 1897, a group of prominent Viennese artists broke with the city's established artistic institutions to form a new group, known as the Secession. Although it lasted for only around eight years, the Secession had a profound impact on European culture, breaking the stifling traditions of 19th-century Viennese art and design.

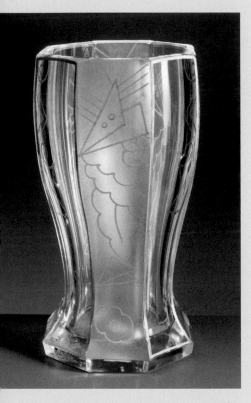

A vase designed by the Wiener Werkstätte

For most of the 19th century, Vienna's art scene was shaped by the Genossenschaft bildender Künstler (Association of Visual Artists; usually known as the Künstlerhaus), an organization associated with the Akademie der Bildenen Künste and the old-fashioned tastes of the Viennese aristocracy.

In the 1890s, however, many of Vienna's younger artists began to come into conflict with the old historicist painters who ran the Künstlerhaus. The breaking point finally came in 1897, when the Künstlerhaus refused to send the work of any of its younger members to an international exhibition in Paris. The disgruntled young artists, led by the 35-year-old painter Gustav Klimt (1862–1918), announced that they were breaking their ties to the Künstlerhaus and starting their own organization. They were joined by the designer Koloman Moser (1868–1918) and the architect Otto Wagner (1841–1918), whose students were already closely involved with the group.

The Secession, as it came to be called, brought together artists, designers, architects, and a host of other creative thinkers. The disparate disciplines were united under the aim of creating what the group referred to as *Gesamtkunstwerk*, or a total work of art. These were events or projects that would involve every member to some capacity, with equal importance being given to every role. They hoped to move art out of galleries and into everyday life, elevating disciplines like product design, while making fine art more widely accessible.

Making Their Mark

The first priority for the group was the acquisition of a space that could be their headquarters and primary exhibition hall. The new mayor of Vienna, Karl Lueger (see p. 30), was persuaded to give them a plot of land on Karlsplatz that had been recently reclaimed from the river. It was a provocative location, close to the city's musty old art institutions and a stone's throw from the historicism pomp of the Ringstrasse.

The design of the building was entrusted to Josef Olbrich (1867–1908), who came up with the bold, minimalist structure. He worked closely with Koloman Moser and Josef Hoffmann (1870–1956), a designer and former student of Otto Wagner, to design the exterior decoration and the layout of the interior spaces, creating a physical embodiment of the Secession's artistic ideas. While it is almost universally loved today, the Viennese people of the time weren't so kind, referring to the building as a "mausoleum" and the gilded orb over the entrance as "the golden cabbage."

While the building was being constructed, the group began to publish a magazine called *Ver Sacrum* (Sacred Spring in Latin), to propagate their ideas. This publication featured innovative graphic design by Moser and Hoffmann, art prints and illustrations by Klimt, and articles by many of Europe's most prominent writers and art theorists.

Exhibitions

Between 1898 and 1905, the Secession organized several major exhibitions every year. Many of these events were devoted to the work of the group's members, but they also put on frequent exhibitions of work by artists they admired or were inspired by. It was at the Secession Building that Austria's first ever exhibition of French Impressionist art took place in 1903.

In keeping with their idea of the Gesamtkunstwerk, every aspect of the exhibition space and its promotional materials was carefully designed to fit in with an overall aesthetic concept. Every design decision, from the hanging of the paintings to the typeface on the tickets, was overseen by the Secession's creative leaders.

The pinnacle of this approach was the 1902 "Beethoven Exhibition." A total of 21 artists, designers, and architects worked to create a so-called designed space around Max Klinger's monumental sculpture of the composer. Klimt painted his "Beethoven Frieze" (which remains in the Secession to this day) as part of this project, while the atonal composer Arnold Schoenberg (who was not officially part of the

Wiener Werkstätte

In 1903, Koloman Moser and Josef Hoffmann left the Secession to form the Wiener Werkstätte (Vienna Workshop)—a design collective inspired by the British arts and crafts movement. They took the aesthetic ideas of the Secession and applied them to the design of everyday objects, such as kitchenware, furniture, and textiles.

The emphasis was always on carefully considered, modern design that avoided the forced economy of mass production as well as the wasteful ostentation of handmade luxury items. They continued to work closely with many members of the Secession, however, on projects like Otto Wagner's Kirche am Steinhof (see p. 217), which featured stained-glass windows and interior decoration by Koloman Moser. The Wiener Werkstätte closed in 1932.

Secession, but agreed with its ideas) wrote and conducted a special variation on Beethoven's Ninth Symphony for the event. The exhibition was seen by around 60,000 people in the few months it was open, and made a lasting impression on Viennese culture.

The End of the Secession

The Secession's glory days ended in 1905, when Klimt and many other prominent members severed their ties with the group to protest the increasing commercialization of its activities. Although the Secession kept going for several more years, it was only as a group of painters, without the interdisciplinary aspect that had marked its most notable achievements. The period of Viennese artistic preeminence associated with the Secession came to a final and tragic end in 1918, when many of the most important figures associated with the movement—including Klimt, Schiele, Moser, and Wagner—died within a few months of each other.

(b. 1930) and Arik Brauer (b. 1929), which combined a finely detailed, traditionalist painting style with surreal subject matter. Another notable movement was Friedensreich Hundertwasser's (see p. 175) transautomatism, which produced colorful abstract paintings filled with swirling lines and spirals. From the 1960s onward the Viennese art scene has taken an abrupt turn toward the conceptual and avant-garde. Starting with movements like Viennese Actionism, which is documented at length in the MUMOK (see p. 118), the emphasis has been on installation and performance art.

Literature

The earliest examples of what can be reasonably defined as Viennese literature were written during the 12th and 13th centuries, by *minnesingers* (troubadours) attached to the Babenberg court. Reinmar von Hagenau was the first of these poets whose work has survived, at least in part, to the present day. He wrote lyric poems and songs about the idealized world of knightly chivalry and courtly love. Reinmar is better known as the mentor of Walther von Vogelweide, another knight-poet who produced a broader and better preserved body of work. In addition to stock poems of courtly love and chivalry, Walther wrote scathing critiques of the powerful men of the time, as well as polemical attacks on what he saw as an overreaching Catholic Church. The last notable court poet was Niedhart von Ruenthal, whose poems broke with the established traditions of chivalry and courtly love, instead focusing on the lives of common people. Although they wrote for the imperial court, these poets' work had a wider influence on Viennese culture, as can be seen from the so-called Niedhart Frescoes (see p. 89) in the Stephansdom Quarter. This initial burst of literary activity came to an end with the fall of the Babenberg dukes in the late 13th century. This marked the beginning of a long period during which Vienna produced little literature, and nothing of any great significance. Although Habsburg rulers like Josef II prided themselves on their erudition and their great libraries, they didn't really do anything to encourage literary culture in their court.

The Art of Defining Austrian Literature

The question of what counts as Austrian literature has long been a source of debate among literary scholars. During the Middle Ages and early Renaissance, Austria was usually thought of as part of a greater Germanic nation, defined by its shared culture and language—the poets and writers of the era traveled freely across political boundaries and rarely associated themselves with any particular place. In more recent centuries the constantly evolving political and cultural landscape of central Europe has made it possible for a writer to have lived his or her whole life hundreds of miles from Austria, yet still be considered Austrian, while another might have spent his or her most productive years in Vienna, yet belong firmly to the German, Czech, or Hungarian literary tradition.

The growth of a literate middle class in the early 19th century encouraged the development of a new literary scene, centered on the Theater-in-der-Josefstadt (see p. 215) and the Theater an der Wien (see p. 203). Unlike the aristocratic Burgtheater, these theaters admitted anyone who could afford a ticket. In addition to staging German plays, these theaters showcased the work of local playwrights, such as Johann Nestroy

(1801–1862), Ferdinand Raimund (1790–1836), and Franz Grillparzer (1791–1872). Works by all three of these writers are still frequently performed at theaters in Vienna, particularly the complex plays of Grillparzer, who used historic settings or mythological subjects to disguise his bitter criticisms of the Habsburg regime.

Vienna's literary culture didn't really come into its own until the early 20th century, when a modern, countercultural style began to emerge from the community of young writers that gathered in the city's coffeehouses. Some of these writers were so immersed in the intellectual social atmosphere of Café Central that they never got around to doing much writing. The fame of the poet Peter Altenberg (1859–1919), for example, rests more on his reputation as a coffeehouse wit than it does on his rather slender poetic output. More heavyweight literary figures included Arthur Schnitzler (1862–1931), a playwright and short story writer; Karl Kraus (1874–1936), a satirist, essayist, and poet; and Felix Stalten (1869–1945), whose prolific output was characterized by a strange mixture of children's stories (most notably *Bambi: A Life in the Woods,* later adapted by Walt Disney), highbrow theater criticism, and pornographic novels.

> **Vienna's literary culture didn't really come into its own until the early 20th century, when a modern, countercultural style began to emerge.**

The literature of the interwar period was defined by the writers Robert Musil (1880–1942) and Joseph Roth (1894–1939). Their masterpieces—Musil's *Man Without Qualities* (written during the 1930s, published after his death) and Roth's *Radetzky March* (1932)—are both epic novels that trace the decline of Vienna's aristocratic elite and the moribund political system that supported it.

Since the Second World War, Vienna has remained the literary center of Austria, home to many internationally renowned writers. The most important of these writers was the playwright and novelist Thomas Bernhard (1931–1989), whose aggressive, experimental plays explored Austria's relationship with its troubled past. Although artistically successful (many of his plays premiered at the Burgtheater), Bernhard was generally disliked in Austria for his harsh criticisms of the country. It would seem that the dislike was mutual, however, as when Bernhardt died he left a will that stipulated that he was to go into "posthumous literary exile"—forever banning the production of his works in Austria. A similarly combative stance has been adopted by the two biggest figures in Austrian literature today—Peter Handke (b. 1942) and Elfriede Jelinek (b. 1946). The former made his debut with a play called *Offending the Audience* (1966), which, as its title suggests, involved four actors alternately discussing the nature of theater and yelling abuse at the audience for over an hour, and hasn't softened with age. The latter was awarded the Nobel Prize for Literature in 2004 for her dense and disturbing psychological novels, but is best known in Austria for her socialist and feminist political activism.

Music

Vienna is arguably the most important city in the history of music, having fostered the creative talents of Mozart, Beethoven, Schubert, Brahms, Strauss (junior and senior), and Schoenberg. Although it's been a long time since Vienna last produced a world-famous composer, the city's musical tradition is a crucial part of its cultural identity, and the city boasts a breathtaking variety of venues for opera and classical music. The city also continues to foster new talent, with a number of internationally renowned schools of music (where more than half the students are from overseas). It's not all orchestral music and opera, however; the city's summer festivals attract bands from all over Europe and internationally famous headliners.

Wiener Klassik: For many centuries Vienna's aristocracy employed musicians to entertain guests at their grand parties and balls. During the baroque era, it became common for wealthy members of the imperial court to commission unique pieces of music from local composers. Over the years this developed into a more elaborate system of patronage, with composers being gradually elevated in social status from something akin to a skilled artisan to that of a modern celebrity. This change took place during the late-18th and early-19th centuries, an era known as Wiener Klassik (classical Vienna), when the city's music scene was transformed by the work of three world-famous composers.

....

The city boasts a breathtaking variety of venues for opera and classical music.

....

The first of these was Joseph Haydn (1732–1809), an innovative composer who is often credited with inventing the symphony and the string quartet as we know them today. He was born in the town of Rohrau (see p. 225), a few miles southeast of Vienna. As a child he was a choirboy at St. Stephen's Cathedral, and spent most of his adolescence working as a musician while teaching himself music theory from old textbooks. In 1761, Haydn was hired by Prince Paul Anton Esterhazy as a *kapellmeister* (musical director), a post that he held for the next 30 years. It is during this period that he wrote most of his important works, including symphonies, concertos, and piano sonatas. He spent the last 20 years of his life as a freelance composer and teacher, whose students included Ludwig van Beethoven. He was highly respected by the musicians and composers of Vienna; Mozart, a friend of his, called him "Papa Haydn."

EXPERIENCE: Vienna's Oldest Marching Band

For an authentic taste of the pomp of imperial Vienna, there are few more evocative spectacles than a performance by the **Hoch und Deutschmeister Band** (www.deutschmeister.at). This 35-member marching band was founded in the late 18th century as part of the Hoch und Deutschmeister Regiment of the Austrian army. Throughout the 19th and early 20th centuries, it was Austria's foremost military band, and its members were sent on tours all over the world. With the breakup of the Austro-Hungarian Empire in 1918, and the disarmament of its army, the Hoch und Deutschmeister Band re-formed as a private organization but kept all of its old traditions.

Between May and October, the band performs a weekly public concert. At 11 a.m. every Saturday, the band's 35 members assemble at the eastern end of the Graben (see p. 124). The musicians, who range in age from 18 to 82, are all dressed in the 19th-century dress uniform of the Hoch und Deutschmeister regiment—a navy blue tunic with a gold-edged peaked cap. After a 40-minute recital the band marches down the Kohlmarkt to Michaelerplatz, in the shadow of the Hofburg.

On October 9, 1762, while Haydn was settling into his job at the Palais Esterhazy, a six-year-old boy from Salzburg, named Wolfgang Amadeus Mozart, gave his first performance in Vienna. Over the next few months the young protégé and his family performed at palaces all over the city, including a performance for Empress Maria-Theresia at the Schönbrunn Palace. Mozart returned to the city as a young man in 1781 as part of the Bishop of Salzburg's entourage. He was utterly overwhelmed by the city and the opportunities it offered him. Within just a few days, the impulsive Mozart had been fired by his patron and thrown out of his lodgings at the Deutschordenhaus (literally, he was kicked out of the front door by the steward).

In Vienna he was exposed to a new and dazzling variety of influences that inspired some of his finest works. For example, the imperial adviser Gottfried van Swieten (son of Gerard van Swieten) lent him a massive sheaf of Bach and Handel pieces from the Hofbibliotek (now the Nationalbibliotek) that he pored over for weeks. In addition to a constant stream of symphonies, masses, concertos, and sonatas, Mozart composed several operas while he was in Vienna, including the *Marriage of Figaro* (1786) and *Cosi fan Tutte* (1787), both of which premiered at the Burgtheater. His last opera, *The Magic Flute* (1791), was written for the newly opened Theater an der Wieden. In Vienna Mozart lived a famously dissolute life, constantly getting into debt and spending his evenings at lavish society events. This extravagant lifestyle, coupled with his exhausting workload, took its toll on Mozart's health, and he died of an unknown illness at the age of just 35. He was buried in St. Marx Cemetery but his gravestone is in the Zentralfriedhof (see p. 179).

In 1787 a young German musician by the name of Ludwig van Beethoven traveled to Vienna from his hometown of Bonn. He hoped to gain a position as Mozart's student, but it is not known if the two men ever met. Some scholars believe that he auditioned for Mozart but was rejected by the already overworked composer; others that he failed to secure a meeting with the great man. He returned to the city five years later, shortly after Mozart's death, to study with Joseph Haydn. Over the next few years he wrote relatively little, instead concentrating on his studies and refining his performances by playing at society parties. From 1795, however, Beethoven began a period of prolific artistic activity, composing numerous symphonies, string quartets, and piano sonatas. He actively cultivated a reputation as the heir to Mozart's genius, writing works that closely followed the late composer's style. It was during this period that Beethoven first noticed that he was losing his hearing. Despite this seemingly insurmountable handicap, Beethoven continued to compose music. In 1805 he moved to Baden (see p. 226) in order to avoid the noise of the city, although

This memorial in Buggarten is one of the many statues of Mozart in the city.

The Waltz

The dance known as the waltz was developed in the late 18th century from the *walzen* (spinning) dances of Austrian peasants. It was accompanied by music distinguished by its use of triple time (usually 3/4) and steady rhythm. When it was introduced to Vienna, the waltz caused something of a moral panic. Its fast pace, combined with the dancers' scandalously close embrace, led to many denouncing it as sinful.

After a few years, these initial objections quieted down and the dance became incredibly popular with the Viennese. New ballrooms were built in the city with enough space for thousands of dancers, and it soon became the dance of choice for everyone from princes to factory workers. The most significant composer of waltzes in this early period was Franz Schubert, who had many popular hits during the 1810s.

While the popularity of the dance and the music waned elsewhere in Europe, Vienna remained the city of the waltz. The rival composers Joseph Lanner (1801–1843) and Johann Strauss the elder (1804–1849) played to packed ballrooms every night. The true golden age of the waltz, however, was brought about by Johann Strauss the younger (1825–1899), who combined his father's rhythmic style with the flowing melodies of his father's rival. His compositions, which include the famous "An der Schönen Blauen Donau" ("The Blue Danube"), made him one of the most popular composers in Viennese history. Today, his music is a symbol of the city, played at civic events, balls, and festivities.

he returned to Vienna a few years later. One of his most famous works, the Ninth Symphony (1824) was composed several years after he had become profoundly deaf. When Beethoven died in 1827 he was one of the most famous men in Vienna, and thousands of people lined the streets for his funeral.

Among the mourners at Beethoven's funeral was a disheveled musician named Franz Schubert. Although his music belongs more to the Romantic era than to the Wiener Klassik period (see p. 58), his short but productive life fell almost entirely within this period. He was born in Alsergrund in 1797, the son of a teacher. Although his talent was evident from a very young age, no wealthy patron ever came and swept the young Schubert into high society. He was noticed, however, by the court composer Antonio Salieri (1750–1825), who arranged for his education at a prestigious choir school.

Although he composed numerous pieces for orchestras or large ensembles, he is best known as a composer of *lieder* (literally "songs")—simple romantic songs usually arranged for voice and piano. At first he performed these pieces among a small group of friends, but they found a wider audience in 1817, when he was introduced to the renowned singer Johann Michael Vogl (1768–1840). Together the two men became fixtures of Viennese high society parties, performing Schubert's lieder and his arrangements of other songs. Toward the end of the 1820s, Schubert began to get some measure of commercial success with pieces such as his song-cycle "Winterreisse" (1827). He had a chance to meet his idol, Beethoven, on a few occasions before the latter's death, reputedly impressing the old composer with his work. Schubert had never been a healthy man, however, and in the summer of 1828 he contracted a severe illness (probably typhoid fever) and died. After his death, his friends collected and organized his vast body of unpublished compositions, which were published a few years later. In 1897, on the centenary of his birth, Emperor Franz-Josef gave a speech hailing Schubert as one of Austria's finest composers, an accolade Schubert could not have imagined in his lifetime.

The Romantic Era: In the second half of the 19th century, while Vienna's ballrooms swayed to the tunes of the "Waltz King," Johann Strauss (see sidebar opposite), its concert halls were under the spell of Johannes Brahms (1833–1897), a German-born composer who settled in the city in 1867. In addition to his own Romantic compositions, Brahms was significant for his efforts to revive baroque music in its spiritual home. He rediscovered long-forgotten compositions by Joseph Haydn, Johann Sebastian Bach (1685–1750), and Mozart, and performed them in Vienna, often for the first time in centuries.

In 1898, composer and conductor Gustav Mahler (1860–1911) was appointed musical director of the Hofoper (now Staatsoper). Although Mahler had trained at the Vienna conservatory, he had spent most of the 1880s and 1890s making a name for himself with short stints at opera houses and orchestras all over Europe. His

The Vienna Boys' Choir singing during the city's Christmas celebrations

The Vienna Philharmonic periodically performs special concerts on the grounds of Schönbrunn Palace.

appointment marked the beginning of a new era for the Hofoper, with the tired repertory of the venue replaced by a constant stream of premieres, creative new stagings, and daring modern interpretations of established works. Although his directorship of the Hofoper was critically and commercially successful, his dictatorial and unreasonable persona made Mahler unpopular with the orchestra and singers. Despite his heavy workload and constant disputes with performers, Mahler managed to find time to write several symphonies and other pieces. His work bridges the gap between the romanticism of Brahms and the experimental compositions of the Second Vienna School.

The Second Vienna School: At the beginning of the 20th century, as the radical ideas of the Vienna Secession spread through the worlds of art and architecture, a similarly radical movement was developing in the world of music. The leader of this new school of composition was Arnold Schoenberg (1874–1951), a largely self-taught musician who hailed from the Viennese Jewish community of Leopoldstadt. Schoenberg learned to play the violin as a child, before progressing to the viola and cello in his teens. His compositions were initially fairly conventional, drawing on the style of the 19th-century Romantic composers, but he soon began to drift into more experimental territory. He attracted a small group of students that included the composers Alban Berg (1885–1935) and Anton Webern (1883–1945). Together these composers developed a style today known as atonal music, which bypasses traditional musical structures and conventions. Initially Schoenberg and his pupils didn't attract much attention beyond a small circle of Viennese concert-

goers, but by the 1930s he was being hailed as one of the most important composers of his generation.

Opera: Vienna is well known for its long association with opera, which enjoys an extraordinary degree of popularity in the city. There are four permanently established opera houses in Vienna (see Travelwise p. 264) and several other theaters that periodically stage opera or operetta. The form has a long history in the city, going back to the 18th century, when it became popular with the imperial court. For many years the only venue for performances was the Burgtheater (which was closed to the general public), but the early 19th century saw the creation of several public opera houses, including the Theater an der Weiden and its successor, the Theater an der Wien. In 1869 the city gained its first purpose-built opera house (the Staatsoper; see p. 127), which continues to be one of Europe's most prestigious venues for opera. Three of Mozart's best known operas—*The Marriage of Figaro* (1786), *Cosi fan Tutte* (1790), and *The Magic Flute* (1791)—premiered in Vienna, as was Beethoven's *Fidelio* (1805) and Johann Strauss's *Die Fledermaus* (1874). Although opera started as an amusement for aristocrats, ordinary Viennese theatergoers took to it quickly, giving it a broad popularity that isn't seen in any other city.

Sacred Music: Although Vienna's musical tradition is often associated with the secular entertainments of the royal court, the city also has a long history of sacred music. The church hierarchy in Vienna and the surrounding region was mostly staffed by minor scions of grand aristocratic families—men with plenty of money to pay for artistic commissions. All the composers of the Wiener Klassik era wrote sacred music. Visitors to the city today can hear masses by Haydn, Mozart, Beethoven, Schubert, and Brahms, often performed in the churches where they premiered. The best known place to hear sacred music is the Burgkapelle (see p. 104), where the angelic voices of the Wiener Sangerknaben (Vienna Boys' Choir, see p. 105) perform in the 12th-century chapel built for the rulers of Vienna.

> Visitors . . . today can hear masses by Haydn, Mozart, Beethoven, Schubert, and Brahms, often performed in the churches where they premiered.

Contemporary Music: There are plenty of events and venues in Vienna where people make music without a grand piano or an orchestra in sight. In addition to a few venues around the outskirts of the city (see Travelwise p. 263), the Vienna contemporary music scene can be experienced at the Donauinselfest (see p. 167), a massive free music festival that takes place on the Donauinsel every summer. ■

The historic core of Vienna: a densely packed maze of baroque
mansions, old-fashioned coffeehouses, and busy shopping districts

Stephansdom Quarter

A statue of Gotthold Lessing, an advocate of religious tolerance, in Judenplatz

Stephansdom Quarter

For many visitors, the Stephansdom Quarter *is* Vienna. Indeed, among its mysterious cobbled backstreets, narrow alleyways, and broad medieval marketplaces you will find enough fascinating attractions to occupy your entire stay.

The towering spire of St. Stephen's Cathedral

The soaring 450-foot (137 m) spire of the Domkirche St. Stephan (St. Stephen's Cathedral; usually known simply as the Stephansdom) marks the geographic and spiritual center of Vienna. This masterpiece of medieval Gothic architecture is one of the finest cathedrals in Europe, and has been at the heart of religious life in the city for more than 800 years.

Today the cathedral stands in a setting that is quintessentially Viennese, a broad public space where the modern and the historic are closely intertwined. The architecture around the cathedral is a mixture of traditional Viennese baroque and eye-catching post-modernism, while beneath the flagstones the tunnels of the modern subway station are routed around, and sometimes through, the eerie passageways of the cathedral's medieval catacombs. Standing at the confluence of the Wienfluss (Vienna River) and Donaukanal (Danube Canal), the Stephansdom Quarter comprises some of the oldest parts of Vienna. It occupies around two-thirds of the city's 1st District (the Innere Stadt). Here the elegant baroque buildings of the 18th and 19th centuries are pressed tight into a road layout that has changed little since the Middle Ages. In fact, two of the neighborhood's main throughfares, the Wollzeile and Kärntner Strasse, closely follow the routes of Roman roads—relics of the ancient settlement of Vindobona.

There is more to this downtown neighborhood, however, than historic sightseeing opportunities. Medieval marketplaces have been assimilated into large pedestrianized shopping districts, where achingly fashionable (and painfully expensive) boutiques stand opposite sprawling craft markets where everything is lovingly handmade.

The Jewish Quarter

Standing on the site of an ancient Roman fort in the northern part of the Stephansdom Quarter are the historic buildings that once formed the core of Jewish Vienna. This district is home to the Jewish Museum and Holocaust Memorial on Judenplatz, as well as the magnificent Stadttempel—the only synagogue in Vienna to survive the systematic destruction of the Holocaust. Today the majority of the city's Jewish community (most of whom are refugees from Iran and the former Soviet Union) live in Leopoldstadt, but the Jewish Quarter remains an important cultural center. ■

Area of map detail

NOT TO BE MISSED:

The cavernous interior of St. Stephen's Cathedral **68**

Taking in the panoramic views of the Innere Stadt and beyond from the cathedral's South Tower **71**

The fine examples of Viennese *Jugendstil* (youth style) around the Fleischmarkt **75**

Watching the noon procession of mechanical figures at the Ankeruhr **80**

Biedermeier grandeur in the Stadttempel synagogue **83–84**

Searching for the enigmatic traces of Vienna's Jewish history below the stones of Judenplatz **86–88**

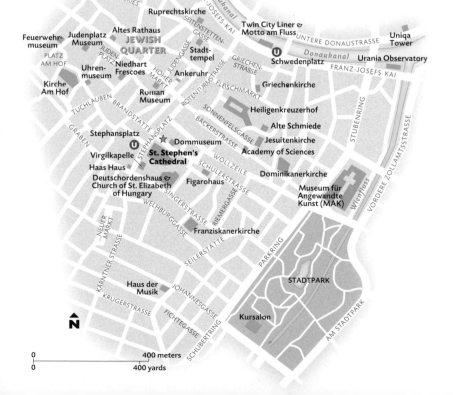

St. Stephen's & Around

From almost every corner of Vienna you can see the spire of St. Stephen's Cathedral—Austria's most visited and much beloved attraction and one of the tallest religious buildings on the planet. Although Austria as a nation is three-quarters Roman Catholic, the Viennese have slowly lost interest in religion over the years—though this hasn't affected how they feel about their adored cathedral.

The view from the South Tower of St. Stephen's Cathedral, looking west

Stephansplatz

 67

Visitor Information

✉ Stephansplatz Visitor Information, Stephansplatz U-Bahn Station

☎ (1) 245 55

🚇 Stephansplatz (U1, U3)

www.wien.info/en

St. Stephen's Cathedral

St. Stephen's Cathedral is without a doubt Vienna's most prominent landmark. It is visible from pretty much anywhere in the city, and the tolling of its bells resonates throughout the Stephansdom Quarter.

The original St. Stephen's Cathedral was built on this site in 1160, but nothing from this phase of construction remains. The oldest parts of the structure that can be seen today are the

13th-century **Riesentor** (Giant's Gate) and the 213-foot-high (65 m) **Heidentürme** (Towers of the Heathens) at the western end of the cathedral. Most of the building that stands today, including its two huge towers, dates from the 14th century, when the church was reconstructed at the behest of Habsburg Duke Rudolf IV—an act that earned him the epithet of "The Founder." Construction stopped in the early 16th century, before the North Tower could be completed. St. Stephen's was badly damaged by the fire that spread through the Stephansdom Quarter in the chaos that followed the capture of the city by Soviet forces in 1945. Decades of painstaking restoration work, however, have made this damage almost impossible to detect.

The Interior: Unlike many other European cathedrals, the interior of St. Stephen's was never scrubbed bare by Protestant iconoclasts. Every one of its vast structural columns is decorated by life-size statues of biblical figures and saints; some are elaborately painted, while others have been carved from colorful and exotic stone.

The decoration, beautiful though it is, takes a back seat to the sheer scale of the interior space—sinuous stone columns branch out and meet in complex vaults high above the nave, and stained-glass windows that stand several stories high flood the space with multicolored light.

Interesting features of the interior include the **Kaiser Oratory;** a private prayer room for the emperor with windows that look out over the nave; and the spectacular **high altar.** On the southern side of the high altar is the **Tomb of Frederick III** (1415–1493), hewn from unusually dense red marblelike stone by sculptor Nikolaus Gerhaert van Leyden (1420–1473). Emperor Frederick is depicted on the lid of the crypt in his coronation finery, amid the coats of arms of all his dominions.

The undisputed highlight of the cathedral's interior decoration, however, is the 15th-century **pulpit** that stands against a pillar in the center of the nave. The pulpit is renowned for the astonishing

St. Stephen's Cathedral

🅰 67

✉ Stephansplatz

☎ (1) 515 52-3526

🚇 Stephansplatz (U1, U3)

www.stephans kirche.at

NOTE: St. Stephen's Cathedral is open 6 a.m.–10 p.m., seven days a week. In practice, however, visitors are discouraged from entering the cathedral when services are taking place, which means that visiting hours are typically restricted to 9 a.m.–11:30 a.m. and 1 p.m.–4:30 p.m. Monday to Saturday, and 1 p.m.–4:30 p.m. on Sundays.

Exploring St. Stephen's Cathedral

Admission to St. Stephen's Cathedral is free, but without a guide you can only walk around the transept and nave. Other areas of the cathedral, including the towers, can be accessed only as part of a guided tour.

The most popular tour is the **Cathedral Tour** *(\$, starts from the pulpit),* which covers the cathedral's interior. It takes around 30 minutes and is held in English at 3:45 p.m. daily from April to October. The English-language tour is often sold out, so it's wise to reserve a place in advance *(tel 1/515 52-3526, www.stephanskirche.at).* Alternatively, visitors can pick up an **audio guide** *(\$\$, available from the counter near the main entrance),* which is available in several languages, including English. The audio guide details the interior of the cathedral, as well as the treasury.

There are also tours of the **Catacombs** *(see p. 70; \$, start from the north transept),* the **North Tower** *(\$),* and the **South Tower** *(\$).* The best of these tours, however, is the **Evening Tour** *(\$\$, starts from the South Tower at 7 p.m., every Sat. June–Sept.),* which takes you up the South Tower, through the attic over the nave, and then out along the parapets around the roof as the sun sets. At present, this tour is offered only in German, but it is still worth going along just to see this otherwise inaccessible part of the cathedral as well as the views.

The Great Bell of St. Stephen's

The largest bell in St. Stephen's Cathedral is the gigantic 22-ton (20 tonne) bell known to locals as the *Pummerin* (Boomer). The Pummerin was cast in 1711 using metal from cannon abandoned by the Ottomans after the failed 1683 Siege of Vienna.

When the bell was first raised into the South Tower, it took a team of 16 men pulling on ropes a quarter of an hour to swing it far enough for the clapper to strike. The forces generated by this massive swinging weight nearly shook the cathedral apart, and from then on it was usually kept still and rung by striking it with a hammer. In 1945 a fire swept through the tower and burned through the beams supporting the bell. The massive Pummerin crashed 230 feet (70 m) through the inside of the burning tower and shattered on the ground below. It was not until 1951 that a new bell was cast. Craftsmen melted down the broken bell and combined it with metal from some Ottoman cannon found in the collection of the Vienna Museum.

The new bell—officially called St. Mary—was even bigger than its predecessor. It was mounted in a special steel cradle and placed in the shorter, stronger North Tower. Even with its modern housing and computer-controlled swinging mechanism, it still vibrates the building so strongly that the cathedral's engineers allow it to be rung only a few times a year. Its low, booming toll can be heard around the city on Catholic feast days and on New Year's Eve, as well as during special civic or ecclesiastical events.

complexity and delicacy of its stonework, thought to be the work of either Anton Pilgram (1460–1516) or Nikolaus Gerhaert van Leyden.

The lower part of the structure is a treelike piece of Gothic tracery, while the upper part holds busts depicting the four Doctors of the Church. The most distinctive feature of the pulpit, however, is hidden under the stairs—here you will see a carving of a man leaning out of a window, staring up at the pulpit with a chisel in his hand. This figure is thought to be a self-portrait of the mason, whomever he was.

The Crypt & Tombs: The cathedral's crypts are a fascinating piece of imperial history, although touring them can sometimes feel a little ghoulish and surreal. They extend in a labyrinthine succession of narrow passages that begin under the nave before continuing beneath the high altar and out under the flagstones of Stephansplatz.

It is well worth taking the English-language guided tour of the catacombs (*$*), which winds its way though a series of vaults and past the sarchophagi of kings, dukes, archbishops, and other notables. One vault contains 78 small bronze urns, each holding the internal organs of Habsburg rulers (their bodies were interred in the Kapuzinerkirche—see p. 126; and their hearts in the Augustinerkirche—see p. 112). Another chamber is home to the stacked bones of more than 15,000 individuals who were re-buried after being removed from St. Stephen's cemetery in the 1700s during the outbreak of the bubonic plague.

The Towers: The towers of St. Stephen's are truly formidable. The **South Tower** (known to locals as Steffl—a diminutive form of Stephen) rises 450 feet (137 m) over Stephansplatz. It was completed in 1433 after 75 years of hard labor.

During the Ottoman siege of Vienna, the tower served as the main observation and command post for the defense of the old walled city. In peacetime it was manned by watchmen who rang bells if anything untoward was spotted in the city, such as a fire—a practice that ended only in 1955. The South Tower has a spiral staircase that ascends 246 feet (75 m) to the cathedral's observation platform.

The observation platform provides great views of the cathedral's famous roof, which is covered by more than 230,000 glazed tiles. On the south side of the building, the mosaic forms the double-headed eagle motif of the Habsburg dynasty while colorful depictions of the coats of arms of the City of Vienna and the Republic of Austria cover the northern side.

The **North Tower** was originally intended to be a mirror image of the South Tower, but construction work stopped when it was only about halfway complete, leaving it just 223 feet (68 m) tall. Although local folklore ascribes its truncated size to the work of the devil,

historical sources state that the money and political support needed to continue the construction simply ran out before it could be finished. The tower-stump was augmented with a Renaissance cap in 1529.

Stephansplatz

For most of its history, St. Stephen's Cathedral was surrounded by a large graveyard. This was where the great and the good of Vienna were buried, close to the tombs of bishops and kings. This custom ended in 1780, when, after a series of devastating plagues, Emperor Franz-Josef closed all the burial grounds within the city limits and converted the area around the cathedral to a public square.

INSIDER TIP:

In the Dommuseum, look for the ninth-century illuminated Gospel, the earliest book in the collection.

—CLIVE CARPENTER
National Geographic contributor

On the northern side of Stephansplatz, the **Dommuseum** (Cathedral Museum) houses the most valuable items belonging to the Archdiocese of Vienna. In addition to holy relics and altar-pieces, the collection includes numerous works of religious art that were donated to the cathedral. Highlights of the collection

Dommuseum (Cathedral Museum)

🅰 67

✉ Stephansplatz 6

☎ (1) 515 52-3300

🕐 Closed Sun. & Mon.

💲 $$

🚇 Stephansplatz (U1, U3)

www.dommuseum.at

Virgilkapelle

🏛 67

✉ Stephansplatz
   U-Bahn Station

☎ (1) 513 58 42

🕐 Usually closed
   Mon.

💲 $$

Ⓜ Stephansplatz
   (U1, U3)

**www.wien
museum.at**

include a pair of 13th-century Syrian glass decanters, the only known portrait of Rudolf IV, and the sword of St. Ulrich.

In the southeastern corner of Stephansplatz the floor plan of a small chapel is marked out on the ground. This outline marks the position of a medieval crypt known as the **Virgilkapelle** (Vergilius Chapel) located around 39 feet (12 m) below the surface of the square.

The crypt was discovered in 1973 during the construction of the U-Bahn. Local historians have dated the structure to the mid-13th century, and many believe it was originally intended to house the body of a saint. The crypt was blocked off and forgotten when the graveyard around the cathedral was leveled to create the square in 1780. Today, the chapel can be accessed through the Stephansplatz U-Bahn Station.

The entire western side of the square was destroyed by Allied bombing raids in early 1945. As a result, the buildings on this side are much newer than the other nearby structures. The most striking of these new constructions is the 1990 **Haas Haus.** The mirrored glass edifice provides a surprising contrast to the medieval and baroque architecture around Stephansplatz. The building is packed with offices but does contain the popular but expensive Do & Co Restaurant *(Stephansplatz 12, tel 1/535 3969, www.doco .com/index_eng.htm)* which offers wonderful views of the cathedral.

EXPERIENCE: Sightseeing in a Vintage Horse-drawn Carriage

When it comes to sightseeing, many cities are always associated with an iconic mode of transport. Venice has its gondolas, Bangkok has its *tuk-tuks,* and London its red buses. In Vienna this role is played by the *fiaker* (traditional Viennese horse-drawn carriages). These open-top carriages are a fittingly grandiose way to tour the baroque edifices of the Innere Stadt.

Fiakers can be hired from stands in certain places around the Innere Stadt, including Stephansplatz, Heldenplatz, Albertinaplatz, Petersplatz, and Burgtheater. Alternatively, you can book a tour in advance with one of the city's established operators, such as **Fiaker Paul** *(Albrechtsgasse 26, tel 1/480 43 05, www.fiaker-paul. at/pages/en/the-company.php?lang=EN, $$$$$),* **Fiaker.co.at** *(Rosaliagasse 19, tel*

1/966 0261, www.fiaker.co.at, $$$$$), or **Fiaker Johann Trampusch** *(Essinggasse 49, tel 0664/302 00 76, www.wien-fiaker .at/en, $$$$$).* Reserving through one of these companies allows you to customize your tour to an extent or request one of their knowledgeable English-speaking guides to accompany you through the city. You can also reserve a romantic evening tour or an extravagant ride from your hotel to the opera.

Regardless of whom you book them with, the fiakers in the Innere Stadt take a fairly standard route through town, avoiding busy roads and pedestrianized areas. A typical tour takes in St. Stephen's Cathedral, the Hofburg, the Opera House, and the neoclassical parliament building before returning to St. Stephen's.

Many of the interactive exhibitions at the Haus der Musik demonstrate music fundamentals.

East Toward the Stadtpark

When standing in Stephansplatz, few visitors pay much attention to the building that occupies the southeastern corner of the square. Indeed, based on its facade, there is no apparent reason to do so. If you head south out of the square and left onto Singerstrasse, however, you will be rewarded with a chance to see one of the more unusual pieces of Vienna's ecclesiastical history. This building is the **Deutschordenshaus**—the headquarters of an organization called the Order of Brothers of the German House of St. Mary in Jerusalem—better known as the Teutonic Knights. This Roman Catholic religious order was founded in the Holy Land during the Crusades, and was

once a powerful military organization that controlled large areas of the Holy Land, as well as territory in Germany, Poland, and the Baltic States.

Although they sound like something out of the *Da Vinci Code,* these days they are a quiet monastic order, whose headquarters contains a church (St. Elizabeth of Hungary); a small hostel; and the **Schatzkammer** (Treasury), which functions as the Order's museum. The museum's collection was gathered by many generations of Teutonic Grand Masters over the order's 800-year history. It contains medieval altarpieces, golden chalices, and exotic Arabian swords.

In the southeastern corner of the old Innere Stadt, on Seilerstätte, lies the **Haus der Musik,** a
(continued on p. 77)

Deutschordenshaus

⚑ 67

✉ Singerstrasse 7/1

☎ (1) 512 10 65-214

🕐 Closed Sun. & Tues.

💲 $

🚇 Stephansplatz (U1, U3)

www.deutscher-orden.at

Haus der Musik

⚑ 67

✉ Seilerstätte 30

☎ (1) 513 48 50

💲 $$$

🚇 Karlsplatz (U1, U2, U4)

www.hdm.at

A Walk Around Stephansplatz

Exploring the area around Stephansplatz will reveal the fantastic architectural and historical patchwork that is the Innere Stadt, where 1900s art nouveau buildings often share walls with Renaissance palaces, and medieval cloisters are hidden behind 1960s commercial buildings.

Street performers in Stephansplatz

NOT TO BE MISSED:

The Dommuseum • Jugendstil architecture on Fleischmarkt • The church of Franziskanerkirche

Begin outside the western entrance to **St. Stephen's Cathedral ❶**, close to the steps that lead up from the U-Bahn station. Head to the left of the cathedral and along its northern side. On the left, built onto the side of the cathedral is the Dombauhütte (Cathedral Workshop)—where a staff of 20 masons and sculptors work year-round to maintain this grand building—while on the right there is the entrance to the **Dommuseum** (see p. 71). Head out of the square along Schülerstrasse and turn left onto Strobelgasse. Cross the lively commercial street of Wollzeile (named for its medieval wool market) and continue down the cobbled alleyway known as the Essiggasse, before turning right onto Bäckerstrasse.

This street soon opens out into **Dr.-Ignatz-Seipel-Platz ❷**, an elegant plaza that houses the Academy of Sciences and the Jesuitenkirche (Jesuit Church). The former is the headquarters of Austria's most prestigious research institution, housed in what was the *aula* (great hall) of the University of Vienna, where several pieces by Beethoven, Haydn, and Schubert had their first public performances.

It is the Jesuit Church (sometimes known as the Universitätskirche—University Church) that is the real highlight, however; this grand building, with its neatly symmetrical facade and copper-roofed towers, is a classic example of early baroque architecture. It was built in 1631 and remodeled by Italian Jesuit brother and multitalented artist Andrea Pozzo (1642–1709) in 1703. Behind the church's relatively austere exterior there is an interior of spectacular—some would say excessive—grandeur. It has a forest of ersatz marble pillars, gilded filigree decoration, and numerous allegorical ceiling frescoes all capped by Pozzo's remarkable trompe l'oeil dome, which is actually painted on a flat part of the ceiling!

From Dr.-Ignatz-Seipel-Platz, head down Sonnenfelgasse until you reach Schönlaterngasse, a narrow little side street that curves sharply to the right. Look for a broad archway set into a yellow building on your left, which leads into the broad courtyard of the **Heiligenkreuzerhof ❸**, a former monastic complex that dates from 1659. Local artisans gather twice monthly in this tranquil courtyard to sell their wares. Go straight across the courtyard and pass through the archway on the western side, which takes you through to Köllnerhofgasse.

Along the Fleishmarkt

Turn right and right again and you'll find yourself on the ancient thoroughfare of the **Fleishmarkt ❹**, a lively jumble of old and new buildings occupied by chic boutiques, cafés, and hotels. In addition to its curious old buildings, the street is also home to two fine examples of the Jugendstil (youth style) art nouveau architecture associated with the Viennese Secession (see p. 54). The first, on the right-hand side of the street at number 14, has a facade adorned with statues and twisting floral designs, all highlighted with

tasteful use of gold leaf. The second, on the left at number 7, was originally owned by Julius Meinl, a famous coffee importer. The art nouveau facade holds three stylized friezes depicting the various stages of coffee production and consumption, including being picked (by scantily clad exotic "natives"), unloaded by dockworkers, and then drunk by high-class Viennese citizens.

Continue east along the street, past the ivy-covered buildings on narrow Griechenstrasse (where an old sign instructs cart drivers to lead their horses by the bridle and watch out for pedestrians) and the spectacular Griechenkirche (Greek Orthodox Church; see p. 80) to Postgasse, a street known for the baroque Dominican church known as **Dominikanerkirche** or St. Maria Rotunda **❺**. Built in the Roman-Lombardic style with

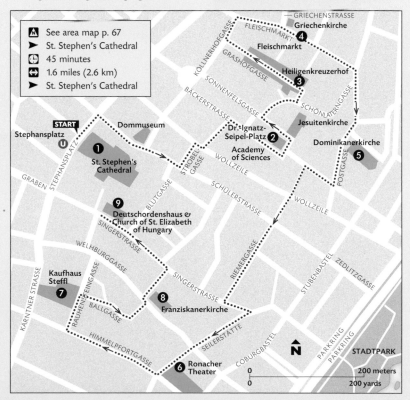

See area map p. 67
► St. Stephen's Cathedral
🕑 45 minutes
↔ 1.6 miles (2.6 km)
► St. Stephen's Cathedral

START
Stephansplatz Ⓤ
❶
St. Stephen's Cathedral

Dommuseum

Dr. Ignatz-Seipel-Platz **❷**
Academy of Sciences

Jesuitenkirche

Dominikanerkirche **❺**

GRIECHENSTRASSE
FLEISCHMARKT
Griechenkirche **❹**
Fleischmarkt
Heiligenkreuzerhof **❸**

❾
Deutschordenshaus & Church of St. Elizabeth of Hungary

Kaufhaus Steffl **❼**

❽
Franziskanerkirche

❻
Ronacher Theater

STADTPARK

0   200 meters
0   200 yards

prominent columns supporting the cornice, the style of the facade dates back to early baroque churches in Rome. Statues top the portico entrance and are set in recessed niches to each side. Inside, the church has a truly resplendent array of frescoes, ornate stucco, and fine religious art. The Dominikanerkirche's imposing architectural features are topped by a richly painted barrel-vaulted ceiling while six separate chapels contain an impressive range of altar paintings.

South of St. Stephen's

From here, turn south from the plaza to crisscross the Wollzeile and follow the examples of Viennese Jugendstil epoque along Riemergasse and Seilerstätte before you reach the corner of Seilerstrasse and Him-

The font inside the Church of St. Elizabeth

INSIDER TIP:

**If you visit the Domini-
kanerkirche, look up as you
approach the west door to
see the exquisitely beautiful
gilt organ.**

—CLIVE CARPENTER
National Geographic contributor

melpfortgasse, where the colorful neoclassical **Ronacher Theater** ⑥ *(Seilerstätte 9, tel 1/588 85, www.musicalvienna.at)* stands. This popular venue hosts big-budget productions of German musicals and broadway imports.

Continue west on Himmelpfortgasse. On the narrow Rauhensteingasse (on the right, just beyond the Ministry of Finance building on Himmelpfortgasse) is the rear entrance of **Kaufhaus Steffl** ⑦, a gigantic modern department store best known for its **Sky Bar** *(Kärntnerstrasse 19, tel 1/513 17 12)* a top-floor café with sweeping views across the Stephansdom Quarter. A small plaque on Rauhensteingasse marks the location of the property where Mozart died in 1791.

Just beyond the Mozart plaque, turn right into a narrow cobbled alleyway called the Ballgasse. This passage emerges opposite Franziskanerplatz and the Franciscan church of **Franziskanerkirche** (Church of St. Jerome) ⑧. This old monastic complex boasts a Renaissance-style exterior but is lavishly baroque inside with a high altar depicting the Virgin Mary, designed by Andrea Pozzo in 1707; and the oldest organ in Vienna, designed by Johann Wockerl in 1642. Exit Franziskanerplatz on the northern side to arrive at Singerstrasse, the home of swanky city apartments, five-star hotels, and the **Church of St. Elizabeth of Hungary** ⑨, identified by its slender white bell tower. It forms part of the headquarters of the Teutonic Order, an 800-year-old monastic order. Just past the church, turn right to get back to Stephansplatz.

The famous gilded statue of Johann Strauss in the Stadtpark

gadget-rich interactive museum that opened in 2000. Building on Vienna's prestigious musical history, it is designed to foster an enthusiastic understanding of music in children and adults. It uses tactile, interactive exhibitions to evoke the emotion and experience of music, as well as to explain the fundamental building blocks of musical composition like melody, rhythm, and counterpoint. The Haus der Musik also houses the historic archives of the Vienna Philharmonic Orchestra and hosts numerous classical concerts and music events in the evenings.

Stadtpark

About 5 minutes' walk east of the Haus der Musik are the carefully landscaped green spaces of the Stadtpark, which stretch over more than 16 acres (6 ha) of land between the Innere Stadt and Landstrasse. The park was created in 1861 as a joint venture between court artist Joseph Selleny and the royal gardener, Rudolf Siebeck. They designed a public park that spanned the east and west banks of the Wienfluss (Vienna River). The western half of Stadtpark is a neatly landscaped space in the style of an English palace garden, while the eastern side is mostly occupied by the Kinderpark (Children's Park), an area of playgrounds, child-friendly play areas, and hide-and-seek foliage.

The Stadtpark is much loved by the Viennese, who come here to relax and to take a walk down by the river. In the summer months, the park fills up with office workers soaking up the sun on their lunch breaks.

Stadtpark
🗺 67
🚇 Stadtpark (U4) or Stubentor (U3)

Kursalon

🏛 67

✉ Johannesgasse 33

🚇 Stadtpark (U4) or Stubentor (U3)

www.kursalonwien.at

Austrian Museum of Applied Arts (MAK)

🏛 67

✉ Stebenring 5

☎ (1) 711 36-248

🕐 Closed Mon.

💲 $$

🚇 Stubentor (U3) or Landstrasse (U3)

www.mak.at

At the southern end of the park is the **Kursalon,** an impressive 19th-century pavilion. This building was originally designed as a mineral healing spa, where people could come to "take the water." Today this opulent location is used to host society events, concerts, weddings, and conferences. When it is not hosting events, the Kursalon is home to Das Johann *(Johannesgasse 33, tel 1/512 57 90, www.restaurantjohann .at, $$$),* a popular restaurant with excellent views over the park from its second-floor terrace. Make sure you don't miss seeing the well known gilded statue of composer Johann Strauss.

Along the Riverfront

The **Museum für Angewandte Kunst** (Museum of Applied Arts; MAK), Vienna's foremost design museum, is located on the Stubenring just north of the Stadtpark. It houses a collection that ranges from Renaissance altarpieces and baroque statues to art deco furniture and 21st-century architecture. There is a guided tour of the museum in English every Sunday at midday *($).* The museum has several other branches around the city (such as the Geymüller Schlössel in Wahring; see p. 217).

A few minutes' farther north along the Stubenring stands the **Urania Observatory.** This much loved Vienna institution is positioned where the Wienfluss meets the Donaukanal. Built in 1910, the observatory was never intended for serious research work (its urban surroundings give off too much light) but rather as a place of education, where children

A view of Motto am Fluss from the artificial beach on Leopoldstadt

INSIDER TIP:

In the MAK, check out the unique Dubsky Porcelain Room, reassembled from a palace in Brno (in the Czech Republic).

—SALLY MCFALL
National Geographic contributor

and students could learn about astronomy.

Today, in addition to continuing its education work, the Urania building acts as a multipurpose cultural center, complete with movie theater, lecture rooms, and the excellent but expensive Bar Urania *(Uraniastrasse 1, tel 1/713 30 66)* café-restaurant.

From the café, diners are treated to an exceptional view along the riverfront, and across the Donaukanal to the newly built **Uniqa Tower.** By day, this structure is home to the workers of the Uniqa Insurance Company; by night, however, the building is transformed by mesmerizing light shows. The exterior of the building is covered by 160,000 computer-controlled LED panels, which are programmed to dance and sway in dizzyingly complex patterns, making the 250-foot-high (75 m) building seem as if it is moving.

Schwedenplatz: Upstream along the Donaukanal from Urania, Franz-Josefs-Kai opens out into the broad public square of Schwedenplatz. Positioned between two of Vienna's oldest river crossings, Schwedenplatz

has long been an important transport hub. Today, it is the meeting point of several tram lines, the U1 and U4 lines of the U-Bahn, and home to the city ferry terminal.

Last year, the rusting barges that had long served as the city's ferry terminal were replaced with an exciting modern building that curves out over the river, supported by slender steel columns. The building houses the ticket office for the **Twin City Liner,** which runs between Vienna and the Slovakian capital, Bratislava, located just over an hour downriver. Most of the building, however, is occupied by the spectacular Motto am Fluss *(see p. 251)*—a popular café, bar, and restaurant. The top floor and its large terrace are home to the café and bar, while the enclosed lower floor, with its floor-to-ceiling windows and panoramic river views, houses the stylish restaurant.

Heading away from the river, Schwedenplatz is typically covered by outdoor cafés and ice-cream stands throughout the summer. The best of these is the long-established Eissalon am Schwedenplatz *(Franz-Josefs-Kai 17, tel 1/533 19 96, www.gelato.at),* a family-run store that sells handmade Italian gelato.

Fleischmarkt

The street to the right of Eissalon am Schwedenplatz leads south toward the Fleischmarkt. At its far end there is a narrow stone staircase that leads up to Griechenstrasse (Greek Street; a reference to the immigrant

Urania Observatory
- 🅰 67
- ✉ Uraniastrasse 1
- ☎ (1) 729 54 94
- 🚇 Stubentor (U3) or Schwedenplatz (U1, U4)

www.urania
-sternwarte.at

Twin City Liner
- 🅰 67
- ✉ Franz-Josefs-Kai/Vorkai
- ☎ (1) 588 80
- 🕐 Operates between April 1 & Oct. 31
- 💲 $$$$$
- 🚇 Schwedenplatz (U1, U4)

www.twincityliner
.com

Motto am Fluss
- 🅰 67
- ✉ Franz-Josefs-Kai/Vorkai
- ☎ Café: (1) 252 55 11
  Restaurant: (1) 252 55 10
- 🚇 Schwedenplatz (U1, U4)

www.motto.at/
mottoamfluss

The Whimsical Ankeruhr

Positioned on a short bridge that connects two office buildings formerly occupied by the Anker Insurance Company, the famous Ankeruhr (Anker Clock) is a whimsical masterpiece of art nouveau design. It was constructed between 1911 and 1914, based on drawings by Viennese artist Franz von Matsch (1861–1942), who was a close friend and collaborator of Gustav Klimt. This unorthodox timepiece doesn't have a conventional clock face—instead of hands, a metal tag marked with the hour moves from left to right across a scale marked with the minutes.

Each hour-marker has a corresponding metal statue that depicts a figure from Viennese history, such as Roman emperor Marcus Aurelius (1 o'clock), medieval lyricist Walther von der Vogelweide (4 o'clock), Empress Maria-Theresia (11 o'clock), and composer Joseph Haydn (12 o'clock).

These figures appear on the left at the beginning of the hour, accompanied by a piece of music related to their lives, and move across the face of the clock as the hour progresses. At noon all 12 figures pass across the face of the clock, accompanied by their music. This entertaining spectacle attracts hundreds of tourists and is probably one of the most frequently photographed sights in Vienna.

Griechenbeisl

🅐 67

✉ Fleischmarkt 11

☎ (1) 533 19 77

🚇 Stubentor (U3) or Schwedenplatz (U1, U4)

www.griechenbeisl.at

Griechenkirche

🅐 67

✉ Fleischmarkt 13

☎ Closed Sat. & Sun.

🚇 Stubentor (U3) or Schwedenplatz (U1, U4)

community that settled here in the early 19th century)—a narrow alleyway framed by old buildings that seem to almost meet above your head. The Griechenstrasse emerges onto the historic Fleischmarkt next to the shambling, ivy covered **Griechenbeisl**—Vienna's oldest traditional inn, established in 1447. It is well-known for its carved sign that depicts *Leibe Augustin* (Dear Augustin), a character from local folklore. The inn has had many famous guests over the years, including the U.S. author Mark Twain. The low-vaulted ceiling of its dining room (called the Mark Twain Room) is covered with the autographs of famous patrons.

Right next to the inn is the Griechenkirche zur Heiligen Dreifaltigkeit (Greek Orthodox Church of the Holy Trinity), better known as the **Griechenkirche.**

It was built in 1861 by Vienna's Greek community, and later refurbished by Theophilus Hansen. The church's gorgeous exterior is covered with densely patterned two-tone brickwork, embellished with gilded archways and topped by a small, tiled dome. It easily outshines many of its better known baroque neighbors. The exterior, however, provides only the merest hint of what lies within. Inside, the church is decorated with frescoes, statues, and gilded Byzantine detailing.

As one of Vienna's oldest commercial streets, the **Fleischmarkt** (Meat Market) has more character than the glossy shopping promenades farther south. There are many interesting little shops located in the numerous narrow alleyways and secluded courtyards just off the main street, making it a rewarding place to spend an afternoon exploring.

Just south of the Fleischmarkt, close to its eastern end, are the charming historic buildings of Schönlaterngasse (Lantern Street). The most notable of these is the **Alte Schmiede** (Old Forge), a former blacksmith's workshop that has been converted into the home of the Kunstverein Wien (Vienna Art Society). Its primary focus is on modern German literature, but it also hosts several musical performances every week, usually avant-garde jazz. The building is also home to the **Schmiedermuseum** (Forge Museum), where the forge and workshop of master blacksmith Otto Schmirler have been preserved exactly as he left them when he laid down his hammer for the last time in 1970.

Hoher Markt

The Hoher Markt (High Market) stands between the Fleischmarkt and the Jewish Quarter, on the edge of what was once the city's textile district. The square's name denotes its former importance as a commercial hub.

The Hoher Markt is the oldest public square in Vienna, but you wouldn't know this from looking at it—all the buildings around the square were destroyed during the Second World War, either by Allied bombing raids or by the artillery bombardment that preceded the arrival of Soviet forces in 1945.

One unexpected consequence of the destruction of the old structures was the discovery of many ruined Roman buildings from ancient Vindobona. Information about this period of Vienna's history can be found in the **Roman Museum** on the south side of Hoher Markt (see p. 90).

Two features of this square survived the the war, although not without some damage. The unique **Ankeruhr** (Anker Clock; see sidebar opposite) is one of these survivors; the other is the baroque **Vermählungsbrunnen** (Wedding Fountain) that stands in the center of the square. Built in 1729 by Joseph Fischer von Erlach (1693–1742), this fountain is capped by a group of statues depicting the marriage of Mary and Joseph. ■

Alte Schmiede & Schmiedermuseum

- 67
- Schönlaterngasse 9
- (1) 512 83 29
- Closed Sat. & Sun.
- Stubentor (U3), Schwedenplatz (U1, U4), or Stephansplatz (U1, U3)

www.alte-schmiede .at

The copper and gold face of the Ankeruhr

The Jewish Quarter

The northern corner of the Innere Stadt is the oldest part of the city. Many different groups have left their mark on this area, from Roman soldiers to medieval salt merchants, but it is the various Jewish communities that have lived here over the centuries that have left the most enduring cultural legacy.

Rachel Whiteread's Holocaust Memorial in Judenplatz

Jewish Quarter

🅰 67

🚇 Schwedenplatz
(U1, U4) or
Stephansplatz
(U1, U3)

Just across the Hoher Markt from the Wedding Fountain, the gentle slope of Judengasse takes you down into the fringes of Vienna's historic Jewish Quarter.

This is not the oldest part of Vienna's Jewish Quarter (that title goes to the neighborhood around Judenplatz), but at its height in the late 19th century it was the most prosperous, influential, and culturally active. The area's Jewish heyday began after the 1782 Edict of Tolerance, passed by Josef I—which allowed Jews many (but far from all) of the same rights as Christians. The community grew

quickly during the 19th century, constructing many of the impressive Beidermeier buildings that can be seen in the area today. In the early 20th century, however, the increasingly hostile local government, led by the openly anti-semitic mayor Karl Lueger (1844–1910), began driving many people away.

In the face of institutional anti-Semitism and frequent mob violence, many thousands fled the city, a movement that accelerated further after the *Anschluss* (see p. 33). Many, however, were either unable to leave or unwilling to abandon the city that had been their community's home for generations. Those who stayed behind were subjected to ever increasing levels of discrimination and violence, before finally being rounded up and sent away to die in the concentration camps of eastern Europe. Only a few hundred survived the war, and almost none of these survivors wanted to return to a city whose people, for the most part, had been at best indifferent to their suffering. By the early 1950s, Vienna's Jewish community had essentially ceased to exist.

The Stadttempel

If you walk down Seitenstetten-gasse today, you will come across a large door with a Hebrew inscription above it, set into the facade of an apartment building. This is the entrance to the Stadt-tempel (City Temple)—once the finest synagogue in Vienna, now the only one. (There are other

Jewish congregations in the city today, but none has a purposely built place of worship.) It was built in 1825, and owes its unusual design (and survival) to a discriminatory clause in the 1782 Edict of Tolerance. This clause allowed only Catholic churches to be built with facades that looked onto main streets, keeping Vienna's religious minorities hidden in backrooms and down alleyways. To comply with this rule, several apartment buildings were constructed along with the Stadttempel to hide it from the street. These buildings are inseparably intertwined with the synagogue, sharing structural supports, foundations, and walls.

The surrounding apartment buildings saved the synagogue from destruction on the night of November 9, 1938 (Kristallnacht) because the synagogue could not be burned down without damaging the nearby homes of non-Jews and risking the Nazi

Stadttempel

⚑ 67

✉ Seitenstetten-gasse 4

☎ (1) 535 04 31

🕐 Closed Fri.–Sun.

💲 $

🚇 Schwedenplatz (U1, U4) or Stephansplatz (U1, U3)

www.ikg-wien.at

Recording Vienna's Jewish Cultural Legacy

The Holocaust extinguished the vibrant, artistic world of prewar European Jewry: a complex and vibrant society whose achievements helped shape modern Vienna. Over the past 30 years various organizations have sprung up across Vienna to help rekindle the city's lost Jewish culture.

Centropa (Pfeilgasse 8, tel 1/409 09 71, www.centropa.org), a digital archive of Jewish history, is one such project. It brings together thousands of family photos and home movies along with the personal memories of individuals interviewed by the organization. It is based

in Vienna and run by Edward Serotta, an American journalist who has spent more than 20 years exploring the region's Jewish history. The images, interviews, and Super-8 film footage gathered by the organization are often displayed to the public in exhibitions and events in Vienna.

The focus is very much on the lives of Austria's Jews, past and present, not on their persecutions or deaths. The light, sometimes heartwarming images are a refreshing change in a city where anything related to the Jewish community is still handled with a cautious, even defensive attitude.

Bermudadreieck

🅰 67

🚇 Schwedenplatz
(U1, U4)

party headquarters, which was only about 100 yards away.

The Stadttempel was extensively restored in 1961 with funding from the city of Vienna. Today it once again functions as a house of worship, serving Vienna's growing Jewish community. Visitors can take a guided tour of the Stadttempel, but they will need to bring a photo-ID for security reasons (the synagogue was the scene of a deadly terrorist attack in the 1980s, so the community is understandably cautious).

INSIDER TIP:

Look for the Turkish cannonball, fired in 1683, embedded in the wall of the Neustadter-Hof Palace near Shakespeare & Company.

—BEATRICE AUMAYR
Viennese tour guide

After the security checks in the entranceway, visitors are led into the large oval hall of the synagogue. On the ground floor there are several rows of seats facing toward the ornate *bimah* (the platform where the person reading from the Torah stands). The central seating area is surrounded by 12 marble columns (representing the 12 tribes of Israel), which support the women's seating galleries on the second and third floors. Above the bimah are two large stone tablets inscribed with the tenets of the Law of Moses, backed by a fanlike

burst of gold and silver decoration. The ceiling of the hall is painted sky blue, and inlaid with hundreds of silver stars.

In the foyer there is a memorial to the Austrian Jews who died in the Holocaust. It consists of a set of slowly rotating stone tablets, engraved with the names of all 65,000 victims, and a broken granite pillar that symbolizes the destruction of the community. Close by there is another, smaller memorial dating from 1934. It commemorates the sacrifice of the young men from the congregation who died fighting for the Austro-Hungarian Empire in the trenches of the First World War.

St. Rupert's & Around

There is more to this area than just its Jewish history, however. It is probably the oldest part of Vienna, having been continuously inhabited since around 14 B.C. Even though few of the buildings visible today are much more than 200 years old, the neighborhood has a quiet, sheltered atmosphere reminiscent of a medieval walled city.

By day this area is home to numerous independent shops, restaurants, and cafés that attract a bookish, bohemian crowd. Highlights for visiting shoppers include the eccentric vintage store **Freistil** *(Judengasse 4, tel 1/535 94 77, www.freistil.at),* the eclectic English-language bookshop **Shakespeare & Company** *(Sterngasse 2, tel 1/535 50 53, closed Sun., www.shakespeare .co.at),* and **Austrian Delights** *(Judengasse 1a, tel 1/532 16 61,*

EXPERIENCE: Get Lost in Vienna's Bermuda Triangle

With its copious number of boisterous bars, the Bermudadreieck (Bermuda Triangle) district is a popular hotspot for local nightlife. But be warned: For Viennese and tourists alike, it's easy to get lost in the small hours in its labyrinthine collection of sometimes rowdy beer joints easy to enter but difficult to leave.

For most of the 20th century anyone trying to get a liquor license in Vienna had to prove to the planning board that there was a need for a bar in the neighborhood they wanted to set up in. This meant that in many areas of the Innere Stadt there was a conspicuous lack of nightlife. When this rule was relaxed in the mid-1980s, numerous bars began to spring up in the old Jewish Quarter, and the area is now one of the city's liveliest and trendiest.

Thanks to its twisting, confusing street layout and plentiful bars, this place soon acquired the nickname Bermudadreieck. Today, the term is often used to describe a large area of the Innere Stadt, but the original bars of the Bermudadreieck were located between Rabenstelg and Seitenstettengasse, with some on Judengasse and Ruprechtsplatz.

The first bar to open in the area was **Krah-Krah** (Rabensteeig 8, tel 1/533 81 93, www.krah-krah.at), which is housed in an old textile warehouse. Today Krah-Krah is renowned for its wide selection of beers (including many locally brewed Austrian ones) and filling home-cooked food.

Many others soon followed, and now there are around 30 establishments in the area, all open until around 4 a.m. on weekends.

These range from the mock-traditional **Bermuda Bräu** (Rabensteig 6, tel 1/532 28 65-14, www.bermuda-braeu .at) to the psychedelic bar and club **Mojo** (Seitenstetten-gasse 5, tel 1/535 43 13) and the classy **First Floor** (Seitenstettengasse 5, tel 1/533 78 66), which has a large aquarium behind the bar. Alternatively, those who want a little fresh air can head around to **Zum Kuchhldragoner** (Ruprechts-platz 4–5, tel 1/533 83 71, www.kuchldragoner.at)—a traditional beer and schnitzel pub with outdoor seating on Ruprechtsplatz—or the brand new waterfront bar at the stylish **Motto am Fluss** (see p. 79).

Friday night crowds at one of the Bermuda Triangle's trendy bars

The simple tower of the Ruprechtskirche

Ruprechtskirche

🚶 67

✉ Ruprechtsplatz

☎ (1) 535 60 03

🕐 By appointment only

🚇 Schwedenplatz (U1, U4)

www.ruprechts kirche.at

Judenplatz

🚶 67

🚇 Stephansplatz (U1, U3)

The building has weathered many storms, wars, and fires over the centuries, meaning that the medieval core of the building has been augmented by a patchwork of repairs, additions, and alterations.

From a distance the Ruprechtskirche looks almost ruined—with its unglazed upper windows and ivy covered tower—but it is still an active church where Mass is said every Sunday. The church isn't often open to the public, but if you can get inside you'll find its interior to be in much the same state as the exterior. Centuries of baroque remodeling and rococo decoration were stripped away in the 19th century, leaving the interior plain and unadorned. The church's only splashes of color come from its large stained-glass windows—which mostly date from the early 20th century, although the middle window in the apse has several panes that date from the 14th century.

Judenplatz

From the 13th to the 15th century, the area around Judenplatz was home to a thriving Jewish community. Although the growth of the district (both in terms of population and area) was severely constricted by discriminatory laws, the relative stability of the Habsburg empire allowed the community to become fairly wealthy and even gain a small amount of political influence. Under Emperor Frederick II, the Jewish population was given a significant degree of autonomy, with its own civil courts, hospital, and kosher

closed Sun., www.austriandelights .at/html/index.html), a fantastic shop filled with high-quality wine, food, beer, and crafts from all over Austria.

At the northern end of Judengasse, on an elevated site that overlooks Franz-Josefs-Kai and the river, stands the sturdy, ivy-covered structure of **Ruprechtskirche** (St. Rupert's Church)—one of the hidden treasures of the Stephansdom Quarter. The extremely plain exterior of this building is testament to its age: The oldest parts date from around 1130, several decades earlier than the first wave of construction at St. Stephen's.

slaughterhouses. The community built what was thought to be the largest and most impressive synagogue in Europe—the bare remains of which can be seen in the basement of the Judenplatz Museum (see p. 88).

In 1421, this period of prosperity came to a terrible and sudden end when Emperor Albert V chose Vienna's Jewish population as a scapegoat to distract people from his disastrous military defeats. He whipped up public outrage about a series of imaginary heresies and Jewish crimes before calling for the expulsion of Austria's entire Jewish population. The hundreds that didn't manage to escape were burned at the stake on the outskirts of town. Vienna became known in medieval Jewish culture as the "city of blood." When Jews were allowed to return to Vienna some 250 years later, they did not settle in this area, but Judenplatz remained an important focal point for the community. Today this broad paved square is home to a trio of important Jewish sights as well as being one of Europe's unique places of remembrance. Visitors can spend time at a Holocaust memorial, the Judenplatz Museum, and witness Vienna's synagogue excavations.

Holocaust Memorial: At the center of the square is Vienna's Holocaust memorial, designed by British artist Rachel Whiteread. The memorial takes the form of a rectangular block of unpainted concrete, covered on all sides with moldings of books with their spines facing inward. The brutally plain appearance of the memorial stands in stark contrast with the traditional architecture around it, drawing in people's attention while remaining inscrutable and enigmatic. An inscription around the base of the structure lists the concentration camps in which Austrian Jews were killed.

Opposite the memorial is a statue of the Jewish playwright, dramatist, and philosopher Gotthold Lessing (1729-1781), erected after World War II. Lessing's witty plays and carefully reasoned philosophy substantially influenced the development of German enlightenment thought.

INSIDER TIP:

On the wall of Judenplatz 2, an ancient inscription commemorates the killing and expulsion of Vienna's Jews in 1421.

—CLIVE CARPENTER
National Geographic contributor

In addition to these larger memorials, the square also holds a few plaques and inscriptions acknowledging the 87 Austrian members of the Righteous Among Nations (gentiles who risked their lives to save Jews from the Holocaust, as designated by Israel) and the Austrian cardinal who formally apologized for the past role of the Catholic Church in anti-semitic persecutions.

Holocaust Memorial
- 🅰 67
- ✉ Judenplatz
- 🚇 Stephansplatz (U1, U3)

Judenplatz Museum

- 🗺 67
- ✉ Judenplatz 8
- ☎ (1) 535 04 31
- 🕐 Closed Sat. & Jewish holidays
- 💲 $
- Ⓜ Stephansplatz (U1, U3)

www.jmw.at

Zum Finsteren Stern

- ✉ Schulhof 8
- ☎ (1) 535 21 00
- 🕐 Closed Sun.
- Ⓜ Stephansplatz (U1, U3)

Uhrenmuseum

- 🗺 67
- ✉ Schulhof 2
- ☎ (1) 533 22 65
- 🕐 Closed Mon.
- 💲 $
- Ⓜ Stephansplatz (U1, U3)

www.wienmuseum.at

Judenplatz Museum:

This museum is an annex of the larger Jewish Museum of Vienna (see p. 125) located on Dorotheergasse. Work on the Judenplatz Museum began in the mid-1990s, when builders working on a nearby parking lot stumbled across the buried ruins of the medieval Jewish ghetto. Archaeologists were brought in and were amazed to find that the medieval synagogue—a structure previously thought to have been lost forever—had been uncovered. It was decided that this site was too important to be simply reburied, and work began to build a museum that could exhibit the ruins and place them in their historical and cultural context.

The exhibitions in this museum focus on the medieval ghetto that once occupied the area. The enigmatic ruins are brought to life by a fascinating video presentation that places the ghetto within the context of medieval Vienna. As part of the presentation, years of archaeological investigation and historical study have been brought together to make a 3-D reconstruction of the ghetto as it would have looked in the early 15th century.

After watching this presentation, visitors should head down to the lower level of the museum, where the remains of the medieval synagogue are on display. You can still see the foundations of the bimah, the Torah shrine, and the walls and floor of the women's section, as well as displays of the artifacts that were found during the course of the excavations.

The well-stocked Dorothy Singer Bookshop is another very good reason to visit the museum and stocks everything from exhibition catalogs, posters, fiction, and reference literature to souvenirs and ritual objects.

Around Judenplatz

Just a few hundred yards southwest of the busy crowds of Judenplatz is the secluded side street of Schulhof. This narrow one-way street passes through an archway next to the Kirche am Hof before curving around its northern side. Where the road takes a sharp turn around the end of the church, the sidewalks broaden out into a small square, shaded by a few pretty old trees and surrounded by 17th- and 18th-century houses. This quiet spot is home

---

EXPERIENCE:
Authentic Walking Tours of Jewish Vienna

In order to fully appreciate the dense history of this small neighborhood, it helps to get a knowledgeable local guide. Several organizations offer guided walking tours of Vienna's Jewish districts, taking you to the well known historic landmarks as well as to more obscure sites like the locations of historic events or homes of notable people. Tours are offered by the **Vienna Guide Service** (tel 1/786 24 00, www.viennaguide service.at), **Vienna Walks** (Wedertofgasse 9/2, tel 1/774 89 01, www.viennawalks .com), as well as several of the independent guides that operate through **Wien Guide** (www.wienguide.at).

to one of Vienna's best kept secrets, the stylish modern restaurant **Zum Finsteren Stern** (The Dark Star). This excellent restaurant is housed in the lower floors of Palais Collato, a 16th-century mansion with an attractive Renaissance facade. In the summer the restaurant sprawls out onto the dappled shade of the little square, offering fine dining in an enchanting setting. (There are only a few tables outside, so it's worth making a reservation.)

Just a little farther along the street is the **Uhrenmuseum** (Clock Museum), an annex of the Wien Museum (see p. 187) that houses a huge and exquisite collection of timepieces. The 3,000 clocks in this unique collection range in size from the open-framed cast-iron mechanism of the old St. Stephen's Cathedral clock to a minuscule "Zappler" pendulum clock that is smaller than a tube of lipstick. Visitors can see elegant masterpieces of mechanical precision alongside almost grotesquely ornate baroque "lantern clocks." All the clocks are kept in working order and fully wound, which means that the rooms are filled with a wonderful cacophony of chimes, whistles, bells, buzzers, and beeps at the top of every hour.

Examples of the clockmaker's art at the Uhrenmuseum

The Niedhart Frescoes: Behind the mundane exterior of Tuchlauben 19, just south of Schulhof, lies a much older building and a fascinating example of medieval secular art. In the late 14th century, this house belonged to a Viennese merchant named Michel Menschein. Around 1400, Menschein commissioned a local artist to paint a series of frescoes for his banquet hall. He asked that the frescoes be based on the songs of Neidhart von Reuental (1190–1241), a famous knight and troubadour who served in the Babenberg court. The rather risqué subject

(continued on p. 92)

Neidhart Frescoes

🅰 67
✉ Tuchlauben 19
☎ (1) 535 90 65
🕐 Closed Mon.
💲 $
🚇 Stephansplatz (U1, U3)

www.wienmuseum.at

Roman Vienna

Austria's fascination with its Roman heritage captured the hearts and minds of everyone in central Vienna in 2008 when the Roman Museum on Hoher Markt threw open its doors for the very first time. On the exact same site, almost 2,000 years earlier, Roman legionnaires rested and prepared for upcoming battle campaigns, repairing their weapons and boosting their physical fitness in the military base of Vindobona.

A section of the Roman ruins at Michaelerplatz, near the Hofburg Palace

Until the 20th century, Vienna's Roman heritage was something of a mystery. Historians knew from references in Roman chronicles and markings on ancient maps that Vienna was once the site of the Roman frontier town of Vindobona, but nobody was sure where exactly this settlement was or what it was like. Construction work in the Innere Stadt often uncovered Roman artifacts, but they were never systematically studied or mapped.

Beginning in the early 20th century, archaeologists began digging in the basements and cellars around the Fleischmarkt and Jewish Quarter, hoping to find some evidence of the old settlement. Gradually, they were able to piece together a rough idea of the location and layout of the Roman city, and they found numerous artifacts that gave clues to what everyday life would have been like in this garrison town. The destruction of the Second World War and construction of the U-bahn also revealed a great deal of Roman material.

Vindobona

It is thought that the walled fortress itself, which was inhabited almost exclusively by the military, occupied a square site in what is now

INSIDER TIP:

The excavations in the middle of Michaelerplatz reveal part of the Roman camp of Vindobona and also part of an 18th-century theater.

—CARL BIELER
National Geographic contributor

the northwestern quarter of the Innere Stadt. The fortress was probably built up against one of the channels of the Donau (Danube), and extended southwest as far as the modern shopping street of the Graben (which means "trench" or "moat"). Its southeastern wall ran along the route of the present-day Rotenturmstrasse, and the northwestern wall followed the route of the modern Tiefer Graben (whose name means "deep trench").

Over time a quite large town grew up around the fortress, surrounding it to the west, south, and east. It grew up along the roads that led out of the settlement, which ran along the same routes now taken by present-day Kärntner Strasse, Herrengasse, and Wipplingerstrasse.

At its largest extent the town probably occupied most of the area now contained within the Ringstrasse and had a population of close to 30,000 people. The inhabitants of the town, as well as the soldiers that manned the fortress, came from all over the Roman world—including as far north as Britain and as far south as North Africa. The town itself, though on the frontier, was comfortable, even luxurious by the standards of the time, with an extensive sewer system, public baths, and theaters.

In recent years, archaeological finds and scientific research have revealed that the community fulfilled a much more complex economic role than just meeting the needs of the garrison. As the town evolved over time it gained a large warehouse district, a community of craftsmen and manufacturers, and even importers of luxury goods and wines.

Roman Museums & Sites

Today, those visitors keen to explore Vienna's Roman heritage should head to the **Roman Museum** *(Hoher Markt 3, tel 1/535 56 06, closed Mon., www.wienmuseum.at, $$)* at the Hoher Markt (once the site of Vindobona's public forum). Here there is a large and informative exhibition centered around the ruins of some Roman garrison buildings. The archaeological finds on display here create an impression of what daily life was like in this town, including household objects: statuettes of gods and goddesses, children's toys, coins, and simple pottery.

Surprisingly, there is very little military hardware, and few spearheads or swords, suggesting that life here was mostly peaceful. The exhibitions are brought to life by an extensively researched and carefully constructed set of models, maps, and 3-D renderings that show various stages of the town's development, and give an idea of what it looked like when it was new. Each aspect of the exhibition is extremely child-friendly due to the use of sophisticated computer animations and a large number of hands-on exhibitions. The museum provides descriptions in English and German and a video guide recorded in sign language.

For those curious to learn more about the Roman settlement, there are two publicly accessible archaeological sites in the Innere Stadt. One is beneath the Fire Department headquarters in the Am Hof (which is currently closed for renovation work) while the other is in an open-air site in the middle of Michaelerplatz, in the Hofburg (see p. 99). The Am Hof site is fairly unimpressive, consisting of a section of **Roman sewer,** but the ruins at **Michaelerplatz** are well worth a look. They consist of a broad exposed section of the Roman **civilian settlement,** including houses and commercial buildings clustered around the junction of two main Roman roads. Smaller collections of Roman artifacts can be found at the **Wien Museum Karlsplatz** (see p. 187) and the **Bezirksmuseum Innere Stadt** (see p. 93).

Archive of the Austrian Resistance

- ✉ Altes Rathaus, Wipplinger Strasse 6–8
- ☎ (1) 228 94 69
- ⏱ Closed Sat. & Sun.
- 💲 $
- 🚇 Schwedenplatz (U1, U4)

www.doew.at

Bezirksmuseum Innere Stadt

- ✉ Altes Rathaus, Wipplinger Strasse 6–8
- ⏱ Open Wed. p.m. & Thurs. p.m.
- 🚇 Schwedenplatz (U1, U4)

Platz Am Hof

- 🚌 67
- 🚇 Schottentor (U2) or Herrengasse (U3)

Feuerwehr-museum (Firefighting Museum)

- 🚌 67
- ✉ Am Hof 7
- ☎ (1) 531 99
- ⏱ Open Sun. a.m. only; Mon.–Fri. by appointment only
- 🚇 Schottentor (U2) or Herrengasse (U3)

matter of the paintings was not popular with later owners of the house, and in the 16th century, when a priest moved in, the frescoes were plastered over and forgotten. In 1979 the frescoes were rediscovered by construction workers renovating an apartment in the building. When the age and significance of the frescoes became apparent, the Wien Museum decided to buy the property and make it into a museum.

The frescoes resemble the margin illustrations found in medieval illuminated Bibles, painted with a simple, almost cartoonlike style. The songs of Neidhart von Reuental were notoriously bawdy and focused on the lives and loves of peasants rather than the delicate world of courtly love. There is nothing edifying or religious about these frescoes. As you walk around the room, the scenes cycle through the seasons, and show the cast of Neidhart's songs—a rabble of young farmers, attractive maidens, and drunken knights—indulging in various seasonal activities. We see young men wrestling, people tobogganing in the snow, and women picking spring flowers. One of the best preserved and largest scenes depicts a party in the forest, complete with dancing, drinking, and couples sneaking off into the trees in various states of undress.

Altes Rathaus: On the opposite side of Judenplatz stands the magnificent baroque facade of the Altes Rathaus (Old Town Hall). This 18th-century building stands on the site of a palace confiscated from a rebellious baron in the 14th century. It served as the town hall from around that time until 1883, when the institution was moved to the neo-Gothic building on the Ringstrasse (see p. 123).

INSIDER TIP:

Ask the attendant for help distinguishing the various Niedhart frescoes. Several of them are difficult for the untrained eye to interpret.

—LARRY PORGES
National Geographic Books editor

At the eastern end of the site is the **Salvador Chapel,** a 12th-century church that has survived from the original palace complex. It has been heavily modified and renovated, but still retains its distinctive medieval Gothic architecture. Most of the building is today occupied by small stores and offices, but there are also two museums that are worth a look if you are not in a hurry.

The first is the **Archive of the Austrian Resistance,** a museum dedicated to the various resistance movements that sprang up to oppose both the Nazis and the Austrian fascist dictatorship that preceded them. It's not easy stuff, but for those with an interest in European history, it shines light on a little-known aspect of the Second World War. Across the courtyard from the archives is the **Bezirksmuseum Innere Stadt,** whose collection covers the history of Vienna's inner city district from Roman times to the present day. There are some interesting exhibitions, and you don't have to pay anything to get in, but it is hardly ever open.

Platz Am Hof

Just southwest of Judenplatz is the largest public square in the Innere Stadt, standing where the heart of the Roman fortress was once located. It gets its name (which means "at court") from the Babenberg royal palace that once stood at the southern end of the square. Although some of the buildings that surround it were badly damaged during the Second World War, it is still in far better condition than the Hoher Markt.

Around the square are a selection of fine 16th- and 17th-century buildings, including the Palais Collalto, where in 1762 a six-year-old Wolfgang Amadeus Mozart made his first public performance. At the center of the square is the baroque Column of Our Lady, which was erected in 1667 to honor the Catholic victory over the Swedish Protestants in the Thirty Years' War (1618–1648). Since 1685, the old civic armory on the western side of the square has been used as a fire station. Today it houses the Viennese fire department's headquarters and the **Feuerwehrmuseum** (Firefighting Museum).

The Am Hof's main attraction is the large baroque church, the

The Column of Our Lady looks down on Platz Am Hof.

Kirche Am Hof, that stands on the eastern side of the square. Behind the ostentatious whitewashed facade, the Kirche Am Hof is actually a very old building, thought to date from the 14th century. The Gothic architecture of the church's interior was given a rather awkward baroque overhaul at the same time as the construction of the facade, making it a slightly peculiar, if not exactly ugly, building. ∎

Kirche Am Hof

🏛 67

✉ Am Hof 1

🚇 Schottentor (U2) or Herrengasse (U3)

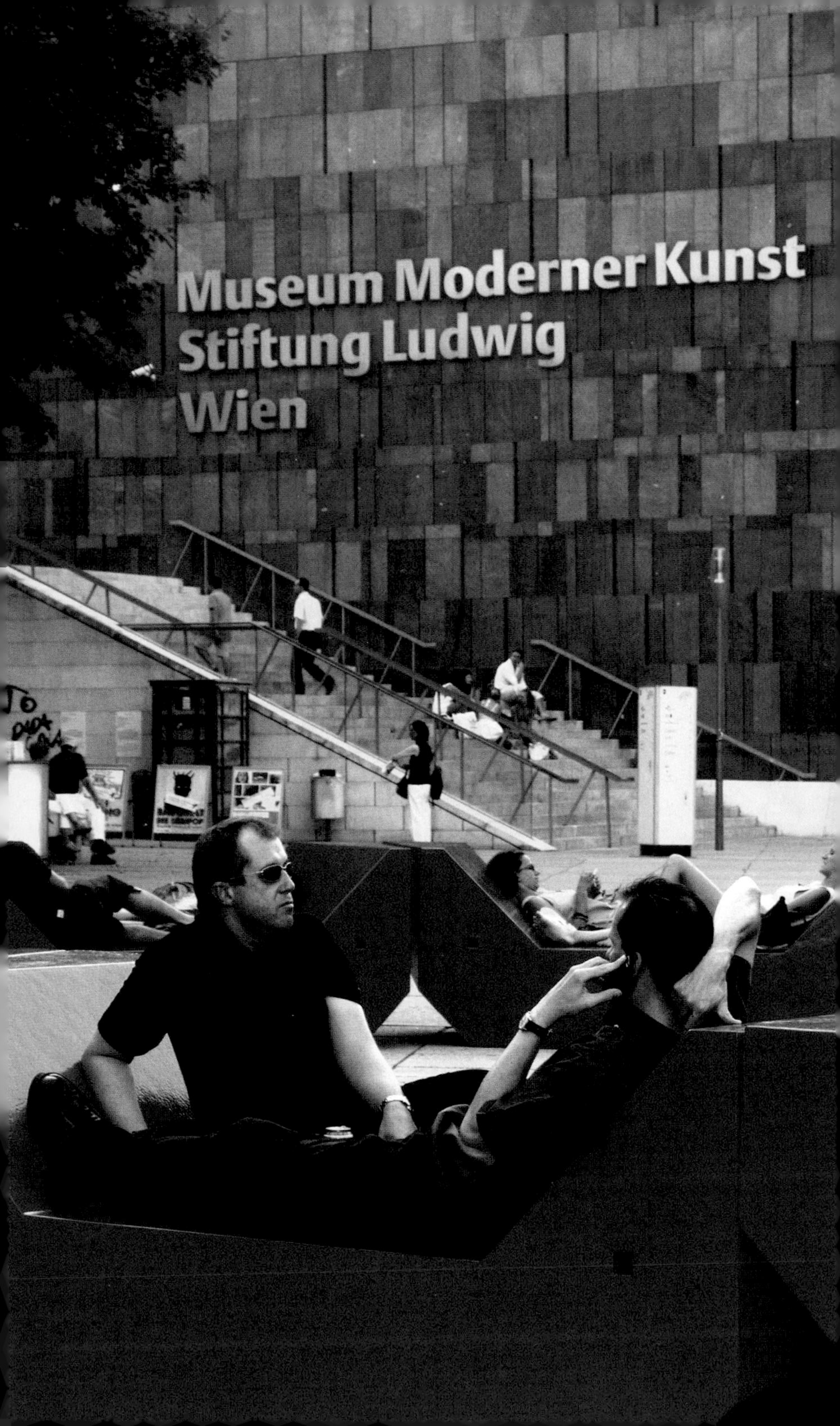

Museum Moderner Kunst
Stiftung Ludwig
Wien

A world-class cultural complex in the former heart of the Habsburg empire—and a few surprises as well

Hofburg Quarter

Quirky modern furniture enhances the MuseumsQuartier courtyard.

Hofburg Quarter

Stretching from the trendy museums and arts venues of the MuseumsQuartier to the glitzy shops on the Graben, the Hofburg Quarter combines the allure of Vienna's imperial past with its vibrant modern cultural scene.

The bustling Rathaus Christmas Market sets up annually near the Burgtheater.

Even by the standards of European royal palaces, the Hofburg is huge. Rather than replacing old parts of the building, the Habsburgs simply added to it—grafting baroque libraries on to Renaissance mansions and neoclassical residences onto medieval cloisters. Over more than seven centuries, the Hofburg complex grew from a small, fortresslike dwelling to a sprawling complex of gilded ornamentation and extravagant architecture. Today the palace's various wings are home to around a dozen museums and cultural institutions, including the Schatzkammer and the Kunsthistorisches Museum, which together form Vienna's largest and most popular tourist attraction.

Imperial Vienna

There is far more to the Hofburg's relationship with the surrounding area, however,
than just its physical presence. For centuries this was the heart of the Habsburg empire, the glittering wellspring from which all political power, cultural patronage, and legal authority flowed. It had a kind of gravity that pulled the rich, the cunning, and the talented into its proximity.

Even though the emperor is long gone, the legacy of his money and influence can be clearly seen in the grand cultural institutions and exclusive boutiques that line the area around the palace. Walk along Kohlmarkt and you'll see many boutiques with "K.K." or "K.u.K." written above the door—these initials stand for *kaiserlich und königlich,* meaning "imperial and royal," and designate an establishment that was once favored by the emperor. The same initials are inscribed on the stonework of the Burgtheater and the Wiener Staatsoper.

The MuseumsQuartier

In many cases, the role of the emperor has been taken up by the Austrian government. This modern form of patronage has given rise to a new kind of cultural institution, one established with a firmly democratic public appeal. The finest example of this is the **MuseumsQuartier,** an assembly of art galleries, theaters, and artistic initiatives that break down the formal boundaries that surround the high art of the Habsburg era. ■

NOT TO BE MISSED:

The glittering crown of Emperor Rudolf and the jewels of the Imperial Treasury **100**

Hearing the angelic voices of the Vienna Boys' Choir **105**

Seeing the elegant Lipizzaner stallions of the Spanish Riding School **106–107**

The artistic treasures at the Kunsthistorisches Museum **114**

Exploring the exciting small galleries of Quartier 21 **119**

The lavish window displays in the Golden U shopping district **124**

The marionettes, costumes, and stage models at the Theatermuseum **126**

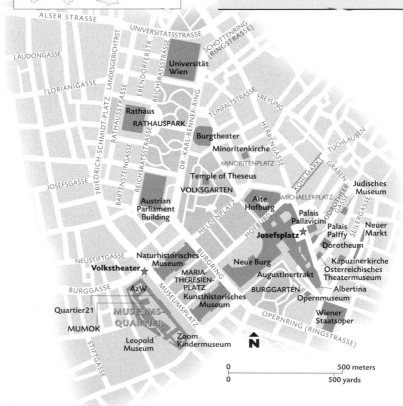

Area of map detail

The Hofburg Complex

On a map, the sprawling shape of the Hofburg looks more like a college campus than a palace. As there is no imperial family to occupy this vast complex (or pay for it to be left empty) the Hofburg's several thousand rooms have been filled by an array of museums that showcase what was once the Habsburg family's hoard of art, jewels, and other finery.

A traditional *fiaker* passes through the Alte Hofburg's In der Burg (Palace Square).

Hofburg Palace Complex

🅰 97

🚇 Stephansplatz (U1, U3), Herrengasse (U3), or Volkstheater (U2, U3)

www.hofburg .vienna.info

Alte Hofburg

The Alte Hofburg (Old Imperial Palace) is the area of the complex located between Michaelerplatz and Heldenplatz. It is the historic core of the Hofburg, home to the rulers of Austria and its empire from the 13th century to the declaration of the Austrian republic in 1918. Each generation extended and added to the Alte Hofburg, either to suit their changing tastes or to accommodate new members of the royal court.

When they were first built, many of the wings of the Alte Hofburg were freestanding buildings, but over the years they have been joined together into one continuous structure. As a result, the Alte Hofburg is a peculiar patchwork of architectural styles, from medieval Gothic to 19th-century baroque. Some buildings have been restored to their original condition and opened to the public, some house museums, and one, the Leopold Wing, houses the Austrian president.

The Michaelertrakt: Coming from the Innere Stadt, the

first part of the Hofburg you'll see is the grand 19th-century facade of the Michaelertrakt (St. Michael Wing). It was designed by the noted baroque architect Joseph Emanuel Fischer von Erlach (1693–1742) in 1726, but was not built until 1893. His fantastically extravagant design—covered with domes, statues, and intricate stucco decoration—is a testament to the lavish tastes of the Habsburg monarchy, and to their willingness to indulge them even as their empire disintegrated.

At the center of the building is the **Michaelertor** (St. Michael Gate), which is the symbolic main entrance to the Hofburg. Here the road passes through an ornate domed chamber before opening into In der Burg (Palace Square).

The Reichskanzleitrakt:
Behind the imposing facade, there really isn't very much to the Michaelertrakt—it's only one room deep. Walk through the door on the right-hand side of the domed chamber and you will find yourself in the Reichskanzleitrakt (Imperial Chancellory Wing), an 18th-century structure that was built to house the apartments and offices of the Lord Vice Chancellor of the Holy Roman Empire (Reichsvisekanzler). In the 19th century Emperor Franz-Josef I moved into this building with his young wife, Sisi. Today the Reichskanzleitrakt houses three visitor attractions. On the ground floor is the Imperial Silver Collection, while the second floor houses

both the Sisi Museum and the Imperial Apartments.

The **Silberkammer** (Imperial Silver Collection) contains 7,000 pieces of tableware, ranging from tiny silver coffee spoons to the 100-foot-long (30 m) Milan Centerpiece—a gold and silver table decoration bristling with candleholders, statuettes, and vases. Everything here was once part of the Habsburg family collection, and the various sets reflect the individual tastes of each ruler—such as the beautiful paintings of flowers on Emperor

INSIDER TIP:

Even if it's out of your way, walking through the Michaelertor is worth the trip—the spectacular domed ceiling inside wouldn't look out of place in a baroque cathedral.

—CLIVE CARPENTER
National Geographic contributor

Franz-Josef's porcelain plates (he was a keen gardener). One of the rooms holds the massive tureens, cooking pots, and cauldrons that were once used by the palace's several hundred kitchen staff—revealing the hard work that was required to maintain all this imperial grandeur.

At the top of the Emperor's Staircase, there is a small exhibition about the history of the Hofburg. In addition to some interesting information about

Silberkammer
- ✉ Michaelerplatz
- ☎ (1) 533 75 70
- 💲 $$$ (also provides access to the Sisi Museum and Kaiserapartments)
- Ⓜ Herrengasse (U3)

www.hofburg-wien .at

Sisi Museum & Kaiserapartments

✉ Michaelerplatz

☎ (1) 533 75 70

💲 $$$ (covers admission to Silberkammer, Sisi Museum, & Kaiserapartments)

🚇 Herrengasse (U3)

www.hofburg-wien.at

the development of the site, it is home to a large architectural model that shows the Hofburg as it would have looked if Archduke Franz-Ferdinand's grand designs had ever been realized: They show another huge colonnaded structure on the eastern side of Heldenplatz that is essentially a mirror image of the Neue Burg. The most surprising thing about Franz-Ferdinand's grand plans is not that they weren't finished, but that they were started at all—such an ostentatious display of wealth was a curious choice for an empire struggling against a tide of popular unrest.

The next room marks the beginning of the **Sisi Museum,** which explores the life and death of Austria's most enigmatic empress, Elisabeth of Bavaria, known to all as "Sisi" (see sidebar

p. 101). Although few non-Austrians will have ever heard of Sisi, this exhibition provides an account of her dramatic life—illustrated with photographs, paintings, and personal effects—that it is hard not to find compelling.

After passing through the Sisi Museum, visitors are ushered through the guard room and into the **Kaiserapartments** (Imperial Apartment). This lovingly restored palatial 17-room apartment was the winter home of Emperor Franz-Josef (r. 1848–1916) and Sisi. Visitors enter the apartments through the audience chamber, where the emperor would once have met with any citizen of his empire who had a grievance to discuss. This room, along with the next two rooms (the conference room and the study), represent the public life of Franz-Josef—a conscientious ruler who scrutinized all new political appointees and read every piece of paper requiring his signature.

The rooms beyond reveal the personal lives of Franz-Josef and Sisi. Visitors pass through his spartan bedroom and the rooms where he once received family and friends, before moving into the half of the apartment occupied by Sisi. Here they can see her more opulent bedroom, the exercise machinery where she maintained her slender figure (she never weighed much over 100 pounds/45 kg),

The crown of Rudolf II, housed in the Hofburg Treasury

Sisi, Empress Elisabeth of Bavaria

Elisabeth of Bavaria (1837–1898), known to all as Sisi, was only 15 years old when she first met the emperor of Austria. The 23-year-old Franz-Josef was supposed to be courting her older sister, but became infatuated with her instead. They married a year later but there was no happily ever after for Sisi, who soon found herself trapped by the rigid protocol and archaic traditions of the Viennese court.

After only six years as empress, Sisi had become desperately miserable in Vienna. Her relationship with Franz-Josef had broken down, she had been ostracized from court society, and she was only rarely allowed to see her own chil-

dren. From 1860 until her death nearly 40 years later, she traveled constantly, only rarely returning to Vienna. She became an advocate of the rights of the Austrian Empire's subject states, which made her popular with the people of the empire.

In 1898, while traveling in Switzerland, she was assassinated by an Italian anarchist. During her lifetime, she was rarely mentioned in the press, having almost entirely retired from public life, but the circumstances of her death brought her a strange kind of fame. Her life was heavily romanticized, and she was transformed into the fairy-tale figure who lives on in Austrian culture today.

and the bathroom where she washed her ankle-length hair (a task that required several helpers and took all day). All the rooms of the apartments are decorated in sumptuous 19th-century style, and filled with fine antique furniture.

Visitors exit the Imperial Apartments through the **Amalienburg**—the pretty 16th-century building that occupies the western side of In der Burg. The most distinctive feature of this wing of the palace is its little clock tower, which has both a mechanical clock and a sundial on it.

Schweizerhof: The oldest parts of the Schweizerhof (Swiss Wing) date from the 13th century. The building is named for the Swiss mercenaries who used to guard the royal family here. It was originally built as a small castle-like building with four defensive towers by one of the last dukes of Babenberg, but

has been heavily modified and added to over the years. Most of the building that stands today dates from the 16th century, when it was reconstructed in a Renaissance style by Emperor Ferdinand I. His personal coat of arms, as well as those associated with his various aristocratic titles, can be seen over the handsome red and black Schweizertor (Swiss Gate) on In der Burg.

Today the Schweizerhof houses the **Schatzkammer** (Treasury) and the Burgkapelle (Palace Chapel). The Schatzkammer is undoubtedly the highlight of the various museums in the Hofburg—a glittering collection of crowns, tiaras, orbs, and scepters, all set with priceless gemstones and covered with a thick layer of gold.

The highlight of the Schatzkammer collection is the crown of (continued on p. 104)

Schatzkammer (Treasury)

✉ Schweizerhof, Hofburg

☎ (1) 525 24-0

🕐 Closed Tues.

💲 $$$$

🚇 Herrengasse (U3)

www.khm.at/en/ treasury

A Walk Around Josefsplatz

This walk starts at the heart of the Hofburg, before moving east and north through the wealthy streets that surround the palace. In this area of the Innere Stadt, the medieval Gothic of the Stephansdom Quarter has been supplanted by the ostentatious baroque architecture of the 17th and 18th centuries.

A tour group crosses the cobbled lane that runs through Josefsplatz.

This walk begins in Josefsplatz, a small square that stands between the Alte Hofburg and Augustinerkirche (St. Augustine's Church). This square's most prominent feature is the life-size equestrian **Statue of Josef II ❶**, which stands on an imposing stone pedestal in the center of the square. The square is surrounded on three sides by the baroque facade of the Hofburg complex; the Reitschulgasse runs along the other.

Across Reitschulgasse from the square, facing the Hofburg, are the **Palais Pallavicini** and the **Palais Palffy ❷**, which were once inhabited by two of Vienna's most powerful aristocratic families. Today the Pallavicini is rented as an exclusive venue for wedding receptions and business conferences, while the Palais Palffy's grand halls are used for art exhibitions and classical music concerts (particularly the music of Mozart, whose opera *The Marriage of Figaro* was first performed here).

NOT TO BE MISSED:

Palais Palffy • The Monument Against War and Fascism • The boutiques of the Golden U

Turn right onto the street that leads out of the square and follow it as it runs alongside the Augustinian wing of the Hofburg Palace. At the end of this street, next to the bastion of the Albertina, is a small public square. This little plaza was once the location of the Philipphof—a palatial apartment building whose basement was used as an air-raid shelter during the Second World War. On March 12, 1945, the building suffered a direct hit during an Allied bombing raid and collapsed, killing around 300 people sheltered inside. Today, the site is the location of the **Monument Against War and Fascism ❸**, a collection of inscriptions and sculptures created by Austrian sculptor Alfred Hrdlicka (1928–2009) to memorialize those killed on both sides of the war, as well as those entombed in the buried rubble below.

Exit the square and head north along Tegetthofstrasse, which soon opens into the **Neuer Markt.** The name of this place, which translates as "New Market," is a bit of a misnomer, as it is actually around 800 years old. It is, however, newer than the Hoher Markt, hence the name. On the left as you enter the square you will pass the 17th-century **Kapuzinerkirche** (Capuchin Church; see p. 126) ❹ before reaching the **Donnerbrunnen ❺** (Donner Fountain) an ornate 18th-century fountain decorated with bronze sculptures.

The Golden U

Head east out of the Neuer Markt along the Donnergasse, a short street that links the Neuer Markt to the pedestrianized shopping precinct of **Kärntner Strasse ❻**. This street forms part of the so-called Golden U (see pp. 124–125)—an upscale shopping area formed by the intersecting streets of Kärntner Strasse, Graben, and Kohlmarkt. Kärntner Strasse, which is probably the most everyday of the three streets, is still a glamorous avenue lined with modern designer clothing stores and cafés.

Keep going north to the edge of Stephansplatz before turning left onto **Graben.** This broad pedestrianized street has long been one of Vienna's most important public spaces—it was once the scene of royal parades and feast day festivities, where minor aristocrats and wealthy merchants had their palatial homes. Today it is a busy commercial street and is vibrantly decorated during the winter months. About halfway down the street is the massive

Pestsäule (Plague Monument) ❼, a spectacular baroque memorial for those who died in the plague of 1679. It is carved to look like a cloud with cherubs and angels emerging from it. The whole thing is adorned with extravagant quantities of gold leaf.

Farther along the Graben, you will pass the short street that leads to the copper-roofed baroque **Petruskirche** (St. Peter's Church) ❽. At the end of the street, turn left onto the **Kohlmarkt** (Coal Market) ❾, where some of Vienna's longest established boutiques are located, and where the most prestigious brands have their flagship stores. Despite its sky-high price tags, Kohlmarkt has a more low-key atmosphere than Graben or Kärntner Strasse.

As you walk south, you can't fail to notice the imposing copper dome of the Hofburg Palace entrance, which is dramatically framed by the buildings at the end of the street. At the end of the Kohlmarkt, head left between the buildings of the **Spanish Riding School ❿** to finish the walk back at Josefsplatz.

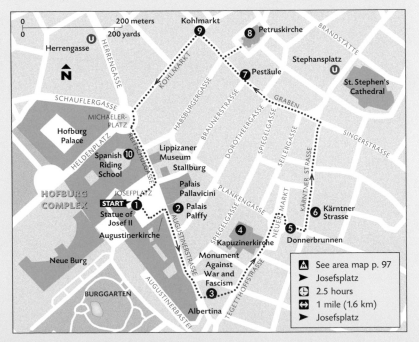

Burgkapelle

 Schweizertrakt, Hofburg

☎ (1) 533 99 27

💲 $ (tours $$$$)

🚇 Herrengasse (U3)

www.hofburg kapelle.at

Wintereitschule (Winter Riding School)

🅰 97

✉ Michaelerplatz

☎ (1) 553 90 31

🕐 Closed public holidays

🚇 Herrengasse (U3)

www.srs.at/en

Rudolf II (*r.* 1576–1612), a delicate crown with a split down the center that recalls a bishop's miter (if that bishop's miter were made from solid gold and encrusted with pearls and gemstones).

Other notable exhibitions include a fist-size emerald, a tenth-century royal crown made from hinged gold panels, and the Vienna Coronation Gospels—the Bible bound with gold and jewels on which Holy Roman emperors swore their oaths. The Treasury also houses some of the more unusual items acquired by Austrian royalty—such as a 500-year-old, 8-foot-long (2.5 m) "unicorn horn" said to bestow magical powers on its owner (it's probably the tusk of a narwhal, a kind of whale that lives in the Arctic Ocean).

The **Burgkapelle** is the oldest surviving part of the Hofburg, built in 1447 and preserved largely untouched. This Gothic structure is best known as the home of the Hofmusikkapelle, or Court Music Orchestra, which embodies a musical tradition that is hundreds of years old. The core of the Hofmusikkapelle is the Weiner Sängerknaben (Vienna Boys' Choir), which was established during the reign of Maximilian I (1459–1519) to sing at religious ceremonies and court events. After the collapse of the monarchy in 1918, the choir began touring internationally to support the choir school—earning it the nickname "singing ambassadors."

For most performances the angelic voices of these sailor-suited singers are accompanied by 42 musicians from the Vienna Philharmonic. They are also sometimes augmented by the Men's Chorus of the Vienna State Opera. The Hofmusikkapelle performs Masses by Mozart, Schubert, and Haydn every Sunday *(at 9:15 a.m.)* in the Burgkapelle, as well as special performances for religious holidays.

INSIDER TIP:

Captions in the Schatzkammer are in German only, so it's worth renting the English audio guide at the entrance.

—LARRY PORGES
National Geographic Books editor

The Winterreitschule:

Just to the north of the Swiss Wing is the Winterreitschule (Winter Riding School), a large indoor area designed by Joseph Emanuel Fischer von Erlach and completed in 1735. It was built as the performance space for the **Spanish Riding School** (Spanische Hofreitschule; see pp. 106–107), which still uses the building today. The nearby 16th-century Stallburg wing—which was originally built as a home for a rebellious prince—now serves as the stable block where the Spanish Riding School's Lipizzaner stallions are kept. Performances at the school attract visitors from all over the world, and are usually booked several months in advance. For those who don't feel they're sufficiently interested in horses to sit through an 80-minute dressage performance but still want to have a look, it is possible to go watch the horses' morning exercise sessions without a reservation. Sessions start at 10 a.m., but you have a better chance of walking straight in if you turn up later, when the early crowd has thinned out.

Leopoldtrakt: This 17th-century residential wing was once the home of Empress Maria-Theresia (1717–1780), who had the interior decorated in the same style as her beloved summer home, the Schönbrunn Palace (see pp. 192–197). It was home to various other members of the royal family over the years before becoming property of the state in 1920. Since 1946, this building has been the official residence of the President of Austria, and is therefore closed to the public most of the time.

Curiously for what was once an imperial palace, the Leopoldtrakt (Leopold Wing) had to be significantly renovated before it was considered inhabitable by the president and his staff. Although luxuriously decorated and furnished, the building had no indoor plumbing and required a small forest's worth of firewood to heat every winter.

Heldenplatz & Around

If you pass through the gate on the southern side of In der Burg, you will find yourself in the broad open space of Heldenplatz.

This rather empty expanse of grass and flagstones was intended to be the centerpiece of Franz-Ferdinand's Imperial Forum, of which the Festsaaltrakt (Ballroom Wing) and the Neue Burg are the only parts that were completed. If the plan had been finished, the Neue Burg would have been matched by an identical building on the right-hand side of the square, and the mismatched buildings of the Alte Hofburg would have been hidden behind a neatly symmetrical neoclassical building.

At the center of the square there are two massive bronze statues. The one closest to the Neue Burg is of Prince Eugene of Savoy (1663–1736), the skilled military commander who drove

(continued on p. 108)

Vienna Boys' Choir

✉ Burgkapelle, Schweizertrakt, Hofburg
☎ (1) 533 99 27
🕐 Hofmusikkapelle High Mass Sun., mid-Sept.–late June
💲 $
🚇 Herrengasse (U3)

www.wsk.at

The Vienna Boys' Choir

The children who make up the Vienna Boys' Choir, or Wiener Sängerknaben, are educated in a private music school housed in the Augarten Palace. Promising boys are admitted to the school's kindergarten at the age of three or four, and most stay there until they graduate from the high school at age 18. Most students go on to become professional musicians, teachers, or choirmasters themselves. Each pupil spends around 11 weeks of the year on tour as part of one of the four touring choirs, each of which has its own choirmasters and tutors. Each pupil takes part in around 80 public performances a year. Hear them at a Mass in the Burgkapelle (9:15 a.m., mid-Sept.–late June).

Lipizzaner Horses

These beautiful white horses are carefully selected from among the healthiest and strongest young animals at the imperial stud farm just outside Graz, Austria. Over the course of years of training they are taught to move with grace and poise and to work smoothly with their riders, and are given a chance to master some of the most challenging movements in haute école dressage.

One of the Spanish Riding School's Lipizzaner horses performing the *levade* during practice

For an hour or so every day, a team of eight horses and riders performs a tightly choreographed series of dressage exercises for a large audience in the baroque Winter Riding School. Each of these displays is the culmination of decades of training—both for the horses and the riders—and, in a broader sense, the result of hundreds of years of selective breeding (just the horses) and equestrian tradition.

The Spanish Riding School was founded in 1735 by Emperor Karl VI, but similar institutions are thought to have existed in Vienna as early as 1572. These earlier academies developed from the rigorous training programs that elite cavalry horses had to complete. Their purpose was to teach discipline and composure that would transfer over to greater agility on the battlefield. By the time of Karl VI, however, haute école was not really intended to be anything other than an art form. The Spanish Riding School was largely freed from the traditional relationship with cavalry horses and began to develop ever more elaborate routines.

Training the Horses

The training of a Lipizzaner stallion begins when the horse is around four years old. The first year or so of training is known as the *remontenschule,* where the horse is taught the fundamentals of poise and obedience. For the first few months of training the horse is kept on a lunge line, without a rider. Later it is familiarized with a bridle and rider before being taught to transition on command among walking, trotting, and cantering. After this first year, some of the school's

INSIDER TIP:

Look closely as the Lipizzaner riders enter the Spanish Riding School arena—each one tips his hat to a portrait of Karl VI, the founder of the school.

—BEN HOLLINGUM
National Geographic contributor

most experienced and skilled riders begin teaching the horses the rudiments of dressage. At this stage of their training, known as the *campagneschule,* the horses are taught to carry themselves with most of their weight on their hind legs, to turn with the correct posture, to move sideways and backward, and to turn on the spot.

After about two years of this training the horses are finally moved on to the very advanced *hohe schule* stage. There, trainers teach the more intricate movements of traditional dressage such as the pirouette (where the horse performs a cantering turn on the spot), passage (a trot with extremely long strides), and *piaffe* (where the horse trots without mov-

ing forward). Once all these levels of training have been completed, experienced trainers assess the horses to see if they are capable of the advanced exercises unique to the Spanish Riding School.

Each horse found to be good enough is then taught one of three movements—the levade (where the horse stands perfectly still on its hind legs), the *croupade* (where the horse leaps into the air with all its legs tucked under its body), or the capriole (a leap into the air with the front legs tucked under the body and the rear legs kicked straight out behind).

The Riders

The riders also spend many years in training before they are allowed to take part in public performances. To attain the level of mastery expected by the Spanish Riding School, riders must train for at least five years, on top of whatever training they have already received. In 2008 the Spanish Riding school began to accept female applicants, and the first woman to pass the entrance exams, Austrian Hannah Zeitlhofer, made her first public appearance at a performance in autumn 2010.

EXPERIENCE: Horse-riding in Vienna

While a hands-on equine experience isn't offered to visitors at the Spanish Riding School, visitors keen to climb into the saddle for a canter across Vienna will find a stable of magnificent rideable beasts in the heart of the Prater (see pp. 162–163): Personalized individual and group lessons at the Reitverein Freudenau (Freudenau Riding School; *the Prater, tel 1/728 95 94, www.reitverein-freudenau .at, $$$–$$$$$*) are tailored for riders of every standard.

Although there will be little opportunity to practice the "airs above the ground"—the perfectly disciplined, spirited kick for which the Lipizzaners are

famous—the Prater's Freudenau school is renowned throughout Austria for its beautiful, graceful, and mild-mannered horses. Riding in the Prater has a long tradition, dating back to the hunting days of Maximilian in 1560. Today riders can experience the glory of the park's meadows on horseback or utilize the Freudenau's state-of-the-art equestrian facility. Dressage and show-jumping arenas offer plenty for the competent rider. Visitors can also help groom the horses or sweep the stables under the guidance of some of Vienna's top equine trainers. A strict reservation system operates at the school, so reservations are essential.

Museum für Völkerkunde (Museum of Ethnology)

✉ Neue Burg

☎ (1) 525 24-0

🕐 Closed Tues.

💲 $$

🚇 Herrengasse (U3)

www.khm.at/en/ the-museum-of -ethnology

NOTE: The Museum of Ethnology was closed for renovations at the time of writing, and only some of the galleries were open. It is due to reopen fully in December 2012.

Sammlung Alter Musikinstrumente (Collection of Ancient Musical Instruments)

✉ Neue Hofburg, Heldenplatz

☎ (1) 525 24-4025

🕐 Closed Mon. & Tues.

💲 $$$

🚇 Herrengasse (U3)

www.khm.at/en/ neue-burg

the Ottoman Turks out of Austria and central Europe. The other statue depicts Archduke Charles of Austria (1771–1847), a military leader who played a decisive role in the defeat of Napoleon.

Today the Ballroom Wing is home to the Hofburg Conference Center—a venue for corporate events, academic conferences, and private functions. It is best known, however, for its annual **Kaiserball,** which has been held on New Year's Eve in the Hofburg ballroom since 1970. It is the modern equivalent of the traditional Hofball, which was traditionally hosted by the empress in early January.

Neue Burg

Even when the Imperial Forum project was first proposed in the late 19th century, it seemed an ill-advised undertaking. By the time the Neue Burg building was completed in 1913—against the backdrop of an empire that was disintegrating and a continent that was arming for war—it was viewed as a baffling anachronism, an ostentatious throwback to the excesses of prerevolutionary France. No member of the royal family ever lived in the Neue Burg, and its only notable appearance in Austrian history was an ignominious one—it was from the building's central balcony that Hitler declared the Anschluss (unification) of Germany and Austria in 1938.

For decades the Austrian government struggled to find a use for this massive building. Beginning in the 1920s, the Kunsthistorisches Museum (see p. 114) began to

INSIDER TIP:

It's worth visiting the Heldenplatz at night, when the Neue Burg's artful exterior lighting really shows off the complexity of the architecture.

—BEATRICE AUMAYR
Viennese tour guide

move more and more of its art collections into the Neue Burg's cavernous halls, and the Austrian National Library (see p. 111) relocated some of its archives (including its collection of ancient papyri) into the rooms at the northern end of the building. Today, most of the building is occupied by museums, whose varied collections sit within lavish interiors designed for the emperor.

Museums of the Neue Burg: The first museum to be installed in this palace was the **Museum für Völkerkunde** (Museum of Ethnology), which was started as a place to exhibit items acquired by Archduke Franz-Ferdinand on his 1908 world tour. These items were supplemented by the collections of several other Austrian travelers and anthropologists, some of which had been sitting in the archives of the Naturhistorisches Museum (see p. 115) since the 1850s. The museum collection includes artifacts from all over the world, such as the feathered headdress of an Aztec priest, a set of beautiful manuscripts from Japan, and ornate gold figurines of Hindu gods.

The second museum to be set up here was the **Hofjagd und Rüstkammer** (Collection of Arms and Armor), established in 1935. The museum's exhibitions are almost entirely drawn from the private collection of the Austrian royal family. The core of the collection comes from the

emonial pieces (covered in gold filigree and plumes of feathers) to plain, battle-ready ones. Given Austria's troubled relationship with its more recent past, it's hardly surprising that this collection of military hardware cuts off in the late 19th century.

Fittingly, the first museum to open in the Neue Burg after the Second World War was

Hofjagd und Rüstkammer (Collection of Arms & Armor)

✉ Neue Hofburg, Heldenplatz

☎ (1) 525 24-4025

🕐 Closed Mon. & Tues.

💲 $$$

🚇 Herrengasse (U3)

www.khm.at/en/ neue-burg

The sweeping curved facade of the Neue Burg dwarfs the statue of Prince Eugene of Savoy.

remarkable collection of Archduke Ferdinand of Tirol (1529–1595). Ferdinand purchased the arms and armor of noted military commanders for display in a museum he called the Heldenrüstkammer (Armory of Heroes). The galleries of the museum are filled with beautifully crafted muskets and rifles, as well as suits of armor that range from slightly ridiculous cer-

neither military nor imperial. The **Sammlung Alter Musikinstrumente** (Collection of Ancient Musical Instruments) showcases the physical relics of Vienna's rich musical history. While many come here to see the instruments played by well-known composers—such as a piano played by Beethoven or a zither on which Anton Karas played the theme to

One of the Hofburg's many formal balls

Burggarten

📍 97

🚇 Volkstheater (U2, U3) or Babenberger-strasse (Strassen-bahn line 2)

Ephesus Museum

✉ Neue Burg, Heldenplatz

☎ (1) 525 24-0

🕐 Closed Thurs.–Sat.

💲 $$$

🚇 Herrengasse (U3)

www.khm.at/en/neue-burg

The Third Man—it is the collection of unusual and archaic instruments that is most fascinating. In the gallery of stringed instruments, for example, visitors can trace the gradual evolution of the violin, or marvel at the many strange fretted instruments that preceded the modern guitar.

The last major museum to open in the Neue Burg was the **Ephesus Museum,** which brought together the artifacts recovered by Austrian archaeological teams working in the ancient Roman city of Ephesus (on the west coast of present-day Turkey) and the island-state of Samothrace. The collection includes fragments of ruined architecture, sections of friezes, and the impressive Parthian Monument—a Roman-era sculpture commemorating a major victory against the Parthians in Asia Minor.

Burggarten

Behind the Neue Burg, where Vienna's fortifications once stood, lies the neatly tended greenery of the Burggarten (Palace Garden). This small public park is a popular spot with those who need a break from sightseeing. Next to the southern entrance to the park there is a large marble statue of Mozart, which overlooks a flower bed that is carefully maintained in the shape of a treble clef. If you head north from here along the shaded paths and past the ornamental pond, you will find yourself at the art nouveau Palmenhaus, an enormous greenhouse designed by the noted *Jugendstil* architect Friedrich Ohmann (1858–1927) and completed in 1906.

Although the building's exterior is impressive, it is the

remarkable ecosystem that thrives inside that is the biggest draw. In 1988, after many years of neglect, the Palmenhaus was rebuilt and reopened to the public as the **Schmetterlinghaus** (Butterfly House)—under its glazed roof thousands of exotic butterflies flutter around a lush collection of tropical plants. In addition to the butterfly house, the Palmenhaus is also home to a café and a popular restaurant.

The Augustinertrakt

In the days when Vienna was still a fortified city, the Hofburg stood right up against the city's southwestern walls. The area where Heldenplatz, the Neue Burg, and the Burggarten now stand was covered by a network of walls, ditches, and triangular bastions that extended out to around where the Ringstrasse now is.

When you bear this in mind, the arrowlike shape of the Augustinertrakt (Augustinian Wing) makes a little more sense—it was built this way because the plot of land it stands on was originally wedged between a major road and the city's inner wall. This is probably also the reason why few members of the royal family ever wanted to live here.

In the 19th century, almost every part of the city's defenses fell to either Napoleon's artillery or Franz-Josef's modernizing zeal. The Augustinertrakt stands on top of the only fragment that survived—a short raised section of what was once the colossal Augusterbasei (Augustinian Bastion).

Most of the Augustinertrakt dates from the mid-18th century, but at its heart there is a much older building—the 14th-century **Augustinerkirche** and its adjoining cloisters. Today this wing is home to the Österreichische Nationalbibliotek (Austrian National Library) and the museums of the Albertina.

Österreichische National-bibliotek (Austrian National Library): Emperor Karl VI founded this institution in the 1730s. In both its function and style, it is a monument to the ideas of the European Enlightenment—a secular

---

Schmetterling-haus

✉ Burggarten, Hanaschgasse

☎ (1) 533 85 70

💲 $$

🚉 Babenberger-strasse (Strassen-bahn line 2)

Österreichische National-bibliotek

✉ Josefsplatz 2

☎ (1) 534 10-394

🕐 Closed Mon.

💲 $$$

🚉 Stephansplatz (U1, U3) or Herrengasse (U3)

www.onb.ac.at/ev/

EXPERIENCE:
Juggle in the Burggarten

To experience the Burggarten in the style of the locals, throw yourself into the hoop-spinning, Frisbee-throwing, stilt-walking, and park-going throng with your own variation on the theme. Pick up some juggling balls (the bean-filled ones are best for beginners) from **Bumfidl** (*Lerchenfeld-strasse 113, tel 1/522 74 82, www.bumfidl .com*) or opt for something braver: They also sell a colorful array of fire-eating gear, jester costumes, modeling balloons, face paints, and acrobatic equipment as well as unicycles.

Vienna's more experienced jugglers, acrobats, and hoop-spinning kings are often in or around the Burggarten and are more than willing to share personal tips to newbies struggling to perfect the art. Juggling balls cost just a few euros, but if you struggle with hand-to-eye coordination, choose a hand pump instead to fill the manicured gardens with giant bubbles—a magical sight on a breezy summer's day.

Papyrus Museum

- ✉ Heldenplatz
- ☎ (1) 534 10-420
- 🕐 Closed Sun. & Mon.
- 💲 $$
- 🚇 Stephansplatz (U1, U3) or Herrengasse (U3)

www.onb.ac.at/ev/ collections/papyrus

Esperanto Museum

- ✉ Palais Mollard, Herrengasse 9
- ☎ (1) 534 10-730
- 🕐 Closed Mon.
- 💲 $
- 🚇 Stephansplatz (U1, U3) or Herrengasse (U3)

www.onb.at/ev/ esperanto_museum

Globe Museum

- ✉ Palais Mollard, Herrengasse 9
- ☎ (1) 534 10-710
- 🕐 Closed Mon.
- 💲 $$
- 🚇 Stephansplatz (U1, U3) or Herrengasse (U3)

www.onb.at/ev/ globe_museum

Augustinerkirche

- 🅰 97
- ✉ Augustiner- strasse
- 🕐 Closed July & Aug.
- 💲 Burial vault of Hearts of the Habsburgs by appointmen
- 🚇 Karlsplatz (U1, U2, U4)

cathedral, dedicated to the advancement of human knowledge rather than the veneration of God. Although the library has spread out considerably over the years, the core of its collection is still held in the jaw-dropping baroque Prunksaal (main hall) on the southwestern side of Josefsplatz.

This building was designed in 1723 by Johann Fischer von Erlach and completed in 1726 by his son Joseph Emanuel. By the standards of Viennese baroque, the exterior of this building is quite restrained—the decoration is restricted to a group of statues on the parapet. "Restrained" is not, however, a word that anyone is likely to use to describe the building's interior. It took the artist Daniel Gran (1694–1757) four years to complete the massive trompe-l'oeil frescoes that adorn the ceiling vaults, and the library's designers took even longer to amass the forest of marble sculptures that populate the ground floor.

Like most national libraries, the Austrian National Library is constantly expanding in an organic and seemingly random fashion. Its archives occupy a maze of rooms spread throughout the Augustinian Wing and Neue Burg, as well as several other buildings around the city center.

Although most of this collection holds little interest to those who don't speak German, there are a few special collections that are worth a look. The best known of these is the **Papyrus Museum,** next to the National Library, which holds an impressive collection of Egyptian papyri. These fascinating documents range in age from the time of the first pharoahs to the early years of the Islamic caliphate. In addition to ancient Egyptian texts, there are also documents in other languages, such as a fragment of a Greek play by Orestes.

INSIDER TIP:

For lovely soft leather goods—handbags, purses, belts, and briefcases—head to Viennese specialist Horn (Mahlerstrasse 5), **a short walk east of the Hofburg complex.**

—BRIGITTA HARTL-WAGNER
National Geographic contributor

There are two other museums located in an annex about 10 minutes' walk to the northeast, on Herrengasse. These are the **Esperanto Museum,** which is dedicated to the history and development of the well-known constructed language (which was developed in Vienna); and the **Globe Museum,** which houses a large collection of antique globes including several by noted Dutch cartographer Gerardus Mercator (1512–1594).

The Augustinerkirche: This church was built in 1339 to serve the royal court, which had recently moved into the Alte

Hofburg. In its capacity as the parish church of the royal court, it was the venue for many royal weddings and funerals. Its interior consists of a single narrow vaulted chamber, painted plain white, with tall windows along each side. The clean flowing lines of the Gothic stonework are a refreshing change from the overwrought baroque decoration that predominates elsewhere in the Hofburg. Over the centuries, this beautiful white vault suffered from a gradual buildup of baroque memorial statues and over-the-top side altars, but these were swept away in the 18th century when the church was restored to something very close to its original 14th-century appearance.

The Augustinerkirche is still an active church, and the adjoining cloister is still home to a small monastic commmunity. Like the nearby Hofkapelle, this church is renowned for its wonderful sacred music, and there is often a large queue outside the doors before Sunday morning Mass. It does not cost anything to attend, but you may have to show up some time in advance to be seated.

The Albertina: This wing of the Hofburg was built for Maria-Christina (the favorite daughter of Empress Maria-Theresia) and her husband, Albert of Saxony. Today their grand residence is home to an art gallery, which holds one of the world's largest collections of etchings, screen prints, sketches, and watercolors—around 1.5 million pieces

Albertina

🅰 97

✉ Albertinaplatz 1

☎ (1) 534 83-0

💲 $$

🚇 Karlsplatz (U1, U2, U4) or Stephansplatz (U1, U3)

www.albertina.at

The Austrian National Library contains more than seven million books and artifacts in its collection.

Kunst-historisches Museum

<A> 97

<✉> Maria-Theresien-Platz, Burgring 5

<☎> (1) 525 24-4025

<⊕> Closed Mon.

<$> $$$

<⊞> Museums-Quartier (U2) or Volkstheater (U2, U3)

www.khm.at

This ancient Egyptian statuette of a hippopotamus, on display in the Kunsthistorisches Museum, is thought to be around 4,000 years old.

in total. Because of the sheer size of the collection, and how easily these artworks fade in sunlight, only a fraction are ever on display—usually grouped into themed exhibitions. In addition to the permanent collection, the gallery hosts numerous exhibitions, showcasing the work of artists as diverse as Roy Lichtenstein and René Magritte.

Maria-Theresien-Platz

Beyond the Burgring, the perfectly symmetrical Maria-Theresien-Platz is another remnant of the Imperial Forum project. Here the street that runs through the Hofburg complex acts as the line of symmetry, with every detail—from the facades of the buildings to the positions of the shrubs in the gardens—mirrored exactly on either side. The square is flanked by two vast museums: the Kunsthistorisches Museum (Museum of Art History) and the Naturhistorisches Museum (Natural History Museum).

At the center of the square is an enormous bronze statue of Empress Maria-Theresia by Kaspar von Zumbuch (1830–1915). It shows Maria-Theresia on her throne, dressed in all her royal finery. Around the base of the plinth there are statues of her trusted advisers and her four finest generals. She would no doubt have approved of this grand tribute, although you can't help but wonder what the notoriously puritanical empress would have thought of the fact that her gaze is eternally fixed on the many nude sculptures that adorn the surrounding buildings.

The **Kunsthistorisches Museum,** on the southern side of the square, was built to display the vast collection of art that the Habsburg family had amassed over the centuries. The collection occupies nearly 100 rooms, spread over all three floors. It would take several trips to see all that the museum has on display.

The ground-floor rooms are divided into three sections: the

collection of Greek and Roman Antiquities, the Egyptian and Near Eastern Collection, and the Collection of Sculpture and Decorative Arts. The Egyptian and Near Eastern Collection was mostly acquired in the late 19th century, and includes a 4,000-year-old burial chamber (belonging to a royal official) that was transported in its entirety from Egypt. Other highlights of the ground-floor collections include a larger-than-life votive statue from ancient Cyprus,

Across the square, in the architectural mirror image of the Kunsthistorisches Museum, is the **Naturhistorisches Museum,** which chronicles the diversity of the natural world. It is a fine museum, though much of its collection can be seen in similar institutions elsewhere. The second-floor rooms are filled with a largely forgettable menagerie of stuffed animals, wired skeletons, and pickled fish. It is worth visiting, however, for the ground-floor

Natur- historisches Museum

97

Maria- Theresien-Platz, Burgring 7

(1) 521 77-276

Closed Tues.

$$

Museums- Quartier (U2) or Volkstheater (U2, U3)

www.nhm-wien.ac.at

The "Venus of Willendorf"

Exhibited in the Naturhistorisches Museum, the "Venus of Willendorf"—a 4.3-inch-high (11 cm) stone statuette carved some 25,000 years ago by an unknown sculptor in eastern Austria—is one of the oldest known depictions of the human form. A group of archaeologists working near Willendorf, a village on the Donau banks some 40 miles (64 km) upriver from Vienna, discovered the piece in 1908. The Venus depicts a nude obese woman standing with her legs together, her arms folded across her breasts, and

her head bowed forward. The statuette has been carved with detailed genitalia and some kind of headdress (or hairstyle) that covers her face.

Although more than 100 years have passed since her discovery, the statue remains an enigmatic and mysterious object. Some believe that she is an idealized "mother goddess" or fertility figure while others argue that the detailed, natural shape of her body implies she was modeled on a real woman, perhaps a priestess or matriarch.

---

and a dazzling array of golden sculptures purchased by generations of Habsburg connoisseurs.

The second and third floors are home to the Picture Collection, which includes hundreds of pictures from all over Europe. The breadth and quality of this collection—which includes masterpieces by Rembrandt van Rijn, Diego Velásquez, Albrecht Dürer, and Peter Rubens—is testament to the excellent taste (and staggering wealth) of the Habsburg monarchy.

collections, which include a glittering selection of minerals, pieces of actual meteorites, and the towering skeletons of dinosaurs. It is the early human collection (rooms 11–13), however, that contains the most compelling exhibitions. Here you will see Bronze Age swords, Iron Age burial goods from the Halstatt culture (which thrived in western Austria from the eighth to fourth centuries B.C.), and the Stone Age statuette known as the "Venus of Willendorf (see sidebar above). ■

The MuseumsQuartier

To the southwest of Maria-Theresien-Platz, the low baroque facade of the old royal stables conceals a vibrant modern cultural complex, the MuseumsQuartier. Inside, the baroque exterior gives way to a striking mixture of old and new architecture that houses several major museums, galleries, performance spaces, and exhibition halls, as well as a cluster of 60 independent creative initiatives brought together as part of the Quartier 21 project.

The Leopold Museum houses the world's largest repository of works by Austrian artist Egon Schiele.

Museums-Quartier

🅰 97 & 121

🚇 Museums-Quartier (U2) or Volkstheater (U2, U3)

Visitor Information

✉ Museums Quartier, Museumplatz 1/5

☎ (1) 523 58 81

www.mqw.at

The core of the Museums-Quartier is the former imperial stable building, designed in 1713 by Johann Fischer von Erlach. His original building (the long, straight wing that faces onto Maria-Theresien-Platz) was repeatedly extended during the 19th century to accommodate more horses and facilities.

After the founding of the Austrian Republic, the stables were converted into an exhibition space for trade shows. It continued to be used for this purpose until the late 1980s, when the Museums-Quartier project got started. After

numerous political squabbles about the size and extent of the proposed cultural complex (particularly the controversial 184-foot-high/56 m tower that was the centerpiece of the original design), construction began on the buildings of the Museums-Quartier in 1998.

The institutions of the Muse-umsQuartier are located around a series of courtyards at the heart of the old baroque stables. The courtyards are connected to the street by long, barrel-vaulted passageways, which run through the old buildings. Several of these passageways are enlivened by mini-museums or art installations showcasing sound design (Volkstheater entrance), comic-book art (Mariahilfer Strasse entrance), street art (Spittelberg entrance), and typography (Quartier 21). These little museums feature playful exhibitions and interactive works by young artists, while discarding the usual trappings of a museum—for example, the programs are dispensed by vending machines and there are no permanent collections.

Most visitors arrive in the central courtyard from Maria-Theresien-Platz, passing through the baroque vaulted entranceway into the broad central courtyard. On the right of the entrance is the loaf-shaped gray stone building of the Museum of Modern Art (see p. 118), while the neat white cube of the Leopold Museum stands on the right; directly ahead is the old winter riding hall, which has been converted to house a number of smaller institutions; as well as the **Halle** *(MuseumsQuartier 1, tel 1/523 7001, ww2.diehalle.at)*, a stylish modern café-restaurant.

The directors of the Museums-Quartier have not wasted any part of the old stable complex, and even the open spaces of the courtyard are often spruced up to serve as an open-air cultural venue. In the summer the courtyard is used for film screenings and open-air theater, while in the winter it houses an ice rink and numerous art installations.

Leopold Museum

The most visited institution in the MuseumsQuartier is the Leopold Museum, a spectacular hoard of Viennese Jugendstil and expressionist art acquired by Viennese collector Dr. Rudolf Leopold (see sidebar below).

Leopold Museum

- 🅰 97 & 121
- ✉ Museumplatz
- ☎ (1) 525 70-0
- 🕐 Closed Tues. (open every day in Aug.)
- 💲 $$$$
- 🚇 Museums-Quartier (U2) or Volkstheater (U2, U3)

www.leopold museum.org

A Controversial Art Champion

Rudolf Leopold, the future champion of early 20th-century figurative painter Egon Schiele (1890–1918), was born in Vienna in 1925. He spent the Second World War hiding from Nazi conscription in an obscure mountain village before returning to Vienna to study medicine.

As a student Leopold became transfixed by Schiele's intense works. He bought his first Schiele painting in 1950 and soon gained a reputation as a zealous collector—spending everything he earned on art and often sinking deeply into debt. In the early 1960s he organized exhibitions of Schiele's work around the world, bringing Schiele a degree of fame he never experienced during his lifetime.

Leopold's obsessive desire to acquire ever more works by Schiele and his contemporaries sometimes led him into dubious moral territory. In the postwar years he bought several works that the Nazis had confiscated from Viennese Jews, allegedly fully aware of their provenance—though he always maintained that he acquired them legitimately.

Less than a month after Leopold's death in June 2010, his namesake museum was forced to pay $19 million to the descendants of Leah Bondi Jaray, a Jewish art dealer who owned the "Portrait of Wally" before the war. The controversy surrounding his collection looks set to endure for years to come.

MUMOK

- 🅰 97 & 121
- ✉ Museumplatz 1, Museums-Quartier
- ☎ (1) 525 00
- 💲 $$$
- 🚇 Museums-Quartier (U2) or Volkstheater (U2, U3)

www.mumok.at

Architektur-zentrum Wien (AzW)

- 🅰 97 & 121
- ✉ Museumplatz, Museums-Quartier
- ☎ (1) 522 31 15
- 💲 $$$
- 🚇 Museums-Quartier (U2) or Volkstheater (U2, U3)

www.azw.at

Tanzquartier Wien

- ✉ Museumsplatz 1
- ☎ (1) 581 35 91
- 🕐 Closed Sun.
- 🚇 Museums-Quartier (U2) or Volkstheater (U2, U3)

www.tqw.at

The museum houses the world's largest collection of Egon Schiele artworks—a total of 44 oil paintings and 180 sketches and watercolors that chronicle his artistic career from 1907 to his death in 1918. The Schiele collection includes portraits of his friends and lovers, stylized male and female nudes, and dozens of self-portraits (Schiele painted and sketched himself constantly).

INSIDER TIP:

The workshops in Quartier 21 are popular with tinkerers and amateur inventors—you'll often see strange homemade robots wandering the halls.

—BASTIAN SCHWARZ
National Geographic contributor

The museum is also home to several masterpieces by the leading lights of the Viennese Secession (see pp. 54–55)—including masterworks by Gustav Klimt, Carl Moll, and Ferdinand Andri. Klimt's 6-foot-high (2 m) painting "Death and Life" (1916) is probably the museum's biggest attraction outside the Schiele collection.

MUMOK

On the opposite site of the courtyard stands the Museums-Quartier's other main attraction: the Museum Moderner Kunst (Museum of Modern Art; more simply known as MUMOK).

This museum was founded in the 1960s as the Museum of the 20th Century (usually known as the 20er Haus), a small institution that had various homes over the course of its history. In the 1980s, the collection of the 20er Haus was combined with the collection of Peter Ludwig (1925–1996), a German businessman and ardent collector of modern art. Ludwig was especially fond of American pop art, collecting works by Jasper Johns, Robert Rauschenberg, Roy Lichtenstein, and Andy Warhol—and today many of these can be seen in the Museum of Modern Art.

The 9,000 works in the museum's collection are grouped into five categories. There is a small collection brought together under the category of Classical Modernism—art from the first half of the 20th century, including prominent works from the cubist, futurist, surrealist, and expressionist movements—while the bulk of the collection is composed of works drawn from four artistic movements that thrived between the 1950s and 1970s: *nouveau réalisme, fluxus,* pop art, and Viennese actionism.

Don't come to the MUMOK expecting to see pretty pictures—with the exception of some of the pop-art exhibitions, the displays are very avant-garde, with frequently disturbing or surreal imagery. Artists earn their place here by doing things like taping fish to their bodies or dressing up in bloody bandages and wandering around Vienna. It's worth checking what exhibitions

EXPERIENCE: Exploring Quartier 21

Occupying most of Johann Fischer von Erlach's original baroque stable block that forms the heart of the MuseumsQuartier, **Quartier 21** (*Museumsplatz 1, http://quartier21.at*) offers space and support to small cultural initiatives and innovative new projects. In the rooms leading off two main passages (named Electric Avenue and Transeuropa), young artists, writers, designers, and hackers are given free rein to create interesting new work. For those who tire of carefully curated museums and galleries, this assortment of workshops, studios, stores, and galleries provides a lively breath of fresh air.

Visitors can wander the halls independently, knocking on doors and browsing the shops, or they can join one of the guided tours of the spaces organized by the MuseumsQuartier (*www.mqw.at*) to learn more about what goes on within the project.

Notable occupants of Quartier 21 include **Subotron** (*www.subotron.at*), a celebration of video-games culture that combines shop, cultural center, and reverential museum of video-games hardware; **Combinat** (*www.combinat.at*), a studio and store that serves as a launchpad for young fashion designers; and the anarchic art collective **monochrom** (*www.monochrom.at*).

---

are taking place, as the museum consistently attracts some of the biggest names in the art world.

Other Institutions

In addition to these two big names, there are several other museums, galleries, and educational centers in the complex, which, while they may not have the broad appeal of the first two, are still fascinating places.

The largest is the **AzW** (Architekturzentrum Wien, or Vienna Architecture Center), an exhibition space, architecture museum, and research center. Housed in the western wing of the baroque stable complex, the AzW arrived at the MuseumsQuartier in 1993. In addition to its permanent exhibition "Viennese Architecture in the 20th and 21st Centuries," the AzW hosts various career retrospectives, student design shows, and architectural contests.

On the opposite side of the complex the stable buildings have been converted to house the **Tanzquartier Wien** (Vienna Dance Quarter), a group of performance spaces and studios devoted to the development of modern dance and performance in Vienna. The main foyer, leading from the central courtyard of the MuseumsQuartier, takes you into an impressive space that has been converted into a performance area, **Hall E+G**, a light, totally white hall that has sweeping staircases. Hall E+G stages concerts, dance shows, and drama.

Throughout the MuseumsQuartier there are cafés, bars, and restaurants. Visitors can settle into the huge squashy sofas at **Kantine** with an art book from the adjoining store, or have lunch at the beautiful **Milo** restaurant (in the AzW), where the vaulted ceiling of the baroque stables has been transformed with traditional Turkish tiles designed by the artist Asiye Kolbai-Kafalier, who lives and works in Vienna. ■

Hall E+G

- ✉ Museumsplatz 1
- ☎ (1) 542 33 21
- 🕐 Closed Mon.
- 🚇 Museums-Quartier (U2) or Volkstheater (U2, U3)

www.mqw.at

Kantine

- ✉ Electric Avenue, Museumsplatz
- ☎ (1) 523 82 39
- 🚇 Museums-Quartier (U2) or Volkstheater (U2, U3)

Milo

- ✉ Architekturzentrum Wien, Museumsplatz
- ☎ (1) 523 65 66
- 🚇 Museums-Quartier (U2) or Volkstheater (U2, U3)

www.azw.at

A Walk Around Spittelberg

Only a handful of neighborhoods in the *vorstädte* (once the suburbs, but now part of
the city center) have retained their authentic 18th-century character. The exception
is Spittelberg, a few blocks of narrow cobblestoned streets located between Burggasse and Siebensterngasse, just west of the MuseumsQuartier.

Several charming outdoor restaurants line the streets of Spittelberg.

The best way to reach the Spittelberg area
is to take the U-Bahn to **Volkstheater
U-Bahn Station ❶**. From the station, head
west along the gentle uphill slope of the
Burggasse, passing the ornate 19th-century
facade of the Volkstheater on your right and
the MuseumsQuartier on your left.

Continue past the entrances to Breite Gasse
and narrow Kirchberggasse and you'll soon
reach the pastel-green **Zum Heiligen Josef
Biedermeier house ❷**, a beautiful little house,
now a restaurant, that is dwarfed by the 19th-
century building next door. Gutenberggasse
is the sort of narrow cobbled street that once
would have been common throughout Vienna.
It survives today thanks to the efforts of local
residents who, in the 1970s and 1980s, resisted
attempts to rebuild or "modernize" the area.

NOT TO BE MISSED:

Zum Heiligen Josef Biedermeier
house • Cobbled Gutenberggasse • Garnisonkirche

Today the street is lined with neat little
stores, art galleries, and traditional restaurants,
the best known of which is the **Witwe Bolte
❸** *(Gutenberggasse 13, tel 1/523 14 50, www
.witwebolte.at)*, which was formerly an inn called
the Six-Legged Lion. Inside the restaurant there
is a plaque commemorating the occasion, in
1778, when a riotously drunk Emperor Josef II
was thrown out of the bar.

There is a short alleyway just north of the

Witwe Bolte that connects Gutenberggasse with Spittelberggasse, the cobbled lane from which the area takes its name. Spittelberggasse is home to a well-known craft market, which is held every Saturday between April and November, then daily in the run up to Christmas. Just to the south of the alleyway is the **Theater am Spittelberg** ❹ (*Spittelberggasse 10, tel 1/526 13 85, www.theateramspittelberg.at*), a modern theater that hosts nightly performances by well-known musicians and up-and-coming theater companies. Spittelberggasse is home to many wonderful pieces of 18th-century architecture. Highlights include the restrained baroque of the house at Spittelberggasse 20, and the playful trompe l'oeil decoration that adorns the facade of Spittelberggasse 9.

Head back onto Burggasse and then back down Schrankgasse, the next street along. At the bottom of this street, where it joins Stiftgasse, is the **Amerlinghaus** ❺ (*Stiftgasse 8, tel 1/523 75 15, www.amerlinghaus.at*), once the home of the painter Friedrich von Amerling

(1803–1887), a lovely 18th-century courtyard house that now functions as the local museum and community center.

Continue south along the Stiftgasse, across the Siebensterngasse, and then south down to where it meets the broad and busy Mariahilfer Strasse. On this corner is the **Garnisonkirche** ❻ (Garrison Church), a chapel traditionally associated with the Austrian military. Its designer managed to squeeze all the architectural motifs of Viennese baroque onto the small structure, creating an effect that can be a little overwhelming up close. Turn left on to Mariahilfer Strasse and walk the 500 yards (460 m) to the MuseumsQuartier U-Bahn Station.

🅜	See area map p. 97
▶	Volkstheater Station
🕐	90 minutes
↔	1 mile (1.6 km)
▶	MuseumsQuartier Station

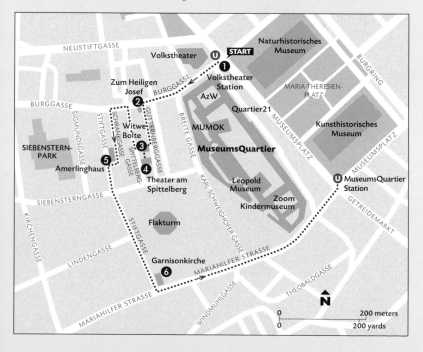

Imperial Vienna

The broad avenues that surround the Hofburg complex have been shaped by hundreds of years of patronage from the royal family and their endless entourage of aristocrats, politicians, and wealthy merchants. Their wealth encouraged the development of theaters, opera houses, and hundreds of high-class boutiques. Even though the royal family is now long gone, the area retains a refined, sophisticated atmosphere.

The Volksgarten on a summer evening, with the Burgtheater visible in the background

Austrian Parliament Building

🏛 97

✉ Dr.-Karl-Renner-Ring 3

☎ (1) 401 10-2400

💲 $$

🚇 Rathaus (U2) or Volkstheater (U2, U3)

www.parlament.gv.at

NOTE: Guided tours are given in English and German, Mon.-Sat., but only when Parliament is not in session, so it's a good idea to call ahead. Visitors are admitted on production of identification papers or a passport.

The Ringstrasse

Moving north along the Ringstrasse (the circular road encircling the Innere Stadt) from the Hofburg, the first major public institution you encounter is the **Austrian Parliament Building.** This massive structure was designed in 1878 by the king of neoclassical architecture, Theophilus Hansen (1813–1891). He pulled out all the stops for this design, basing the style of the enormous porticoes on the Parthenon and covering the pediments in gilded allegorical statues. It's not always entirely clear what these statues are allegories for, nor—to give one example—how a seminude woman can be an allegory for the legislative branch of government, but the sheer quantity of carved marble on display certainly makes an impression.

The visitors' entrance is behind a large marble statue of the Greek goddess Athena, who represents wisdom (locals often joke that she appears to be walking away from the building). In this recently renovated space you can purchase tickets for one of the guided tours of the building's interior (in English and German), which take you through the spectacular halls and chambers where Austrian politicians hold their debates.

A good spot to take in the broad facade of the Parliament Building is from the **Volksgarten,** a pleasant former royal garden located where the city's battlements once stood. The centerpiece of the park is the **Temple of Theseus,** an exact copy of the Thission in Athens. This was built to house Antonio Canova's "Theseus and the Minotaur," which was brought to the city by Napoleon. Since 1890, however, this work of art has stood by the main staircase of the Kunsthistorisches Museum (see p. 114) and the interior of the temple has been closed to the public. In the southern corner of the park is a large café, the **Tanzcafé** (Dance Café), which holds events with live music and dancing every Sunday evening during the summer.

Beyond the Parliament Building stands Vienna's **Rathaus** (Town Hall). This massive piece of Gothic revival architecture was designed in 1872 by Friedrich von Schmidt (1825–1891). The handsome facade is capped by five stone towers, the largest of which is 325 feet (115 m) tall. The building's 1,600 rooms house Vienna's local government, the mayor's offices, and various other administrative departments. Visitors can go on a guided tour around the building's sumptuous interior, which takes in its stone halls (home to the famous Opernball); grand council chambers; and quiet, cloister-like courtyards.

The Burgtheater

Directly opposite the Rathaus is the elegant facade of the Burgtheater, built in the 1880s to house Vienna's premier theater company. As with the other buildings along this stretch

Tanzcafé
- ✉ Volksgarten
- ☎ (1) 532 42 41
- 🚇 Rathaus (U2) or Volkstheater (U2, U3)

www.volksgarten.at

Rathaus
- 🚋 97
- ✉ Friedrich-Schmidt-Platz 1
- ☎ (1) 525 50
- 🚇 Rathaus (U2)

www.wien.gv.at/ english/cityhall

NOTE: Guided tours of the Rathaus are free and start at 1 p.m. on Mon., Wed., & Fri. Visitors can also explore the building with a multilingual audio guide (free, if you deposit your photo ID at reception). Tours aren't held when the council is in session, so check before visiting.

EXPERIENCE: Running the Ringstrasse

For one day every year, usually in April or May, the entire Ringstrasse is transformed from a busy road to a colossal running track. The **Vienna City Marathon** (tel 1/606 95 10, www.vienna-marathon.at) provides a unique way to experience the city, whether you do the full marathon, the half marathon, or the 2.5-mile (4 km) run along the Ringstrasse.

The two longer events start by UNO City (see p. 169) and head through the Prater (see pp. 161–165) toward St. Stephen's Cathedral. Half-marathon runners finish at Heldenplatz, while the marathoners continue past the Parliament Buildings and back over the river before returning to the Ringstrasse and the finish line at Heldenplatz.

While this is a serious athletic event, one that requires training, things are still done with a distinctively Viennese touch of class. The night before the marathon there is a huge party in the great hall of the Rathaus, with a carb-heavy banquet of pasta and bread. The marathon also has a fine musical accompaniment, including the Ringstrasse's "melodious mile," where runners are treated to everything from gentle Strauss waltzes to bouncy modern pop.

For those who want to see the city and do a little training at the same time, **Vienna Sight Jogging** (tel 1/504 51 31, www.viennasightjogging.co.at) provides guided jogging tours of the city—typically covering 2.5–4.5 miles (4–7 km) of historic streets in around an hour.

Burgtheater

 97

✉ Dr.-Karl-Lueger-
Ring 2

☎ (1) 514 44-4140

🚇 Rathaus (U2) or
Schottentor (U2)

www.burgtheater.at

NOTE: Guided tours
of the Burgtheater are
interpreted in English
and German at 3 p.m.
Fri.–Sun.

of the Ringstrasse, no expense
was spared in its construction or
decoration.

The most impressive features
of this remarkable building are the
two huge entrance halls on either
side of the main auditorium. Both
are decorated with ceiling frescoes
painted by Gustav Klimt, his
brother Ernst, and their friend and
collaborator Franz Matsch. Guided
tours of the theater are available,

The Burgtheater, a symbol of Vienna's cultural heritage and
a major donor to the Theatermuseum

Minoritenkirche

 97

✉ Minoritenplatz
2a

☎ (1) 533 41 62

🚇 Herrengasse
(U3) or Rathaus
(U2)

**www.minoriten
kirche-wien.info**

including one that pays special
attention to the Klimt frescoes
and their history. This tour takes
in the "Klimtraum," where the
artist's full-size preparatory drawings (found in the theater's attic in
1999) are on display.

About 2 minutes' walk to
the east of the Burgtheater, on
Minoritenplatz, stands the strange

and wonderful medieval-Gothic
Minoritenkirche (Minorites'
Church, named for the Friars
Minor, a Franciscan monastic
order that came to the city during
the time of the Babenberg Dukes).
The core of the church you see
today was built by King Ottokar
of Bohemia (see p. 24) in 1276. It
was periodically added to during
the 13th and 14th centuries, giving
the church its current irregular
appearance. Its octagonal tower
was once capped by a Gothic
spire, but this was blown off
by cannon fire during the first
Ottoman siege of Vienna and was
never replaced.

The Golden U

On nearby Michaelerplatz, the
bold modern design of the 1909
Loos Haus (which is sometimes
open to the public for architectural exhibitions) marks the
beginning of the Kohlmarkt—the
western arm of the Golden U
shopping district (see p. 103).
The name is a reference to the
intersecting streets of Kohlmarkt, Graben, and Kärntner
Strasse, which form the core
of the area. These three broad
pedestrianized streets are home
to Vienna's finest traditional
boutiques and flagship stores,
from relics of Vienna's imperial
past like **Knize**—whose clothes
have been worn by archdukes
and aristocrats—to modern
international fashion houses like
Gucci, Armani, and Chanel.

Kohlmarkt is Vienna's answer
to Rodeo Drive in Los Angeles
or Bond Street in London, where
the stores cater to an extremely

Fine Architecture in the Golden U

Starting with the daring minimalist landmark that is Adolf Loos' Loos Haus, the Golden U is an architectural feast, with every style from 18th-century baroque to late-20th-century postmodernism on show. Highlights include the metal and stone facade created by Hans Hollein (designer of the Haas Haus; see p. 72) for the Schullin jewelry store at number 7, and Max Fabiani's beautiful art nouveau Ataria Haus at number 9.

This architectural splendor is not restricted to the high-end stores, however—Adolf Loos is also often credited with having designed the underground public toilets on the Graben (although there is some confusion on this point, with some sources ascribing them to Franz Krasny or Wilhelm Beetz). This may seem unlikely, but Adolf Loos was known for his very strong opinions about plumbing. He was convinced that Austria and Germany could never achieve cultural and political greatness until they had better toilets than the British.

Whoever designed them, their elegant art nouveau interiors—with gilded faucets, patterned tiled floors, and inlaid wooden stalls—make them worth a visit, even if you don't need to use them.

wealthy clientele. Still, thousands of people flock here every day to admire the opulent window displays and stunning architecture (see sidebar above). As you continue around the Golden U, the stores become gradually more affordable, the Graben is home to high-end consumer fashion stores, and on Kärntner Strasse the shops become quite reasonably priced.

Dorotheergasse

This side street, which branches off to the south about halfway along the Graben, is home to one of Vienna's most important museums—the **Judisches Museum** (Vienna Jewish Museum). The first incarnation of this museum was founded in 1896 and focused on the history of Austrian and Czech Jews. It was closed down in 1938 by the Nazis, who burned or confiscated most of its exhibits. The museum reopened in its current home, the 17th-century Palais Eskeles, in 1992. It houses a broad collection of artifacts relating to Austrian Jewish history, including some from the original museum's collection. The curators of the new museum decided that the focus of its collections and exhibitions should be the society and culture of Viennese Jews and not the circumstances of their deaths. In addition to the permanent collection, the museum often hosts short-term exhibitions that examine particular periods or profile notable figures from Viennese Jewish history.

Dorotheergasse is also known as the home of Vienna's antiques business. The numerous little stores that line the street, selling everything from fine jewelry to huge mahogany furniture, are satellites of the gigantic **Dorotheum**—Vienna's premier auction house. This venerable Viennese institution was established in

Judisches Museum

🅰 97

✉ Dorotheergasse 11

☎ (1) 535 04 31

🕒 Closed Sat. & Jewish holidays

💲 $$

🚇 Stephansplatz (U1, U3)

www.jmw.at/en

Dorotheum

🅰 97

✉ Dorotheergasse 17

☎ (1) 515 60-0

🕒 Closed Sun.

🚇 Stephansplatz (U1, U3)

www.dorotheum .com

Österreichisches Theatermuseum

🅰 97

✉ Lobkowitzplatz 2

☎ (1) 525 24-3460

🕐 Closed Tues.

💲 $

🚇 Karlsplatz (U1, U2, U4)

www.khm.at/en/ austrian-theatre -museum

1707 on the site of the Dorotheer Abbey by Emperor Josef II. The Dorotheum holds almost daily antiques auctions, where all manner of items are put up for sale. Visitors who don't feel the need to bid on anything can explore the building's exhibition halls (where items are displayed before sale) or pause at the traditional **Dorotheum Café** *(tel 1/515 60-395, closed Sun.)* on the second floor.

Just around the corner from the Dorotheum, in the sumptuous Lobkowitz Palace, is the most interesting of the Kunsthistorisches Museum's various annexes—the

INSIDER TIP:

Don't be put off by the Kapuzinerkirche's plain facade. Go inside and look for the ornate Kaisergruft.

—SALLY MCFALL
National Geographic contributor

Österreichisches Theatermuseum (Austrian Theater Museum). Thought to be one of the largest such museums in the world, its collection includes more than a thousand stage scenery models, hundreds of thousands of photographs, and several thousand items of theater memorabilia (this collection includes beautifully made costumes and props).

The museum's vast collection was brought here in the late 1970s, when the Burgtheater's private museum was combined with the collection of theater memorabilia that the national library had

inherited from the royal family. It's not just about Vienna's historic theatrical tradition, however—the museum holds many exhibitions focusing on new developments in Austrian theater or retrospectives examining the work of a particular designer or director.

The Kapuzinerkirche

Established in 1627 with funds donated by Empress Anna, this small Capuchin monastery is just around the corner, off the Neuer Markt on the southern end of Kärnter Strasse. The church presents an extremely plain facade to the street—just a low, adobe structure with a faded fresco above the main door—and is only slightly more ornate on the inside. Certainly, by Viennese standards, this church is almost puritanically unadorned.

It is this highly visible air of humility that made the Kapuzinerkirche the preferred resting place of the Habsburg family: a tomb here, rather than in the cathedral, served as a symbolic renunciation of their worldly wealth.

That's not to say there's anything humble about the **Kaisergruft** (Imperial Crypt)—far from it—here the dead rulers of Austria lie in an astonishingly ostentatious selection of tombs and sarcophagi. The tombs of the 18th-century Habsburgs (such as Karl VI and Maria-Theresia) are particularly impressive. On their sarcophagi carved figures swoon over coffins in dramatic gestures of grief, and likenesses of the dead sit in saintly poses over their remains. While it seems a little strange to be touring a family crypt, the monuments here were clearly built to be publicly admired. To fit all this in, the crypt has been extended several times over the course of its history. The tombs are arranged with clear reference to the importance of the individuals within—emperors and empresses get whole rooms to themselves, while minor royals are jumbled together in small rooms and alcoves off corridors.

Wiener Staatsoper

The Wiener Staatsoper (Vienna National Opera) is one of the city's most renowned cultural institutions. When it opened in 1869, the former K. K. Hofoper (Imperial and Royal Court Opera) was the first major public building on the Ringstrasse. In 1945 the Staatsoper suffered a direct hit that destroyed the original auditorium and sets for hundreds of operas. Luckily the foyers and stairs, which are decorated with frescoes, statues, and ornate stucco, survived the blast and ensuing fire.

During the day, visitors can take a guided tour of this remarkable neo-Renaissance building and its lavishly decorated interior. Tours start at the **Opernmuseum** *(Opera Museum; Goethegasse 1, tel 1/51444 2100, closed Mon., $$, www.wiener-staatsoper.at)* on nearby Goethegasse, which houses a collection of memorabilia and historic photographs.

In addition to being one of the best known opera houses in Europe, the Wiener Staatsoper is also one of the busiest. It stages around 50 productions every year, often with several shows running on alternating nights of the week. Despite its prestigious reputation and opulent setting, however, the Staatsoper continues to offer cut-price tickets to anyone willing to queue up beforehand. Standing-room tickets, in particular, can be purchased only immediately before the show, and are inexpensive ($). People sometimes camp out for days to get standing tickets for opening nights, but typically you have to show up only an hour or so in advance to have a good chance of getting in. ∎

The Kapuziner-kirche & Kaisergruft
🅰 97
✉ Tegetthoff-strasse 2, Neuer Markt
☎ (1) 512 68 53
💲 $$
🚇 Stephansplatz (U1, U3)

Wiener Staatsoper
🅰 97
✉ Opernring 2 (for tickets: Bestellbüro der Wiener Staatsoper, Hanuschgasse 3)
☎ (1) 513 15 13
💲 Tickets: $–$$$$$, Tours: $$
🚇 Karlsplatz (U1, U2, U4)
www.wiener -staatsoper.at

Travel by Segway in Vienna

The public square around the Wiener Staatsoper serves as the meeting point for Vienna's growing number of Segway tour operators. For those who find the idea of a jogging tour (see sidebar p. 123) disturbing, these nimble electric scooters can whisk you around the sights of historic Vienna in record time. Tours typically take around three hours, and cover the sights of the Ringstrasse, including the Burgtheater and Rathaus, before heading into the Innere Stadt. Operators include **Vienna Sightseeing Tours** *(tel 1/712 46 83-80, $$$$$, www .viennasightseeingtours.com)* and **Pedal Power** *(Ausstellungsstrasse 3, tel 1/729 72 34, $$$$$, citysegwaytours.com/vienna)—* who, as its name suggests, also runs cycle tours of the city. These are a cheaper option that allow you to avoid the lengthy familiarization process that visitors have to go through with a Segway.

A more open, varied urban landscape and an informal, youthful vibe just north of the Innere Stadt

Alsergrund

The eccentric Spittelau incinerator, designed by Viennese architect Friedensreich Hundertwasser

Alsergrund

The district of Alsergrund is roughly triangular in shape, bounded by the Gürtel on its northwestern side, the Donaukanal to the east, and the Schottenring in the south. Within these borders lies a patchwork of different eras of development, with shiny modern skyscapers overlooking 18th-century country houses.

Historically, most of what is now Alsergrund was positioned between the main city walls (where the Ringstrasse now stands) and the outer ring of defenses (which ran along the route of the Gürtel). This area was part of the *vorstädte* (outer city).

During Roman times Alsergrund was a rural area, probably mostly occupied by vineyards and farms. One of the major Roman routes through central Europe, the Limestrasse, ran through the area (along the route now taken by Währinger Strasse and Boltzmanngasse). The area developed into a small satellite settlement of Vienna during the early Middle Ages, and by the late Middle Ages, Alsergrund was home to several small villages (whose names have been preserved as the names of Alsergrund's neighborhoods, such as Rossau, Alservorstädte, and Althangrund).

The area was devastated during the Ottoman sieges of Vienna, which took place in 1529 and 1683. In 1683 the entire neighborhood was demolished before the Ottomans arrived in order to provide clear lines of fire for the defenders. From the 18th century onward, Alsergrund expanded quickly, developing into a fashionable residential district and center of medical science. The first major public institution to move to the area was the Grossarmenhaus (Great Poorhouse), a colossal complex of workhouses and almshouses where the poor, orphaned, or insane from Vienna ended up. This was later joined by the Josephinum (a military hospital) and the Rossauer Kaserne (Rossau Barracks).

Schottenring

The oldest parts of the district are those located close to the old Innere Stadt, alongside the Schottenring. Here you will find Vienna's main financial district—a neatly ordered grid of office buildings that surround the Wiener Börse (Vienna Stock Exchange). It is dominated by the Ringturm, a 1950s office block that served for many years as a symbol of Vienna's postwar reconstruction. On the edge of this area is the Freyung—an attractive public square and marketplace, home to Vienna's famous Café Central coffeehouse. On the northern side of the Schottenring stands the Votivkirche, a massive 19th-century church, built to commemorate Franz-Josef's lucky escape from death at the hands of a Hungarian assassin.

NOT TO BE MISSED:

The huge, redbrick Rossauer Kaserne **133**

The elegant churches and traditional coffeehouses around the Freyung **133–138**

The Votivkirche's spectacular neo-Gothic architecture **139, 142**

Exploring the quiet, little-known area near the Servitenkirche **143–144**

The fascinating but slightly eerie anatomical models in the Josephinum **146–147**

Admiring the priceless paintings and opulent interiors at the Liechtenstein Museum **148–150**

Catching a modern production at the Volksoper **150–151**

Modern Alsergrund

Today the character of this district is strongly influenced by the two major public institutions that are located here: the Allgemeines Krankenhaus (General Hospital; usually known as the AKH) and the Universität Wien (Vienna University). The AKH is one of the largest hospitals in the world, occupying a vast and extremely ugly complex of buildings on the western side of the university campus (which was once also part of the AKH). The university is Vienna's oldest and most prestigious institute of higher education, whose campus has gradually expanded from a single building on the Ringstrasse to a sprawling campus with buildings and departments scattered into every corner of the district.

There are around 11,000 medical students working at the AKH, and tens of thousands more students at the

university. This enormous student population means that Alsergrund has no shortage of bars, cafés, and inexpensive restaurants.

Unlike many other areas of the vorstädte, Alsergrund is very heavily developed. There are few green spaces or public parks. The only significant green space in the district is the garden of the Liechtenstein Museum—an 18th-century palace belonging to the Prince of Liechtenstein, which has gradually been enveloped by the expanding city of Vienna. Beyond the grounds of the palace lie the enormously popular Volksoper (People's Opera) and the weird and wonderful Spittelau Incinerator. ∎

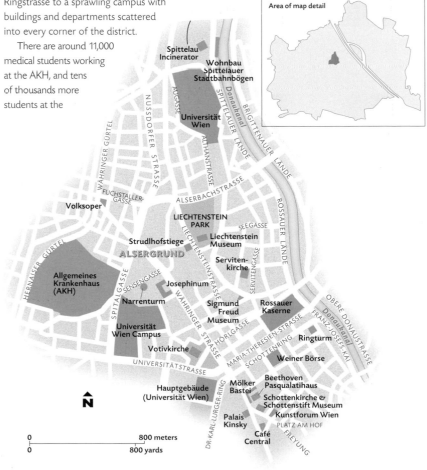

Around the Schottenring

Most of Alsergrund's major attractions are within 10 minutes' walk of the Schottenring (the northernmost section of the Ringstrasse). It is this area of Alsergrund that contains its great educational institutions, and where the city's intellectual elite once met.

The twin spires of the Votivkirche lit up at night

The Schottenring

The Schottenring is bordered to the south by Vienna's main business district. This area, while containing some interesting architecture, isn't particularly visitor-friendly, as most of the buildings are closed to the public. The area's most distinctive landmark is the **Ringturm** office building, which stands at the end of the Schottenring, alongside the Donaukanal. This simple 23-story building was built in 1955 on the site of a building destroyed in an Allied bombing raid. As the first modern, high-rise building to go up in the Innere Stadt, the construction of the Ringturm marked an important turning point in the process of Vienna's reconstruction, and served as a symbol of the new, changed city that Vienna was striving to become.

At night, the mast on the roof—known as the Wetterturm (Weather Tower)—displays basic information about the next day's weather. Red lights refer to the temperature (if they are rising, it means it will be warmer tomorrow; if they are falling, cooler) while green lights refer to general weather (as with the red lights, rising lights mean an improvement; falling lights mean it will get worse). If the lights on the tower flash red then it means there will

INSIDER TIP:

Don't miss the Ringturm if you're visiting in summer—the building is often entirely hidden behind giant works of art printed onto fabric panels mounted to its side.

—TIM HARRIS
National Geographic contributor

be a storm tomorrow, and if they flash white it means there will be snow and ice.

Across the Schottenring from the Ringturm is the **Rossauer Kaserne** (Rossau Barracks), a large 19th-century redbrick building that resembles a Renaissance country house or fortress. Emperor Franz-Josef ordered the construction of this barracks following the social unrest of 1848, which saw rioting in the streets of Vienna and a very real threat of revolution.

Franz-Josef was a staunch conservative, bitterly opposed to political reform of any kind. Rather than institute even a vaguely representative government to placate his dissatisfied people, he decided to build a series of military installations around the edge of the city so that he could use the army to put down any attempted revolutions. Today the building is home to the Vienna Police headquarters, as well as a few other government offices, and is therefore closed to the public.

The **Wiener Börse** (Vienna Stock Exchange) is a little farther west along the Schottenring. This grand building is another example of Theophilus Hansen's historicist designs. This one is notable for being executed in a neo-Renaissance style rather than his usual grand neoclassicism. Sadly the original interior of the building, including the spectacular trading hall, was destroyed by a fire in 1956, so even if it were possible to get inside, there wouldn't be much to see.

The best part of the Börse is **Hansen,** a unique combination of high-end florist and modern restaurant, located in the exchange's vaulted basement. Diners are surrounded by blooming plants and greenery in a surprisingly light and airy space. At lunchtime, especially during the week, the restaurant fills up with the movers and shakers of Vienna's business world, but remains fairly calm during breakfast and dinner.

Alternatively, hungry visitors can head across the street to **Café Schottenring** *(Schottenring 19, tel 1/315 33 43, www.cafe-schotenring.at),* a traditional Viennese *kaffeehaus* (see pp. 140–141) that first opened in 1879. The café's unique selling point is its house pianist, who plays requests every afternoon from 3–7 p.m.

Freyung

A few minutes' walk south of the Börse, the grid-pattern streets of the financial district give way to the twisting street layout of the medieval old

(continued on p. 136)

Schottenring

 131

🚇 Schottenring (U2, U4), Schottentor (U2)

Visitor Information

✉ Vienna Tourist Office, Schottentor U-Bahn Station

☎ (1) 245 55

🕑 Closed Sat. & Sun.

www.vienna.info

Ringturm

🅰 131

✉ Schottenring 30

🚇 Schottenring (U2, U4)

Rossauer Kaserne

🅰 131

✉ Rossauer Länder 1

🚇 Schottenring (U2, U4)

Wiener Börse

🅰 131

✉ Wallnerstrasse 8

🚇 Schottenring (U2, U4), Schottentor (U2)

Hansen

✉ Wiener Börse, Wiplingerstrasse 34

☎ (1) 532 05 42

🕑 Closed Sun.

🚇 Schottenring (U2, U4), Schottentor (U2)

www.hansen.co.at

Walk: Southern Alsergrund

This walk takes you from the business district on the banks of the Donaukanal into the historic heart of Alsergrund. The buildings on this walk represent centuries of Viennese architectural fashion, from the clean lines of the Ringturm to the early baroque of the Servitenkirche.

Franz-Josef built the imposing Rossauer Kaserne in reaction to the revolutionary fervor of 1848.

This walk starts from **Schottenring U-Bahn Station ❶** on Franz-Josefs-Kai. The first thing you see as you emerge from the station is the looming form of the Ringturm, a 23-story building that would pass entirely unnoticed in most U.S. cities, but seems like a vast skyscraper against the low skyline of the Innere Stadt. Cross the road to the riverfront section of Franz-Josefs-Kai, and head north toward the Rossauerbrücke bridge. On your left you will see the fussy redbrick architecture of the **Rossauer Kaserne ❷** (Rossau Barracks), one of Emperor Franz-Josef's bulwarks against the tide of political reform. The high, crenellated walls of this building would be useless against a military assault, but they could hold back a revolutionary mob for weeks.

NOT TO BE MISSED:

The Rossauer Kaserne
• Servitengasse • Palais
Liechtenstein • Votivkirche

After passing the barracks, cross the road at Türkenstrasse and then head west along Porzellangasse. The end of this street is marked by another landmark of Vienna's postwar architectural revival, the minimalist form of the 1959 Pensionsversicherungsanstalt building. About 300 yards (275 m) farther on you reach Jörg-Mauthe-Platz, where Porzellangasse meets with Servitengasse, Schlickgasse, and Berggasse. A few yards down Berggasse lies the **Sigmund**

Freud Museum **3** (see pp. 142–143), in the building where Freud once practiced.

If it's a nice day and you don't feel like visiting this rather musty museum, then turn onto the pedestrianized street of **Servitengasse,** where there are numerous outdoor cafés and restaurants. Turn left at the **Servitenkirche 4** (see p. 144), a pretty example of 17th-century baroque architecture, and continue down Grünentorgasse. At the far end of the street lies the **Liechtenstein Museum 5** (see p. 148), an 18th-century palace and art gallery owned by the Prince of Liechtenstein.

On the other side of the palace, go up Vienna's most famous staircase, the delightfully art nouveau **Strudlhofstiege 6**, and then left past the leafy grounds that surround the Josephinum. Continue south past the numerous buildings of the university campus and the striking modern **Österreichisches National-**

bibliotek offices 7 on Garnisongasse. Turn onto Ferstelgasse and you'll be presented with a view of the **Votivkirche 8**—a forest of flying buttresses, Gothic spires, and weatherworn carvings. If you walk around to the front of the church you will be able to admire its perfectly symmetrical, unified design (a feature that also makes it seem rather inauthentic when compared with the architectural patchwork of the medieval cathedrals it imitates). From **Sigmund Freud Park 9** in front of the church you can either walk across the Ringstrasse and back into the Innere Stadt or along Maria-Theresien-Strasse to Schottentor U-Bahn Station.

> ⚠ See also map p. 131
> ➤ Schottenring U-Bahn
> 🕐 45 minutes
> ↔ 1.7 miles (2.7 km)
> ➤ Schottentor U-Bahn

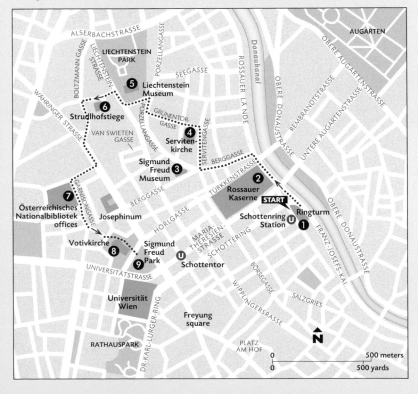

Freyung

🅰 131

🚇 Schottentor (U2), Herrengasse (U3)

town. The streets around here converge at the **Freyung,** a medieval marketplace that is surrounded by fine palaces and churches.

The square's name, which roughly translates as "freeing," is a reference to the fact that it was originally outside the jurisdiction of the city's law enforcement. As it stood on the land controlled

by the Schottenkirche, it was a place where fugitives could be granted asylum. A thriving market grew up in this legal gray area, and although this still operates in the square today, the merchants are more reputable than their medieval predecessors.

The square is the venue for two popular markets: On Tuesday, Wednesday, and Thursday there is a general food market, while on Friday and Saturday the square hosts an organic food market. In the winter, the square is home to a long-running (since 1772) **Christkindlmarkt** (Christmas market), where piped Christmas music, reindeer, and images of Santa Claus are banned. The market's managers decided that both the retailers and the customers were probably thoroughly sick of these tacky holiday clichés, and would be happier without them.

The area around the Freyung was once very popular with Vienna's aristocratic families, who built enormous palaces around the square. The most impressive is the **Palais Kinsky,** designed in the early 18th century by Johann Lukas von Hildebrandt (1668–1745). For this building, Hildebrandt had to try to squeeze all his usual grandeur into a plot of land just 30 yards by 100 yards (27 m by 91 m). He created an imposing facade that manages to be fabulously ornate while at the same time almost completely flat (he needed to make the rooms inside as large as he could). Today, the lavish interior of the building is home to an auction house, a club, and several restaurants.

The opulent vaulted roof of the Freyung Passage

The similarly grand **Palais Ferstl,** on the southern side of the square, shows a different method of fitting an aristocratic palace into an urban setting. Here the palace sits on top of an arcade of shops known as the **Freyung Passage.** This beautiful vaulted passageway, lit by a glass-roofed atrium in the center, is probably the closest thing to a shopping mall that the Innere Stadt will ever see.

In addition to a number of attractive little boutiques, the Freyung Passage is home to the rear entrance of the famous **Café Central** (see p. 140), which faces onto Herrengasse. This Viennese institution is famous for its popularity with a range of fin-de-siècle intellectuals—everyone from Leon Trotsky to Sigmund Freud used to gather here to drink coffee, read the papers, and argue vociferously over the issues of the day.

Just across the Freyung from the Palais Ferstl is the old headquarters of the Austrian Bank of Trade and Commerce. This building, which dates from 1914, is of little architectural interest but houses one of Vienna's most important and dynamic cultural institutions. The **Kunstforum Wien** was founded in the 1980s as an exhibition space—it is not a gallery or a museum in the traditional sense because it has no permanent collection. Instead, this space plays host to touring exhibitions, short-term loans, and private collections. Famously, its first major exhibition (held in 1989) was "Egon Schiele and His Era"—the first time that the

remarkable collection of Rudolf Leopold (see p. 117) had been shown in its entirety.

The Schottenstift: The northern side of Freyung's square is dominated by the buildings of the Schottenstift (Scottish Monastery), a complex of beautiful baroque structures. The monastery was founded by a group of Irish—not Scottish—monks in 1155 (in medieval Vienna *Schotten*—meaning "Scottish"—was used as a generic name for Celtic Christians). The monks remained in Vienna until 1418, when dwindling numbers forced them to leave, and the monastery was passed to the Benedictine order that remains in residence to this day. Under the Benedictines the monastery was rebuilt and expanded to

---

EXPERIENCE: Stay in a Benedictine Monastery

For those looking for somewhere unusual (and cheap) to stay in Vienna, the **Schottenstift Benediktushaus** (*Freyung 6a, tel 1/534 98-900, www.benedicktushaus.at, $*) is certainly worth considering. This isn't a hotel converted from an old monastery; it is a set of rooms within the active monastery. The rooms, as you'd expect, are spartan, but not old-fashioned or cramped. Each room is a pleasing example of minimalist modern design, with single beds, nice bathrooms, and wireless Internet. Don't come here for a romantic getaway with a boyfriend or girlfriend or a hedonistic weekend break, however—the monks don't approve of unmarried couples, and they expect their guests to adhere to their high moral standard while staying in the hotel.

Palais Kinsky
- 🅰 131
- ✉ Freyung 4
- ☎ (1) 532 42 00
- 🚇 Schottentor (U2), Herrengasse (U3)

www.imkinsky
.com/en

Kunstforum Wien
- ✉ Freyung 8
- ☎ (1) 537 33 26
- 💲 $$
- 🚇 Schottentor (U2), Herrengasse (U3)

www.bankaustria
-kunstforum.at

Schottenkirche

- ⚑ 131
- ✉ Freyung 6
- ☎ (1) 534 98-200
- 🕐 Closed Tues., Fri.–Sun.
- 🚇 Schottentor (U2), Herrengasse (U3)

www.schotten pfarre.at

Schottenstift Museum

- ✉ Freyung 6
- ☎ (1) 534 98-600
- 🕐 Closed Sun., Mon., & Fri.
- 💲 $$
- 🚇 Schottentor (U2), Herrengasse (U3)

www.schottenstift .at

Beethoven Pasqualatihaus

- ⚑ 131
- ✉ Mölker Bastei 8
- ☎ (1) 535 89 05
- 🕐 Closed Mon.
- 💲 $$
- 🚇 Schottentor (U2), Herrengasse (U3)

www.wienmuseum .at

Hauptgebäude (University of Vienna)

- ⚑ 131
- ☎ (1) 4277-17525
- ✉ Dr.-Karl-Lueger-Ring 1
- 🚇 Schottentor (U2), Rathaus (U2)

www.univie.ac.at/en

occupy a large area extending to the north of the Freyung.

The centerpiece of the complex is the **Schottenkirche,** a fine piece of baroque design that dates from the mid 17th century. Although you can get a good look at the church from the square, it's worth going inside to see the lavish, but not overwhelming, interior decoration. The columns and arches are painted in pastel shades and capped with decorative stucco work, while the barrel-vaulted ceiling is covered by several large frescoes depicting biblical scenes.

Also worth visiting is the adjacent **Schottenstift Museum,** one of Vienna's hidden treasures. This small collection, gathered by the Benedictine monastery over the centuries, includes paintings by Peter Paul Rubens, Jan Cossiers, and many others. There is also a fascinating collection of medieval illuminated manuscripts, including official documents, bibles, and other religious texts.

Toward the Ringstrasse

The road to the right of the 18th-century baroque pile of Palais Kinsky leads to the **Mölker Bastei,** the only remaining fragment of Vienna's fortifications. Above the sturdy walls of the old bastion stands a group of 18th-century houses, among them the building that Beethoven lived in for many years. Today the **Beethoven Pasqualatihaus** (named for Johann Baptist von Pasqualati, the wealthy patron of the arts who owned the building) is open to the public, although its

fairly small collection has little of interest to any but the most hard-core Beethoven fan.

The **Hauptgebäude** (main building) of the University of Vienna stands on the opposite side of the Ringstrasse from the bastion. This large baroque edifice completes the trio of monumental public buildings on this stretch of the Ringstrasse (the others being the Parliament and Rathaus; see p. 123). It was constructed in 1884 as the new home of the university

INSIDER TIP:

The Schottenstift Museum—with its faded medieval manuscripts, religious paintings, and holy relics—feels like a forgotten secret.

—MATTHIAS BRÜCKNER
National Geographic contributor

(which was previously crammed into the Academy of Sciences in the Stephansdom Quarter; see p. 74) but was itself soon outgrown. Today very little teaching actually takes place here, but the university retains the building as its administrative headquarters and as a venue for conferences and events. A **guided tour** (http://event.univie.ac.at/fuehrungen, $$) of the building's interior (every bit as grand as its Ringstrasse neighbors) is held in English every Saturday at 11:30 a.m.

Walk north from the university

The Origins of the Votivkirche

The Votivkirche is a peculiar structure—a cathedral-like church that was built in the late 19th century for a city that already had one of Europe's finest cathedrals and no need for another. Furthermore, when it was built, it stood on a sparsely populated suburb of Vienna that had neither the funds nor the inclination to undertake such a major project.

As its name suggests, the church was intended as a kind of votive offering, a symbol of thanks for an act of what was seen by many as divine intervention. The incident that motivated its construction took place on the Mölker Bastei (next to Beethoven's old home) in 1853. Emperor Franz-Josef was watching a parade on the old city wall with one of his officers when János Libényi, a Hungarian tailor (who was either a nationalist militant or a lunatic, depending on whom you choose to believe), tried to stab Franz-Josef in the neck. His knife was deflected by the heavily starched collar of the emperor's uniform, and Libényi was restrained by a passerby before he could strike Franz-Josef again.

The emperor's brother, Maximilian, saw this event as a perfect piece of propaganda for the beleaguered empire, which was troubled by growing nationalist movements in almost every one of its subject-states. He immediately began publicly praising it as proof that God approved of the Habsburg monarchy, and proposed that a great church be built close to the site where this "miracle" happened. After a blaze of patriotic support from the papers and pulpits of Vienna, the people of the city donated huge sums of money to fund its construction.

Maximilian did not live to see the completion of his grand project, however; he was chosen as Emperor of Mexico by Napoleon III in 1864, and soon left Austria to rule his new kingdom. In 1867 he was deposed by a popular revolution in Mexico and executed.

and you'll find yourself in the leafy environs of the Votivkirche. These lush city parks (Sigmund Freud Park and Votiv Park) were created in the 1870s, shortly after the demolition of the city's fortifications, when this area was still mostly undeveloped. In the summer Sigmund Freud Park fills with sunbathing students and city workers on their lunch breaks. The centerpiece of the park is a giant granite table, with ten granite chairs, surrounded by a circle of 15 trees. The trees were planted in 1997 to mark the 40th anniversary of the European Union. Each EU state is represented by a species of tree native to that country. The table and chairs in the center were added in 2004 as an inventive way to symbolically include the ten new states that joined the EU that year, without ruining the symmetry of the existing installation.

The Votivkirche

This massive neo-Gothic church was designed in the 1860s by historicist architect Heinrich von Ferstel (1828–1883). Ferstel was inspired by the original plans for St. Stephen's Cathedral (see pp. 68–71), which featured two tall symmetrical towers (the north tower was never finished because the builders ran out of money). Working with the advanced technical knowledge

(continued on p. 142)

Votivkirche
- 131
- Rooseveltplatz 8
- (1) 408 11 92
- $$
- Schottentor (U2), Rathaus (U2)

www.votivkirche.at

Vienna's Coffeehouse Tradition

Long before Starbucks spread across the world, the Viennese were devoted patrons of their coffeehouses. Many of these august institutions have changed little since the 19th century, serving their communities as homes away from home.

A cup of Viennese coffee known as a "Mozart" (coffee with whipped cream and cherry brandy)

The average Austrian consumes about 42 gallons (162 liters) of coffee every year—that's enough to fill a bathtub. You'll understand why after a short stay in Vienna. Coffeehouses first appeared in the city in the late 17th century and quickly became an established part of the culture. Their heyday was probably around the end of the 19th century, when they were at the heart of Viennese intellectual life. The Viennese poet Peter Altenberg (1859–1919) famously gave "Café Central, Wien" as his home address.

Although international chains have managed to get a foothold in the city, most Viennese still prefer the traditional *kaffeehäuser*. These cafés are opulent, sometimes rather gloomy places, with cane chairs and dark,

wood-paneled walls covered with heavy gilded mirrors. With no public smoking ban in force, Vienna's coffeehouses are often very smoky places—the larger ones are required to have a space nominally designated a smoke-free area, but this is not mandatory for smaller cafés, and many prefer to allow smoking.

The oldest surviving Viennese coffeehouse is just north of the Haus der Musik (see p. 73):The **Café Frauenhuber** (*Himmelpfortgasse 6, tel 1/512 53 53, www.cafe-frauenhuber.at/index -en.php*) first opened in the 18th century. Most of the coffeehouses that exist today were founded in the late 19th century. Although many were lost during the economic slump of the 1950s, there are still more in Vienna than there is space to mention.

The most famous of them all is probably **Café Central** (*Herrengasse 14 tel 1/533 37 63, www.palaisevents.at/en/cafecentral.html*), whose beautiful neo-Renaissance interior has welcomed patrons as diverse as Sigmund Freud and Leon Trotsky. It can be found between Platz Am Hof (see p. 93) and the Minoritenkirche. Close to the Burgtheater, the **Café Landtmann** (*Karl-Lueger-Ring 4, tel 1/2410 01 00, www.landtmann.at*) has maintained the same exclusive, aristocratic atmosphere that it has had since the days of imperial Vienna. The relatively modern **Café Hawelka** (*Dorotheergasse 6, tel 1/512 82 30, www.hawelka.at*), a short walk from the Judisches Museum (see p. 125), is still run by Leopold Hawelka, the sprightly centenarian who opened the café as a young man in 1939. It has a friendly, arty atmosphere. While other bohemian hangouts have become upmarket, international places, the **Café Alt Wien** (*Bäckerstrasse 9, tel 1/512*

52 22), which was founded by Hawelka in 1936, has maintained its traditional style (which might be too gloomy and smoke-filled for some). It is a hop and a skip from St. Stephen's Cathedral (see pp. 68–71) and is a perfect place for hanging out with friends—or making new ones.

The trendiest café in Vienna is also the smallest—the **Kleines Café** (Franziskanerplatz 3), which manages to be the favorite of artists and students despite being about the size of a motel room. It is a short walk east of the Friedensbrücke bridge.

INSIDER TIP:

Don't come to a kaffeehaus expecting to be able to rush in, grab your coffee, and leave—these are slow, old-fashioned institutions that don't like doing anything in a hurry.

—BEATRICE AUMAYR
Viennese tour guide

Kaffeehaus Options

These institutions are generally rather more formal than cafés and coffee shops in the U.S.—rather than walking up to the counter, in Vienna you pick a table and wait to be served by one of the tuxedo-clad waiters. If you ask the waiter for "coffee" he will stare at you in blank incomprehension—in Vienna, this is the equivalent of going into a restaurant and trying to order "food." Coffee comes in dozens of different styles, strengths, and sizes and you'll rarely see anything as simple as filter coffee. The most common types are listed below:

Brauner: Black coffee served with a small jug of coffee-flavored cream. Can be large (grosser brauner) or small (kleiner brauner).

Fiaker: A brauner with a shot of rum. Once the favorite drink of carriage drivers.

Milchkaffee: Very milky coffee, essentially the same as café latte.

Kapuziner: Black coffee with a shot of milk or cream.

Konsul: Black coffee with a dash of cream.

Mélange: Strong milky coffee topped with frothed milk, like a cappuccino.

Mozart: Large mocha with cherry brandy and whipped cream.

Schwarzer: Very strong black coffee.

Verlängerter: A weaker, watered-down version of the brauner, looked on by many Viennese as a child's drink.

Although the immaculately presented waiters may seem a little intimidating, they are usually helpful and more than willing to guide you through the menu (a decent grasp of English is expected for staff in many Innere Stadt kaffeehäuser).

In addition to their dizzying range of coffees, most Viennese coffeehouses serve snacks and small meals. This being Vienna, the emphasis is of course on things that are sweet and unhealthy—a display case filled with cakes, tarts, and pastries is a standard feature of the Viennese coffeehouse. In many of the traditional cafés, these cakes and pastries are made on site, often to recipies unique to that particular café. In case anything on the shelves might be seen as healthy (some of the pastries are mostly fruit, after all) nearly all cakes and pastries are served with a large blob of whipped cream.

For some cafés it is their cakes rather than their coffee that is the main draw—the **Sacher Café** (Philharmonikerstrasse 4, tel 1/514 56-0, www.sacher.com), almost adjacent to the Albertina (see p. 113), is best known as the birthplace of the rich chocolate cake with apri-cot jam known as the Sacher torte; while the **Café Demel** (Kohlmarkt 14, tel 1/5351 71 70, www.demel.at), close to the Winter Riding School (see p. 104), still proudly displays its credentials as the K.u.K. Hofzuckerbäcker und Chocoladerfabrikant (Royal and Imperial Confec-tioner and Chocolate-maker).

Sigmund Freud's waiting room re-created at the Sigmund Freud Museum

Sigmund Freud Museum

🅰 131
✉ Berggasse 19
☎ (1) 319 15 96
💲 $$$
🚋 Schlickgasse (Strassenbahn line D), Schottenring (U2, U4)

www.freud-museum .at

and mechanized building techniques of 19th-century engineering, he was able to create a light, open design that seems almost like a frame for something more substantial.

The interior of the church sticks to the studied Gothic style of the exterior, with a high vaulted ceiling, huge stained-glass windows, and a highly ornate altar. In a nod to the forgotten craftsmen who built St. Stephen's, a depiction of Heinrich von Ferstel is carved into the stone under the steps of the pulpit (see p. 70). There is a small museum on site that houses artifacts relating to its construction as well as to the religious history of the area. Despite the best intentions of the people who built it, however, the Votivkirche's modern construction and unified design

leave it feeling rather characterless. In a neighborhood of medical students and scientific researchers, a church this size is always going to be mostly empty, and this is somehow reflected in the atmosphere of the building.

The Sigmund Freud Museum

A few minutes' walk to the northeast of the Votivkirche is the Sigmund Freud Museum, which is located in his old consulting office. Freud lived and worked in Alsergrund for most of his life, first at the University of Vienna, and later in his own private practice. It was here that he developed his ideas on psychoanalysis and the unconscious mind, and where these ideas began to gain adherents.

Despite the importance of this site to Sigmund Freud's career and ideas, very little of his old workplace has been preserved. This is because Freud was forced to flee Vienna in 1938, shortly after the *Anschluss*. His personal belongings, including all his books, his furniture, and the entire contents of his consulting room were either sold or shipped to his new home in London—where they remain in an independent museum.

The waiting room has been re-created with period furniture, and there are around 80 items from Freud's collection of art and antiques within the rooms of the museum. The rather paltry collection of artifacts relating to Freud's work here is compensated for by a comprehensive archive of film footage, interviews, and temporary exhibitions examining his ideas and the effect they had on Western culture.

Servitengasse

With its trendy restaurants, stylish boutiques, and historic architecture, Servitengasse has an atmosphere reminiscent of the Neubau's Spittelberg district (see pp. 120–121). It is located just around the corner from the Sigmund Freud Museum, on the northern side of Jörg-Mauthe-Platz.

Most of the buildings along this leafy pedestrianized street date from the mid to late 19th century, although the street's major landmark (and namesake), the **Servitenkirche,** is significantly

Psychotherapy & Neurology in Vienna

In medieval Vienna, the mentally ill were not generally treated as a distinct group within society—they weren't treated, nor were they persecuted. Unless they were wealthy enough to be labeled as eccentric or religious enough to be called visionaries, they were usually simply ignored. The construction of the Narrenturm asylum (see p. 146) in 1782 marked a significant change in attitude. The mentally ill were stigmatized, seen as a dangerous group that needed to be separated from the rest of society.

By the mid-19th century Vienna was at the forefront of efforts to better understand and treat mental illness. One of the most important figures in this effort was the German-born neurologist Richard von Krafft-Ebing (1840–1902), who lived and practiced in Vienna from the 1880s to his death. Krafft-Ebing was instrumental in establishing the Purkersdorf Sanatorium, a large mental institution just outside Vienna. Here, by contrast to the prison-like conditions of the Narrenturm, patients lived in stylish, bright, and airy rooms, designed by the *Jugendstil* architect Josef Hoffman. They were encouraged to work in the gardens and take up painting and writing.

In the late 1890s, another lecturer at the University of Vienna, Sigmund Freud, was developing ideas that would revolutionize the treatment of the mentally ill. Although many of his ideas have since been discarded, and his research methods were dubious at best (he often based his theories of the mind on the mind of a single research subject—himself), many of the techniques developed by Freud while working in Vienna have become mainstays of modern psychotherapy.

Servitenkirche

[A] 131
[✉] Servitengasse 9
[☎] (1) 317 61 95-0
[🚊] Schlickgasse
(Strassenbahn
line D), Rossauer
Lände (U4)

www.rossau.at

Serviten Stüberl

[✉] Servitengasse 7
[☎] (1) 317 53 36
[⊕] Closed Mon.
[🚊] Schlickgasse
(Strassenbahn
line D), Rossauer
Lände (U4)

www.serviten
stueberl.at

Die Serviette

[✉] Servitengasse 4
[☎] (0) 664 808 20
82
[🚊] Schlickgasse
(Strassenbahn
line D), Rossauer
Lände (U4)

www.die-serviette.at

older. Servitengasse is an excellent place to go on a warm summer evening, when the many restaurants and cafés move their tables outside. Popular choices include the traditional Viennese bistro **Serviten Stüberl** and the trendy modern restaurant **Die Serviette.**

The construction of the Servitenkirche was an important event in Vienna's architectural history. It was designed in the style pioneered by the Italian architect Andrea Palladio (1508–1580), whose classically influenced architecture emphasized symmetry and simple external decoration. Work began on the church in the 1660s and was completed in 1677. It was the only church in the vorstädte to survive the Siege of Vienna. Features of the Servitenkriche, such as the twin towers set into the facade or the elliptical domed nave, were later incorporated into the design of both Karlskirche (see p. 187)

and Petruskirche (see p. 103).

Outside the Servitenkirche there is a moving memorial to the hundreds of Jewish families who were driven from their homes and businesses on this street in 1938. Before the Anschluss more than half the population of this street was Jewish, but after the Nazi takeover of Austria they all either fled the country or were deported to the death camps. In 2004 a group of local residents started a research project, called Servitengasse 1938, to learn more about their "lost neighbors." The memorial, called Keys Against Forgetting, is a glass case set into the paving outside the Servitenkirche. Inside there are hundreds of house keys, each attached to a tag with the name of one of the street's former residents.

The University of Vienna

With more than 85,000 students and nearly 9,000 staff, the Uni-

---

EXPERIENCE: Make Your Own Chocolates

Vienna is a city with a notorious sweet tooth; almost every street in the Innere Stadt has at least one confectioner, ice cream store, or patisserie. In recent years the boutique chocolatier Xocolat has become a firm favorite with the Viennese, winning several awards. The main store is located in Freyung (see p. 133), but true chocolate fanatics should instead head to **Xocolat Manufactur** *(Servitengasse 5, tel 1/310 00 20, www.xocolat.at, closed Sun., $$$$$)* on Servitengasse, where their chocolates are made.

Here the chocolatiers Christian Petz and Thomas Scheiblhofer run weekly workshops where they teach small

groups the tricks of their trade. Several different workshops are offered, catering to everyone from experienced chefs to absolute beginners. Participants in these workshops will learn the techniques needed to work with fine-quality chocolate and how to make delicacies such as truffles.

For those who don't want to pay the high fees for the workshops or who don't feel they have enough self-control to work with chocolate without immediately eating it, the kitchens at the store have glass walls, so you can watch the chefs at work while you browse their wares.

Early evening ambience outside the Servitenkirche

versity of Vienna needs a lot of space. Walk for just a few minutes through any part of Alsergrund and sooner or later you will see buildings marked with the university logo. Academic departments and administrative offices are housed in everything from 19th-century town houses to modern tower blocks.

The heart of this institution is the **Universität Wien Campus** (also known as the Altes AKH Campus) in the southwestern quarter of Alsergrund. Visitors often assume that this leafy campus, much of which dates from the 18th century, has always been part of the university. In actuality, the university has occupied this campus since only the 1990s.

The oldest parts of this campus were built in the late 17th century as a home for disabled soldiers.

The complex, often referred to as the Grossarmenhaus (Great Poorhouse), grew throughout the 18th century and soon incorporated charity hospitals, orphanages, and almshouses. This adminstration of the Grossarmenhaus was riddled with corruption and in 1783 the reforming Emperor Josef II had it closed down and replaced with a new institution: the Allgemeines Krankenhaus (AKH). During the 19th and early 20th centuries, this hospital was one of the great centers of medical research in Europe, where discoveries such as the existence of blood groups were made and the principles of surgical hygiene were established. By the 1950s the AKH had outgrown its original home (now the Altes AKH University Campus), and by the 1980s had moved all its operations to the huge new hospital

Universität Wien Campus

🅰 131

🚃 Bauernfeldplatz (Strassenbahn line D), Schottentor (U2)

www.univie.ac.at

EXPERIENCE: Learning German in Vienna

In summer, when the regular students have gone home, the University of Vienna operates a large and highly regarded language school in the Altes AKH Campus. This school is known as the **Deutschkurse** *(Campus der Universität Wien Hof 1, tel 1/4277-24101, deutschkurse. univie.ac.at, $$$$$)* and is open to everyone from absolute beginners to near-fluent German speakers who just want to put a bit of polish on their pronunciation.

The different courses are divided according to the CEFR (Common European Framework of Reference) system—where a beginner takes the A1 course, then the A2 course, then B1, and so on. The highest level is C2, which denotes complete fluency. Students can take evening classes or intensive one-month courses that take place three times a year (July, August, and September). Cheap housing is offered in the student dorms nearby.

Vienna is a wonderful place to learn to speak German and there are several other institutions around the city. These include **Berlitz** *(Graben 13, tel 1/512 82 86, www.berlitz.at, $$$$$)*, **Cultura Wien** *(Bauernmarkt 18, tel 1/533 24 93, www.culturawien.at/eng, $$$$$)*, and the **Internationales Kulturinstitut** *(Opern-ring 7, tel 1/586 73 21, www.iki vienna.at/en, $$$$$)*.

No matter which they choose, those who come to Vienna to learn German have the advantage of being immersed in the language and culture from dawn to dusk every day. The more daring student might try to learn the dense Viennese dialect (known as *Wienerisch*) that is still spoken in some parts of the city. This dialect is a strange mixture of archaic, formal phrases, loanwords from other languages, and inpenetrable slang. It is hard for Germans to understand and confusing even to some Austrians.

Universität Wien Campus Tours

- ✉ Universität Wien Campus, Spitalgasse 2
- ☎ (1) 4277-17525
- 💲 $$
- 🚋 Lange Gasse (Strassenbahn lines 5, 43, & 44)

Narrenturm

- 🅰 131
- ✉ Universität Wien Campus
- ☎ (1) 406 86 72-2
- 🕐 Open Wed., Thurs., & first Sat. of each month
- 💲 $
- 🚋 Lange Gasse (Strassenbahn lines 5, 43, & 44)

www.narrenturm.at

complex on the other side of Spitalgasse. The move was controversial, as the final cost of the new hospital building was many times higher than the original estimates. There were widespread allegations of corruption among both the contractors who built the hospital and the politicians who ordered it.

Outside term time, the Altes AKH University Campus tends to be almost completely deserted, while in the spring and fall its courtyards are turned into what is essentially a giant outdoor bar. **Guided tours** of the campus are available, but the main attraction for visitors is the **Narrenturm** (Fools' Tower), located in the north of the campus. This strange round building was constructed in 1782 as an insane asylum (see sidebar p. 143). Today this building holds the Museum of Pathological Anatomy, a grotesque collection of strange fleshy things kept in jars of formaldehyde. For those with a strong stomach and an interest in medical history, the place is fascinating; for everyone else it is probably best avoided, especially if you've just eaten.

The Josephinum

In addition to overhauling the Grossarmenhaus, Emperor Josef II opened a new school for the instruction of military surgeons on the edge of the AKH campus. This school, known as the Josephinum, was completed in 1785. Thanks to generous funding, it was able to acquire hundreds of fabulously detailed wax anatomical models from Italy, as well as a large library of medical textbooks. Because of this support the Josephinum became an important institution on the cutting-edge (no pun intended) of surgical science. It continued to expand until the school's syllabus overlapped so much with that of the University of Vienna's medical school (which trained civilians) that it was decided the two institutions should be merged. Today this grand baroque building houses the **Museum of the Medical University,** whose collection includes the Josephinum's unsettlingly lifelike original wax anatomical models. There are also many beautifully illustrated medical textbooks, and numerous cabinets filled with scary-looking surgical tools.

If you're going from the Josephinum or the AKH campus to the Liechtenstein Museum (see pp. 148–150) it is worth heading north along Boltzmanngasse and then down the picturesque street of Strudlhofgasse. The 19th-century town houses along this street are home to the various departments of the University of Vienna's faculty of physics. The street terminates at the **Strudlhofstiege,** a beautiful art nouveau staircase that zigzags its way down to the western side of the Liechtenstein Museum. The staircase was designed by Theodor Jaeger (1873–1943) in 1905. ■

Josephinum / Museum of the Medical University
- ⊠ 131
- ⊠ Währinger-strasse 25
- ☎ (1) 4277-63422
- 🕐 Closed Sat. & Sun.
- 💲 $$
- 🚃 Bauernfeldplatz (Strassenbahn line D)

Strudlhofstiege
- ⊠ 131
- ⊠ Strudlhofgasse
- 🚃 Bauernfeldplatz (Strassenbahn line D)

The Strudlhofstiege's elegant art nouveau ironwork

Liechtenstein Museum & Northern Alsergrund

As you move farther north, Alsergrund's visitor-friendly attractions thin out, and the historic buildings give way to modern ones, of which only a few are worth seeing. The exception to this is the Palais Liechtenstein—a beautiful 17th-century palace and art gallery that seems rather out of place in the modern suburban district that now surrounds it.

The Liechtenstein Museum displays the personal art collection of the Prince of Liechtenstein.

Liechtenstein Museum

- 🏛 131
- ✉ Fürstengasse 1
- ☎ (1) 319 57 67-0
- 🕐 Closed Wed. & Thurs.
- 💲 $$$
- 🚉 Bauernfeldplatz (Strassenbahn line D)

www.liechtenstein museum.at

Liechtenstein Museum

This beautiful Gartenpalais (Garden Palace) was commissioned in the late 17th century by Johann Adam I of Liechtenstein. Johann wanted to build a palace that would reflect his rising political influence, as well as his enormous wealth. He asked many of the leading architects of his day to come up with designs for this palace, among them Johann Fischer von Erlach (designer of many grand buildings in the Hofburg Quarter). Initial work on the palace was done according to the plans of Italian architect Domenico Egidio Rossi (1659–1715), but he was soon replaced by fellow Italian Domenico Martinelli (1650–1718), who substantially altered the original designs.

Over the next decade, Martinelli coordinated a workforce that included the finest craftsmen and artists in Vienna. The interiors were covered with stucco decoration by Santino Bussi (1664–1736) and huge frescoes by Johann Rottmayr (1656–1730) and Andrea Pozzo (1642–1709), whose distinctive style can also be seen in the Jesuitenkirche (see p. 74). A large formal garden and a smaller Upper Palace (today used as a private conference center) were also built under Martinelli's direction.

In the late 18th century, Prince Johann I Josef began to move the Liechtenstein family's vast art collection into the palace. He bricked up windows and blocked off doors in order to make space on the walls to hang his huge paintings. Pictures from the early 19th century show the galleries to have been absolutely crammed with art of every shape, size, and style—from giant oil paintings to fine china plates.

After the Liechtenstein family fled the country in 1938, the building was put to a number of different uses, the most notable being the period from 1979 to 2000, when it was the home of the MUMOK (see p. 118). From 2000–2004, the building was extensively renovated—stucco work was repaired, frescoes were restored, and the building was generally brought up to the standards required by a 21st-century museum.

Today, visitors enter the building through the *sala terrena*— a bright colonnaded terrace that was originally open to the elements. This space is dominated by the absurdly ornate French carriage that is covered with gold leaf, painted panels, and hundreds of carved figures. On either side of this space a pair of large marble staircases lead up to the main galleries. The ceilings over these stairways are decorated with frescoes by Austrian baroque artist Johann Rottmayr—one shows the Prince of Liechtenstein being

The Princely Family of Liechtenstein

The nation of Liechtenstein, sandwiched between Austria and Switzerland, is something of a geopolitical anomaly. It has a population of only 35,000 and covers an area slightly smaller than Washington, D.C. It came into existence in the early 18th century because the Liechtensteins, an incredibly wealthy Austrian aristocratic family, wanted more influence in the Habsburg court. They decided the best way to get more influence was to become the rulers of a sovereign state, so they bought the two small regions of Vaduz and Schellenberg and renamed them Liechtenstein.

Though they styled themselves the princely family of Liechtenstein, they continued to live in their palaces in Vienna and work in the Habsburg court. No Prince of Liechtenstein so much as visited his kingdom until about 150 years after it came into existence. The Liechtenstein family didn't actually take up residence in their own country until the Nazis arrived in Vienna, forcing them to flee across the border with their vast collection of art and antiques. After the Second World War, the Austrian government maintained that this flight constituted illegal export of Austrian cultural property and demanded it be returned to Vienna. This decades-long legal battle concluded in 2004, when a significant proportion of their collection was returned to Vienna and the Palais Liechtenstein was converted into a museum and art gallery.

Volksoper

- 131
- Währinger Strasse 78
- (1) 514 44-3670
- Währinger Strasse-Volksoper (U6)

www.volksoper.at

carried up to Mount Olympus; the other depicts a battle between the gods of ancient Greece. These frescoes were rediscovered during the 2000–2004 restoration effort, after having been concealed behind heavy oil paintings for more than a century.

The collection itself, which has been acquired over the past 400 years by successive generations of princes of Liechtenstein, is one of the finest private art collections in the world. It includes several works by Peter Paul Rubens (1577–1640) as well as works by Anthony van Dyck, Lucas Cranach the Elder, Raphael, Rembrandt van Rijn, and Salomon van Ruysdael. The museum also houses a large collection of fine china, bronze statues, and furniture.

Every Sunday afternoon the museum's spectacular Hercules Hall is used as a venue for informal classical music concerts. These afternoon concerts are rather more varied and modern than the

helpings of Strauss and Mozart routinely dispensed by other concert venues in the city.

Volksoper

A few minutes' walk to the west of the Liechtenstein Museum, on the border between Alsergrund and the neighboring district of Währing, stands one of Vienna's most popular cultural institutions, the Volksoper. Founded in 1903, the Volksoper gained popularity with the Viennese as an alternative to the Staatsoper that was less formal, less exclusive, and more willing to experiment with new ideas.

The Volksoper's repertoire is drawn from the worlds of opera, operetta, and classic musical theater, with the emphasis placed very much on entertainment and fun. English-language subtitles are available for most productions, although generally it's no great loss if they aren't. Although there are no bargain standing-room

Architecture Tours in Vienna

Ever since the Jugendstil architects broke up the city's love affair with pompous historicist buildings, Vienna has been at the forefront of several important movements in modern architecture. While it is large prestige projects like Zaha Hadid's Wohnbau Spittelauer Stadtbahnbögen (2005) or Friedensreich Hundertwasser's Spittelau Incinerator (1987; see p. 151) that attract the most attention, Alsergrund is filled with lesser known architectural gems like the elegant Haus der Forschung (House of Research; designed by Mascha & Seethaler in 2004), located on the edge of the university campus.

For those who want to explore the city's rich architectural history, the **Architekturzentrum Wien** (Vienna Architecture Center) conducts guided tours *(tel 1/522 31 15-11, www.azw.at, $$$$)* around the city. Some of its tours are part of a fixed program (the Sunday tours and summer excursions) while others can be arranged by appointment. Alternatively, visitors can map out their own tours of Vienna's architectural highlights on **Wien Architectur** *(www.wienarchitectur.at),* an innovative online project funded by Vienna City Council and the Architektzentrum Wien.

Zaha Hadid's Wohnbau Spittelauer Stadtbahnbögen, near Spittelau's famous incinerator

places, like those offered at the Staatsoper, the ticket prices at the Volksoper are significantly lower than at its better known rival.

Spittelau

The northernmost region of Alsergrund, known as Spittelau, is not the most attractive part of the city. It is dominated by the monolithic and extremely ugly buildings that make up the campus of the Universitätzentrum (housing several departments of the university but mostly occupied by the business school).

Those with an interest in architecture might want to head north along the riverside road to go see two of Vienna's most significant modern buildings—Iraqi architect Zaha Hadid's **Wohnbau Spittelauer Stadtbahnbögen** (Spittelau Railway Arch Apartments), which stand on stilts over an old railway viaduct; and the playfully strange **Spittelau Incinerator** designed by Austrian architect Friedensreich Hundertwasser. Some parts of the incinerator are open to the public, and the local utility company offers guided tours of the facility by appointment. Those thinking of going on the tour might be disappointed to know that Hundertwasser's involvement with the project was limited to the facade of the building (which is probably just as well, given his notorious dislike of any kind of precision engineering). Inside it is a state-of-the-art but nonetheless purely functional industrial building. ■

Spittelau Incinerator

🅰 131

✉ Spittelauer Lände

☎ (1) 313 26 27-05

🚇 Spittelau (U4, U6)

The city's youngest and most vibrant neighborhoods, beautiful riverside parks, and the glittering towers of the UNO City

Eastern Vienna

The Schwimmende Brücke on the Copa Cagrana, or Donauinsel

Eastern Vienna

The mostly residential districts of eastern Vienna aren't going to be at the top of anyone's must-see list, but if you have more than a few days to tour the city, it's certainly worth making a trip across the Donaukanal.

River views at one of the cafés on the Donaukanal waterfront in Leopoldstadt

For many centuries, the development of Vienna was limited to the western bank of the Donaukanal—the land to the east was too risky an investment as it was frequently inundated by the unpredictable waters of the Donau (Danube) River. Today, though it has been more than a hundred years since the Donau was tamed and the eastern bank settled, many Viennese still stand by the old adage that everything east of the Donaukanal is "the Orient."

While it is true that the four districts that make up eastern Vienna (Leopoldstadt, Brigittenau, Donaustadt, and Floridsdorf) are more sparsely populated and can't match the old city for cultural institutions or historic landmarks, eastern Vienna is not without its charms.

Leopoldstadt & Brigittenau

These two districts occupy an island located between the Donaukanal and the main branch of the Donau. Although they are neighbors, the two districts are almost completely cut off from each other by two massive rail yards and the leafy Augarten.

Both districts are largely residential, but they have different characters. Brigittenau is still very much a working-class neighborhood, with a large population of recent immigrants and few notable attractions. Leopoldstadt, on the other hand, is an area very much on the rise, with a creative young population and many independent stores, bars, and restaurants. Beyond downtown Leopoldstadt, almost the entire southeastern third of the island is occupied by the Prater—a public park and recreation area known for its fairs and as the location of the famous Riesenrad (Ferris wheel).

East of the Donau

Just north of Vienna the main branch of the Donau River divides into two parallel courses—known as the Donau and the Neue Donau—which were created when the river was regulated (see p. 157). Between these two channels and the Alte Donau (a branch of the Donau that is now a lake) there are several islands, ranging from the long, thin Donauinsel to the large island of Kaisermüh-len that houses UNO City.

Beyond the various courses of the river lie the two massive districts of Floridsdorf (in the north) and Donaustadt (in the south). These two districts are home to miles and miles of suburbs that gradually give way to farms and open land. The U-Bahn network extends only a few stops into this part of Vienna, but you aren't likely to want to go farther than that. ∎

NOT TO BE MISSED:

Exploring the glory days of the waltz at the Johann Strauss Museum 157

Eating at some of Vienna's finest new restaurants 158

The beautifully tended formal gardens of the Augarten 160

A ride in the iconic Riesenrad Ferris wheel in the Volksprater 161–162

A journey into the heart of the wild Grünprater on the Liliputbahn 164

Going for a swim at one of the Alte Donau's lakeside beaches 168

Looking out over Vienna from the top of the Donauturm 169

Area of map detail

```
0 ————————————— 1500 meters
0 ————————————— 1500 yards
```

FLORIDSDORF

N

Alte Donau
ARBEITERSTRANDBADSTRASSE
Kagran School Gardens
HANDELSKAI
BRIGITTENAUER BRÜCKE
Donauturm
DONAUPARK
A22
WAGRAMER STRASSE
ERZHERZOG-KARL-STRASSE
Millennium City
Dresdner Strasse
UNO City
Blumengarten Hirschstetten
BRIGITTENAU
REICHSBRÜCKE
DONAUSTADT
NORDBAHNSTRASSE
Augarten Contemporary
Donau
Strandbad Gänsehäufel
Donaukanal
AUGARTEN
LASSALLESTRASSE
HANDELSKAI
Alte Donau
DONAUSTADTSTRASSE
A23
OBERE AUGARTENSTRASSE
Porzellan-manufaktur Augarten
Donauinsel
Neue Donau
A22
Karmelitermarkt
TABORSTRASSE
Wien Praterstern Station
AUSSTELLUNGSSTRASSE
PRATERSTRASSE
Karmeliterkirche
Johann Strauss Museum
LEOPOLDSTADT
Church of St. Johann Nepomuk
UNTERE DONAUSTRASSE
Volksprater
WEISSGERBERLÄNDE
Sofitel Vienna
HANDELSKAI
PRATERBRÜCKE
INNERE STADT
PRATER PARK
LANDSTRASSER HAUPTSTRASSE
RÜSTENSCHACHERALLEE
HAUPTALLEE
A23
ERBERGER LÄNDE
Lusthaus

Leopoldstadt & Around

Just across the bridge from the Innere Stadt, the district of Leopoldstadt is home to some of the city's most exciting neighborhoods and distinctive landmarks. While the summer crowds flock to the lights of the Volksprater, much of this area is still off the tourist trail.

The artificial beach bars along the Donaukanal are an expression of Leopoldstadt's youthful, creative character.

Leopoldstadt

If you ignore the area covered by the railyards, the Augarten, and the Prater, Leopoldstadt is about the same size as the Innere Stadt. It is often thought of as one of Vienna's *vorstädte* (inner suburbs), but its densely packed, narrow streets reveal that Leopoldstadt has far more in common with its southwestern neighbor than it does with districts like Wieden or Neubau.

Praterstern: The western edge of old Leopoldstadt is marked by the Praterstern railroad station, a massive glass and steel building that replaced the old Nordbahnhof station in 2008. From the mid-19th century to the 1930s, this station was the point of entry for numerous immigrants hoping to start a new life in Vienna. Buildings throughout Leopoldstadt were turned into tenements to accommodate the constant stream of new arrivals, and the area gained a reputation as one of the most deprived in Vienna.

Today, however, the neighborhood around the Praterstern is a bustling commercial district, a self-contained "downtown" area where many companies have moved in recent years to escape the limited space and high rents in the Innere Stadt. The center of this neighborhood is the **Prater-strasse,** where the rows of 18th-century buildings are punctuated by high-rise office buildings, such as the **Galaxy Tower** on Nestroy-platz or the **Uniqa Tower** (see p. 79) by the Aspernbrücke.

In addition to being convenient to the Prater, the area does have a few attractions for visitors. The most popular of these is the **Johann Strauss Museum,** which is located in the apartment that was the famous composer's home from 1863 to 1870. It was here that he wrote many of his most famous waltzes, including the unofficial Austrian national anthem "An der Schönen Blauen Donau" ("At the Beautiful Blue Danube," better known simply as "The Blue Danube").

The museum's collection includes paintings from the period, a number of manuscript versions of Johann Strauss's most popular pieces, and several of his instruments, including a few of his prized violins. (Johann Strauss's father, who was also a noted composer, refused to allow his son to study music, thinking he'd be

better off training as an accountant. As a result Johann Strauss received his early musical training in secret from a violinist in his father's orchestra.) The museum's collection of photographs, ball gowns, and highly ornate dance cards paint an evocative portrait of life in imperial Vienna, making it worth seeing even if you're not a fan of Strauss waltzes.

Directly opposite the museum is the 19th-century neo-baroque **Church of St. Johann Nepomuk** (*Nepomukgasse 1, tel 1/214 64 94, www.pfarre-nepomuk.at*). Although this church isn't of any major historic or cultural significance, the cool, attractively decorated interior (dominated by a huge fresco of St. Johann ascending into heaven) provides a calming break from the busy street outside.

Leopoldstadt

🗺 155

🚇 Praterstern (U1, U2), Nestroyplatz (U1), or Taborstrasse (U2)

Visitor Information

✉ Vienna Tourist Information, Praterstern Station

☎ (1) 245 55

🕐 Closed Sat. & Sun.

www.wien.info

Johann Strauss Museum

✉ Praterstrasse 54

☎ (1) 214 01 21

🕐 Closed Mon.

💲 $$

🚇 Nestroyplatz (U1)

www.wienmuseum.at

Taming the Donau River

If you look at a map of Vienna today, the Donau appears as a pair of parallel channels running straight through the city from the northwest to the southeast. Vienna's oldest neighborhoods, and indeed most of the city's districts, are located some distance south of the main course of the river—a strange detail considering how important rivers have traditionally been to trade and commerce.

The reason for this unusual pattern of development is that the Donau was channeled into this regular course only in the late 19th century. For most of Vienna's history, the river split into many smaller channels (a phenomenon known as braiding) just north of the city. These channels created a complex and constantly changing landscape of islands and marshes that was around 3 miles (5 km) wide at its

broadest point. The branch of the Donau now known as the Donaukanal marked the southern bank of this braided river, and the (now dammed) Alte Donau was the farthest north.

After a series of severe floods in the 19th century, plans were put in motion to regulate the flow of the river. Work began in 1870 and was finished in 1875 to much fanfare. Not only was the river less prone to flooding but it was also now usable as a shipping channel, allowing large boats to travel from Vienna all the way through the major cities of the Austrian Empire (e.g., Bratislava, Budapest, and Belgrade) and out to the Black Sea. The flow of the river was altered again in the 1970s, when the parallel stream of the Neue Donau and the artificial island known as the Donauinsel were created.

Stilwerk Vienna

✉ Praterstrasse 1

🚇 Schwedenplatz (U1, U4)

www.stilwerk.at/en

Le Loft Restaurant

✉ Stilwerk, Praterstrasse 1

☎ (1) 906 16-0

🚇 Schwedenplatz (U1, U4)

www.sofitel.com

Karmeliterkirche

✉ Karmelitergasse 10

☎ (1) 214 58 26

🕐 Open in the morning Mon.– Sat., as well as for services.

🚇 Karmeliterplatz (Strassenbahn lines N & 21) or Taborstrasse (U2)

www.st-leopold.at

The Praterstrasse terminates on the northern bank of the Donaukanal, opposite Schwedenplatz. Here, among the modern office buildings that replaced those destroyed in the Vienna offensive of 1945, stands the city's latest and most futuristic architectural landmark. Designed by the French architect Jean Nouvel (b. 1945) and completed in 2010, the **Stilwerk Vienna** is a glass tower that rises out of an asymmetrical base of jagged polygonal shapes. Inside this building there is an upscale shopping mall filled with stylish design boutiques and a large hotel.

The building has won praise from architecture critics, but the Viennese remain unconvinced by its design. The top floor is home to a gourmet restaurant, **Le Loft**, which has glass walls that give an unobstructed view across the city and a ceiling covered by a huge abstract painting (which can be seen from outside the building).

Karmeliterviertel: If you walk for a few minutes up Taborstrasse the glass towers of the Donaukanal waterfront give way to a much older neighborhood. Here the buildings are as much as 400 years old, and huddled together in a maze of narrow streets that resemble the older parts of the Innere Stadt. They date from the time before the Donau was regulated (see p. 157), when the island on which Leopoldstadt stood was much smaller and Brigittenau was a swamp. This neighborhood is known as the Karmeliterviertel (the Carmelite Quarter), a name it takes from the white **Karmeliterkirche** (properly known as St. Josef) on Karmelitergasse. This white baroque church was built in the 18th century as the center of a Carmelite monastery but is now a regular parish church.

EXPERIENCE: Karmelitermarkt for Foodies

During the regeneration of the Karmelitermarkt in the 1990s, several small retail units were built on the western half of the old marketplace. Their low rents attracted a crop of young restauranteurs who transformed this collection of little square buildings into one of Vienna's culinary highlights.

Visitors to the Karmelitermarkt can sample Georgian cuisine at **Madiani** (Karmelitermarkt 21–24, tel 0/664 456 12 17, www.madiani.com), get a filling lunch of locally sourced schnitzel at the delicatessen/café **Kaas am Markt** (Karmelitermarkt 33–36, tel 0/669 1814

0601, www.kaasammarkt.at, closed Mon.), or have something a little more healthy at **Tewa** (Karmelitermarkt 26–32, tel 0/676 792 22 14, www.tewa672.com)—one of the few establishments in Vienna that sells vegan food. If you venture a little farther north, there are a few larger restaurants along Leopoldsgasse, including **Skopik & Lohn** (Leopoldsgasse 17, tel 1/219 89 77, www.skopikundlohn.at, closed Sun.), **Schöne Perle** (Grosser Pfarrgasse 2, 0/664 243 35 93, www.schoene-perle.at), and **Einfahrt** (Haidgasse 3, tel 1/942 68 86, www .einfahrt.at, closed Sun.)—well known for its excellent live jazz nights.

During the 19th century, the Karmeliterviertel was the heart of Jewish Leopoldstadt, where thousands of eastern European Jews first settled after arriving in Vienna. Although they were no wealthier than the other impoverished immigrant groups in Leopoldstadt, they worked to establish a number of religious and social institutions in the neighborhood, including several synagogues, kosher butchers, and a Hebrew school.

The majority of Leopoldstadt's inhabitants were not Jewish, but Vienna's anti-semitic political establishment perceived the area to be a wholly Jewish enclave. They saw its poverty as evidence of the Jews' degeneracy (using the same twisted logic that saw the success of any Jew as evidence of their greed). With the rise of the Nazi party, the situation in Leopoldstadt deteriorated rapidly. The Jewish population here was generally too poor to flee the country or buy the protection of the local police, and so they suffered the worst of the mob violence. In just one night (1938's *Kristallnacht;* see p. 34) every synagogue in Leopoldstadt was burned to the ground, and within a year or two, the entire Jewish population had been sent off to concentration camps.

After the war the enormous void left by the loss of the Jewish community was filled by refugees fleeing Soviet-controlled eastern Europe, and the area remained one of the most deprived in Vienna. In the late 1980s, however, the situation began to change. Young professionals and artists

Saturday-morning shoppers at the Karmelitermarkt

began to move into the neighborhood's semiderelict Biedermeier buildings and turn them into apartments and studios. A few years later they were joined by a small but culturally active Jewish community from the former Soviet Union. Today, the Karmeliterviertel is a vibrant young neighborhood with trendy cafés, restaurants, and bars; several small art galleries; and a plethora of independent stores. The heart of this revitalized neighborhood is the **Karmelitermarkt,**

Karmelitermarkt

- ✉ Corner of Krummbaumgasse & Leopoldgasse
- 🕐 Closed Sun.
- 🚊 Karmeliterplatz (Strassenbahn lines N & 21) or Taborstrasse (U2)

Augarten
- Ⓐ 155
- 🚊 Heinestrasse (Strassbahn lines N & 21) or Taborstrasse (U2)

Porzellan-manufaktur Augarten
- ✉ Augarten, Obere Augarten-strasse 1
- ☎ (1) 211 24-201
- 🕐 Closed Sat. & Sun.
- 💲 $$$$
- 🚊 Heinestrasse (Strassenbahn lines N & 21) or Taborstrasse (U2)

www.augarten.at

Augarten Contemporary
- ✉ Scherzergasse 1a
- ☎ (1) 216 86 16-21
- 🕐 Closed Mon.–Wed.
- 💲 $$
- 🚊 Heinestrasse (Strassenbahn lines N & 21) or Taborstrasse (U2)

www.belvedere.at

Brigittenau
- Ⓐ 155
- 🚊 Järgerstrasse (U6), Dresdner Strasse (U6), Handelskai (U6)

Millennium City
- ✉ Handelskai 94–96
- ☎ (1) 24000 1160
- 🕐 Closed Sun.
- 🚊 Handelskai (U6)

www.millennium -city.at

an organic food and craft market with lots of interesting semi-permanent stores.

Augarten: This 128-acre (51 ha) park started life as a densely forested royal hunting ground. It was converted into a baroque formal garden in the early 18th century, and opened to the public by Emperor Josef II a few decades later. The park is divided into numerous flower gardens and crisscrossed by picturesque avenues of chestnut and ash trees.

Unfortunately, the most prominent features of the park are its two enormous *flaktürme* (antiaircraft towers; see p. 34), which at around 180 feet high (55 m) dwarf even the largest trees in the park. Curiously, the flaktürme stand at the park's focal points, with avenues of trees and flower beds radiating out from them in all directions. It is not clear whether this odd juxtaposition is the result of a bizarre aesthetic choice by Nazi military engineers or a postwar attempt by the park's gardeners to make the towers fit into the park's design.

In the southeastern corner of the park stands the **Porzel-lanmanufaktur Augarten** (Augarten Porcelain Factory), a centuries-old Viennese company that makes porcelain tableware and ornaments. Visitors can go on a factory tour or look around the showroom (located in the old Augarten ballroom). Just to the north is **Augarten Contempo-rary** (also known as the Gustinus Ambrosi Museum), a small

open-air sculpture museum and art gallery. Behind the Augarten Contemporary are the grounds of the **Schloss Augarten,** a former royal palace. This building was the seat of the Congress of Vienna— an international conference held in 1814, which redrew the map of Europe after the Napoleonic Wars. Today it houses the school of the Vienna Boys' Choir (see p. 105) and is closed to the public.

INSIDER TIP:

On summer days, it's best to skip the crowded Volksprater and head straight for the peaceful parkland of the Grünprater—the number 21 streetcar will take you there from Schwedenplatz.

—TOM JACKSON
National Geographic contributor

If you get caught in the rain or need to warm up in the winter, the **Gasthaus am Nordpol** (*Nordwest-bahnstrasse 17, tel 1/333 58 54, www.amnordpol3.at*), just outside the park's northeastern gate, is a charming modern café with comfy chairs and a variety of traditional board games (all in German though, which can make things a little confusing). Alternatively, you can head to **Bunkerei** (*Obere Augartenstrasse 1a, tel 0/6769 724 370, www.bunkerei.at*), a café located in an old air-raid shelter on the southern side of the park.

Brigittenau

The northwestern side of the Augarten marks the border between Leopoldstadt and Brigittenau. This district, which is farther from the city center and doesn't have much in the way of public transport infrastructure, has not been able to reinvent itself in the manner of its southern neighbor.

Most of the district is residential, with lots of rather shabby apartment blocks inhabited by students and recent immigrants. The only reason anyone might want to visit Brigittenau is to go to the **Millennium City,** a shopping mall and multiplex cinema built around the base of the Millennium Tower—which, at 663 feet tall (202 m), is one of Vienna's few proper skyscrapers.

The Prater

This massive public park covers 1,500 acres (600 ha) of former floodplain between the Praterstern and the southeastern tip of the island. Like the Augarten, the Prater was originally a royal hunting ground, and it was also opened to the public by Emperor Josef II. It is best known for the amusement park at its northwestern end, known as the Volksprater (People's Prater), which has been an important part of Viennese life for centuries. The park extends for several miles to the southeast beyond this point, however, through a lovely natural landscape of lakes, forests, and meadows known as the Grünprater (Green Prater).

A porcelain figure of a Spanish rider, made in Augarten

Volksprater: When Josef II opened the Prater to the public in 1766, he allowed cafés and public entertainments in the park. Over the course of the 19th century the original crop of bowling alleys, coffeehouses, and beer gardens was joined by colorful carousels, ice cream stands, and fairground rides.

Then, as now, warm summer days brought the Viennese here by the thousands—it was the place where courting couples went to get away from their parents, where parents went to get away from their children, and where people of every age and class went to escape the stuffy

(continued on p. 164)

Prater

- 🅼 155
- 🚇 Praterstern (U1, U2), Messe Prater (U2), Stadion (U2), or Prater Hauptallee (Strassenbahn line 1)

Visitor Information

- ✉ Prater Service, Prater 123
- ☎ (1) 729 20 00
- **www.prater service.at**

Walk: The Prater

The sheer size of the Prater can make it a slightly intimidating place for first-time visitors to the city, many of whom never venture beyond the flashing lights of the Volksprater, but those who continue farther south are rewarded with an unexpected slice of the Austrian countryside right near the center of the city.

The iconic Riesenrad, a simple fairground ride, has become a symbol of the city.

It's best to treat the route described in this walk as a broad suggestion, as the sights mentioned all take something of a backseat to the beauty of the park itself. Enter the Prater at the northern end of the **Hauptallee,** which can be accessed by a pedestrian underpass on the southern side of Praterstern station. The first thing you see when you emerge from this tunnel is the slowly rotating wheel of the **Riesenrad** ❶, the Prater's most famous landmark. At 212 feet (65 m), this towering steel structure is the most famous of the Volksprater's hundreds of attractions.

Continue along the tree-shaded avenue, past the **Prater Museum** (see p. 164) and the various whirling fairground rides of the Volksprater. Toward the southern end of the Prater a strange spherical structure, about 25 feet (9 m) high, can be glimpsed through the trees. This is not a fairground ride but the **Republic of Kugelmugel** ❷. It was built in 1972 by the Viennese artist Edwin Lipburger, and it originally stood in the countryside outside Vienna. When it was pointed out that he didn't have any planning permits for his unorthodox home, Lipburger declared it to be an independent country, and started printing his own stamps.

The plan didn't work, however, and the building ended up in the Prater after Lipburger was sent to prison for tax evasion. Today it stands inside a barbed wire "border" fence as a monument to one man's eccentricities. Lipburger still stops by from time to time, usually to add more names to his rambling and strange blacklist of government officials and "traitors to the Republic of Kugelmugel" that stands next to the building.

A few minutes' walk farther down the Hauptallee, the steep little hill known as the **Konstantinhügel** ❸ rises over a small pond on the right of the street. Like all the hills in the Prater (which was originally a low-lying river island), the Konstantinhügel is entirely artificial—under the turf and trees lie a few thousand tons of rubble created by the demolition of the buildings used in the 1873 Great Exhibition. Climb the hill and then walk around the pond to the south. Turn left past the sports complex and continue under the tramlines to the **Jesuitenwiese** ❹. This large open

NOT TO BE MISSED:

The weird, spherical Republic of Kugelmugel • Quiet woodland south of the Jesuitenweise • The quaint Church of Maria Grün

meadow is used for music festivals in the summer and sledding in the winter (see p. 165). Follow the path that cuts through the woods on the southeastern side of the meadow to the **Heustadelwasser ⑤**, a long-since isolated section of the old Donau.

Toward the Unterer Prater

The café at the northern end rents out small rowboats in the summer, but it's pretty rare to see anyone in them, as the rather murky waters of the lake aren't particularly enticing. In the spring and early summer it's worth giving the Heustadelwasser a wide berth, as it is often surrounded by clouds

of biting insects. On the other side of the Hauptallee are the much cleaner waters of the Stadionbad, a huge outdoor swimming pool complex.

Continue south along the banks of the Heustadelwasser, following the path as it passes beneath the stretch of autobahn that cuts through the park. Cross the Hauptallee at the southern end of the Heustadelwasser, and walk for a few minutes through the woods to the **Church of Maria Grün ⑥** (you'll need to take the path under the railroad tracks to reach it).

This little schoolhouse-church, built in the late 19th century, feels perfectly in keeping with its pastoral surroundings, and if it weren't for the occasional sound of a passing train, you'd be forgiven for thinking you'd somehow walked into a picturesque corner of the Wienerwald. Close by is the **Lusthaus ⑦** (*Freudenau 254, tel 1/728 95 65, www.lusthaus-wien.at*), a 19th-century hunting lodge that is home to an excellent restaurant. From here visitors can either walk back up to the entrance, along the Hauptallee, or keep exploring the woods.

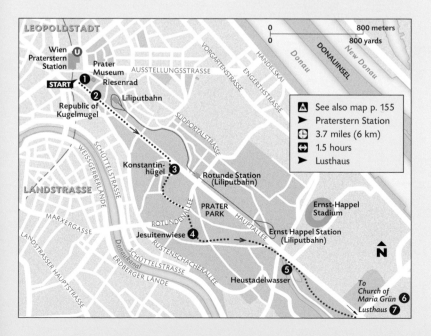

The sinister streets of postwar Vienna as seen in the 1949 movie *The Third Man*

Prater Museum

✉ Oswald-Thomas-Platz 1
☎ (1) 726 76 83
🕒 Closed Mon.–Thurs.
💲 $
🚇 Praterstern (U1, U2)
www.wienmuseum.at

Riesenrad

✉ Prater 90
☎ (1) 729 54 30
💲 $$$
🚇 Praterstern (U1, U2)
www.wiener riesenrad.com

Liliputbahn

✉ Prater 99
☎ (1) 726 82 36
💲 $
🕒 Closed Mon.–Fri. bet. Oct. & May.
🚇 Praterstern (U1, U2)
www.liliputbahn.com

formality of imperial Vienna. The air was always full of music, whether it was the noisy steam organs of the carousels or the gentler tones of Johann Strauss' orchestra, which was a regular fixture at the Prater's ballrooms and bandstands. This golden age of the Volksprater is documented in the **Prater Museum,** where a collection of strange and wonderful artifacts (the giant shoes of the world's tallest man, dragons from an old carousel, a fortune-telling machine) are displayed alongside photographs of the fair in the late 19th century.

Very little about the Volksprater is permanent, however, and so, besides the museum, only one or two objects remain from the park's heyday in the early 1900s. The most visible of these is the **Riesenrad** (which means "giant wheel"), a 212-foot-high (64 m) Ferris wheel built in 1897. It has become an iconic symbol of Vienna, thanks in part to its prominent role in the 1949 hit movie *The Third Man* (see sidebar opposite). Although it feels a little rickety as it slowly lurches its way around, there are few better places to see Vienna than from the pine-clad interiors of the Riesenrad's boxes.

Close to the Riesenrad is the northern terminal of the **Liliputbahn,** a miniature railway that whisks visitors out to the wide-open spaces and natural beauty of the Grünprater. Trains run between the Volksprater and the southern station (about half a mile/1 km away) every 15 minutes during the summer, and on weekends the trains are pulled by adorable half-size steam locomotives (which were built in the 1920s).

Grünprater: As its name suggests, the southern half of the Prater is a peaceful stretch of parkland, similar in both atmosphere and size to New York's Central Park. The upper half of the Grünprater is occupied by numerous sports grounds and athletics clubs, while the lower section is mostly meadows and woodland. Connecting these two halves is the Hauptallee, a tree-lined promenade that runs straight down the center of the park from the Praterstern.

The best known of the Grünprater's landmarks is the **Lusthaus,** a pretty octagonal building surrounded by a two-story veranda. This particular structure dates from the mid-19th century, but various hunting lodges and cafés have stood on this spot for centuries. Today the building houses a popular café

and restaurant. Nearby, in a small forest clearing off the Aspernallee, stands the quaint little chapel of **Maria Grün,** a popular spot for weddings in Vienna.

The Grünprater isn't really a place for sightseeing, however. The best thing to do is just to go for a walk or get on a bike (see p. 264 for bicycle rental companies in Vienna) and explore the scenery. In the summer the woods and meadows on either side of the Hauptallee are a great spot for a picnic or a bit of sunbathing, while in the winter, families flock to the **Rodelhügel** (sledding hill; actually a mound of turfed-over rubble cleared from the city after the bombing raids of the Second World War), just south of the sporting grounds. There, snow machines make sure there are good sledding conditions even when it doesn't snow. ■

Lusthaus

- ✉ Freudenau 254, Prater
- ☎ (1) 728 95 65
- ⏰ Closed Wed.
- 🚃 Stadion (U2) or Prater Hauptallee (Strassenbahn line 1)

www.lusthaus-wien.at

Kirche Maria Grün
- ✉ Aspernallee 1, Prater
- 🚃 Stadion (U2), or Prater Hauptallee (Strassenbahn line 1)

Rodelhügel

- ✉ Rotundenallee, Prater
- 🚃 Prater Hauptallee (Strassenbahn line 1)

EXPERIENCE: In the Shoes of Harry Lime

Anyone who has seen *The Third Man*, the 1949 classic film noir of black-market intrigue in post-WWII Vienna, will instantly recognize the Riesenrad Ferris wheel from the tense scene where the protagonist, Holly Martins, meets his mysterious old friend Harry Lime. If you re-create the characters' ride on the wheel, you will see that Vienna has changed dramatically from the bombed-out city of the late 1940s.

Despite the city's reconstruction, however, many of the locations used in the film remain largely unchanged today. These include the Palais Palffy (which served as Harry Lime's apartment building) and the Zentralfriedhof. Visitors can take a guided

tour of the aboveground locations used in the film through **Vienna Walks** (*Werdertorgasse 9, tel 1/774 89 01, www.viennawalks .com, $$$$*) or, for those with a sense of adventure, **Third Man Tours** (*tel 1/4000 30 33, www.drittemanntour.at, $$$*) offers a chance to explore Vienna's sewers. Given the tour's high demand, and the fact that it takes place only between May and October when the water levels are reliably low, it's best to make reservations.

Enthusiasts can also head to the excellent **Third Man Museum** (*Pressgasse 25, 1/586 48 72, www.3mpc.net, $$*) in Wieden or go see the film at one of the frequent screenings at the **Burgkino** (*Opernring 19, tel 1/587 84 06, www.burgkino.at, $$*).

East of the Donau

This leafy suburban area, divided between the two large districts of Floridsdorf and Donaustadt, is where Vienna comes to unwind. There's not much here for those who have only a few days in Vienna, but it's a great place to explore if the weather is too nice for museums.

Joggers getting their morning exercise on the Donauinsel

Donauinsel

🏛 155

🚇 Donauinsel
(U1), Neue
Donau (U6),
Kaisermühlen-
VIC (U1), or
Alte Donau (U1)

Beyond the Donau, eastern Vienna is divided equally between the districts of Floridsdorf and Donaustadt. The border between the two runs northeast from the Brigittenauer Brücke (Brittenau Bridge), dividing the islands of the Donauinsel and the Kaisermühlen into roughly equal halves. The northwestern half of the islands is in Floridsdorf and the southeastern half is in Donaustadt. Past these islands the districts continue into Vienna's eastern suburbs, which are home to 286,000 people.

Most of the sites worth visiting in these districts are located fairly close to the Innere Stadt, either on the Donauinsel, the Kaisermühlen, or within walking distance of the Alte Donau. The suburbs beyond hold little of any cultural or historical interest.

Donauinsel

This strangely shaped island— 12 miles (19 km) long but only about 300 yards (274 m) wide at its broadest point—is a byproduct of the city's efforts to control the flow of the Donau (see p. 157). While the Neue Donau was being excavated in the 1970s it was decided that the island created by the new flood defenses should be made into a recreation area for the

Viennese, complete with bars, clubs, and—this being Austria—large nudist areas in the north and south. Few Viennese ever use its rather generic sounding official name, instead preferring one of its many nicknames. The most commonly used are "spaghetti insel" and "Copa Cagrana" (an ironic reference to the Copacabana beach in Rio de Janeiro and the nearby neighborhood of Kagran).

The quickest way to reach the island is to take the U-Bahn to Donauinsel Station. This station is located on the lower deck of the Reichsbrücke bridge, over the Neue Donau, and offers impressive views along the riverfront. A few hundred yards away to the north is the blue-and-yellow footbridge known as the **Schwimmende Brücke** (floating bridge), which connects the clubs and bars of the Donauinsel with other venues on the opposite bank. As its name would suggest, this is a pontoon bridge, and everything other than the large yellow columns in the center can be dismantled and floated away when the river floods. Given the highly variable water level in the Neue Donau, this design is a popular one for riverside buildings, and many of the bars and restaurants on the waterfront also rise and fall with the varying water levels.

The best way to explore the island is to head to **Copa Cagrana Rad und Skaterverhleih,** near the Schwimmende Brücke, which offer half- or full-day rental of a wide variety of wheeled transport, including bikes, pedal carts, inline skates, skateboards, scooters, and roller skates.

Kaisermühlen

The Kaisermühlen is a semicircular patch of land that was reclaimed from the river in the 1870s. It stands between the straight, artificial channels of the Donau and Neue Donau, and the curved, shallow lake known as the Alte Donau. The latter was once the river's main course but is now cut off from the Donau by two high embankments. To the Viennese the Kaisermühlen is best known as the location of various swimming areas and recreational facilities (see p. 168), but it is also home to a large UN office complex and a growing business district.

Copa Cagrana Rad und Skaterverhleih

- ✉ Donauinsel
- ☎ (1) 263 52 42
- 🕐 Closed Nov.–April
- 💲 $$$$–$$$$$
- 🚇 Donauinsel (U1)

**www.fadrradverleih
.at**

EXPERIENCE:
Donauinselfest

For one weekend in June, the Donauinsel hosts a giant open-air music festival known as the **Donauinselfest** *(www.donauinselfest
.at)*. This festival was first held in 1984 to entice the Viennese out to their newly opened island park. Over the years it has grown from a small local festival to one of Europe's biggest music events, drawing an estimated two to three million visitors every year. Dozens of venues dot the island, from little stages in marquees to gigantic stadium-size arenas. Walking around the island you will hear everything from European trance pop to the Vienna Philharmonic. Even though the festival attracts the big names in European pop and rock, all the outdoor events remain completely free. If you're planning on going, make sure that you make hotel reservations a long way in advance.

EXPERIENCE: Summer on the Alte Donau

In 1875, the Donau was diverted into its current straightened course, cutting off a 3.5-mile-long (5.7 km) stretch of the old riverbed from the river. This section, known as the Alte Donau, is now the city's favorite spot for various water sports and summer recreation. It remains popular with a broad cross-section of Viennese society, although it can get rather crowded in the summer.

Little dinghies sailing on the Alte Donau

The Alte Donau is a very shallow lake, rarely more than 8 feet (2.5 m) deep, with water so clean that you can usually see the lake bottom in all but the deepest parts. The Kagraner Brücke (Kagran Bridge) divides the lake into two halves—the Obere Alte Donau and the Untere Alte Donau.

Public Beaches

All along the lakeshore you'll find large recreational facilities and beach areas, ideal for those looking to sunbathe or go for a swim. In a throwback to the days of Red Vienna (see pp. 31–33), many of these bathing areas are run by labor unions or professional societies, which charge a small fee for non-members. Almost all of the recreation areas have several outdoor (and sometimes indoor) swimming pools and children's play areas in addition to their beaches.

Popular facilities include the **Angelibad** (Oberen Alten Donau, tel 1/263 22 69, $$), a large complex that is very popular with families; the **Strandbad Alte Donau** (Arbeiterstrandbadstrasse 91, tel 1/263 65 38, $$), which has a long wooden boardwalk that dates from the 1920s; and the **Strandbad Gänsehäufel** (Moissigasse 21, tel 1/269 90 16, www.gaensehaeufel.at), a massive recreational complex located on its own private island in the Alte Donau, close to the UNO City.

Other Activities

There is much more to do on the Alte Donau than just lie around soaking up the sun. Numerous little marinas on the lakeshore offer boat hire and sailing lessons. Most of these marinas are run by restaurants and bars.

For a few euros, you can rent a rowboat or pedal boat from **La Creperie** (Oberen Alte Donau 6, tel 1/270 31 00, www.lacreperie.at, $$), a French restaurant at the lake's northern end; **Seepferdchen** (Oberen Alte Donau 6, tel 0/664 222 59 44, $$), a garden restaurant that offers picnic baskets for those going out in their boats; or **Zum Schinakl** (Laberlweg 19, tel 1/263 36 56, www.schinakl.com, $$), a traditional-style heurigen (see p. 229) opposite the Grosses Gänsehäufel at the lake's southern end.

At several sailing schools, beginners of any age can spend a day (or more) learning to sail small dinghies. The best of these are the **Segelschule Hofbauer** (An der Oberen Alten Donau 191, tel 1/204 34 35, www.hofbauer.at, $$$$$), just north of the Kagraner Brücke; and **Segelschule Irzl** (An der Unteren Alten Donau 29, tel 1/203 67 43, www.irzl.at, $$$$$), just over the bridge.

Getting off the U-Bahn at Kaisermühlen-VIC, the first thing you'll see is the striking modernist towers of **Vienna International Center,** more commonly known as UNO City, the home of the United Nations in Vienna. This complex of offices and conference rooms houses the International Atomic Energy Agency (IAEA), the United Nations

INSIDER TIP:

The rather ugly buildings of the UNO City are enlivened inside by an impressive collection of European modern art and sculpture.

—BEATRICE AUMAYR
Viennese tour guide

Office for Outer Space Affairs (UNOOSA), and a host of other agencies with even longer, more indecipherable acronyms. Guided tours of the complex are held in many languages several times a day, although you will need to bring your passport with you—by entering the UNO City you're technically leaving Austria.

Behind UNO City lies the **Donaupark,** a pleasant patch of greenery that was laid out on an old landfill site in the 1960s. Like the Prater, the Donaupark can be traversed by miniature train, the **Donauparkbahn.** Looming over all this is the 827-foot-high (252 m) **Donauturm.** This needle-like tower was built in 1964 and offers panoramic views over Vienna. Visitors can either head to the

observation deck or to the even higher restaurants (both of which revolve) on the upper floors—the lower one is fairly reasonably priced, while the upper caters to the fine-dining crowd. For a few days in the summer you can bungee jump off the tower's observation deck (which is nearly 500 feet/155 m high). For details and tickets call **Jochen Schweizer** *(tel 0/820 220 211, www.jochen -schweizer.at, $$$$$).*

The East Bank

On the far eastern side of the Alte Donau lies the neighborhood of Kagran, a traditionally working class suburb of Vienna. Unless they live in the area, few Viennese come out here unless they need to pay a visit to the gigantic shopping mall known as the **Donauzentrum.**

The only other attractions that draw visitors out this far are the area's two botanical gardens. The **Kagran School Gardens** comprise 14 acres (5.6 ha) of beautifully tended gardens in the heart of Kagran, and are adjacent to the **Österreichisches Gartenbaumuseum** (Austrian Horticulture Museum), which houses an extensive collection of gardening tools, paintings, and landscape plans for some of the city's lost baroque gardens. A little farther away, near the suburb of Aspern, lie the **Blumengarten Hirschstetten** (Hirschstetten Botanical Gardens), which feature plants from all over the world (including many tropical varieties in the palm house) as well as 1,700 different varieties of roses. ■

Vienna International Center

- ✉ Wagramer Strasse 5
- ☎ (1) 260 60-5270
- $ $$
- Ⓜ Kaisermühlen-VIC (U1)
- **www.unvienna.org**

Donauturm
- ✉ Donauturm-strasse 4
- ☎ (1) 263 35 72
- Ⓜ Kaisermühlen-VIC (U1)
- **www.donauturm.at**

Donauzentrum
- ✉ Wagramer Strasse 81
- ☎ (1) 203 47 22
- Ⓜ Kaisermühlen-VIC (U1)
- **www.donauzentrum .at**

Kagran School Gardens
- ✉ Donizettiweg 29
- ☎ (1) 4000 80 42
- 🕐 Closed Thurs.–Sun. & Nov.–March
- Ⓜ Kagran (U1)

Österreichisches Gartenbaumuseum
- ✉ Siebeckstrasse 14
- ☎ (1) 4000 42 27-0
- 🕐 Closed Sat. & Sun.
- Ⓜ Kagran (U1)

Blumengarten Hirschstetten
- ✉ Quadenstrasse 15
- ☎ (1) 4000 42 19-0
- 🕐 Closed Mon.–Wed. (palm house only during the winter)

Vienna's finest palaces, the Schönbrunn and the Belvedere, as well as some of the city's most important cultural institutions

Southern Vienna

Mozart's monument stands in massive Zentralfriedhof cemetery

Southern Vienna

From the built-up southern bank of the Wienfluss to the leafy avenues of the Zentralfriedhof, Vienna's southern districts offer a wide range of attractions, including the beautiful Belvedere and Schönbrunn palaces and the wacky apartment buildings of Friedensreich Hundertwasser.

One of Otto Wagner's *Jugendstil* pavilions in Karlsplatz

Looking across the Wienfluss from the Innere Stadt, the southern districts do not look particularly enticing—a colossal wall of government office buildings shields most of Landstrasse from view, and the roaring traffic of Lothringerstrasse sets the scenic buildings around Karlsplatz apart from the historic center of the city.

Beyond this unfriendly facade, however, the eight districts that make up southern Vienna offer some of the most beautiful sights in the city, including the pinnacle of Jugendstil design in Karlsplatz, modern architecture in the Gasometers, and baroque splendor at the city's two finest palaces: the Belvedere and Schönbrunn.

Landstrasse

Like Leopoldstadt to the north, this area's proximity to the Innere Stadt makes it a desirable residential area for young profes-

sionals and families. In the north of the district is the neighborhood of Weissgerber. Here the buildings date from the second half of the 19th century but are laid out on a maze of narrow streets that are much older. The area is home to the eccentric art galleries of the KunstHausWien and the Fälschermuseum, as well as the stark modernist architecture of the Haus Wittgenstein.

As you head farther south toward the district of Simmering, the 19th-century town houses give way to former industrial buildings and the massive housing projects of the Red Vienna era (see pp. 31–33). Out here visitors will find the Heeresgeschichtliches Museum (Military History Museum), the glossy modern architecture of the Gasometer complex, and the serene Zentralfriedhof (Central Cemetery)—where Vienna's love affair with the rites and rituals of death can be most clearly seen.

The Belvedere & Karlsplatz

In the western corner of Landstrasse lies the Belvedere, once the home of Prince Eugene of Savoy and now the home of Austria's national gallery. Here you can see the world's largest and most comprehensive collection of works by the Viennese painter Gustav Klimt, as well as works by numerous other Austrian and European artists. This impressive collection has to compete for visitors' attention with the stunning architecture of the palace itself. Set within several acres of carefully landscaped grounds and botanical gardens, the palace is a masterpiece of Viennese baroque design, crafted by Johann Lukas von Hildebrandt (1668–1745) in the early 18th century.

walk from the main square you'll find the fascinating Wien Museum, the Akademie der Bildenden Künste (Academy of Fine Arts), and the gallery of the Generali Foundation.

Schönbrunn

The former summer home of the Habsburg family is a pleasure palace built on a quite extraordinary scale. Since the abolition of the monarchy in 1918, the Austrian government has converted the palace into a museum where the royal family's apartments have been preserved as they were when they were occupied. Out in the former servants' quarters visitors can view the decorated coaches that played a prominent role in the pageantry of imperial Vienna. Outside, the grounds feature a zoo, vast formal gardens, and a few strange architectural follies. ∎

Located between the neat symmetry of the Belvedere and the historicist pomp of the Ringstrasse, the area around Karlsplatz is a curiously unplanned and disorganized looking place. It makes up for this lack of stylistic unity with some of the most important architectural landmarks in Vienna—including the spectacular baroque Karlskirche and the bold Jugendstil design of the Secession. Just a few minutes'

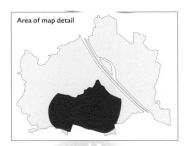

Area of map detail

Landstrasse & Simmering

These two districts stretch from the eastern border of the Innere Stadt to the sparsely developed outskirts of the city. Within them you will find baroque palaces, fascinating museums, and the imposing gravesites of anyone who was anyone in Vienna.

The weird and wonderful facade of the Hundertwasserhaus in Weissgerber

Weissgerber

 173

🚇 Landstrasse
(U3) or
Schwedenplatz
(U1, U4)

Visitor Information

✉ Landstrasse
Visitor
Information,
Landstrasse U-
Bahn Station

☎ (1) 245 55

🕐 Closed Sat. &
Sun.

www.wien.info

**Hundertwasser-
haus**

🅰 173

✉ Kegelgasse 35

🚇 Landstrasse
(U3)

Weissgerber

The first area of Landstrasse that most visitors see is the densely packed 19th-century residential neighborhood of Weissgerber. The area is named for a small village that once stood at the confluence of the Wienfluss and the Donau (Danube), and occupies the broad peninsula formed by the curving course of the Donaukanal. This gradually gentrifying neighborhood is home to a few sights of interest and borders downtown Landstrasse and the Belvedere to the south.

The area's biggest attractions are two apartment buildings designed by the eccentric Viennese architect Friedensreich Hundertwasser. The first of these, known as the **Hundertwasser-haus,** was built on Kegelgasse in 1983. Hundertwasser transformed a dull early-20th-century block of social housing into a dazzling riot of color, covered with onion domes, swirling mosaics, and mismatched windows. The apartments in this building are still occupied, so the building is not open to the public.

To see a Hundertwasser-designed interior, you will have to walk a few minutes north to the **KunstHausWien,** designed in 1988. This similarly eye-catching building is home to a museum devoted to Hundertwasser's life and work. In addition to a large collection of his visual art, there is a selection of architectural models (including one of the Spittelau Incinerator) and readable summaries (in German and English) of his outlandish architectural manifestos. While the museum is certainly worth visiting, the self-conscious quirkiness that infuses the whole place can get a little tiresome after a while, especially in the lumpy-floored shop (a conscious design decision) and rather expensive café.

One other sight in the area that's worth a look is the **Fälschermuseum,** located just across Löwengasse from the Hundertwasserhaus. This idiosyncratic little museum is devoted to the world of art forgery. It houses paintings, sketches, and sculptures by noted forgers like Tom Keating (1917–1984), Eric Hebborn (1934–1996), and Han van Meegeren (1889–1947). The museum offers an English-language guide that discusses the techniques and materials used by these forgers, as well as their fascinating stories—van Meegeren, for example, was too skilled for his own good. He was arrested after the Second World War and charged with selling priceless Dutch cultural property (actually his own forgeries) to the Nazis. He escaped a long prison sentence only by publicly revealing his career of deception.

A few blocks to the south, on Kundmanngasse, stands a building that is the antithesis of Hundertwasser's lively architectural style. The **Haus Wittgenstein** *(Parkgasse 18, tel 1/713 31 64, closed Sat. & Sun)* is an utterly unadorned, minimalist building

KunstHausWien

- 🅰 173
- ✉ Untere Weissgerberstrasse 13
- ☎ (1) 712 04 91
- 💲 $$$
- 🚇 Radetzkyplatz (Strassenbahn lines 0 & N)

www.kunsthauswien.com

Fälschermuseum

- 🅰 173
- ✉ Löwengasse 28
- ☎ (1) 715 22 96
- 🕐 Closed Mon.
- 💲 $$
- 🚇 Hetzgasse (Strassenbahn line N)

www.faelschermuseum.com

Vienna's Most Colorful Architect

As Vienna's favorite (and only) psychedelic artist/architect, Friedensreich Hundertwasser left a unique mark on the city's cultural and physical landscape.

Hundertwasser first attracted attention in the early 1960s for his bold, brightly colored paintings. His early involvement with architecture was as a critic, known for delivering long lectures about the evils of modernism (which he delivered with no clothes on, for some reason). He later published a manifesto that detailed his vision of architecture as a vehicle for its occupants' artistic expression. He believed that buildings should be constructed and decorated in an organic, haphazard way—with each occupant customizing the living space to his or her needs and decorating it, inside and out, according to their taste. It was better, he argued, for a building to be handcrafted and dangerously unstable than to be carefully engineered and impersonal. He put these ideas into practice in Vienna when he redesigned several buildings in the city, including the so-called Hundertwasserhaus and KunstHausWien in Landstrasse as well as the Spittelau Incinerator (see p. 151).

Among the Viennese, his work tends to divide opinion: Some think he was a playful, people-friendly visionary, while others argue that his architectural style amounts to nothing more than a coat of paint, some colored tiles, and a lot of shameless self-promotion.

Rabenhof Theater

🅰 173

✉ Rabengasse 3

☎ (1) 712 82 82

Ⓜ Kardinal-Nagl-Platz (U3)

www.rabenhof.at

Strassenbahn-museum

🅰 173

✉ Ludwig-Koessler-Platz

☎ (1) 786 03 03

🕐 Closed Mon.–Fri. & Nov.–April

💲 $$$

Ⓜ Schlachthaus-gasse (U3)

www.wiener-tramwaymuseum.org

that was designed in 1925 by Paul Engelmann (a student of Adolph Loos) for Margaret Wittgenstein (1882–1958), a prominent member of the Viennese intelligentsia. Margaret's brother, the philosopher Ludwig Wittgenstein (1889–1951), essentially took over the project soon after it started, obsessively redesigning everything from the door handles to the exact proportions of the rooms. Under his guidance the project ran several times over its original budget and wasn't finished until 1929. It was widely praised as a perfectly composed piece of minimalist architecture, but even Ludwig admitted it was a horribly impersonal place to live.

Today the building is part of the Bulgarian Embassy, hosting cultural events and meetings, but is open to the public during the week. It's worth having a look inside at the rooms that seem so utterly simple and yet managed to torment one of the greatest minds of the 20th century for the best part of four years.

Erdberg

The neighborhood known as Erdberg occupies the southeastern third of Landstrasse. This was formerly an area dominated by heavy industry, and a stronghold of Red Vienna. Although most of the factories have gone, this period of the area's history can be seen in the massive public housing projects that are dotted throughout the area. The largest of these, the Rabenhof, has maintained its radical character and is the home of one of Vienna's most politically active and daring cultural institutions—the **Rabenhof Theater.** This small theater stages German-language plays and also hosts touring companies from around the world.

Erdberg is also home to two large museums. Neither is likely to be on anyone's must-see list, but they offer a fascinating few hours for those already interested in their contents. The first is the **Strassenbahnmuseum** (Streetcar Museum), which is housed in a huge old streetcar garage near the river. As the name would suggest, the exhibitions here are the city's streetcars—from steam-powered 19th-century models to the familiar red-and-white ones that you see on the streets today.

On the other side of the Rabenhof Theater you'll find the

Youth Culture in Erdberg

About 600 yards (548 m) from the Erdberg U-Bahn Station stands the **Arena** (Baumgasse 80, tel 1/798 85 95, www.arena .co.at), one of Vienna's most important venues for alternative culture and live music. This cultural complex first opened in the summer of 1976, when a group of young artists and activists took up residence in the abandoned slaughterhouse buildings on the site. They were tired of the fact that Vienna had more venues for opera and orchestral music than it did for local bands. Today, the Arena is operated as a nonprofit youth culture center—it has a concert hall, several smaller rooms used for live music and theater, and a large central courtyard that hosts open-air concerts, mini-festivals, and screenings of cult movies throughout the summer.

The Skywalk connecting two of the newly renovated Gasometers in Simmering

Heeresgeschichtliches Museum (Museum of Military History), an institution with a rather broader appeal, if only for its odd architecture. This large museum is located in the Arsenal—the Rossauer Kaserne's southern counterpart.

It was designed by the historicist architect Theophilus Hansen, who deviated from his usual neoclassical style to design something that has been variously described as Moorish, neo-Byzantine, and orientalist. It is certainly hard to pin down exactly what he was trying to do with this building, which has rounded Byzantine arches, intricately carved Moorish windows, castle-like crenellations, and copper-roofed domes. Inside, the museum houses a large collection of weapons of war (including tanks, artillery pieces, and more guns than you can shake a sword at), as well as exhibitions about famous Austrian generals and

military campaigns. The museum's strangest (and most popular) exhibitions, however, are the artifacts relating to various famous political assassinations—including the car in which Archduke Franz-Ferdinand and his wife, Sophie, were murdered—the event that triggered the First World War.

Simmering

Simmering is one of Vienna's youngest and fastest growing districts, home to around 88,000 people. In recent years it has seen several landmark building projects and the development of Vienna's equivalent of Silicon Valley in the offices along the Donaukanal. This urban development is largely confined to the northern third of Simmering, however, and more than half of the district is still occupied by green spaces and public parks.

Heeresgeschichtliches Museum

173

Arsenal Objekt 1

(1) 795 61-0

$$

Erdberg (U3) or Südtiroler Platz (U1)

www.hgm.or.at

Vienna Gasometer Tours

- ✉ Gasometer C, Guglgasse 6
- ☎ (0) 660 748 48 00
- 🕐 By appointment only
- 💲 $$$ (guided tour)
- 🚇 Gasometer (U3)

www.wiener -gasometer.at/en

The Gasometers: When they were built in 1896, these four huge gas storage tanks were a symbol of Vienna's growing industrial and economic prowess. Standing around 230 feet high (70 m), they are Simmering's most prominent landmark, easily visible from the air during the approach to Vienna's international airport. They remained in use until the early 1980s, when they were replaced by modern underground facilities. By this time, however, the tanks—with their distinctive neo-Gothic brick exteriors (yes, in imperial Vienna, architects could even make historicist gasometers)—were protected landmarks, safe from the wrecking ball.

For a long time, the buildings lay empty—the huge echoing spaces of the old tanks used only for illegal raves—but in 1999 work started on an ambitious renovation project that saw the four buildings transformed into a vibrant new commercial and residential district. Several of Vienna's most prominent architects were recruited to think of innovative new uses for the gasometers.

The work took place between 1999 and 2001. Each gas tank was divided into apartments, offices, and commercial areas. While the offices and apartments have proved highly desirable, the shopping malls haven't taken off in quite the way the planners hoped. Visitors should head to the Skywalk that connects the shopping areas in Gasometers C and D for a great view over Simmering and the Donau River. A group of residents runs guided tours of the gasometers for those interested in modern architecture.

The glossy modern shopping complex inside Gasometer C

Mozart's Grave & Monument

Mozart's empty grave in the Zentralfried-hof—marked by a grand monument and attended to by legions of fans—is often seen as a symbol of the adage that genius is appreciated only after death. The oft-recounted story goes that Mozart died in poverty and was buried in an unmarked pauper's grave, where he lay unappreciated and unnoticed until a more fitting memorial was unveiled decades later. While this is undoubtedly the sort of romantic story that Mozart would have liked, it is a myth, and Mozart's two graves (the unmarked one in St. Marx and the grand one in the Zentralfriedhof) tell more about changing Viennese attitudes to memorials than the social status of artists.

First of all, it's not true to say that Mozart died in poverty or that he was buried in a pauper's grave. Mozart bounced into and out of debt constantly,

and while he was short of cash when he died, he had plenty of friends and patrons who owed him favors. His memorial service, for example, was one of the grandest events Vienna had seen in decades—paid for by Emmanuel Schikaneder (director of the Theater an der Wien). He was buried in an unmarked grave not because he was poor and forgotten but because that was standard practice at the time. Only the extremely wealthy were interred in individual marked tombs; everyone else had to share mass graves. As attitudes about burial changed in the decades after his death, and grand gravesites became more common, many felt he should have a monument of some kind. Some of his admirers went as far as to exhume dozens of bodies in the St. Marx Cemetery, looking for Mozart. In the end they settled for a memorial in the Zentralfriedhof.

Zentralfriedhof

Despite the rapid development of the area in recent years, Simmering is still best known to locals and visitors alike as the home of the Zentralfriedhof—Vienna's enormous main cemetery, which opened in 1875. Indeed, despite the growth of the area, the dead still vastly outnumber the living.

The Viennese are often characterized, not entirely unfairly, as a people obsessed with death. The city is filled with tombs and memorials, ranging from humble graveyards to grotesquely ostentatious family vaults. To the Viennese, it is important that you are interred with dignity and with a level of pomp that befits your wealth and social standing.

Cremation is rare in this city, and many older citizens still keep a special savings account to ensure their funeral is sufficiently grand. It is this macabre cultural fixation that has fueled the expansion of the city's cemetery into a kind of parallel shadow-city, with its own ethnic enclaves, fashionable districts, and celebrity hangouts.

The entrance is flanked by a pair of tall art nouveau columns designed by the Jugendstil architect Max Hegele (1873–1945), which give you an idea of what to expect inside. Guards at the gates sell annotated maps to the cemetery, which are invaluable if you're planning on exploring far. All around the entrance and the two large gatehouses there are numerous stalls selling everything

Zentralfriedhof

🅰 173

✉ Simmeringer
  Hauptstrasse
  230-244

☎ (1) 760 41-0

NOTE: The best way to reach the Zentral-friedhof from the Innere Stadt is to take the U-Bahn as far as Simmering Station (U3) and then catch streetcar number 6 or 71, getting off at 2. Tor station outside the main entrance.

Karl-Lueger-Kirche

✉ Zentralfriedhof

☎ Guided tours:
   (1) 535 34 73

www.luegerkirche.at

Feuerhalle Simmering

✉ Simmeringer
   Hauptstrasse
   337

🚋 2. Tor (Strassen-
   bahn lines 6
   & 71)

from single roses to huge, shrub-like wreaths of flowers. These stalls are a reminder of the fact that this cemetery is still active, and many of the visitors—especially on Sundays and religious holidays—are visiting the graves of loved ones, rather than sightseeing.

INSIDER TIP:

Be sure to pick up a map from the information office when you enter, as the Zentralfriedhof is far too big to navigate without one.

—LARRY PORGES
National Geographic Books editor

The Ehrengräber: Passing through the main gates, visitors are greeted by the sight of the elegant copper dome of the Karl-Lueger-Kirche. The view of the church is framed by a red-brick arcade that houses a group of elaborate marble memorials erected by wealthy Viennese.

Between this arcade and the church lies the most frequently visited avenue in the cemetery, the **Ehrengräber.** The plots here are occupied by Vienna's finest composers, artists, and architects. Famous residents of this area include the architect Theophilus Hansen; the sculptor Fritz Wotruba; and a cast of world-famous composers, including Ludwig van Beethoven, Johann Strauss (father and son),

and Franz Schubert. As a general rule the grave markers are fairly traditional affairs, with neoclassical sculptures and elegant bas-reliefs, but it's worth having a look at the fittingly abstract gravestone that Fritz Wotruba made for Arnold Schoenberg, as well as the jagged obelisk he made for himself.

At the far end of the Ehrengräber stands the **Präsidentengruft**—the final resting place of the presidents of the Austrian Republic.

The Karl-Lueger-Kirche: This large white marble church (officially called the Friedhofskirche zum heligen Karl Borromäus) was designed by Max Hegele in 1905. It is a perfectly symmetrical basilica, with sturdy buttresses and understated Jugendstil decoration. It shows the influence of Hegele's mentor, Otto Wagner—particularly his famous Kirche am Steinhof (see p. 217)—but takes a slightly more traditionalist approach. The interior of the Friedhofskirche is beautifully decorated in a style reminiscent of Byzantine cathedrals, with icon-like mosaics of saints around the base of the dome.

There are four broad avenues radiating out from the Karl-Lueger-Kirche. The eastern avenue leads to the Muslim, Protestant, and new Jewish sections, while the western avenue takes you to the old Jewish section. If you continue past the Karl-Lueger-Kirche, the southern avenue takes you into the area occupied by war memorials and soldiers' graves—including the graves of the Soviet soldiers who fell in the Vienna Offensive of 1945 and the imposing memorial to the Viennese men who died in the First World War.

The Feuerhalle & Schloss Neugebäude: Just across the street from the main entrance of the Zentralfriedhof lies the **Feuerhalle Simmering,** Vienna's main crematorium.

This curious piece of expressionist architecture, which looks a little like a Moroccan desert fortress, was built in 1922 as the political culture wars were gaining momentum in Vienna. In a city divided between conservatives and socialists, every action became politicized—even the manner in which a person chose for his or her remains to be handled. Burial in the Zentralfriedhof became viewed as the conservative option, while cremation was seen as socialist. The construction of this grand crematorium was supported by the Workers' Undertaking Association and given the go-ahead by the city's socialist mayor.

The memorial gardens that surround the Feuerhalle are actually significantly older than the building—older, in fact, than pretty much anything still standing in Simmering. They were laid out in the late 16th century as part of Vienna's great lost palace, **Schloss Neugebäude,** which was built by Emperor Maximilian II in 1568. At the northern end of the gardens you can see the partially ruined remains of this building, which

has been largely forgotten since the royal family abandoned it in favor of the even more luxurious Schönbrunn (see pp. 192–197) during the 18th century.

It is only in the last decade that any serious attempt has been made to preserve this remarkable Renaissance building, which is one of the only surviving examples from this period. Outdoor concerts and film screenings are regularly held in the courtyard during the summer to raise money for the restoration work. ∎

Schloss Neugebäude

- 173
- ✉ Otmar-Brix-Gasse 1
- ☎ (0) 664 574 52 10
- 🚊 2. Tor (Strassenbahn lines 6 & 71)

www.schloss neugebaude.at

EXPERIENCE: Prayers for the Nameless

If you share the Viennese fascination with the rites and rituals of death and you happen to be in town around All Saints' Day (November 1), you might want to make the trip out to Simmering to witness an authentically Viennese event. At the far end of the district near the river port of Albern *(catch streetcar 76A from Haide-strasse U-Bahn Station)* lies the overgrown **Friedhof der Namenlosen** (Cemetery of the Nameless). Between 1840 and 1940, this small graveyard was the final resting place of the unidentified bodies that were fished out of the Donau around Vienna. It is a quiet, slightly eerie place most of the time, but on the Sunday after All Saints' Day the local community descends on the small graveyard with gardening tools and bunches of flowers. Each of the neglected graves is spruced up and cared for, flowers are placed, and prayers are said for these forgotten souls. At the end of the day a small raft decorated with flowers and crosses is floated off down the river as a memorial to the unknown dead.

The Belvedere

Johann Lukas von Hildebrandt, one of the masters of Viennese baroque, designed this elegant *gartenpalais* as the summer home of Austria's greatest military leader, Eugene of Savoy. Since Prince Eugene's death in 1736, the palace has been only intermittently occupied, and today stands open to the public as one of the city's best preserved baroque palaces and the home of the Austrian national gallery.

The Belvedere Gardens with the Unteres Belvedere in the background

Unteres Belvedere

- ✉ Rennweg 6
- ☎ (1) 795 57-134
- 💲 $$$$
- 🚇 Am Heurmarkt (Strassenbahn line 71) or Karlsplatz (U1, U2, U4)

www.belvedere.at

The Belvedere comprises two separate palaces, joined by a large formal garden. The Unteres Belvedere (Lower Belvedere) is the older of the two—built between 1712 and 1717 on a plot that fronted onto the Rennweg. The larger Oberes Belvedere (Upper Belvedere) stands up the hill at the southern end of the site and was built between 1717 and 1723. Between the two lie the magnificent 18th-century formal gardens, designed by the French landscape architect Dominique Girard (1680–1738).

Unteres Belvedere

This palace was intended to be Prince Eugene's private residence, and as such the rooms are not as cavernous as those in its southern counterpart. What they lack in size, however, they make up for in ornamentation. While the Oberes Belvedere was extensively redecorated in the late 19th century, the interiors here have been left largely untouched.

The highlight of the building is the **Marmorsaal** (Marble Hall), which features a massive trompe l'oeil ceiling fresco depicting

Prince Eugene as Apollo, ascending into heaven with a floating entourage of gods and goddesses. Other notable features include the **Groteskensaal,** which is decorated with gloomy and grotesque images of animals and mythical beasts (apparently once the height of fashion, although it's hard to see why); and the **Goldkabinett,** a room whose walls are paneled with sheets of highly polished gold.

The Gardens

Laid out on a terraced slope, the Belvedere's gardens are some of the best preserved in the city. The garden is divided into three terraced sections, designed around a series of cascades, pools, and fountains. The planting consists of neatly tended lawns, hedges, and narrow flower beds, laid out in complex swirling patterns that can only really be appreciated from a viewpoint in the Oberes Belvedere. The gardens are actually the oldest part of the Belvedere, having been laid out more than a decade before work started on the rest of the palace. Originally the gardens would also have contained a small forest of classical statuary and plants from Prince Eugene's exotic botanical collection.

Under Empress Maria-Theresia the gardens were opened to the public, and another garden, the **Botanischer Garten,** was established in the large plot next door. The Botanischer Garten, accessed from an entrance near the Oberes Belvedere, is still maintained by the Universität Wien (University of Vienna). Its walled gardens and hothouses contain plants collected from all over the world—it's the ideal place to go if you find the gravel, grass, and fountains of baroque gardens a little sterile.

Botanischer Garten

- ✉ Rennweg 14
- ☎ (1) 42775 4100
- 🕐 Closed Dec. & Jan.
- 🚋 Am Heurmarkt (Strassenbahn line 71) or Südbahnhof (Strassenbahn lines D & 18)

www.botanik.univie .ac.at

Prince Eugene of Savoy

As a minor member of a French aristocratic family, Eugene of Savoy (1663–1736) did not initially seem destined for greatness. He always wanted to be a soldier, but was notoriously ugly and physically weak—a perfect candidate, his parents felt, for the priesthood. After being rejected by the French army at the age of 19, he traveled to Austria, where Emperor Leopold I was assembling an army to drive back the Ottoman invasion.

Eugene's first taste of warfare was as a cavalryman in the 1683 Battle of Vienna. His front-line heroics earned him the command of his own regiment, which was the beginning of a rapid rise through the ranks that would see him made a general at 23. In the years following the Battle of Vienna, Eugene commanded a massive counterattack into Ottoman territory, retaking Hungary and capturing the city of Belgrade (in present-day Serbia).

He returned to Vienna in around 1700, as a hero and a very wealthy man. He commissioned the two finest architects of his age, Johann Fischer von Erlach (1656–1723) and Johann Lukas von Hildebrandt (1668–1745), to design his city and country palaces, respectively. Eugene also became an influential patron of the arts, financially supporting many writers and philosophers, commissioning paintings and sculptures, and amassing one of the largest private libraries in Europe.

Oberes Belvedere

 173

✉ Prinz-Eugen
Strasse 27

☎ (1) 795 57-134

💲 $$$$

🚋 Schloss
Belvedere
(Strassenbahn
line D) or
Südbahnhof
(Strassenbahn
lines D & 18)

www.belvedere.at

The Oberes Belvedere

This palace was built as a venue for grand parties, masked balls, and other aristocratic social events. Von Hildebrandt was instructed to design something that would reflect his client's wealth and fame, so the opulent design contains many allusions to Prince Eugene's military successes. The roofline, for example, was designed to look like the tents of the Ottoman army that Prince Eugene drove from Vienna in 1683. Sadly, most of the original interiors were lost when the building was renovated to serve as the home of Archduke Franz-Ferdinand in 1897. Today, the Oberes Belvedere is occupied by Austria's national gallery.

Visitors enter through the *sala terrena*—once an open terrace where the prince's guests would have pulled up in their gilded car-

riages—a hall with a vaulted ceiling supported by muscular marble statues. Most of the ground floor is occupied by the Belvedere's shop and café, although several rooms on the northern side are used for temporary exhibitions.

After climbing the grand marble staircase, you find yourself in the **Marmorsaal**—a larger and brighter version of the hall in the Unteres Belvedere. This spectacular room serves as the lobby for the Belvedere's two main galleries, although the few pieces that adorn the walls of the room—including works by van Gogh, Renoir, and Rodin—would be the undisputed highlights of many a museum's collection. The doorway to the right leads into the 20th-century collection of works by Klimt, Schiele, and their less well known contemporaries, while through the opposite doorway lies the collection of

The elaborate ceiling fresco of the Marmorsaal

INSIDER TIP:

Don't miss von Hildebrandt's baroque interior chapel, which can be seen from a mezzanine balcony in the farthest room of Klimt paintings.

—CLIVE CARPENTER
National Geographic contributor

19th-century historicist, realist, and Impressionist paintings.

Most visitors head straight into the right-hand gallery, but it's worth having a look through the massive gilt-framed paintings of the 19th-century collection. Their style isn't to everyone's taste, but it's hard not to be impressed by the sheer scale and complexity of the historical and mythical scenes. One artist worthy of note is the Viennese painter Hans Makart (1840–1884), whose sensual, highly decorative paintings were an important early influence on Gustav Klimt and the artists of the Viennese Secession.

Across the Marmorsaal in the early 20th-century collection lie the gallery's undisputed highlights, including the world's largest collection of Gustav Klimt paintings. Many of these paintings have been in the possession of the gallery since they were first exhibited in the early 20th century.

The Klimt collection is spread over several rooms, and includes well-known masterpieces like "Judith I" (1901) and "The Kiss" (1908), as well as obscure but equally impressive landscapes and portraits. The museum's collection of Egon Schiele paintings is not as comprehensive as that of the Leopold Museum (see pp. 117–118), but it includes some of his most acclaimed works, such as the haunting "Death and the Maiden" (1915); "The Artist's Wife" (1917); and his last great work "The Family" (1918), which was left unfinished at the time of his death.

In addition to the work of these two famous figures, the gallery has many paintings by their lesser known contemporaries, such as Oskar Kokoshka's (1886–1980) ominous "Tigerlion" (1926); and the warm-toned "Laughing Self-Portrait" (1908) by the brilliant but troubled painter Richard Gerstl (1884–1908), painted as the artist sank into suicidal depression.

On the top floor of the Oberes Belvedere, two more small galleries exhibit neoclassical and Biedermeier Austrian art. There's not much of note up here, although it's worth going to see the "Portrait of Joshua Reynolds" (1794) by Swiss-Austrian painter Angelica Kauffman (1741–1807) .

The last of the Belvedere's galleries is the recently opened medieval collection, which is housed in the former stable block opposite the entrance. The art here is packed in quite tightly, with little wall space left blank—it's a worthwhile stop for those with an interest in medieval culture, but most would probably prefer to see their medieval art with a little more context in one of the city's cathedrals or treasuries. ■

Karlsplatz & Around

Karlsplatz is characterized by two distinctive features. The first is the Karlskirche, Johann Fischer von Erlach's finest baroque church; the other, sadly, is the roaring traffic of the area's busiest road. Those willing to spend some time ducking in and out of subways, however, will discover a wealth of stunning architecture and fascinating cultural institutions.

The playful and unique facade of the Karlskirche

Karlsplatz U-Bahn Station—a maze of underground passages, elevators, and escalators linking the platforms of the U1, U3, and U4 lines. Visitors will want to pass through the large but unremarkable concourse area to the southernmost exit of the station: Resselpark. This route allows you to avoid the traffic on the Rechte Wienzeile but, slightly unnervingly, does take you under the Wienfluss.

Otto Wagner's Pavilions

The subway emerges at the western end of the Resselpark, a small island of green space that fills the eastern half of the square. The park is best known for the Otto Wagner–designed pavilions that were once the main entrance to the Karlsplatz U-Bahn Station. Wagner designed them during his time as the chief architect of the Stadtbahn in the late 1890s. The two pavilions were built using iron frames and thin marble panels. He used sunflowers as a decorative motif, which appear (in various stylized forms) all over the buildings.

Today one of the pavilions houses the **Otto Wagner Pavilion** exhibition (part of the Wien Museum) where visitors can view a collection of artifacts and docu-

Karlsplatz is an easy walk from the Innere Stadt (just two blocks south of the Staatsoper) and is well connected to Vienna's streetcar network. Many visitors, however, will arrive via

ments relating to Otto Wagner's life and work. The other pavilion is home to the **Otto Wagner Pavilion Café** *(Karlsplatz, tel 1/505 99 04, www.otto-wagner-pavilion.at).*

Karlskirche

Set back a short distance from the other buildings around the square, the Karlskirche is the most spectacular baroque church in Vienna. Designed by Johann Fischer von Erlach, the exterior of the Karlskirche combines his usual baroque style with elements of classical design—including a Greek-style portico and a pair of enormous freestanding columns, modeled after Trajan's column in Rome.

The church is dedicated to St. Carlo Borromeo (known as Karl Borromäus in Austria), but was probably intended to glorify Emperor Karl VI as much as it was the Italian saint. This dual purpose can be seen clearly in the details of the two columns—they are carved with friezes depicting the good deeds of St. Borromeo, but topped by carvings of eagles: the symbol of the Habsburg emperor.

Inside, the church has been decorated with breathtaking flair by Fischer von Erlach (who made use of highly polished marble and lots of gold leaf) and by the painter Johann Rottmayr, whose huge ceiling fresco here is arguably his finest work. On the right-hand side of the nave there is a 105-foot-high (32 m) scaffolding tower that goes up to the top of the dome. This utilitarian structure looks like something that has been left there by restorers, but

is actually open to the public, and provides an excellent opportunity to view the intricate detail and clever perspective effects that Rottmayr put into his work.

Wien Museum Karlsplatz

At the east end of the square, next to the Karlskirche, stands the Wien Museum Karlsplatz. This light, modern building houses the main collection of the Wien Museum, a public institution that operates numerous museums around the city.

The exhibitions here trace the history of the city from pre-Roman settlements to the present day. The highlight of the permanent collection is the exhibition **"Vienna Around 1900,"** which showcases paintings by Gustav Klimt, Egon Schiele, and Richard Gerstl, alongside furniture from the Wiener Werkstätte and an interior designed by Adolph Loos. In addition to the permanent exhibitions, much of the museum is used for temporary exhibitions—sometimes showcasing art and artifacts loaned from other institutions, but often simply drawing from the museum's vast archives. In recent years the exhibitions have included Viennese street photography, 19th-century fashions, and the original architectural plans for St. Stephen's Cathedral.

The Kunsthalle & Kunstlerhaus

The Kunstlerhaus, artists' house, was built on the northern side of Karlsplatz in 1868 as the home of the Viennese artists'

(continued on p. 190)

Karlsplatz

Ⓜ 173

🚇 Karlsplatz (U1, U2, U4)

Visitor Information

✉ Vienna Visitor Information, Karlsplatz U-Bahn Station

☎ (1) 24 555

www.wien.info

Otto Wagner Pavilions

✉ Karlsplatz 1

☎ (1) 505 87 47-85177

🕐 Closed Mon. & Nov.–March

💲 $

www.wienmuseum.at

Karlskirche

✉ Karlsplatz 10

☎ (1) 504 61 87

💲 $$

www.karlskirche.at

Wien Museum Karlsplatz

✉ Karlsplatz 8

☎ (1) 505 62 94

🕐 Closed Mon.

💲 $$

www.wienmuseum.at

Kunstlerhaus

✉ Karlsplatz 5

☎ (1) 587 96 63

💲 $$

www.k-haus.at

Walk: South From Karlsplatz

The area around the Belvedere, stretching as far west as Karlsplatz and as far east as Ungargasse, is Vienna's unofficial diplomatic quarter. Here you will find an internationally varied range of architectural styles, as well as the beautiful surroundings that drew the embassies here in the first place.

The Heldendenkmal der Roten Armee, a memorial to those who died in the 1945 Vienna Offensive

Start outside the **Secession** (see pp. 190–191), where the breakaway art collective made its most prominent statement of artistic intent.

Head across the street and into the Resselpark, pausing to admire Otto Wagner's 1894 **Pavilions ❶** (see pp. 186–187). At the southeastern end of the square, pass by the **Karlskirche ❷** (see p. 187), stopping for a while to admire its grand facade. If you get up close you can make out the frieze depicting St. Borromeo's life and work. Most of this beautiful frieze is too high up to see clearly, or facing the wrong way—it is testament to the dedication of the craftsmen that they would lavish such careful detail on something no one would see.

Walking round behind the church, turn left onto Mattiellistrasse and then right onto Bruck-

ner Strasse. As you walk out into the wide-open space of Schwarzenbergplatz, pause to examine the building on your right. This is the **French Embassy ❸**, built in 1905 by the art nouveau architect Paul Chedanne. Note how the flowing organic shapes differ from the cleaner lines favored by the Jugendstil architects.

In the center of the square, and rather hard to miss, is the **Heldendenkmal der Roten Armee ❹** (see sidebar p. 191), an incongruous slice of socialist realism built as a memorial to those who died in the 1945 Vienna Offensive. Behind it is the **Palais Schwarzenberg**—an 18th-century palace built for Prince Eugene's political rival, Count Heinrich-Franz of Mansfield. Determined to outdo Prince Eugene, Mansfield bought the plot right next to the Belvedere and hired the same architect, Johann

NOT TO BE MISSED:

**Karlskirche • The Heldendenkmal
der Roten Armee • Russische Kirche**

Lukas von Hildebrandt. The results are impressive, although ironically neither Mansfield nor Prince Eugene lived to see it finished. Today the building is occupied by a luxury hotel.

Continue along Rennweg and you'll see the **Polnische Kirche ⑤** (Polish Church), a pretty Catholic church built for the Polish Embassy's staff. There are several more of these international churches in the area, including the humble redbrick **Englische Kirche** and the fabulous **Russische Kirche ⑥** (Russian Church) on Jauresgasse. The latter—a beautiful orthodox church topped with gilded onion domes—is one of the area's highlights.

Head south down Reisnerstrasse and cross Rennweg onto Praetoriousgasse. At the end of the street lies the main entrance to the **Botanischer Garten ⑦** (see p. 183), an oasis of greenery managed by the Universität Wien.

Nearby is the construction site where the Sudbahnhof is being rebuilt as Vienna's main train station. As part of the project (which is due to finish in 2015), the builders have erected a 210-foot-high (64 m) wooden tower, called the **Bahnorama ⑧** *(Favoritenstrasse 49–53, www.hauptbahnhof-wien.at),* from which you can see the developing site, as well as great views over southern Vienna.

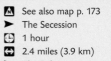

- See also map p. 173
- ► The Secession
- 🕓 1 hour
- ⬌ 2.4 miles (3.9 km)
- ► The Bahnorama

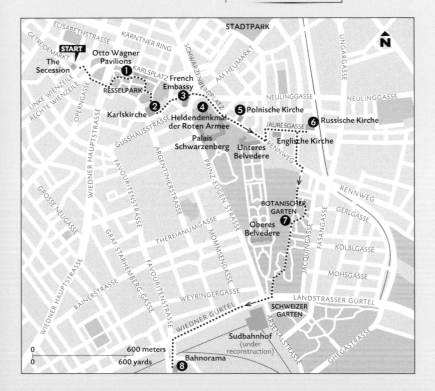

The floral gold leaf patterns and stone carvings that decorate the entrance to the Secession

Kunsthalle Karlsplatz

✉ Treitlstrasse 2
☎ (1) 521 89 33
**www.kunsthalle
wien.at**

The Secession

✉ Friedrichstrasse 12
☎ (1) 587 53 07
🕐 Closed Mon.
💲 $$
🚇 Karlsplatz (U1, U2, U4)
www.secession.at

Akademie der Bildenden Künste

✉ Schillerplatz 3
☎ (1) 588 16-0
🕐 Closed Mon.
💲 $$
🚇 Karlsplatz (U1, U2, U4)
www.akbild.ac.at

association. This organization was very much part of the Viennese cultural establishment, promoting the solid values of classicism and historicism among the city's painters. Today it is best known for being the organization that the Viennese Secession was breaking from, rather than for the work of any of its members. Today the building houses a movie theater and a few exhibition spaces. With so much competition in the immediate area, it's not always at the top of people's itineraries, but it does sometimes have interesting exhibitions.

Across the square, at the western end of the Resselpark, stands a more modern equivalent, the Kunsthalle. This contemporary glass and steel pavilion is used as an exhibition space by the Kunsthalle-Wien, which also operates a hall in the MuseumsQuartier. It hosts exhibitions by young Austrian artists, performance pieces, and other cultural events.

The Secession

Other than the Karlskirche, the most famous building on Karlsplatz is the Secession—a jewel of Jugendstil design, sadly driven to the margins of the area by the busy traffic of the Rechte Wienzeile. It stands at the western end of the square as a kind of architectural response to the Karlskirche (the original plans called for the construction of a broad avenue between the two buildings).

The design of the building, which was drawn up by one of the co-founders of the Secession movement, Joseph Maria Olbrich (1867–1908), embodies the radical architectural ideas of the Secession. The flowing ornamentation of Viennese baroque has been stripped away; the front walls are mostly blank—no columns, no statues, not even any windows on the facade—and the decoration is limited to stylized versions of forms found in nature.

It's worth walking all the way around the building to appreciate the thought that went into the building's design, and the elegant decorative touches like Koloman Moser's sculpted owls and the great gilded orb over the entrance. Inside, the Secession is still used as an exhibition space, housing works by contemporary artists and designers. In addition to the temporary shows, there is a small permanent collection of works crafted for the original Secession shows that took place in the first few years of the 20th century. This collection includes Gustav Klimt's "Beethoven Frieze," a large painting with three allegorical tableaux depicting themes from Beethoven's work.

Around Karlsplatz

Behind the Secession stands the **Akademie der Bildenden Künste** (Academy of Fine Arts), Vienna's oldest and most prestigious college of art and design. There are two galleries in the building that are open to the public: the Graphic Collection and the Paintings Gallery. The Graphic Collection houses the school's archive of sketches, prints, and photographs (around 160,000 pieces in total), and frequently holds themed exhibitions. Larger portions of this collection are often put on display in the Albertina Gallery (see pp.

113–114). The Paintings Gallery has been refurbished and hosts exhibitions by the school's talented students, as well as by artists-in-residence and alumni.

Another nearby institution that is worth a visit is the **Generali Foundation** gallery, located south of Karlsplatz on Wiedner Hauptstrasse. This gallery is part of a nonprofit organization established and funded by the Austrian-Italian insurance company Generali. The foundation's gallery is at the heart of its efforts to promote contemporary visual art, particularly conceptual art, in Austria. ∎

Generali Foundation

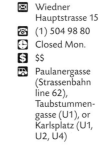

✉ Wiedner Hauptstrasse 15
☎ (1) 504 98 80
🕐 Closed Mon.
💲 $$
🚋 Paulanergasse (Strassenbahn line 62), Taubstummengasse (U1), or Karlsplatz (U1, U2, U4)

http://foundation .generali.at

The Soviet War Memorial

One of the most incongruous sights around Karlsplatz is the enormous Soviet War Memorial on Schwarzenbergplatz. The **Heldendenkmal der Roten Armee** (Monument to the Heroes of the Red Army) was unveiled in August 1945, four months after Vienna was captured. It consists of a curved marble colonnade surrounding a 39-foot-high (12 m) bronze statue. Over the colonnade there is an inscription in Russian, which translates as "Eternal glory to the heroes of the Red Army who fell in the fight against the German-fascist invaders for the freedom and independence of Europe."

Although the city's political leaders turned out to pay their respects, the attitude of the Viennese public was less than enthusiastic. They knew the Red Army as a heavy-handed occupying force, riddled with corruption and prone to acts of violence and looting. To them, this monument, with its triumphant inscriptions, was an insult. Even today, the monument is commonly known by the disrespectful nickname *denkmal des unbekannten plünderer* (tomb of the unknown looter).

Schönbrunn Palace

In a city as filled with aristocratic extravagances as Vienna, the royal family had to make an extraordinary effort to impress anyone. With the Schönbrunn Palace and its adjoining gardens, no one can doubt the supreme wealth or power of its occupants. Uninhabited since the abolition of the monarchy in 1918, today the palace is open to the public, allowing visitors to tour the finest rococo interiors in Vienna as well as its extensive gardens.

One of the many grand halls in the Schönbrunn's Imperial Apartments

Schönbrunn Palace

✉ Schönbrunner Schlossstrasse 47

☎ (1) 811 13

💲 $$$$

🚇 Schönbrunn (U4) or Hietzing (U4, Strassenbahn lines 10 & 58)

www.schoenbrunn.at

The area around Schönbrunn has been associated with the Habsburg family since the 16th century—they used it as a hunting ground, and built a succession of lodges. The idea of building a grand summer palace here, however, has its origins in the late 17th century, when Emperor Leopold I commissioned Johann Fischer von Erlach to design a palace for his son, Prince Josef. Fischer von Erlach's designs—which included a gigantic hilltop palace and a series of terraced formal gardens on the slopes below—were a

little more grandiose than the emperor had perhaps expected. The plans were shelved for more than a decade, and when they were eventually built it was on a far smaller scale than originally intended. Only the central section of the palace was built, in a more practical location at the bottom of the hill, and the plans for the terraced gardens were ignored entirely.

Around 40 years later, however, Empress Maria-Theresia discovered the original plans and found them very much to her liking. Her court architect, Nicolo

Palassi, was instructed to add an extra floor to the existing building and update the architecture to the fashionable style of the day. From this time until the collapse of the Austrian Empire in 1918, the Schönbrunn was one of the principal residences of the Habsburg family. It was not universally liked, however—the famously ascetic Emperor Josef II had the palace boarded up during his reign.

At the height of the palace's importance, during the reign of Maria-Theresia, the Schönbrunn was like a small city all of its own, with a population of more than a thousand servants, gardeners, and gamekeepers making sure that the lives of the royal family ran smoothly.

The Palace

If you're coming from the nearby Schönbrunn U-Bahn Station, the first glimpse you'll get of the palace is through the imposing iron gates that face onto Schönbrunner Schlossstrasse. From here you can see the mustard-yellow facade of the Schönbrunn framed by the eagle-topped obelisks on the entrance.

After boggling at the sheer size of the place, the first thing most visitors notice is how plain the architecture is—compared with the complex tentlike roofs of the Belvedere or the colonnades of the Palais Liechtenstein, the Schönbrunn looks a bit like an office building. Any impression of austerity, however, instantly vanishes the moment you head inside to view the Imperial Apartments.

The Imperial Apartments:

Inside, every room is decorated with breathtakingly lavish rococo detailing, richly colored paintings, and acres of gold leaf. The only way to see the Imperial Apartments is by guided tour—these are almost always heavily booked, so if you haven't made reservations online it's a good idea to head straight for the reception area in the eastern wing when you arrive. This way you can get yourself onto a tour group later in the day. There are two tours: The Imperial Tour takes 35 minutes and works its

Emperor Franz I Stephan

The most significant figure in the creation of the Schönbrunn Palace as it stands today was Franz I Stephan (1708–1765), the husband of Empress Maria-Theresia. Though technically Maria-Theresia's co-regent, the amiable but politically apathetic Franz I Stephan happily left the business of governing the empire to her, even after he had been granted the title of Holy Roman Emperor. As the French conquered his own duchy shortly after his marriage, he usually had a lot of time on his hands.

He was closely involved with several decisions relating to the Schönbrunn Palace's construction and played a key role in the design of the gardens. In 1753 he purchased a large meadow from a neighboring farm and had it made into a botanical garden where he could indulge his interest in plants. A few years later he had many of the animals from Prince Eugene's old menagerie at the Belvedere brought to the Schönbrunn. Here they were housed in the Tiergarten (see pp. 196–197), and were soon joined by other exotic animals acquired by the inquisitive emperor.

way through 22 of the rooms, and the Grand Tour takes around an hour and includes all 40 of the preserved rooms. Unless you're short on time, the Grand Tour is the logical choice, as the difference in price is small. Both tours begin by taking in the rooms occupied by Emperor Franz-Josef and his wife, Sisi. Like their apartments in the Hofburg, the rooms here are characterized by Franz-Josef's plain tastes and unwillingness to change the decor put in by his predecessors. Sisi barely left any evidence of her time here—hardly surprising as the Schönbrunn was the favored home of her mother-in-law, the Archduchess Sophie, whom she avoided like the plague.

After making its way through their apartments, the Grand Tour passes through a series of spectacular staterooms dating from the time of Maria-Theresia. These include the **Hall of Mirrors,** where the six-year-old child prodigy Wolfgang Amadeus Mozart performed for the empress in 1762; the **Blue Chinese Salon,** where the last Habsburg emperor signed away his claim to the empire in 1918; and the **Great Gallery,** whose crowd of golden rococo cherubs once looked down on grand state banquets. Although these are the palace's highlights, even the smallest, most insignificant rooms typically boast a few trompe l'oeil frescoes; stucco cherubs; or large, gilt-framed oil paintings.

EXPERIENCE: Summer at the Schönbrunn

During the Austrian school system's summer vacation (usually the months of July and August) the Schönbrunn opens a special **Kindermuseum** *(Schönbrunn Palace, tel 1/811 13-239, www.kaiserkinder .at, $$)* for children between 4 and 12 years old. At the museum, kids get to dress up in period clothing and learn about the lives of the people who lived and worked at the Schönbrunn, from the empress herself to the lowliest servants. Guided family tours of the museum are available in English by appointment.

One of the main venues for cultural events at the Schönbrunn is the **Palace Theater,** located in the western wing of the main building. Although many 19th-century theaters called themselves palaces, this one is the real thing—the marble isn't artfully disguised wood, and the golden cherubs aren't just plaster cov-

ered with yellow paint. During the academic year, this decadent addition to the palace is used by a local theater school, but during the summer months it hosts a variety of orchestral performances, operas, and theatrical productions. Prominent users of the space include the **Wiener Kammeroper** (Vienna Chamber Opera; *www.kammeroper.at*) and the **Marionettentheater** (Puppet Theater; *www .marionettentheater.at*).

On hot summer days, there are few better places to go than the **Schönbrunner Bad** *(Schlosspark 1, tel 1/817 53 53, www.schoenbrunnerbad.at, $$$),* a large outdoor swimming pool and sports complex on the eastern side of the palace grounds. This attractive and well-maintained complex was built around the royal family's private swimming pool and offers impressive views over the gardens.

The Outbuildings: On either side of the main building there is a cluster of low structures that once housed the palace's army of servants, as well as the kitchens, stables, and other important facilities.

Today the buildings on the western side of the palace (on the right as you enter the complex) are home to the **Wagenburg,** a museum that showcases the absurdly ornate carriages that once conveyed the royal family; and the colorful uniforms that their servants had to wear. The highlight of the collection is undoubtedly the huge carriage used by Empress Maria-Theresia for state events—this gold and carved wood behemoth is about 20 feet (6 m) long and weighs more than 4 tons (3.6 tonnes). On the opposite side of the palace is the Orangery, which was built to keep the palace supplied with fruit and flowers even during the harsh Austrian winter. Today, part of the Orangery is used as a cultural venue (it hosts the Schönbrunn Palace Concert series in the summer, see sidebar p. 194), while the rest has been restored to its original state.

Schönbrunn Gardens

Covering around 160 acres (65 ha) of gently sloping hillside, the gardens of the Schönbrunn Palace have no equal anywhere in Vienna. Within the boundaries of the estate, there is a baroque formal garden, lush woodland, open parkland, a zoo, and a palm house, as well as numerous pavilions, grottoes,

Looking over the formal gardens and the palace from the Schönbrunn's Neptune Fountain

and architectural follies. The line of symmetry that runs through the center of the palace is continued in the gardens, forming a broad central avenue around the Neptune Fountain and then all the way up to the Gloriette (see p. 197).

The lowest section, laid out in the shadow of the palace, is a neatly tended baroque formal garden, similar to that of the Belvedere (see pp. 182–185), but many times the size. The garden is laid out around the central line of symmetry, with additional tree-lined avenues (similar to

Wagenburg

✉ Schönbrunn Palace, Schönbrunner Schlossstrasse 47

☎ (1) 525 24-0

💲 $$

🚇 Schönbrunn (U4) or Hietzing (U4, Strassenbahn lines 10 & 58)

www.khm.at

Tiergarten Schönbrunn

✉ Schönbrunn Palace, Schönbrunner Schlossstrasse 47

☎ (1) 877 92 94 0

💲 $$$

🚇 Hietzing (U4, Strassenbahn lines 10 & 58)

www.zoovienna.at

those found in the Augarten) stretching off to the left and right. It's well worth taking some time to explore these gardens, even if you're not hugely interested in plants, as the designers laid them out around a series of odd decorative features.

INSIDER TIP:

The woods to the north of the Tiergarten are home to a colony of completely fearless red squirrels that will follow you around in the hope that you'll feed them.

—TOM JACKSON
National Geographic contributor

From the central avenue of the gardens, for example, you can see the iron onion dome of the **Taubenhaus** (Dovecote) peeking over the trees on your left. Walk a little farther and you'll find the **Roman Ruins,** which were built in 1778 using bits of the old Schloss Neugebäude (see p. 181); and beyond that the **Obelisk Fountain,** which features marble sculptures of ancient Greek river gods and an Egyptian-style obelisk, which is decorated with meaningless pretend hieroglyphics.

On the right of the central avenue there is a small enclosed area that houses the Irrgarten, Labyrinth, and a children's playground. The Irrgarten is a rough re-creation of the 18th-century maze that once stood on the same plot. It is made from tall yew hedges and overlooked by an observation platform. The Labyrinth is a smaller maze, with low box-hedge walls, suitable for small children.

The Palmenhaus: This impressive iron-and-glass building was constructed in 1882 on the site of an earlier botanical garden. It was one of the last palm houses of its type to be built, long after the initial fashion for such buildings had subsided. It made up for its lateness, however, by being one of the largest, and is definitely among the most handsome buildings of its type in Europe. Inside it is divided into three separate areas, each with its own climate: cool in the northern pavilion, temperate in the center, and tropical at the southern end.

The Tiergarten: Established in the 1750s by Emperor Franz I Stephan, the Tiergarten is one of the world's oldest surviving zoos. At the center of the site stands the original 18th-century animal enclosures (which now house sick or elderly animals that require constant care) and the lovely baroque pavilion (now a café) that was built for the royal family to have lunch in. The Tiergarten is a very well funded and modern institution, where the animals are kept in much more comfortable conditions than in many other city zoos. The star attraction of the zoo is its family of giant pandas:

Yang Yang, Long Hui, and their cub Fu Hu (who was born in August 2010).

The Gloriette & Around:

The upper section of the Schönbrunn gardens is almost entirely covered by woodland. Here you are less likely to encounter crowds of people and more likely to encounter some of the local wildlife. On the wooded slopes directly above the zoo is the curious **Tyrolean Cottage**—an Alpine chalet that was commissioned by an eccentric brother of Archduke Franz II in 1800. He thought it would be good for the royal family to come here and live a simple pastoral lifestyle from time to time (few of his relatives agreed). Today it houses a small restaurant selling stodgy Tyrolean fare.

At the southern end of the great central avenue stands the Gloriette, a massive colonnaded structure that offers commanding views over the Schönbrunn and beyond. Like the Roman Ruins, the Gloriette was constructed mostly from architectural salvage brought up from the Schloss Neugebäude. Visitors who manage to walk all the way up here can either take a break in the café, situated in the central section of the building; or pay two euros to climb up the spiral staircase for an even better view from the roof terrace ■

The iron-framed Palmenhaus at Schönbrunn

Bustling shopping streets, Vienna's biggest outdoor market, an energetic nightlife, and some fine historic churches

Western Vienna

Inside Café Sperl, one of the traditional *kaffeehausers* in Mariahilf

Western Vienna

Stretching from the bright lights of Mariahilfer Strasse to the suburban foothills of the Wienerwald, the city's western flank is a richly diverse urban landscape. The small, densely populated districts of Mariahilf, Neubau, and Josefstadt are havens of relaxed bohemian culture, while the large suburban districts of Ottakring, Währing, and Döbling are dotted with historic sites and architectural landmarks.

Mariahilf

The district of Mariahilf consists of a narrow wedge of the city's *vorstädte* (inner suburbs), bounded to the south by the Wienfluss and to the north by the broad thoroughfare of Mariahilfer Strasse.

Although for much of its length Mariahilf is only around 500 yards (460 m) wide, it contains a surprisingly large number of trendy shopping precincts, cultural institutions, and historic buildings. Most Viennese know Mariahilf as a place to go shopping—whether for fresh produce and ethnic cuisine in the Naschmarkt, or apparel, gadgets, and, well, just about anything else on Mariahilfer Strasse. In between these two streets lie the attractive sur-

roundings of Gumpendorfer Strasse, a wealth of top-notch theaters, and the unique Haus der Meeres—an aquarium in a massive concrete bunker.

Neubau

On the northern side of Mariahilfer Strasse lies the arty Neubau district. Here the major brands and department stores of Mariahilf give way to independent boutiques and funky vintage shops. The heart of the district is the historic Spittelberg neighborhood, a cluster of pedestrianized cobbled streets that were saved from the developers' wrecking ball in the 1980s. In both Spittelberg and the nearby St.-Ulrichs-Platz, you will find a wide range of interesting stores, restaurants, and fascinating old churches.

Josefstadt

Neighboring Josefstadt boasts the distinction of being Vienna's smallest district. It is an area with a genteel middle-class character, renowned for its thriving performing arts scene, cozy cafés, and smart but unpretentious bars. The area doesn't have many landmark attractions—just the Maria Treu Kirche and the rather musty Österreichisches Museum für Volkskunde (Austrian Folklore Museum)—so is usually bypassed by tourists. However, its theaters make it enormously popular with a cultured Viennese crowd.

The Vororte

Out beyond the unenticing Gürtel ring-road and its seedy environs, lie the huge, sprawl-

Area of map detail

a few genuine highlights,
such as the Brunnenmarkt's
small independent restaurants, the
majestic *Jugendstil* architecture of the
far-distant Kirche am Steinhof, and the stern
expressionist architecture of the Karl-Marx-
Hof—one of the most enduring symbols of
Vienna's socialist past. ■

ing districts of the vororte (outer suburbs).
The sights in these areas are rather few
and far between, and probably won't be
on most people's must-see list, but include

Mariahilf

Southwest of Vienna's Innere Stadt, Mariahilf is synonymous in the hearts and minds of most Austrians as the spiritual home of retail therapy on a grand scale. There is much more to the district, however, and it takes on a new, vibrant character at night.

Shopping on Mariahilfer Strasse

Mariahilf
🅜 201
🚇 Gumpendorfer Strasse (U6), Kettenbrücken-gasse (U4), Museums-Quartier (U2), Neubaugasse (U3), or Ziegler-gasse (U3)

Naschmarkt
🅜 201
🚇 Kettenbrücken (U4)

Mariahilf is a tightly packed commercial district southwest of Vienna's center, positioned between Karlsplatz and the trendy residential district of Neubau. At its heart is Vienna's most popular shopping precinct, located in the streets around the Naschmarkt. Mariahilf stands on the site of a village that grew up in the Middle Ages around a small church. Every part of this village was devastated during the 1683 Siege of Vienna, but the peace that followed enabled the area to develop into something larger and more closely connected to the city. The district was on the route used by the

imperial family as they traveled between the Hofburg Palace and their summer residence at Schönbrunn, and so became a fashionable spot for business-men hoping to attract an impe-rial patron.

Today, Mariahilf is packed with neon-lit bars, clubs, cafés, restau-rants, bookshops, and hundreds of clothing stores. It is also home to Vienna's largest gay and lesbian community.

Naschmarkt

A good place to start an inves-tigation of the area is around Kettenbrückengasse U-Bahn Station (on line 4). Just by the

U-Bahn station is the **Schubert Museum,** located in the house where Franz Schubert (see p. 60) died in 1828. A short walk from here is the Naschmarkt, Vienna's biggest and liveliest fresh food market.

The market, which is located between Linke Wienzeile and Rechte Wienzeile, dates back to the 16th century. It was once the place to buy and sell wooden flagons for holding milk. (The flagons were made from the wood of ash trees, hence the original name Aschenmarkt). From 1793, growers and farmers began to bring carts of fruit and vegetables to the Wienzeile, establishing the market you see today. Stalls are piled high with breads, fish, meats, cheeses, unusual spices, and hot food. Numerous small eateries and cafés serve all manner of international cuisines, from Turkish kebabs to Japanese sushi. Simply grab a table in the midst of the stalls and absorb the aromatic atmosphere. Delve into the cluttered side streets to discover more small cafés, curious little plazas, bars, galleries, and specialist stores.

At **Linke Wienzeile 38** and **Linke Wienzeile 40** are two examples of Jugendstil design in domestic architecture. These buildings, which are not open to the public but certainly worth viewing for their superb exteriors, were designed by Otto Wagner and date from 1899. Number 40 is named the **Majolikahaus** for its facade of colorful majolica tiles.

A little way east of here is **Café Drechsler** (*Girardigasse 1, tel 1/581 20 44, www.cafedrechsler*

.at), a great place to stop for a rest. This traditional *kaffeehaus* was established by Engelbert Drechsler in 1919 as a convivial meeting place and was reopened in 2007 to provide fine coffee, hot food, newspapers, and a relaxed atmosphere 23 hours a day.

Theater an der Wien

A little way east of Café Drechsler, along Linke Wienzeile, is Theater an der Wien. Built in 1801, it once had Beethoven (see pp. 59–60) as part-time lodger, and today the building has a memorial room dedicated to the composer's life and work. The theater was

Schubert Museum

- ✉ Kettenbrücken-gasse 6
- ☎ (1) 581 67 30
- ⏰ Closed Fri.–Tues.
- 💲 $
- 🚇 Kettenbrücken-gasse (U4)

Theater an der Wien

- Ⓐ 201
- ✉ Linke Wienzeile 6
- ☎ (1) 588 30-200
- 💲 $$$$$
- 🚇 Kettenbrücken-gasse (U4)

www.theater-wien.at

Night Owls of Mariahilf

In Mariahilf the streets brim with energy when the sun goes down. The district is home to numerous bars and clubs where parties rage until sunrise, though many are hidden away in backstreets and basements. To hot DJ beats, crowds of Mariahilf's trendsetters fill stylish lounge **Bar Italia** (*Mariahilfer Strasse 19–21, tel 1/585 28 38*), where cube-shape furnishings, cream leather, and glowing red mood lights lie tucked behind a well-concealed entrance. Equally well hidden is ultra-arty **Elektro Gönner** (*Mariahilfer Strasse 101, tel 1/208 66 79*), an offbeat place named for an electrical store that once occupied the premises. Popular with an oddball crowd, this Berlin-style bar has retained the look of a retail outlet selling washing machines and TVs. It may take a while to locate the tiny music bar **Luftbad** (*Luftbadgasse 17, tel 0/664 451 36 10, www.luftbad.at*)—but the search is worthwhile. Regular live funk and jazz and a friendly vibe give this place a relaxed, cozy ambience, and there are DJs and groove nights on weekends.

Flohmarkt

- ✉ Rechte Wienziele
- 🕐 Open Sat., 6:30 a.m.–6 p.m.
- 🚇 Kettenbrücken-gasse (U4)

the brainchild of Viennese theatrical impressario Emanuel Schikaneder (1751–1812), who collaborated with Mozart on the opera *The Magic Flute* (1791). Many of Schikaneder's performances were grand-scale spectacles with outlandish props and scenery requiring a large and well-equipped venue. Architect Franz Jager (1780–1839) was commissioned, and the theater was built in Empire style, opening with a lavish performance of the opera *Alexander,* to a standing ovation. Since then, its fortunes have been mixed. It survived the economic collapse that followed the Second World War, thanks to the tenancy of the Vienna State

Opera, whose own building had been destroyed by bombing. Although the Theater an der Wien fell into disrepair in the late 1950s, performances resumed in the 1970s, and since then it has reestablished itself as an energetic, vital part of Vienna's theater scene.

Just north of here is perhaps the most famous of all the old Viennese coffeehouses—**Café Sperl** *(Gumpendorfer Strasse 11, tel 1/586 41 58, www.cafesperl.at),* which has been making its patrons feel at home since 1880. It was said to have been Adolf Hitler's favorite café, but don't let that put you off. It has cherubs on the ceiling, magnficent chandeliers, and an ambience worth savor-

---

EXPERIENCE: Haggling at the Flohmarkt

At the Naschmarkt's western end, far from the stalls selling Indian fabrics, Asian beads, and trashy bejeweled trinkets, Vienna's Flohmarkt, or Flea Market *(Rechte Wienziele, www.flohmarkt .at)* comes into its own each and every Saturday, rain or shine. In Austria's biggest yard sale, one of Europe's best collections of stalls—piled high with an eclectic mix of curios, valuable antiques, clothing, and junk—attract the crowds.

Running along Rechte Wienziele, adjacent to the Naschmarkt, this Saturday institution opens around 6 a.m. and closes near 6 p.m. Flanked by gorgeous Otto Wagner–designed architectural masterpieces, the setting is congested with browsers and rummagers, especially if the sun's shining. Established more than 30 years ago, the Flohmarkt always amazes, intrigues, astounds, and puzzles with its sellers hawking books, clothes,

records, old postcards, ornaments, carpets, broken crockery, single items of footwear, and elderly washing machines. Each vendor is allocated a designated spot; some are occupied by a stand or cart while others simply dump their wares on the ground. Expect to find homemade biscuits and old bicycle pumps next to antique coins and medals from past military campaigns. Take your time and don't be afraid to haggle! Bargaining is part of the fun, so remember always to start at half the amount on the price tag—then be prepared to patiently work your way up.

Once you've stopped trawling the jumble, head on over to the Naschmarkt to grab a bite to eat and a drink at one of the many ethnic cafés, sizzling food stalls, and snack bars. Reach the Flohmarkt via the U1, U2, or U4 metro lines to Kettenbrückengasse.

ing. If you're in this area in the evening, try a very different experience at **Aux Gazelles** *(Rahlgasse 5, tel 1/585 66 45)*, where hookah pipes, floor cushions, and North African music provide a relaxed souk-style ambience.

Haus des Meeres & Around

Take a stroll west along Gumpendorfer Strasse from Café Sperl. Where Schadekgasse branches to the right, you will see the looming mass of one of Vienna's *flaktürme*. Like its counterparts in Landstrasse and Leopoldstadt, this reinforced concrete tower was built in 1944 to bolster the city's antiaircraft defenses. It is one of a pair—the other is located just south of the Spittelberg neighborhood in Neubau (see p. 213)—intended to protect the approach to the city.

In the late 1950s someone realized that these indestructible towers were more than up to the task of containing thousands of gallons of aquarium water. After many years of work, the Esterhazy Park flakturm was converted into the **Haus des Meeres** (House of the Sea), an aquarium and aviary. Today it is one of Vienna's most popular attractions. It houses more than 10,000 aquatic creatures, including sharks, as well as birds and reptiles.

There is something else quirky about the construction: A banner around the top (designed by Lawrence Weiner) proclaims "Smashed to Pieces . . . In the Still of the Night," a memorial against

Fresh fruit and vegetables in Mariahilf's Naschmarkt

war and fascism. It was supposed to be only a temporary message when it was erected in 1991 but is now preserved. There is a small museum of Second World War exhibitions on the tenth floor, while the viewing platform on the level above (complete with telescopes) offers panoramic views of the city. The exterior walls are fitted with anchor rings, handholds, and marked routes that have transformed this gray monolith into an inviting climbing wall.

A very short distance away, on Mariahilfer Strasse, is one of Vienna's classic cafés. **Café Ritter** *(Mariahilfer Strasse 73, tel*
(continued on p. 208)

Haus des Meeres (House of the Sea)

 201

✉ Fritz-Grünbaum-Platz 1

☎ (1) 587 14 17

💲 $$$$

🚇 Neubaugasse (U3)

www.haus-des-meeres.at

A Walk Around Gumpendorfer Strasse

Spend a few hours wandering along Gumpendorfer Strasse and the surrounding streets, where chic shops, hip bars, and retro furniture stores stand side by side with fascinating architecture, old and new. This mishmash neighborhood was once the medieval village of Gumpendorf.

The magnificent frontage of the Majolikahaus

This area is an up-and-coming hot spot for Vienna's young and trendy. Start the morning with a cup of thick and creamy chocolate-sprinkled coffee at historic **Café Sperl** ❶ *(Gumpendorfer Strasse 11, tel 1/586 41 58, closed Sun. in July & Aug., www.cafesperl .at)*, one of the district's oldest cafés and a former social hub for Vienna's intellectuals, arty folk, and literati. One of the city's much loved coffeehouse landmarks, the Sperl (the nearest metro station is MuseumsQuartier) is surrounded by some glorious buildings with ornate stained glass, rococo ornamentation, and iron filigree at every turn. Although renovations in the 1960s ripped out many of the café's original features, the owners have combined this stripped-down

modern look with a love of tradition and all things truly Austrian—to dramatic effect. The people who gather here seem blessed by a spirit that transcends the boundaries of time and trend. The interior mirrors this, with a wreath of ceiling cherubs, brass chandeliers, and antique glass intermingled with contemporary touches.

From the Café Sperl's main door, walk southwest along Gumpendorfer Strasse, admiring the eclectic Ringstrasse-style houses and ornately decorated facades of the apartment buildings that line the street. Look out for the small **brass plaques** on the wall of number 24. These are part of the *Stolpersteine* project, commemorating people who were taken from their homes and murdered by the Nazis.

NOT TO BE MISSED:

Café Sperl • Otto Wagner architecture • Mariahilfer Kirche

At **Köstlergasse ❷**, turn left and walk for about a block past some more ornate 19th-century architecture and cozy family-run eateries. These neighborhood institutions offer daily menus at shoestring prices. At the end of Köstlergasse you will see a string of apartment blocks boasting Jugendstil facades designed by Otto Wagner. You'll find more Wagner splendor around the corner at Linke Wienzeile 40. It is impossible to miss this building, so distinctive is its flower-motif facade, known to architecture students around the world as the **Majolikahaus ❸**. Built in 1898, the exterior is glazed with ornamental weather-resistant tiles of exquisite beauty, complimented by green-painted iron balconies and grilles.

Next to the Majolikahaus, at Linke Wienzeile 38, is the **Medallion Haus.** Along with the Majolikahaus, this was once owned by Otto Wagner. Its Secession-style floral display crafted

from tiles set into its facade was designed by Koloman Moser (1868–1918), creator of the stained-glass windows in the Am Steinhof church (see p. 217). Continue west on Linke Wienzeile and turn right along Eggerthgasse. Pass the 1940s flakturm, which now houses the **Haus des Meeres ❹** (see p. 205). If you are particularly interested in architecture, walk farther west along Gumpendorfer Strasse to see the **Arik Brauer House** (*Gumpendorfer Strasse 134–138*), which was constructed as public housing between 1991 and 1994 and features two large ceramic friezes by Brauer. The building itself was designed by architect Peter Pelikan (b. 1950). Otherwise, turn right when you get to Mariahilfer Strasse to look at the fine two-towered 17th-century church of **Mariahilfer Kirche ❺** (see p. 209), then retrace your footsteps a little way to Neubaugasse U-Bahn Station.

> ▲ See also area map p. 201
> ► Café Sperl
> ⊕ 2–3 hours
> ⬌ 1 mile (1.5 km)
> ► Neubaugasse U-Bahn

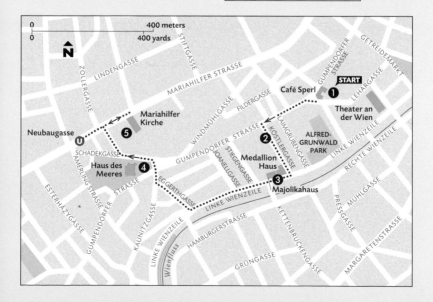

Generali-Center

 201

✉ Mariahilfer
Strasse 77

🚇 Neubaugasse
(U3)

**www.generalicenter
.at**

1/587 82 38, www.caferitter.at)
was established in 1867, though
it didn't move to this location
for another 30 years. It has high,
stuccoed ceilings, marvelous wood
paneling, and 1950s tables and
chairs. Entering the Ritter is like
turning back time. You can read a
newspaper while drinking one of
a bewildering array of coffees and
teas. The salads and soups are also
recommended.

A few blocks to the south
of the Haus des Meeres is the
very beautiful **Fillgraderstiege**
staircase, which links Fillgrader-
gasse and Theobaldgasse. It was
designed by a student of Otto

Wagner and dates from 1907.
There is now an art gallery and
café beneath the staircase: **Das
Fillgrader** (Fillgraderstiege, tel
0/650 850 55 60).

Mariahilfer Strasse

This is Vienna's equivalent of
Fifth Avenue, a buzzing hub
of ringing cash registers and
bag-laden shoppers. The stores
here offer the latest fashion
trends, electronic goods, and
jewelry. This mile-long (1.6 km)
shopping stretch—between
the MuseumsQuartier (see pp.
116–119) at the eastern end
and Westbahnhof U-Bahn Station to the west—boasts chain
stores with big-name brands
sitting side by side independent
retailers selling original Austrian
goods. Dozens of cafés provide
much needed rest stops along
Vienna's longest and most lively
shopping street. Mariahilfer
Strasse continues beyond Westbahnhof, but with fewer shops.

Halfway along this retail
paradise is the smart new
Generali-Center mall with
Levi's, Nike, Swarovski, and other
familiar names. While these may
be the new kids on the block, the
legendary department stores of
the 19th century were **Herzman-
sky** (Mariahilfer Strasse 26–30),
Gerngross (Mariahilfer Strasse
42–48), and **La Stafa** (Mariahilfer
Strasse 120)—and these names live
on in Mariahilf.

In the monthlong run-up to
Christmas, Mariahilfer Strasse
devotes itself to the Advent
season and becomes a garishly
decorated traffic-free zone to

**The climbing wall on the side of the Mariahilf flakturm,
which now houses the Haus des Meeres**

INSIDER TIP:

As you approach the Mariahilfer Kirche, walk slowly and look at the carved angels—they appear to be lowering a crown onto the head of the Virgin Mary.

—CLIVE CARPENTER
National Geographic contributor

accommodate hordes of shoppers in search of gifts, baubles, and cards (see sidebar p. 210).

Mariahilfer Kirche: Tucked away in a quiet corner of busy Mariahilfer Strasse, the twin-towered pilgrim church of Mariahilfer Kirche is often overlooked by passing shoppers hell-bent on maxing out their credit cards. Yet Vienna's 6th district is named for this fine-looking place of worship. It was built between 1686 and 1689 for Barnabite monks, whose religious order was an important ally of the Habsburgs in the counter-reformation. The Mariahilfer Kirche has been continuously maintained—and frequently remodeled and embellished—over the course of the past 325 years, most recently in 2008–2010. A lavish interior, mainly late baroque and rococo in style, contains a copy of a famous painting of the Virgin Mary in Byzantine style from the Basilica in Passau, Bavaria. In the church's left tower is Vienna's second largest bell, the *Schustermichel.* While it can't compare with Stephansdom's *Pummerin* bell (see p. 70), it is still a giant, weighing in at 4.5 tons. Look carefully at the church's facade and you may notice tension cracks in the ancient walls. These were created during the building of the Mariahilfer Strasse U-Bahn (U3). Indeed, the digging of the tunnels so disrupted the church towers that they began to lean toward the road. To rescue the building, city workers implanted robust steel supports in the church's structural framework. Scrutinize the towers closely and you will see that they aren't absolutely perpendicular.

A small Viennese food market is held in front of the church, close to a **memorial to Joseph Haydn** (see pp. 58–59), who lived (and died, in 1809) locally. Financed by a fund-raiser among Haydn's many admirers, the memorial was made by sculptor Henrich Natter (1844–1892) and unveiled in 1887 with a pedestal by Viennese architect Otto Hieser (1850–1892). Distinctive for Haydn's lifelike, amazed expression, the sculpted monument looks down on Mariahilfer Strasse's chaotic hustle and bustle in utter wonderment.

Hofmobiliendepot: A little way farther west along Mariahilfer Strasse, just a couple of minutes' walk from Neubaugasse U-Bahn Station, is one of the most important furniture collections in the world, the

Mariahilfer Kirche

🅰 201

✉ Mariahilfer Strasse 55

☎ (1) 587 87 53

🚇 Neubaugasse (U3)

Hofmobiliendepot

🅰 201

✉ Andreasgasse 7

☎ (1) 524 33 57-0

🕐 Closed Mon.

💲 $$$ or $$$$ (with guide)

🚇 Zieglergasse (U3)

EXPERIENCE: Christmas in Vienna

Vienna's pre-Christmas preparations transform the city into a spellbinding magical wonderland. Carols and harp music fill the air and childlike excitement reigns supreme at the beginning of Advent. Baubles, tinsel, and twinkling fairy-lights engulf every building amid life-size Christmas Nativity scenes, fir trees, and giant holly wreaths.

To meander through Vienna's thrilling festive spectacular is to absorb some of its captivating Yuletide romance. Glitter-frosted fairies and snow-covered elves rub shoulders with Austrian brass bands and tinkling sleigh bells to the mouthwatering aroma of cinnamon-baked apples, chestnuts, and marzipan.

Vienna's centuries-old Christmas tradition dates from the Middle Ages when festive pageantry were a welcome distraction from the long, dark, and, above all, cold winter. Snow-weary villagers found joy in gathering with their neighbors in pre-Christmas celebrations. Today

old-fashioned Christmas cheer characterizes the city's festive markets as traders, artisans, and wood-carvers warm their hands around wood-burning stoves.

Jugs of hot spiced *gluhwein* and *punsch* help keep shoppers warm at Christmas markets across the city. The Adventmarkt in the small square in front of **Mariahilf Kirche** (*Mariahilfer Strasse 55*) is not the biggest of these, but it's a great place to soak up the atmosphere and buy *lebkuchen* (gingerbread), *mandeln* (toasted almonds), decorations, and original gifts. It is open from mid-November to Christmas Eve, between 9

a.m. and 8 p.m. Other Christmas fairs—all open daily from mid-November to Christmas—are held at the crowded **Rathauplatz,** opposite the Burgtheater (*10 a.m.–10 p.m.; www.christkindlmarkt.at);* **Spittelberg** (*2 p.m.–9 p.m.; see pp. 213–214*); **Schönbrunn Castle** (*10 a.m.–9 p.m.; see pp. 192–197*); **Freyung** (*10 a.m.–9 p.m.; see p. 136*); **Maria-Theresien-Platz** (*11 a.m.–10 p.m.; see pp. 114–115*); **Karlskirche** (*noon–9 p.m.; see p. 187*); **Vienna University** (*2 p.m.–10 p.m.; see pp. 145–147*); **Belvedere** (*11a.m.–9 p.m.; see pp. 182–185*); and **Am Hof** (*10 a.m.–9 p.m.; see p. 93*).

An Adventmarkt display near Mariahilfer Strasse

Hofmobiliendepot (Imperial Furniture Collection). This is part repair workshop, part store-room, and part museum. Special exhibitions are displayed on the first floor, imperial interiors are shown on the second, and the emphasis is on the Biedermeier era on the third floor.

Haydn Museum: Within walking distance of Mariahilfer Strasse, south of Zieglergasse U-Bahn Station, is the house in which Joseph Haydn spent his dying days. It is now maintained by the Wien Museum as one of the city's popular *musikerwoh-nungen* (composers' homes). This was Haydn's home for 12 years, and it was here that he created most of his late work, including the great oratorios *The Creation* and *The Seasons.* Haydn's apartment is believed to have been on the upper floor while Johann Elssler, his valet and copyist, occupied the ground floor. Elssler was the father of the celebrated dancer Fanny Elssler (1810–1884). Haydn's fortepiano is on display, as well as his clavichord. There is also a memorial to Johannes Brahms (1833–1897), who was a pas-sionate admirer of Haydn.

Raimund Theater: At the western end of Mariahilf, this theater is named for the Austrian actor and theatrical producer Ferdinand Raimund (1790–1836), who performed at the Theater-in-der-Josefstadt (see p. 215) and the Leop-oldstadter Theater (once an important cultural institution, but demolished in 1847) in the early 19th century. The Raimund Theater forms an important part of the district's small but lively performing arts scene, together with the Theater an der Wien (see p. 203), **TAG** (*Theater an der Gumpendorfer Strasse, Gumpen-dorfer Strasse 67, tel 1/586 52 22, www.dastag.at),* and the **Theater Brett** *(Munzwardeingasse 2, tel 1/587 06 63, www.theaterbrett.at).*

INSIDER TIP:

Look out for the special folding throne in the Hofmobiliende-pot (Imperial Furni-ture Collection)—a travel necessity for an emperor on the move.

—MATTHIAS BRÜCKNER
National Geographic contributor

Originally a trainee baker, Raimund abandoned his apprenticeship to try his hand at acting, eventually landing a role at the Theater an der Wien. As a writer, Raimund was a master of Viennese *posse,* or farce, and his works are frequently performed in Austria today. They include *Der Alpenkönig und der Menschen-feind (The Mountain King and the Misanthrop), Das Mädchen aus der Feenwelt oder Der Bauer als Millionär (The Girl From Fairy Land or the Farmer as Millionaire),* and *Der Ver-schwender (The Dissipate).* Raimund shot himself and died after being bitten by a dog that he mistakenly believed was rabid. ■

Haydn Museum
- 201
- Haydngasse 19
- (1) 596 13 07
- Closed Mon.
- $$
- Zieglergasse (U3)

www.wienmuseum.at

Raimund Theater
- 201
- Wallgasse 18–20
- (1) 588 30-200
- $$$$–$$$$$
- Gumpendorfer Strasse (U6)

www.musicalvienna.at

Neubau, Josefstadt, & the *Vororte*

The two small districts of Neubau and Josefstadt, which were the city's outer suburbs in the 19th century, are now home to some of Vienna's most vibrant and culturally active neighborhoods. Beyond their western borders lie the vororte, or outer suburbs, a set of large residential districts with a friendly atmosphere and a great deal of open space.

The charming streets of Spittelberg evoke an earlier era.

Neubau
201
Museums-Quartier (U2), Neubaugasse (U3), or Volkstheater (U2, U3)

St. Ulrichskirche
St. Ulrichs Platz 3
(1) 523 12 46
Volkstheater (U2, U3)

Neubau

Sandwiched between the districts of Mariahilf to the south and Josefstadt to the north, Neubau was once the center of Vienna's textile industry. Parts of the area once had a dubious reputation, but now it is known for its young, liberal, educated population and large congregation of students. Reflecting this there are dozens of quirky bars, student coffeehouses, and overcrowded Internet cafés.

St. Ulrichs Platz: A good place to start any investigation of the area is St. Ulrichs Platz, just off Burggasse. The centerpiece of the square is **St. Ulrichskirche,** which has a very interesting history. The original church was destroyed in a storm in 1473, the collapsing roof killing the priest and 30 members of his congregation. The rebuilt church was then demolished during the First Siege of Vienna in 1529—and badly damaged again during the Second Siege of Vienna in the late 17th century. Since the most recent incarnation of Ulrichskirche was built in 1721, most changes have involved additions: A second tower was added later in the 18th century.

Around the plaza are narrow streets and alleyways with restaurants, bars, and small shops. For reasonably priced authentic Austrian food, try **Spatzennest** (*St. Ulrichs Platz 1, tel 1/526 16 59, closed Fri. & Sat.*), which is a family-owned restaurant with a loyal local clientele. A neighboring alternative is **Café Morgenstern** (*St. Ulrichs Platz 5, tel 1/522 35 28, www.morgenstern.at*). There's a small gallery

INSIDER TIP:

For an unusual dining experience, try Centimeter in Spittelberg, a quirky restaurant where everything on the menu is priced by its length.

—SALLY MCFALL
National Geographic contributor

at the north end of the square, **Galerie St. Ulrich** *(Neustiftgasse 27, tel 1/522 48 78).*

Spittelberg: Southeast of St. Ulrichs Platz lies the charming historic neighborhood of Spittelberg, which has changed surprisingly little since the late 18th century. The core of this area consists of four parallel pedestrianized streets—Gutenberggasse, Spittelberggasse, Schrankgasse, and Stiftgasse—but the historic atmosphere lingers for a few blocks to the east and west. (See also walk pp. 120–121.)

The area long ago shook off its unsavory reputation for illegal booze dens, brothels, and crime to become an oasis of design stores, photography studios, art and sculpture galleries, and chichi lounge bars. Here, small independent shops sell antiques and handmade items ranging from dolls to silver and leather goods. A **craft market** trades on Saturdays *(and Wed. in July and Aug.).* Restaurant and bar options include **Witwe Bolte** *(Guttenberggasse 13, tel 1/523 14 50, www.witwebolte.at),* with a pleasant beer garden, for Austrian cuisine; and **Plutzer Bräu** *(Schrankgasse 2/Stiftgasse, tel 1/526 12 15, www.plutzerbraeu.at)* for homebrewed beer (including honey ale) and food. In the evenings the **Theater am Spittelberg,** located in a renovated building on Spittelberggasse, offers a varied program of live music, exciting new theater, and art installations.

Strolling in the other direction from St. Ulrichs Platz, a few yards west along Neustiftgasse is **Otto Wagner Wohnung** (Otto Wagner's Apartment), which was designed by Wagner himself in 1912 and features lots of blue tile work and aluminum.

Spittelberg
- 201
- Volkstheater (U2, U3)

Theater am Spittelberg
- 201
- Spittelberggasse 10
- (1) 526 138 5
- Volkstheater (U2, U3)

www.theateram
spittelberg.at

Otto Wagner Wohnung
- 201
- Döblergasse 4
- (1) 523 22 33
- Closed Sat. & Sun.
- Volkstheater (U2, U3)

Centimeter
- Stiftgasse 5
- (1) 470 06 06

www.centimeter.at

Restoring Spittelberg

The regeneration of the historic Spittelberg district, which began in the 1980s, was an important early victory for the conservation movement in Vienna. For most of the 20th century, Spittelberg's attractive Biedermeier buildings had been allowed to fall into a state of terrible disrepair and were barely inhabitable. In 1982 the local authorities gave the go-ahead to a development plan that involved demolishing several of the old buildings.

A loose association of local residents' groups quickly mobilized to prevent this, occupying several buildings scheduled for demolition. Eventually the local authorities relented, and the community was given time to rebuild the neighborhood in a more sympathetic manner. The extraordinary success of this project has had a profound influence on the attitude that the city authorities now take to regeneration projects.

Altlerchenfelder Kirche

- 🔼 201
- ✉ Lerchenfelderstrasse 103–109
- ☎ (1) 523 32 10
- 🚉 Schottenfeldgasse (Strassenbahn line 46) or Volkstheater (U2, U3)

www.pfarre
altlerchenfeld.at

Josefstadt

- 🔼 201
- 🚉 Josefstädter Strasse (U6), Lederergasse (Strassenbahn line 2), or Rathaus (U2)

Maria Treu Kirche

- 🔼 201
- ✉ Piaristengasse 43–45
- ☎ (1) 405 04 25
- ⏱ Open weekday mornings and for services

www.mariatreu.at

Another 10 minutes' walk west takes you to the **Altlerchenfelder Kirche,** located on the border between Neubau and the neighboring district of Josefstadt. Behind its fairly unremarkable brick facade, this church boasts one of the most spectacular interiors in Vienna. It was designed in 1843 by the historicist architect Eduard van der Nüll (1812–1868), who was later responsible for the Staatsoper. Basing his designs on Byzantine and early Christian churches, van der Nüll covered nearly every part of the church's interior with religious frescoes, colorful patterns, and gilded decoration.

Josefstadt

Tucked away behind the most colossal and pompous buildings of the Ringstrasse, the picturesque yet trendy district of Josefstadt often feels like a misplaced section of the Stephansdom Quarter. The relaxed atmosphere and pretty 18th- and

INSIDER TIP:

The Maria Treu Kirche, with its beautiful facade and spectacular interior decoration, is one of Vienna's little-known highlights.

—BEN HOLLINGUM
National Geographic contributor

early 19th-century architecture make this one of Vienna's most sought-after residential districts, popular with arty young professionals and tightly packed colonies of students.

Often, when people talk about Josefstadt they are referring to the historic neighborhood that occupies the maze of streets directly behind the Rathaus. The main focal point of this area is the **Maria Treu Kirche,** a twin-towered baroque church designed by Johann Lukas von Hildebrandt

Theater in Josefstadt

To the Viennese, Josefstadt is, first and foremost, a theater district—home to numerous mostly low-budget theater companies and cabaret venues.

The cornerstone of this theater district is the Theater-in-der-Josefstadt, a grand Viennese institution that has existed, in various incarnations, since 1788. The theater's current home is an attractive Biedermeier building designed in 1822 by Josef Kornhäsl (architect of the Stadttempel in the Jewish Quarter; see pp. 83–84).

For those who do not speak fluent German, there is Vienna's English Theatre, which stages high-quality English-language productions. The theater was founded in the 1960s by an Austrian director who planned for it to be a summer enterprise for tourists. He soon realized, however, that the English-speaking community in an international city like Vienna is easily large enough to sustain an English-language theater year-round. In addition to importing productions from London and New York, the theater often stages original material by respected playwrights and attracts internationally known actors.

in 1716. Because of various financial setbacks, however, the church took several generations to complete—the right-hand tower wasn't added until the 1850s. The gently curved facade of the church overlooks a small square framed on either side by the buildings of the Piarist monastery attached to the church.

They let you try on the hats, so if you've ever wondered what you'd look like wearing a 19th-century Austrian cavalry helmet or an enormous and frilly ladies' hat, this is the place to go.

A few hundred yards' walk north, on the far side of the attractive little Schönborn Park, stands the Palais Schönborn—yet

Österreichisches Museum für Volkskunde

🅰 201
✉ Laudongasse 15–19
☎ (1) 406 89 05
🕐 Closed Mon.
$ $$
www.volkskunde museum.at

Dining alfresco at a Spittelberg restaurant

The northern wing of the old monastery is home to the **Piaristenkeller** (*Piaristengasse 45, tel 1/406 0193, www.piaristenkeller .com, closed Sun.*), a rather kitsch traditional restaurant with two slightly eccentric on-site museums. The first of these is devoted to the imperial wine collection—pretty boring for those who prefer drinking wine to looking at the bottles—while the other museum houses all manner of headgear from the days of imperial Vienna.

another Johann Lukas von Hildebrandt design. Today this small building (well, small for a palace) is home to the **Österreichisches Museum für Volkskunde** (Austrian Folklore Museum). The museum celebrates all things humble, rustic, and handmade—an unusual preoccupation in this gilded baroque city.

The Vororte

On the far side of Vienna's outer ring road (see sidebar

Theater-in-der-Josefstadt

🅰 201
✉ Josefstädter Strasse 26
☎ (1) 427 00
www.josefstadt.org

Vienna's English Theatre

🅰 201
✉ Josefsgasse 12
☎ (1) 402 12 60-21
www.englishtheatre .at

Ottakringer Brauerei

 Ottakinger-strasse 95

☎ (1) 491 00-2344

🕒 Closed Fri.–Sun.

💲 $$$

🚇 Johann-Nepomuk-Berger-Platz (Strassenbahn lines 2, 9, & 44)

www.ottakringer.at

Kirche am Steinhof

✉ Baumgartner Höhe 1

☎ (1) 910 60-11007

🕒 Open 3 p.m.–5 p.m. Sat.

🚌 Bus 48a runs to the gates of the complex from Ottakring (U3).

💲 $$

p. 217) lie the so-called vororte (outer suburbs), a group of pleasant residential neighborhoods that contain a few notable attractions.

Ottakring: The largest and busiest of these outer districts is Ottakring, a traditionally working-class area to the west of Josefstadt. For many Viennese the area's main attraction is the **Brunnenmarkt,** a huge open-air market that rivals the better known Naschmarkt in terms of size and variety. The market runs for half a mile (0.8 km) along Brunnengasse from Thaliastrasse to Yppenplatz, where it spreads out into a broad square. On weekends the area is home to a farmers market, where you can get fresh produce, wonderful meats, and cheeses bigger than your head.

At the northern end of the market, Yppenplatz is one of the city's little known gastronomic highlights. Like the Karmelitermarkt in Leopoldstadt (see p. 158) the small and inexpensive properties on and around the square are popular with independent delicatessens, cafés, and trendy new restaurants. Notable residents include the **Café C.I.** (Payergasse 14, tel 1/403 18 27), **An-Do** (Yppenplatz 11-15, tel 1/308 75 75), and the famous **Staud's** (Hubergasse 3, tel 1/406 88 05-0, www.stauds.com)—a small family run store that sells hundreds of different homemade preserves, chutneys, and sauces.

Farther out, the large **Ottakringer Brauerei** provides Vienna with its most popular beer, Ottakringer Helles. There are guided tours around the brewery during the week, and there is

Karl-Marx-Hof, a survivor of the 1930s housing program, contains nearly 1,400 apartments.

a brewery shop that sells the company's more unusual varieties of beer.

About a mile (1.6 km) beyond Ottakring's western border, in the suburban district of Penzing, stands what is arguably Otto Wagner's greatest work, the **Kirche am Steinhof.** This beautiful Jugendstil church, made with Wagner's signature combination of copper and marble, was built in 1907 as part of the Steinhof Mental Hospital. For this project, Wagner was clearly influenced by Johann Fischer von Erlach's Karlskirche (see p. 187), although the details of his design are pure art nouveau. The church was extensively renovated in 2005, a project that included re-covering the copper dome with 5 pounds (2.2 kg) of gold leaf. The church interior is equally stunning—with mosaics and stained-glass windows designed by fellow Secession artist Koloman Moser.

Währing & Dobling: Visitor attractions are rather thin on the ground in western Vienna's northernmost districts, where monumental social housing projects loom over the genteel homes of the city's doctors, diplomats, and lawyers.

The best known landmark in the area is the **Karl-Marx-Hof,** the most ambitious of the city's 1930s *gemeindebauten* (housing projects). As the name would suggest, this project was funded by the Social Democratic Workers' Party as a "workers' palace." The showpiece central block of the complex, with its plain modern-

The Gürtel

Running along the western side of the vorstädte districts is Vienna's outer ring road, the Gürtel. Like the Ringstrasse farther in, the Gürtel was built over part of the city's demolished defenses. It runs along what was until 1892 the official outer limit of Vienna. In the 1950s and 1960s, when cars became a common sight in Vienna, the Gürtel was widened and made into the noisy and dirty highway you see today. The area around it has something of a seedy reputation, with red-light districts and abandoned buildings. It is prevented from improving itself because every ten years or so the Viennese government toys with the idea of demolishing the buildings on either side and making the Gürtel into an eight- or ten-lane freeway—which promptly crashes property values in the area.

ist facade supported on broad concrete archways, rises over Heligenstadt U-Bahn Station. During Austria's extremely brief 1934 civil war (see p. 33), the Karl-Marx-Hof was one of the last pockets of socialist resistance to fall to the forces of the fascist government. During the fighting the fortress-like building was badly damaged by government artillery.

The most notable sight in neighboring Währing is the **Geymüller Schlössel,** a Biedermeier villa on the western edge of the district. This attractive early 19th-century building is today home to an annex of the MAK (see p. 78), where a selection of historic furnishings from the museum's collection is on display in the villa's restored period interiors. ∎

Karl-Marx-Hof
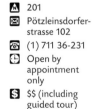
🅰 201

🚇 Heligenstadt U-Bahn (U4)

Geymüller Schlössel

🅰 201

✉ Pötzleinsdorfer-strasse 102

☎ (1) 711 36-231

🕐 Open by appointment only

💲 $$ (including guided tour)

www.mak.at

NOTE: To reach Geymüller Schlössel, take Strassenbahn line 41 from Währinger-strasse-Volksoper (U6) and then either walk (10 mins.) or catch bus 41A up the hill from Pötzleinsdorf.

The blue Donau meandering through forested hills, past spas, monasteries, and wineries galore

Day Trips

The Steiner Tor, a medieval gatehouse in the town of Krems, 55 miles (89 km) northwest of Vienna

Day Trips From Vienna

The name given to the northeast of Austria, encircling Vienna, is Niederösterreich (Lower Austria), and it has plenty to excite the traveler. Within 50 miles (80 km) of the city center are rolling hills, clothed in forest and hiding towns with histories stretching back to medieval times. There are also fine spas, and many wineries, castles, and monasteries. And, of course, there is the mighty Donau (Danube) River.

A Little History

The history of the region is long and turbulent, not least because of its strategic importance, straddling the Donau. Carnuntum was founded as a military base on the river's south bank in the first century B.C. It grew to be one of the most important metropolises in the northern Roman Empire, with a population of more than 50,000. So important was the city that it became the capital of the province of Upper Pannonia and hosted the Emperors' Conference of A.D. 308. However, with the demise of the empire, Carnuntum

faded into obscurity. During the 15th century there was constant unrest in the region around Vienna as different factions of the Habsburgs squabbled over succession rights. The first Ottoman siege of Vienna in 1529 marked a new threat, reminders of which exist to this day—for example, in fortified churches such as at Weissenkirchen (see p. 233). Just over a century later the Swedish invaded the region in 1645; the battered ruins of Dürnstein Castle (see p. 236) bear witness to that military campaign. In 1809 Napoleon's Donau (Danube) Campaign suffered a major setback at the Battle of Aspern (see sidebar p. 223). Those with an interest in battlefields can walk the Napoleon Trail and see for themselves where the emperor's mighty army suffered the loss of more than 20,000 men. More than a century later parts of Lower Austria were once again a theater of war as Soviet troops of the Red Army advanced across the Vienna Basin in April 1945 to surround and eventually liberate the city from German Nazi forces.

From River to Forest

East of Vienna the Donau Valley is broad and gentle, with the forested Donau-Auen National Park (see pp. 222–224) tracking the river's every bend downstream to the border with Slovakia. If you have the time, a river cruise from Vienna to the national park, or on to Hainburg, is thoroughly recommended. Otherwise, the area is well connected by public transport. South of the river are the vineyards and agricultural country of the Carnuntum district. Here you

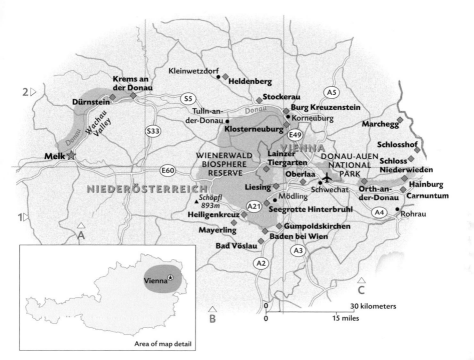

will find a fine archaeological museum and the excavated remains of the former Roman city. Nearby are Haydn's birthplace in the charming town of Rohrau and the medieval walls of Hainburg.

The border with Slovakia is just 30 miles (48 km) from the heart of Vienna, and it is worth visiting some of the towns along the border—places such as Marchegg with its 18th-century castle, its amazing colony of storks, and its bird-rich nature reserve.

The fertile Vienna Basin sweeps around the south of the city before butting up against the wooded hills and spa country of the Baden bei Wien and Heiligenkreuz districts. For those wishing to get the full relaxation experience, this is thermal spring country—and Oberlaa and Baden both have highly recommended spas (see pp. 227 and 229). Several towns in this area are within an hour's travel time from Vienna by bus, tram, or train. The beautiful

Wienerwald (Vienna Woods) are also nearby. Beloved of composers from Beethoven to Strauss, and probably at their most dramatic in fall, this belt of forest loops around the west of the city, offering innumerable opportunities for walking, cycling, and nature-watching.

As the forest continues north it eventually reaches the Donau Valley again, but this time it is a narrower, steeper-sided, and more dramatic affair. This is a region of scenic hilltop castles such as that at Dürnstein, magnificent monasteries such as the one at Melk, and pretty riverside towns that can be reached easily by train and bus. Again, if you have the time, take a cruise along a section of the river or—if you feel a little more energetic—hire a bike and cycle one of the trails running alongside the Donau. There is so much to see and do within easy reach of Vienna that you should plan your itinerary carefully—or you could forget about an itinerary and just see where you end up! ■

East of Vienna

Although much of the countryside between Vienna and the border of Slovakia is flat and uninteresting, for those with a fascination for nature, castles, battlefields, or wine it is worth investigating the area.

An entrance to the magnificent Schlosshof palace, north of Hainburg

Donau-Auen National Park

- ⛰ 221 C1–2
- ✉ Schloss Orth National Park Center, Orth-an-der-Donau
- ☎ (2) 2212 35 55
- 🕐 Closed Dec.– mid-March

www.donauauen.at

East of Vienna, the Donau winds its way through a broad, fertile floodplain that has been inhabited since Roman times (see pp. 224–225). In the past this strategically important area has been fiercely contested, hence its historically important battlefields and numerous fortifications. These include the Roman garrison town of Carnuntum and the Renaissance castle of Schloss Orth. Today much of the area is occupied by a large national park, the Donau-Auen, which covers both sides of the river between Vienna and the Slovakian border.

Donau-Auen National Park

Known locally as the Lobau, or "water wood," the national park stretches along the Donau floodplain (mainly on the north bank of the river) from the edge of Vienna to the Slovakian border 38 miles (60 km) to the east.

Orth-an-der-Donau: The best way to reach the Lobau from Vienna is to take the **National Park Boat** *(departs 9 a.m. from Franz-Josefs-Kai, tel 1/4000 49-495, operates May–Oct., reservations required)* that runs from the city center to

INSIDER TIP:

At Schloss Orth (castle), don't miss the underwater observation station of Donau fauna on Schlossinsel (Castle Island).

—CHRISTIAN BAZANT
National Geographic contributor

the picturesque town of Orth-an-der-Donau. Since 2005 the national park's visitors' center has been housed in **Schloss Orth,** the town's Renaissance castle. Here you'll find a fascinating overview of the flora and fauna of the Donau floodplain, as well as practical information about exploring the national park. In addition to the park's headquarters, Schloss Orth has

an interesting museum that traces the history of the castle and the surrounding town.

Down by the riverside south of Orth, close to where the ferries dock, stands the **Schiffmühle** (Boat Mill), a modern reconstruction of a traditional Donau water mill. This unique floating mill is an example of a design once common throughout this region. Water levels on the Donau used to vary dramatically from season to season, meaning that water mills made from bricks and mortar couldn't work. To solve this problem, local craftsmen built their water mills on barges moored to the shore. The Schiffmühle near Orth-an-der-Donau was built by a group of local enthusiasts and first opened in 2008. Sadly it was in operation for less than a year before it was struck by a piece of

Schloss Orth
✉ Orth-an-der-Donau
☎ (2) 2212 35 55
🕐 Closed Dec.–mid-March
www.orth.at

Schiffmühle
✉ Fadenbachstrasse 6, Orth-an-der-Donau
☎ (0) 664 334 14 22
🕐 Closed Nov.–March
💲 $$$ (boat tours)
www.schiffmuehle.at

Napoleon's Donau Campaign

Just outside the boundaries of the Donau-Auen National Park is the place where French Emperor Napoleon Bonaparte suffered his first major defeat, at the hands of a Habsburg army in the Battle of Aspern.

After taking Vienna in spring 1809, Napoleon was determined to prevent the two Habsburg armies of Archduke Charles and Archduke John from combining their forces. He chose to attack the former, which was close but on the opposite (north) side of the Donau. After much deliberation, he crossed the Donau from Kaiser Ebersdorf to Lobau island and then to the north bank using rafts and pontoons. Once Napoleon had established a bridgehead, engagements took place between French and Austrian

forces around the villages of Aspern and Essling on May 21–22. A combination of fireships and logs sent downriver by the Austrians—and the turbulent floodwaters of the river itself—repeatedly damaged Napoleon's makeshift bridge, starving him of reinforcements of supplies and men. Archduke Charles's numerically superior forces were able to hold their ground, and Napoleon had to retreat south of the Donau.

The defeat was to be temporary, however. Later in the summer the French emperor crossed the river in the same place, but this time using a more secure bridge. On July 3 he engaged the Austrian forces a few miles north, at Wagram. The French were victorious in a battle that involved more than 300,000 soldiers.

Hainburg
⚑ 221 C1

Carnuntum Archaeological Park
⚑ 221 C1
✉ Hauptstrasse 1, Petronell-Carnuntum
☎ (0) 2163 33 77-99
$ $$$ (includes Museum Carnuntum)
www.carnuntum.co.at

floating debris and sank. It was salvaged, however, and is being slowly brought back to working condition by a dedicated team of volunteers. The owners also operate cruises on the Donau in a traditional wooden riverboat.

Exploring the Lobau: The Donau-Auen National Park has plenty of walking and cycling trails to explore, and mountain bike runs for the more adventurous. Some areas are suitable for swimming, and a campsite offers

A swallowtail butterfly in Donau–Auen National Park

visitors a chance to spend a few nights under canvas.

One of the best hiking trails in the area is the history-rich 7-mile (11 km) **Napoleon Rundwanderweg** (Napoleon Loop), just south of Grossenzersdorf, which

runs past Napoleon's headquarters during his campaign of 1809 (see sidebar, p. 223). The Forstverwaltung Lobau *(Lobau Forestry Service, tel 0/2249 23 53)* provides a leaflet detailing the route and key features of the trail, such as the French powder magazine; the point at which Napoleon's troops crossed the river; and the **Lion of Aspern** sculpture, built to commemorate the Allies' first major victory over Napoleon at the Battle of Aspern.

To travel farther, hop aboard the *Admiral Tegetthoff* on the first Sunday of the month *(DDSG Blue Danube, tel 1/588 80, www.ddsg-blue-danube.at, $$$$$)* from May to September. The boat leaves central Vienna *(Handelskai 265, Schifffahrtszentrum)*. This service takes you as far as the town of **Hainburg,** which faces the eastern end of the park, south of the river. Fragments of Hainburg's medieval walls survive, including the **Ungartor tower** (dating from around 1230) and the **Fischertor,** scene of a massacre during the Ottoman invasion of 1683. In **Hauptplatz** there is a fountain dedicated to the composer Franz Josef Haydn (see p. 59).

Carnuntum & Rohrau

Just to the south of Hainburg are the ruins of the Roman city of Carnuntum, where the Emperor Vespasian built a walled settlement and river port between A.D. 69–79. This was once the capital of the Roman province of Upper Pannonia. The **Carnuntum Archaeological Park** has reconstructed

INSIDER TIP:

At Carnuntum, don't worry if you don't understand German: There are plenty of signs and descriptions in English.

—SONJA WEGENSTEIN
National Geographic contributor

buildings and open excavations, and offers guided tours. The most important surviving structure in the town is the **amphitheater,** which once held 15,000 spectators. Other important buildings include the **House of Lucius,** which has been reconstructed; and the **Heidentor gate,** built as a triumphal monument for Emperor Constantius II.

A few miles south is the old town of **Rohrau,** a small place with more than its fair share of attractions. It is dominated by **Schloss Rohrau,** a 16th-century baroque palace that today houses an interesting private art collection. Nearby is the small thatched cottage that was **Haydn's Birthplace** in 1732.

Schlosshof & Marchegg

If you travel north from Hainburg you enter the flat, featureless agricultural plain of Marchfeld—featureless, that is, except for its fine old buildings. **Schloss Niederweiden,** 7 miles (11 km) from Hainburg, was designed by baroque architect Johann Fischer von Erlach (see p. 50) in the last years of the 17th century. Former owners include Prince Eugene of Savoy and Empress Maria-Theresia. Its gardens and Schloss Patisserie—for delicious pastries—are open daily.

Even more impressive is **Schlosshof,** 2.5 miles (4 km) to the northeast. It was built as a home and hunting lodge for Prince Eugene in the 1720s. This fine baroque palace, with gardens on seven descending terraces, was designed by architect Johann Lukas von Hildebrandt and loved by Empress Maria-Theresia. It fell into disrepair after the fall of the Austro-Hungarian Empire in 1918, but has been restored superbly. The nearby **Zum Weissen Pfau** (*The White Peacock, Meierhof Manor Farm, Schlosshof, tel 0/2285 20-000 to book*) serves Austrian and Slovakian culinary classics.

Continue north for 5 miles (8 km) to the March River, which separates this part of Austria from Slovakia, and you will reach the village of **Marchegg.** It is only an hour's drive from Vienna if you travel directly, and there is also a rail link with the city, although the station is 1 mile (1.6 km) south of the village. **Schloss Marchegg** has an interesting, small museum, although not one for the squeamish: the **Jagdmuseum** (Hunting Museum), with stuffed animals and antique hunting weaponry. One of Europe's largest stork colonies sits in trees near the schloss, and from there trails lead into the World Wide Fund for Nature's reserve of **Marchauen-Marchegg** (*www.marchegg.at*), which has many breeding birds. ∎

Schloss Rohrau

- ▲ 221 C1
- ✉ Rohrau
- ☎ (0) 2164 22 53
- 🕐 Closed Mon. & winter months
- 💲 $$$

www.schloss-rohrau
.at

Haydn's Birthplace

- ▲ 221 C1
- ✉ Obere Hauptstrasse 25, Rohrau
- ☎ (0) 2164 22 68
- 🕐 Closed Mon.
- 💲 $$

www.haydngeburts
haus.at

Schloss Niederweiden

- ▲ 221 C2
- ✉ Niederweiden
- ☎ (0) 2285 20-000
- 🕐 Closed Nov.– early April

Schlosshof Palace

- ▲ 221 C2
- ✉ Schlosshof
- ☎ (0) 2285 20-000
- 🕐 Closed Nov.–early April
- 💲 $$$$

www.schlosshof
.at/cms-en

Jagdmuseum

- ▲ 221 C2
- ✉ Schloss Marchegg-Jagdmuseum
- ☎ (0) 2285 71 00-11
- 🕐 Closed Mon. & winter months
- 💲 $

South of Vienna

Less than an hour south of the city are small historic towns, nestled in the folds of the hills; the beautiful, forested Wienerwald Biosphere Reserve, an important wine-growing area; and a variety of thermal spas. Any of these places can be visited on a day trip from Vienna. Alternatively, the towns of Baden bei Wien or Mödling can be used for overnight stays.

Overlooking the Donau River and Vienna from a terrace café inside the Wienerwald

Baden bei Wien

 221 B1

Visitor Information

✉ Brusattiplatz 3, Baden bei Wien

☎ (0) 2252 22 600

www.badenonline .at/en

Beethovenhaus (Haus der Neunten)

✉ Rathausgasse 10, Baden bei Wien

☎ (0) 2252 86 800

🕐 Closed Mon.

💲 $$

Although it is just 16 miles (26 km) southwest of downtown Vienna, the small town of Baden bei Wien couldn't feel farther from the city. It sits on the edge of the Wienerwald and makes a good base for exploring the surrounding districts. Baden is easily reached by car, bus, or train and has enough attractions to keep visitors interested for a generous half day.

Baden & Around

Start in the main square, **Hauptplatz,** where the **Rathaus**

(dating from 1815) still functions as a seat of local administration. In the square is the striking **Holy Trinity Column,** which was designed by the sculptor Giuseppe Stanetti and erected in 1714 to commemorate deliverance from a plague. The **Kaiserhaus** (*Hauptplatz 17*) is another Hauptplatz landmark, a grand building where Emperor Franz I vacationed, but it is not open to the public. Leaving the square, stroll along Rathausgasse to **Beethovenhaus** (or Haus der Neunten, House of the Ninth), a mustard-colored building that Beethoven visited several times between 1821 and 1823 and where he composed his seminal Ninth Symphony. The building's small museum, **Beethoven Schäuraume,** is open to the public. Just north of the town center is **Kurpark,** a tree- and flower-filled open space laid out to honor Empress Maria-Theresia in 1792. It now hosts summer concerts at the music pavilion and operettas in the glass-roofed **Sommerarena.**

INSIDER TIP:

Visit Baden's Doblhoff Park in the summer, when 20,000 roses of 600 varieties bloom.

—KRISTIAN DAVIDEK
National Geographic contributor

People have been bathing in the town's thermal springs since Roman times, when it was known as Thermae Pannonicae. The largest of the 14 springs supplies therapeutic sulfurous water to the **Römertherme Thermal Baths** *(Brusattiplatz 4, Baden, tel 0/2252 45030, www.roemertherme.at, $$$$)* and the **Badener Hof Hotel** *(Pelzgasse 30, Baden, tel 0/2252 48580, www.badenerhof.at, $$$$$).*

Another nearby spa town is **Bad Vöslau,** just south of Baden (and 22 miles/35 km south of Vienna). Though the town's first public baths opened in 1822, the spa complex that stands in the town today, the **Thermalbad Bad**

Vöslau *(Maital 2, Bad Vöslau, tel 0/2252 76266, www.thermalbad -voeslau.at, $$–$$$$),* dates from 1926. This establishment boasts pristine modern facilities, including a very good restaurant and bar, alongside stunning art nouveau fountains and pools that look like sets for a 1930s Hollywood musical. Therapists also offer an array of massage treatments as well as wraps and facials.

If traveling to Baden by car, take the A2 south from Vienna and leave at the Baden exit. There are plenty of public transport options: the Badner Bahn tram leaves from the Opernring, opposite the Vienna Opera (see p. 127), and arrives an hour later in central Baden. Faster trains leave Vienna's Südbahnhof Station but passengers have to disembark a little way to the east of Baden center, adding to the 25-minute rail journey. The bus journey from Vienna takes around 40 minutes.

Nearby there are hiking and biking trails in the **Wienerwald Biosphere Reserve,** and the charming baroque town of **Heiligenkreuz,** just a few miles to the west. This town grew up around **Stift Heiligenkreuz** (Abbey of the Holy Cross), a huge medieval monastery. The original abbey was destroyed during the Ottoman invasion of 1683, hence the 18th-century baroque architecture of the structure that stands today. The abbey is still home to a small community of Cistercian monks.

Three miles (5 km) to the west of Heiligenkreuz is a Carmelite convent, **Karmeliten Kloster Mayerling,** where nuns give

Wienerwald Biosphere Reserve

🅐 221 B1

Visitor Information

✉ Wienerwald Tourist Office, Hauptplatz 11, Purkersdorf

☎ (0) 2231 62 17-6

🕐 Closed Sat. & Sun.

www.wienerwald .info/default.asp

Heiligenkreuz

🅐 221 B1

Stift Heiligenkreuz

✉ Heiligenkreuz im Wienerwald

☎ (0) 2250 07 03

🕐 Prebooked tour groups only

💲 $$

www.stift-heiligenkreuz.org

Karmeliten Kloster Mayerling

✉ Mayerling

☎ (0) 2258 22 75

💲 $

Gumpolds-kirchen

◭ 221 B1

Gumpolds-kirchen Rathaus

✉ Wienerstrasse, Gumpolds-kirchen

☎ (0) 2252 86800

🕐 Closed Mon.

Seegrotte Hinterbrühl

✉ Grutschgasse 2A, Hinterbrühl

☎ (0) 2235 26364

💲 $$$$

guided tours. The convent is on the site of a hunting lodge where Archduke Rudolf, the heir to the Habsburg crown, and his mistress Baroness Mary Vetsera both committed suicide in 1889.

The attractive old town of **Gumpoldskirchen** is a few miles north of Baden and is linked to the latter and Vienna by rail. This area was the scene of bitter fighting between German and Soviet forces at the end of the Second World War, but is now better known as a wine-growing area. There is a **Wine Museum**

Rathaus was built in 1559 and once housed a courthouse, whose old prison cells can still be seen.

A few miles north of Gumpoldskirchen is Europe's largest underground lake, **Seegrotte Hinterbrühl.** This former gypsum mine flooded after work there ceased, and visitors can now tour parts of the subterranean workings in a motorboat.

Liesing

This town offers the best of both worlds: It is less than an hour by S-Bahn train from the center of Vienna and forms the city's 23rd district, but it is also close to some beautiful countryside. Liesing is not the most attractive of towns but in its favor are the beautifully rugged **Kalksteinwienerwald** (Northern Chalk Alps) and the Wienerwald (Vienna Woods), both close by and worth a visit.

Liesing's **Schloss Rodaun Palace** is not open to the public. Not far away, in Mauer, on the edge of the Wienerwald, is a building of real architectural note: the highly individual and unusual **Wotrubakirche.** This modern church sits in a magnificent setting atop a hill with trees all around. Created on a vast scale from rectangular gray stone slabs, this abstract, sculptural building is the work of Fritz Wotruba (1907–1975), an Austrian artist of Czech-Hungarian descent (see sidebar this page). The church opened to the public in 1976, a year after Wotruba was buried in the Zentralfriedhof (see p. 180).

Fritz Wotruba

Fritz Wotruba was one of the greatest sculptors of the 20th century. Born and educated in Vienna, he trained as an engraver before studying sculpture at the Vienna School for Decorative and Applied Arts in the 1920s. He went into self-imposed exile in Switzerland during the Second World War but returned in 1945. Much of Wotruba's work can be seen in public spaces in Vienna, including "Men, Condemn War" (1932) to commemorate those who died in the First World War, which stands in the Belvedere (see pp. 183–185); and "Large Standing Figure" (1962), at Friedrich-Schmidt-Platz 6. His best known work, however, is the Wotrubakirche in Liesing, which he was working on when he died in 1975.

Liesing

◭ 221 B1

Wotrubakirche

✉ Georgsgasse, Mauer

☎ (1) 881 61 85

(Bergerhaus, Schrannenplatz 5, tel 0/2252 63536, closed Nov.–March) and you can sometimes catch a wine-tasting in the **Hotel Winzer-hotel Vohringer** (Wienerstrasse 26, tel 0/2252 607400, www.winzer hotel.at). A **Wine Festival** is held in the town every August. The Renaissance building housing the

Oberlaa

A few miles away, about 10 minutes east of central Liesing, the Oberlaa area on Vienna's southeastern outskirts is a popular destination for visitors keen to enjoy an excursion involving gardens, parks, spas, and wineries. Armed with picnic blankets and hampers in summer, Viennese families descend on **Kurpark Oberlaa,** where enchanting floral displays in a million bright hues surround sunbathing lawns scattered with deck chairs. A petting zoo for children and a skateboard park for teens keep younger visitors entertained while half a dozen themed gardens—including an aromatic floral labyrinth; a film city; and a romantic, velvet-petal garden of love—invite exploration. Created by the Vienna International Garden Show in 1974, this beautiful green area adjoining the Oberlaa health resort is navigable via undulating, meandering paths and trails.

Close by are some of outer Vienna's famed *heurigen* (wine taverns). Just south of Kurpark Oberlaa, **Buschenschank Manhardt** and **Winzerhof Franz Wiesenthaler** tempt wine connoisseurs, the thirsty, and the curious. Look out for signs by the roadside for these and other taverns. Most serve accompanying plates of Austrian fares at outside wooden tables to complement carafes of fresh, young, home-produced wine.

Only half an hour by U-Bahn and streetcar from the city center, Oberlaa's own "liquid gold" isn't reserves of oil but thermo-mineral spring water. **Therme Oberlaa** *(Kurbadstrasse 14, tel 1/680 09 96-00, www.oberlaa.at)* may not be Austria's swankiest spa, but heavy investment has ensured this health resort boasts plenty of stylish touches. Two indoor and two outdoor thermal baths each have jet showers, a fizzing pool, a large swimming bath, and a huge sauna complex. Visit in winter and swim outside in steaming thermal waters amid a blanket of new snow while lights illuminate the surrounding trees. Oberlaa's healing springs spout sulfurous mineral water at 129°F (54°C). There is also a new hotel and health care center. ■

Kurpark Oberlaa

🅰 221 C1

✉ Between Kurbadstrasse, Filmteichstrasse, & Laaer-Berg-Strasse, Oberlaa

☎ (1) 4000 80 42

Buschenschank Manhardt

✉ Liesingbach-strasse 51

☎ (1) 688 69 67

www.manhardt.co.at

Winzerhof Franz Wiesenthaler

✉ Oberlaaerstrasse 71

☎ (1) 688 47 16

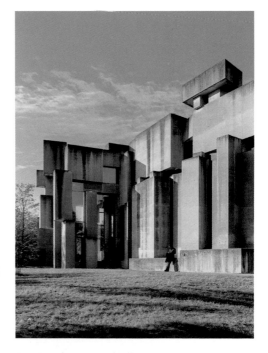

Fritz Wotruba's unique church design in Liesing

West & North of Vienna

West and north of Vienna, the Wienerwald forms an important part of the capital's arc-shaped green belt. Gentle hills, rocky gorges, deep forests, grassy meadows, and sheltered floodplains draw thousands of Viennese urbanites on weekends—keen to breathe in pure, fresh air and take in the spellbinding views. Farther north is one of the most beautiful sections of the Donau Valley, with monasteries, vineyards, and castles.

A vineyard in the Wachau Valley, northwest of Vienna

Lainzer Tiergarten
🅰 221 B1

Wien Museum Hermesvilla
✉ Lainzer Tiergarten
☎ (1) 804 1324
🕐 Closed Mon. & Nov.–early April
💲 $$
🚌 Lainzer Tor (60B)

www.wienmuseum.at

Wienerwald Tourism
www.wienerwald.info

Rising up from the Donau floodplain to the west of the city, the forested peaks of the Wienerwald are as important a part of the Vienna skyline as the Donauturm or the spire of St. Stephen's. For more than a thousand years the Wienerwald has been protected from urban development and intensive forestry, making it a rich and unspoiled landscape positioned uniquely close to a major city.

Beginning in the early Middle Ages, the Wienerwald was used as a royal hunting ground, which kept it safe from development. In 1512 the rules that protected the forest were made into law, with severe punishments for those found felling trees in the area. Many trees were cut down during the rebuilding of Vienna after the Ottoman sieges (see pp. 25–26), but they were allowed to regrow during the reign of Empress Maria-Theresia, who went as far as banning wooden fences in order to protect the forest.

Lainzer Tiergarten

Not far from the city, a little way west of the city, beyond the Schönbrunn Palace (see pp. 192–197) is the part of the Wienerwald called the Lainzer

Tiergarten. This area was fenced off by Emperor Ferdinand I in 1561 for use as a private hunting park. With the fall of the Austro-Hungarian Empire, it became a public open space. Although some parts have been lost to development, it still covers a massive 6,000 acres (2,428 ha).

There are seven entrances to the Lainzer Tiergarten, but most visitors will arrive via the Lainzer Tor, where the streetcars stop. The park boasts an extensive network of footpaths and cycle trails, but no public roads. Walk up to **Hubertuswarte,** a tower set atop the highest point in the park (1,667 ft/508 m). Climb the narrow spiral staircase for unrivaled views over the northern Wienerwald, to the west and north, and the city of Vienna to the east. Then walk down to the **Wien Museum Hermesvilla,** which is housed in a 19th-century building designed in the romantic style for Empress Sisi (see p. 101). There you can look at the cultural exhibitions and rest your legs in the restaurant before continuing on your way. It is 1.4 miles (2.2 km) back to Lainzer Tor. In addition to its lovely scenery, the Lainzer Tiergarten also has wild boars, deer, mouflons (wild sheeplike animals with long, curved horns), and plenty of birdlife (see sidebar).

To the Donau

To the north is the town of Klosterneuburg, known mainly for its monastery, **Stift Klosterneuburg,** and its wine. The monastery, which stands on a hill overlooking the river, was founded in the early 12th century by St. Leopold III, the patron saint of Austria. Most of what you see today was constructed in the 18th century, but parts of the building are older. The **Chapel of St. Leopold** contains the gilded copper plates of the **Verdun Altar,** dating to 1181. The monastery library contains 30,000 volumes, and the wine cellars are immense. The monastery's vineyards are situated in several localities around Vienna; those nearby grow *grüner veltliner,* riesling, and sauvignon blanc grapes.

On the opposite side of the Donau, a little upstream and perched on a hill, is the fairy-tale castle of **Burg Kreuzenstein.**

(continued on p. 234)

Stift Klosterneuburg

- ✉ Stiftsplatz 1, Klosterneuburg
- ☎ (0) 2243 41 10
- 🕐 Closed Nov.–April
- 💲 $$$

www.stift -klosterneuburg .at/en

NOTE: To get to Klosterneuburg by public transport, take the S-40 train to Klosterneuburg-Kierling Station; alternatively, take the U4 service to Heiligenstadt, then bus service 238 or 239 to Klosterneuburg-Niedermarkt.

EXPERIENCE:
Wildlife-watching in Lainzer Tiergarten

Lured by deciduous and coniferous forest, meadow grassland, and small lakes, a wide range of wildlife, especially birds, have made Lainzer Tiergarten their home. Take a pair of binoculars, enter the park at the Nikolaitor entrance, and take one of the many walking trails, either to complete a circuit or leave by the Hermesstrasse gate. Watch for wild boars and red deer at any time of year. If you visit in spring or summer, watch for unusual species of birds, including black storks, honey-buzzards, six species of woodpeckers (including middle spotted and black), golden orioles, and red-backed shrikes. For more information, ask at the **visitor center** (Hermesstrasse, tel 1/4000 49200).

The Donau Bike Trail

A great way to experience the beautiful Donau Valley is to cycle the route between the historic towns of Melk and Krems, west of Vienna. Forested hills, vineyards, and orchards hug the slopes, but you have the luxury of cycling a virtually flat trail.

Pausing for a rest near Spitz

The Donau Bike Trail (Donauradweg) runs from the source of the Donau River in Germany, passing through Austria, to the point at which it spills into the Black Sea. Since there are plenty of small towns along the route, you can pick and choose your day's itinerary according to how far you wish to cycle and how much time you want to linger and admire the views, learn about the history, or simply enjoy the cuisine.

Melk to Krems

One particularly attractive section, easily cycled in a day, is the 24-mile (40 km) stretch between Melk and Krems. It is generally flat, dedicated cycle route, usually close to the Donau, with forested and vineyard-laced hillsides and orchards on either side of the river.

Start at the station in Melk, which is well connected by trains from Vienna. Cycle through the town, pausing to look at magnificent **Melk Abbey** ❶ (see pp. 236–237). Pass through the town square and then head toward the bridge that crosses the Donau River. A steep, but thankfully short, section of path leads onto the bridge, which takes you over the Donau. From the traffic circle on the far side, cycle southwest a short distance to investigate the town of **Emmersdorf** ❷, which has some fine old buildings.

Retrace your route, cycling northeast from the traffic circle as the track climbs higher and away from the river. In spring or summer you will be treated to fine displays of wildflowers. You will soon reach the town of **Willendorf** ❸, where the small **Venusium Museum** (Willendorf, closed Mon. & Oct.–April) has a replica of

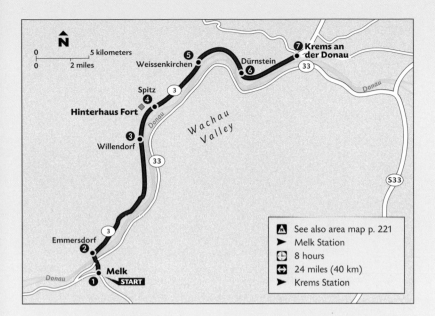

NOT TO BE MISSED:

Melk Abbey • Wildflowers north of Emmersdorf • The view from Hinterhaus Fort • The cobbled streets of Dürnstein

the famous limestone "Venus of Willendorf" figurine (see p. 115) that was found nearby.

Continue to the larger town of **Spitz** ❹. Since you are now halfway to your destination, maybe this is a good time to stop for lunch. For something a little special—good food and good wine—try the **Gasthof Goldenes Schiff** (*Mittergasse 5, Spitz an der Donau, tel 0/2713 2326, www.goldenesschiff.at*). After a suitable rest, make a slight detour and climb the steep hill to the ruins of the 12th-century **Hinterhaus Fort.** Time to push on, so cycle northeast once more, through the village of **Weissenkirchen** ❺, where the 14th-century **church** is worth a few minutes of your time. A defensive tower was added in the 16th century so the building could operate as a place of worship and a

fortification. The river—and your route—swing quite sharply to the southeast and the path climbs to **Dürnstein** ❻ (see p. 236), perched on a cliff overlooking the river. If you have time, investigate the cobbled streets and the ruined **castle,** largely destroyed by the Swedish army in 1645.

Leave the town for the final stage of the ride—to **Krems** ❼. There is plenty to see here (see pp. 235–236), but don't miss the charming old square in the center. If you're looking for an evening meal, try **Gasthaus Zum Elefanten** (*Schurerplatz 9, Krems an der Donau, tel 0/2732 85016, $$$–$$$$*). Trains to Vienna leave from Krems Station.

Bike Rental

For self-guided or guided tour options (from single days to seven days and including bike rentals, hotel reservations, and baggage transport), contact **Vienna Explorer** (*tel 1/890 96 82, www.viennaexplorer.com*). If you are planning a DIY ride, tourist offices provide free maps and booklets.

Burg Kreuzenstein

✉ Kreuzensteiner Strasse, 2 miles (3 km) north of Korneuburg

☎ (0) 664 422 5363

🕐 Closed Nov.–March

💲 $$$

www.kreuzenstein.com

Siegfried Marcus Automobil-museum

✉ Schiessstattgasse 9, Stockerau

☎ 0226 664 5642

🕐 Open Sat. & Sun.

💲 $$

www.siegfried-marcus.at

NOTE: To get to Stockerau by train, take the S-9 service from Landstrasse to Stockerau Station.

Heldenberg

✉ Wimpffen-Gasse 5, Kleinwetzdorf

☎ (0) 2956 81240

🕐 Closed Mon.

💲 $$$ (combined ticket for Radetzky Memorial, Neolithic Village, Koller's Oldtimer, and Lipizzan Spanish Riding School

www.derheldenberg.at/English

It looks like a late-15th-century castle, but all is not quite what it seems. While there was a medieval fort on the site, it was destroyed by Swedish forces in 1645. The present edifice was made in the late 19th century when the millionnaire Johann Wiczek collected parts of other—truly old—castles and put them together to produce this convincing reproduction. It is easy to drive to Kreuzenstein from Vienna, but public transportation is a little trickier. Catch an S-Bahn train from the city to Leobendorf-Kreuzenstein and then it's a 30-minute walk.

Three miles (5 km) to the west of Kreuzenstein is Stockerau, which has little to detain the traveler for long apart from the **Siegfried Marcus Automobil-museum,** named for the Austrian pioneer of automobile development. Exhibitions of classic motors change on a regular basis.

Wachau Wines

The Wachau Valley, particularly the region around the town of Dürnstein, is one of Austria's most highly regarded wine-producing regions. The landscape shelters the vineyards from the worst of the Austrian winter, and the rich alluvial soil gives the grapes a distinct flavor known by connoisseurs all over the world. For more information about the area's wines, visit **Domäne Wachau** (*www.domaene-wachau.at*).

Leaving the valley behind and heading northwest, Kleinwetzdorf is 14 miles (22 km) from Stockerau. There's enough here, particularly in the **Heldenberg** complex, to keep the visitor occupied for a good half day. Named for the greatest Austrian soldier, Field Marshall Radetzky (1766–1858), the **Radetzky Memorial** is in the grounds of Kleinwetzdorf's castle. It was created in 1849 and has statues and busts of many Austrian rulers and generals. Nearby are a reconstructed **Neolithic Village,** the **English Gardens** (now restored to their former glory), **Koller's Oldtimer** (a vintage car museum), and the **summer quarters** of the Spanish Riding School's Lipizzan horses (see pp. 106–107). The horses are given a break here in July and August, when it's possible to watch them in training.

The Wachau

West again, and straddling the banks of the Donau, the Wachau Valley region is a designated UNESCO World Heritage site blessed with a fine wine-making tradition, a pleasant climate, ancient customs, and steep hills with an abundance of fortifications. The Wachau Valley is one of the oldest wine regions of Europe, with 3,706 acres (1,480 ha) of vines and a history of viticulture dating back more than 2,000 years. The thousand-year-old town of Krems marks the beginning (or eastern end) of the valley, and the Benedictine monastery at Melk represents its western

Dürnstein's magnificent *pfarrkirche*

extremity. And there's much to commend what lies between the two, even though the distance between them is only 20 miles (33 km).

The Wachau's healthy wine industry owes much to the post-glacial silty sediment (known as loess) deposited on the hillslopes. Warmth-storing rocks make the most of hot, dry summers and cool winters with crisp down-slope winds and tepid breezes that generate a complexity in the region's grapes. Historic wine villages are home to high-profile winemakers, Wachau's renowned top chefs, and delicious native cuisine. Crack open a bottle of aromatic *grüner veltliner* or riesling in a wine-growing wonderland that boasts the distinction of being the westernmost (and therefore the coolest and highest) of Austria's vineyard regions. Here, shaped by the picturesque banks

of the Donau, fertile lands sprout fruit tree orchards and vegetables.

Krems an der Donau:

One of Lower Austria's most beautiful towns, Krems was first documented in the 12th century, and is famous for its annual wine festival and quaint heurigen (wine taverns). Located at the confluence of the Donau and Krems Rivers, 55 miles (88 km) northwest of Vienna in the easternmost part of the Wachau Valley, the town boasts plenty of thousand-year-old charm with its elegant streets of impressive historic buildings. It was designated a UNESCO World Heritage site in 2000. A collection of bars, restaurants, shops, and cafés boasts a laid-back feel in this hot spot of wine tourism and folk heritage. Krems is as renowned for its folkloric culture, songs, and musical

Krems an der Donau

Visitor Information

- ✉ Krems Tourist Office, Undstrasse 6, Krems
- ☎ (0) 2732 82676
- 🕐 Closed Sat. & Sun., & Nov.–April

www.tiscover.com/ krems

Karikatur-museum

✉ Steiner Landstrasse 3a, Krems

☎ (0) 2732 90 80-20

www.karikatur museum.at

Dürnstein

🅰 221 A2

Visitor Information

✉ Dürnstein Tourist Office, Dürnstein-Bahnhof

☎ (0) 2732 82676

🕐 Closed mid-Oct.–mid-April

www.duernstein.at

NOTE: To get to Dürnstein by car from Vienna, take Route 3 west to Krems, then continue driving west along Route 3 for 5 miles (8 km). To get there by train go from Vienna to Krems where buses link to Dürnstein (a 20-minute ride).

Melk

🅰 221 A2

Visitor Information

✉ Melk Tourist Office, Babenberger Strasse 1

☎ (0) 2752 52307

🕐 Closed Oct.–March & Sun. in April

Mariä-Himmelfahrt-Kirche

✉ Hauptplatz 5

☎ (0) 2752 52448

🕐 Open for services only

tradition as it is for its fine, fresh wines. It is also the home of the rib-tickling **Karikaturmuseum** (Museum of Caricature).

Dürnstein: Staying on the north bank of the Donau, this old town (7 miles/11 km west of Krems) is a typical Wachau community. It is crowned by the ruins of the mighty **castle** where English King Richard I (Richard the Lion-Hearted, 1157–1199) was incarcerated by Austrian Emperor Leopold V while Richard's was en route to England after a crusade in the Holy Land. Richard was accused by Leopold of ordering the murder of his cousin Conrad of Montferrat, and was released only once a huge ransom had been paid. (Emperor Leopold is believed to have spent much of the cash to finance the construction of Wiener Neustadt, south of Vienna.)

With its towering stone walls, the fortress sits atop granite cliffs 520 feet (159 m) above the village. It suffered considerable damage at the hands of the Swedish army, in 1645, but it is no less dramatic for that. Reach the ruins via one of a trio of charming paths through a belt of forest.

Dürnstein's fine 15th-century **pfarrkirche** (parish church) is also an inviting place to visit. Originally part of an Augustinian monastery, the chapel was reconstructed in baroque style. Its slender pale-blue and white tower is without doubt one of the finest architectural landmarks in the Donau Valley.

INSIDER TIP:

The restaurant at Stift Melk is surprisingly good, offering excellent local cuisine and wine from the abbey's own vineyards.

—TOM JACKSON
National Geographic contributor

Melk: A few miles farther upstream, on the southern bank of the Donau, stands the picturesque baroque town of Melk. Take some time to explore the historic town center, where you'll find the grand 18th-century **Rathaus** and the slender white spire of the **Mariä-Himmelfahrt-Kirche.**

Melk's best known attraction, however, is the majestic **Stift Melk** (Melk Abbey), a huge baroque monastery that sits on top of a rocky promontory at the edge of the town. It was founded in the 11th century on the site where the region's patron saint, Koloman, was buried. Over the next few centuries Stift Melk grew in power and importance, acquiring a formidable collection of holy relics and a vast library. In the 15th century it was the birthplace of the so-called Melk Reforms—a set of rules that changed the way that monasteries were run in Europe.

The abbey that stands today was built in the early 18th century after the original buildings were destroyed during the 30 Years' War. The abbot commissioned Austrian architect Jakob Prandtauer (1660–1726) to build a new abbey that would impress on the locals the power and wealth of the Church. Over the years the abbey has lost none of its power to impress. Visitors enter the complex from the east, walking up to the grand entrance (which is easily the equal of any royal palace in Vienna) past a pair of enormous stone bastions.

The grand **Stiftskirche** (Abbey Church) is the centerpiece of the complex. Its two orange-and-white towers and tall copper-roofed dome can be seen for miles in every direction. Its main facade is covered with carved angels, stucco decoration, and lavish quantities of gold leaf. The interior is decorated with the same level of pomp, featuring tall marble pillars and a massive trompe l'oeil fresco by Johann Michael Rottmayr.

The other highlight of the abbey complex is its **library,**

which houses one of Europe's most important collections of medieval manuscripts. The ceiling is covered by another huge trompe l'oeil fresco, this time by Paul Troger (1698–1762). Visitors can admire a selection of the library's collection of illuminated manuscripts here. The abbey's most jaw-droppingly luxurious room is the **Marmorsaal** (Marble Hall), which stands on the other side of the scenic clifftop terrace from the library. It was intended as a banqueting hall where the abbot could entertain important guests, including the royal court.

Another area worth visiting is the **Stiftmuseum,** whose exhibitions include historic artifacts and some of the abbey's prize possessions. The rooms of this museum are decorated in a jarringly modern style, with brightly colored walls and lots of glass. ∎

Stift Melk

- 221 A2
- Abt-Berthold-Dietmayer-Strasse 1, Melk
- (0) 2752 55 50
- Closed Nov.–Feb.
- $$$$ with guided tour; $$$ without tour

www.stiftmelk.at

NOTE: To get to Melk, take the U4 subway line to Spittelau train station. Trains to Melk from Spittelau run every hour (journey takes around 1 hour).

The over-the-top baroque architecture of Stift Melk

TRAVELWISE

Vienna has an efficient metro (U-Bahn) and an extensive streetcar (Strassenbahn) network.

PLANNING YOUR TRIP

When to Visit

Vienna has a distinct seasonal character that offers visitors a very different experience depending on when they arrive in the city. With its fairy-tale Christmas markets, mulled-wine stalls, and candlelit concerts, wintering in Vienna is highly popular. However, while it is typically warmer in the city than elsewhere in the country, winter temperatures can drop as low as 5°F (-15°C) as bitterly cold winds blow down from the mountains.

From the end of November through mid-February, thick, thermal layers are a must, even among the relative warmth of the Christmas market crowds. Also

note that many of the city's tourist attractions close during the winter, so it might not be possible to see everything you want to see.

Spring is Vienna's off-peak season, when visitor numbers are fairly low and many hotels offer reduced rates. If you're thinking of traveling during this period, however, it's worth checking the opening times of the sights you'd really like to see, as some remain closed, or open only a few days a week, until April or May. Note: The weather can be variable in spring, so don't assume it will always be warm and sunny. There may be cool and wet days.

Early summer is probably the time when Vienna is at its most beautiful, with flowers in bloom and the city's social life moving outside to the city's pavement cafés,

alfresco restaurants, and parks. At the height of the Viennese summer, however, it can be stiflingly hot, with temperatures soaring to the mid-90s (around 35°C) and no breeze to cool you. During this period almost every Viennese resident who can afford to do so abandons the city for the cooler air of the mountains, meaning that many family-run restaurants, bars, and cafés close.

In the fall the Viennese return to Vienna, ready for the pleasures of the city's "Indian summers." This is another good time to visit the city, although the weather can be a little unpredictable. November 11 is traditionally the first day that Vienna's *heurigen* (wine gardens) are allowed to sell young wine from that year's harvest (*heuriger*), an event that draws many Viennese out to the inns on the edge of the Wienerwald.

What to Take

Even if you're not planning on venturing beyond the Gürtel ring road at any time during your stay, a sturdy pair of comfortable shoes is essential. You'll cover many miles on your wanderings, and the medieval cobbles of the Innere Stadt are not easy on the feet. If you're thinking of heading to some of the city's classier establishments, such as the Staatsoper, it's worth bringing some stylish clothes so you can look the part. In fact, it's a good idea to err on the more formal side when packing for Vienna—appearances still count for a lot in many parts of town. A compact umbrella or folding rain jacket is also a good idea, as weather conditions can change quickly, especially in the spring and fall. When exploring, it's a good idea to make a photocopy of your passport so you can identify yourself, if needed, to the authorities.

Also, it is important to bring the documentation for your travel insurance, or—if you're an EU citizen—an EU Health Care Card, in case of medical emergencies. Certain aspects of medical care may need to be paid in advance, so be sure to retain all receipts and invoices in order to claim costs from the insurance company. Although you'd be hard-pressed to find such activities in a sedate city like Vienna, it's worth remembering that many adventurous leisure activities are not covered by regular travel insurance.

Entry Formalities

Passports & Visas

As long as they're not planning on remaining in the country for more than three months or working during their stay, citizens of the United States, Canada, and almost all European countries do not need a visa to visit Austria. All they need is a passport valid for at least the period of their intended stay and at least one blank page for the entry stamp. While these rules have been in place for a long time, it's worth remembering that visa requirements are often changed with little warning so you should double-check these details before you leave.

Austrian Embassies

United States

3524 International Court, N.W. Washington, D.C.
(202) 895-6700
www.austria.org

Canada

445 Wilbrod Street, Ottawa
(613) 789-1444
www.bmeia.gv.at/en/embassy/ottawa

United Kingdom

18 Belgrave Mews West
London
(020) 7344 3250
www.bmeia.gv.at/en/embassy/london

Customs

For most visitors, customs checks are just a simple formality, requiring you to do nothing more than sign a short declaration. Coming into the country, you are subject to tariffs only if you're carrying more than 200 cigarettes, 1 liter (around 1 quart) of liquor, or goods with a value of more than 175 euros. Tariffs also apply to those entering or leaving with more than 10,000 euros (or equivalent in another currency) in cash. Plants, and most products of animal origin—milk, meat, etc.—cannot be brought into the country. Visitors with prescription medicines will need to have the relevant medical documentation.

HOW TO GET TO VIENNA

Airports & Airlines

Vienna's international airport, **Flughafen Wien-Schwechat** (VIE; www.viennaairport.at), is located around 12 miles (20 km) to the southeast of the city center, close to the banks of the Donau (Danube) River.

Only Austrian Airlines flies nonstop between Vienna and North America (serving Washington-Dulles, New York–JFK, and Toronto-Pearson), but Vienna airport is served by a vast array of carriers flying from every major airport in Europe. Generally the cheapest way to get to Vienna from the United States or Canada is to fly to one of the major northern European terminals (London-Heathrow, Amsterdam-Schiphol, or Paris–Charles de Gaulle) and transfer to a budget flight to Vienna.

The airport is conveniently served by several different forms of public transport, as well as a large fleet of spacious taxis. All the public transport options are cheaper if you show a Vienna Card (see p. 240) so it's worth buying one of these from the visitor information kiosk at the airport; or ordering one online before you arrive.

The fastest and most comfortable public transport option from the airport is the **City Airport Train** (www.cityairporttrain.com, $$$$), which runs every 30 minutes and takes 16 minutes to reach Wien Mitte Station in Landstrasse, where you can connect to the U-Bahn. There is also the option of a **CAT-CAB** ticket, which includes a shuttle from Wien Mitte Station to your hotel. A slightly slower but much cheaper option is to take the **S7 Express** ($) S-Bahn train, which runs every 30 minutes and takes 26 minutes to reach Wien Mitte. This service also stops at various stations in Landstrasse and Leopoldstadt, which may be more convenient for some hotels.

Another option is the **Airport Express Bus** (tel 1/7007 32300, www.postbus.at, $$), which runs from the airport to three different destinations around the city: Schwedenplatz in the Innere Stadt (20 minutes), the Westbahnhof train/U-Bahn Station in Meidling (45 minutes), or the Vienna International Center/UNO City (about 40 minutes) east of the Donau.

Another option for those who are traveling through one of the major European airports is to get a flight to M. R. Stefánik Airport in Bratislava. Flights to Bratislava are usually significantly cheaper and the airport is usually less crowded. Although this airport is in a different country (Slovakia), it is only about 34 miles (55 km) farther from the city center than Flughafen Wien-Schwechat—making it a feasible alternative for those on a tight budget. The best way to get from Bratislava's airport to Vienna is to catch an Airport Express Bus (tel 1/7007 32300, www.postbus.at, $$$), which runs every hour between the two cities, stopping at Flughafen Wien-Schwechat on the way.

By Boat

For visitors arriving via Bratislava, there is another, more scenic way to arrive in Vienna—the **Twin City Liner** (tel 1/588 80, www .twincityliner.com, $$$$$). This fast twin-hulled ferry whisks passengers from the heart of Bratislava's old town to the newly built city pier on Schwedenplatz, Vienna, in little more than an hour. A ticket on the Twin City Liner is about three times the price of the train but offers a much more relaxing experience, with a sun deck, small bar, and lovely river views.

By Train, Bus, or Car

At the moment, Vienna doesn't really have a "central station" or railroad hub—trains to and from the city arrive at a number of smaller terminals positioned on or near the Gürtel ring road. For the past few years the Austrian government has been building a new international railroad station for Vienna on the site of the old Südbahnhof (in Weiden). As a result of the closure of the old station, services to other city terminals have been augmented to take up the shortfall. When the project is completed in 2012, many of the services that currently run to the Westbahnhof and Bahnhof Meidling will be diverted to the glossy new Hauptbahnhof Wien (Vienna Central Station). Traveling across Europe by train isn't generally particularly fast, nor particularly cheap—although rail passes provided by companies like **Interrail** (www.raileurope.co.uk) and **Eurail** (www.eurail.com) do reduce the cost significantly—but it is generally more comfortable, relaxed, and scenic than traveling by car or bus. Vienna is served by high-speed and sleeper services from Germany, Switzerland, Italy, Hungary, and the Czech Republic.

Vienna is also connected to the other cities of Europe, particularly Germany, by a network of well-maintained autobahns (freeways) that allow fast and easy travel by car or coach. **Eurolines** (www .eurolines.co.uk) runs regular coach services to Vienna from several European cities, including London, Amsterdam, Munich, Berlin, Prague, and Salzburg.

GETTING AROUND
Public Transport

Vienna has one of the most extensive and efficient public transport systems in the world, consisting of an expertly integrated network of buses (autobus), streetcars (trams, Strassenbahn), and subways (U-Bahn). Detailed route maps and timetables for all these services can be found on the **Wiener Linien** website (www.wienplan.com).

Compared with those of many other European cities, Vienna's public transport system is very cheap. Children under the age of six travel free on Viennese public transport, and during school holidays this is extended to anyone under the age of 15. During the rest of the year there are reduced rates for children under 15.

The best deal for visitors is the **Vienna Card** (www.wien.info/en/ travel-info/vienna-card), which costs €18.50. This is a 72-hour netzkarte (network card; see below) that also grants the user significant discounts at almost all the major sights in the city. Although it is slightly more expensive than a regular transport-only network card, the discounts earn back the difference even if you visit only a few sights during your stay. The Vienna Card also allows free travel for one person under the age of 15 when accompanied by the cardholder.

Aside from the Vienna Card, the most cost-effective way to get around Vienna is to buy a transport-only network card, which allows unlimited travel on public transport for a set period. The **Vierundzwanzig Stunden Wien-Karte** ("24-hour Vienna" ticket) costs €5.70. Tickets can also be bought that last 48 hours (Achtundvierzig Stunden Wien-Karte; €10) and 72 hours (Zweiundsiebzig Stunden Wien-Karte; €13.60). If you're going to be staying in the city for a longer period, it's worth getting a **Wochenkarte** (weekly ticket), which costs €14 and is valid from 9 a.m., after the morning rush hour has finished. Alternatively, a more flexible solution is the **Acht**

Tage Klimakarte (8-day climate card; €28.80), which functions like a set of eight 24-hour network cards that can be used by more than one person and not necessarily on consecutive days.

All these tickets can be bought from convenience stores and U-Bahn stations. It is also possible to buy **Einzelfarschein** (one-way single tickets), which cost €1.80 if you buy them in advance or €2.20 if you buy them on board a bus or tram. However, these are a much less convenient and usually more expensive way to get around.

Surprisingly, the otherwise sleek and modern U-Bahn sticks with a distinctly old-fashioned system of paper tickets and punch-card machines. If you're using single tickets, you must punch your ticket in one of the blue machines on entry to the U-Bahn or before you get on the bus. If you have a network card then you'll need to punch it at the beginning of your first journey to activate it. There are no turnstiles or barriers in most stations, but ticket inspectors are a common sight and the fines for traveling without a ticket are high (usually around €70). Remember to punch in and make a note of when you validated your ticket.

U-Bahn

Vienna's U-Bahn is the backbone of the city's public transport system, carrying around 1.3 million passengers every day. It consists of five lines, numbered U1, U2, U3, U4, and U6 (strangely there is no U5). The system as it exists today dates from the 1970s, but large sections of it were adapted from older constructions—including the two lines of the Otto Wagner–designed Stadtbahn (city railway), built in 1898, which became lines U4 and U6. A map of the U-Bahn system is included on the inside back cover

of this guide. U-Bahn trains run from around 5 a.m. to midnight between Sunday and Thursday. On Fridays and Saturdays, and on the eve of public holidays, the trains run all night.

Tram

Vienna is one of the few major cities that has kept its tram (streetcar) network, known as the Strassenbahn (many locals call it the *Bim,* for the sound of the chime that goes off when it stops). The Strassenbahn is most useful for getting around the *vorstädte* and *vororte* suburbs, where the U-Bahn stations are farther apart. On most Strassenbahn routes the streetcars run every 15 minutes or so, but there the timetables vary more than those of the U-Bahn, so it's worth checking before you head out. The best known Strassenbahn route is number 1, which is a good way to see the historicist buildings around the Rathaus.

S-Bahn

The S-Bahn (short for Schnellbahn) describes the over-ground railroad services that run out of Vienna's primary rail terminals. These services, which carry hundreds of thousands of commuters into the city every day, aren't likely to be used very often by visitors. Often the only time that visitors to Vienna find themselves riding the huge two-deck trains of the S-Bahn is on the trip to and from the airport. If you're heading to the picturesque towns of the Wachau Valley, however, the S-Bahn is the fastest and most comfortable way to get there.

Getting Around the Innere Stadt

In the historic core of Vienna, often the best way to get around is on foot. Trams don't run inside

the Ringstrasse, and the U-Bahn stations are too far apart to be much use. The Innere Stadt holds a wealth of fine architecture and fascinating old buildings that is simply too extensive to mention in this guide: Almost every street has some unique marvel to admire. Even if you're going from one side of the Innere Stadt to the other, it's better to take an extra 10 or 15 minutes (it's rarely more than that) to walk to a destination than to take the U-Bahn and miss out on these off-the-beaten-track sights.

That said, city buses manage to squeeze their way down a surprisingly large number of the Innere Stadt's narrow streets, so if you're not up to hiking backward and forward around the old town all day, these are a reliable alternative.

Three bus routes serve the Innere Stadt: **Line 1A** starts from Schottentor and heads south past the Freyung, then along Herrengasse to Michaelerplatz and the Hofburg. From there it turns north and crosses the Graben before going round St. Peter's Church and on to Stephansplatz. It continues east along Wollzeile before turning around at Stubentor (next to the Stadtpark) and returning to Stephansplatz. It then heads to Schottentor via the Hoher Markt, Wipplingerstrasse, and the Börse.

Line 2A runs southwest from Schwedenplatz, past the Hoher Markt and the Am Hof. It passes through the Michaelertor, and cuts through the center of the Hofburg complex, emerging on the Ringstrasse on the far side of Heldenplatz. From here it heads southwest into Mariahilf and Neubau. It passes the MuseumsQuartier and travels along Mariahilfer Strasse as far as Neubaugasse, before returning to the Innere Stadt via Spittelberg and the Volkstheater. It then returns to Schwedenplatz via St. Peter's Church and Stephansplatz.

Beginning at Schottenring, **Line 3A** heads along the waterfront as far as Heinrichsgasse. It then goes down Salzgries, past the Hoher Markt, and south along Tuchlauben. From here it follows route 2A as far as Michaelerplatz, before passing through the Winter Riding School and Josefsplatz. From Albertinaplatz it goes east, past the Staatsoper to Schwarzenbergplatz. It then goes along the Ringstrasse as far as the Staatsoper before heading into the Innere Stadt. It passes through Albertinaplatz and the Neuer Markt before crossing Dorotheergasse and turning north toward the Graben. It follows the same route as the 1A from Stephansplatz to the Börse, before turning north back up to Schottenring.

Driving in Vienna

You don't need a car to get around Vienna, nor do you really need one to reach the various attractions mentioned in the Day Trips chapter. Nonetheless, if you plan on traveling beyond Lower Austria or are planning to arrive in the city by car, it's worth bearing the following in mind. There are several car rental agencies at Vienna's international airport, including **Hertz** (tel 1/7007 32661, www.hertz.at), **Avis** (tel 1/7007 32700, www.avis.at), and **Budget** (tel 1/7007 32700, www .budget.at).

On-street parking in Vienna is heavily restricted, and fees at parking garages are typically high. In almost the whole of downtown Vienna—including the Innere Stadt, Leopoldstadt, and all the vorstädte suburbs—parking is allowed only within designated *kurzparkzonen* (short-term parking zones). These zones are typically marked by signs that show a red and blue circle with a line through the center. Information on each particular parking zone is usually written on a smaller white sign: The first line of these indicates if it is *gebührenpflichtig* (subject to charge); the second lists the maximum stay (for example, "2 std." or "2 hours"); and the third lists the days on which these charges apply. To park in these zones you'll need to get a *parkscheine* (parking voucher), which has to be placed in plain sight on the dashboard. These can be bought from most convenience stores, gas stations, and tobacconists.

In order to drive on the highways and freeways outside Vienna you'll need to buy a toll sticker (*€23 for a 10-day pass*), sold at most gas stations. These have to be affixed to the inside of the windshield in order to be valid.

Taxis, *Faxis,* & *Fiakers*

Vienna has a large and modern fleet of taxis that offer a quick, if expensive, way to get around the city. They are especially useful if you're out after the U-Bahn has shut down, or weighed down with shopping or luggage. Taxis in Vienna can't be hailed from the sidewalk—if you want to get a taxi you'll have to either go to a taxi stand or call one of the city's dispatch offices. Taxi stands are located in many of the city's main squares and railroad terminals, and outside the larger U-Bahn stations. The three main taxi companies in Vienna are all named for their phone numbers—**Taxi 60160** (tel 60 160, www.taxi60160.at), **Taxi 40100** (tel 40 100, www.taxi40100.at), and **Taxi 31300** (tel 31 300, www .taxi31300.at). The minimum fare is around €3, with a €1 surcharge if you phone the taxi company. After that, the usual rate is around €1 for every few minutes' travel.

Within the Innere Stadt, there is also a fleet of bicycle rickshaws known as faxis—a contraction of *fahrradtaxi* (bike taxi). Faxis are rather more high tech than most rickshaws, with a sleek aerodynamic design, an electric motor (to help the rider keep his or her energy up), and brakes that recharge the batteries. These vehicles hold two passengers and cost slightly more than taxis and can be hailed from the street or hired from **Faxi** (tel 0699/1200 5624, www.faxi.at).

The least practical but most atmospheric form of transport in Vienna is fiakers—old fashioned horse-drawn carriage. These can usually be seen waiting at stands in Stephansplatz and Heldenplatz, with their smartly dressed, English-speaking coachmen. The main operators are **Fiaker Paul** (Albrechtsgasse 26, tel 1/480 43 05, www.fiaker-paul.at, $$$$$), **Fiaker .co.at** (Rosaliagasse 19, tel 1/966 02 61, www.fiaker.co.at, $$$$$), and **Fiaker Johann Trampusch** (Essinggasse 49, tel 1/0664/302 00 76, www.wien-fiaker.at, $$$$$). For more information, see p. 72.

Cycling in Vienna

The number of bikes on the road in Vienna has increased dramatically over the past ten years, although it is still not particularly high by European standards. Cyclists now make up around 8 percent of the city's road users. Vienna is generally a safe place to ride, with around 620 miles (1,000 km) of cycle routes, but the busy traffic can be intimidating to those with only a little experience cycling in large cities. Even experienced urban cyclists should be wary of the sometimes unpredictable traffic flows in the narrow streets and blind corners of the Innere Stadt and vorstädte districts. And always be sure to stop at red light signals. Helmets are strongly recommended but are not compulsory.

The **Citybike** (www.citybikewien .at) scheme is one of the main factors to have encouraged cycling in Vienna. This has placed thousands of low-cost rental bikes at special terminals around the city. In order to use these bikes, you'll need to rent a Citybike tourist card (€2 per day)—these are available from two outlets in Vienna: **Royal Tours** (Herrengasse 1–3, tel 1/710 46 06, www.royaltours.at), located just off Michaelerplatz; and **Pedal Power** (Ausstellungsstrasse 3, tel 1/729 72 34, www.pedalpower.at), near Praterstern Station (U-Bahn and S-Bahn). With this card you can rent a bicycle from any Citybike terminal as many times as you want, and as long as you return the bike to a terminal within an hour, there is no additional cost.

Citybikes are a fairly expensive and uncomfortable option for those who want to travel longer distances, however. A better alternative is to rent a conventional bike from Pedal Power or one of the other providers listed on page 265.

PRACTICAL ADVICE
Addresses

The most commonly used format for addresses in Vienna is to write the district number first (for example, 1 for the Innere Stadt or 9 for Alsergrund), followed by the street name, then the property number. In many residential addresses, this property number is followed by a slash, and then another number—this is the apartment number. After this usually comes the postal code (a four-digit number, often preceded by "A-" for Austria); and lastly the city's name in German: Wien. The address of St. Stephen's Cathedral, for example, would usually be written as 1, Stephansplatz 1, A-1010, Wien.

If you're unsure where a place is, type the street name and property number into the unfailingly accurate Vienna City Map (www .wien.gv.at/stadtplan/en) and it will place a marker over the property.

Communications
Internet

Vienna is an exceptionally well connected city, where almost every café, restaurant, and shop has its own well-maintained website. The local government also has an extensive and extremely helpful website (www .wien.gv.at/english).

It is possible to use most foreign smart phones in the city, but doing so will expose you to painfully high roaming charges. It is better to leave the 3G turned off and use the local wireless networks described below. The online mapping service A nach B (www.anachb.at) offers a free iPhone app that gives users an English-language route planner that can be customized for cyclists, drivers, and users of public transport.

For those bringing their laptops, for around €50 it is possible to get a USB mobile broadband modem, SIM card, and 1.5 GB of prepaid data credit (no contract required) from A1 telecom (www.a1.net), Austria's largest telecom company. Given the sheer abundance of Wi-Fi hot spots in Vienna, however, it is unlikely that this expenditure will be necessary—almost all cafés, bars, hotels, and many museums have free Wi-Fi networks (known in Austria by the more technically correct name of WLAN). In most places you'll need to ask the staff of the café or bar for the network password, but sometimes the networks are left unsecured and open to all.

Cell Phones

Cell phones in Austria use the GSM transmission protocol on the European standard 900 and 1800 MHz bands. This means that many U.S. and Canadian cell phones (which run on the 850 and 1900 MHz bands) will not work in Austria, even with a replacement SIM card. Tri-band phones will have limited but usable reception in Vienna, and quad-band phones should work perfectly. Most phones provided by the U.S. carriers Sprint and Verizon will not work at all in Austria as they use different transmission technology.

While many U.S. phones will work in Austria, as noted, the roaming charges are often high for overseas use, and so are best reserved for emergencies only. If you think you're going to be using your phone a lot during your stay, the best option is to get a prepaid SIM card (and a cheap phone—known locally as a handy—if yours won't work in Austria) from one of Austria's main cell phone operators. These prepaid phones can be bought for as little as €20 (plus however much prepaid credit you want to put on it) from A1 telecom (www.a1.net), T-Mobile Austria (www.t-mobile.at), and Orange (www.orange.at).

Phone Numbers

To an outsider there is no discernible logic to Austrian phone numbers—they vary in length from 4 to 13 digits, and can include any number of extension codes. This apparent lack of structure comes from the fact that, as far as anyone can tell, there isn't any. Regional and local codes vary in length from one digit to four—with the shortest code 1 reserved for the capital—while individual subscriber numbers appear to be allocated entirely at random.

Many telephone numbers follow fairly regular patterns—such as the three-digit local code, followed by four-digit subscriber number format widely used in Vienna—but for every rule that has been suggested there seem to be as many exceptions as there are examples that follow it. The international access code for Austria is +43 followed by 1 for Vienna and then the local number. When making outgoing calls to an international number, dial 00 followed by the relevant country code.

Electricity

Austrian outlet power is rated at 220 volts/50 Hz AC, which is the European standard. North American appliances will need a transformer to work here—although many electronic devices, such as laptops, have one built into their power supply. The sockets are the standard two-pin, rounded-prong design used throughout continental Europe. Most electronics shops sell inexpensive adapters.

Etiquette & Local Customs

Although Viennese social customs would be considered quite formal by U.S. standards, few Viennese would recognize the rigid aristocratic etiquette that many visitors expect. Even among the extremely old-fashioned aristocracy, for example, kissing a lady's hand would be considered an eccentric and anachronistic greeting. For most people in Vienna, social formalities don't go much further than using proper titles (*herr* for men and *frau* for women); always saying please and thank you (*bitte* and *danke*, respectively); and, above all, always being scrupulously punctual. German speakers will be expected to have a slightly more nuanced understanding of the social conventions (including the use of formal and informal modes of address), but most Viennese will be very patient and forgiving of tourists' social mistakes.

Liquor Laws

In Austria, liquor laws are regulated by individual states rather than by the federal government. This means that the minimum drinking age (or ages; some states have different minimum ages for different types of alcohol) varies from one part of Austria to another. In Vienna people can buy and consume wine and beer from the age of 16, although some stores might not be willing to sell distilled spirits to people under 18, as is the law in many other parts of Austria. Traditionally, as long as teenagers are with their families, few establishments are particularly bothered about ID. In recent years, however, media coverage of teenage binge drinking (known by the evocative name of *komatrinken* or "coma drinking") has led to this traditionally relaxed attitude tightening somewhat.

Media

Vienna is a very international city with a large English-speaking population, so there are plenty of English-language papers available. Some newspapers from the United States and Britain can be found at newsstands around the city (although they're usually a day old by the time they reach Vienna). The *International Herald Tribune* (www.iht.com) is generally available on the day of printing, and there is a locally printed weekly English-language news magazine called *Austria Today* (www.austriatoday.at), although this will be of little interest if you don't much care about Austrian politics. The city's oldest newspaper is the *Wiener Zeitung* (www.wienerzeitung.at), which also has an English edition.

The publication that may be of most interest to visitors is the weekly listings magazine *Falter* (www.falter.at), a well-written and edgy publication known for its wry take on Viennese society and politics. Although it's published only in German, the listings section isn't hard to decipher.

The state-run broadcaster (Österreichischer Rundfunk, or ÖRF) still accounts for the majority of mainstream TV programming, but most hotels now have CNN, BBC News, and a few other English-language channels.

Money Matters
Austrian Currency

The local currency is the euro (€), the same currency used throughout western Europe (with the exception of Switzerland). Eight kinds of euro coins are in wide circulation: small copper coins for one, two, and five cents; larger gold-colored (actually an alloy of copper, aluminum, and zinc) coins for 10, 20, and 50 cents; and thick bimetallic coins for €1 (a ring of brass around a nickel core) and €2 (a ring of nickel around a brass core). Each coin has a European standard on one side while the reverse is different from country to country. Euro coins are legal tender across Europe, regardless of where they were minted.

Euro bills come in seven different denominations (€5, €10, €20, €50, €100, €200, and €500). You're likely to encounter only the smallest five on a regular basis, and even then the €100 is something of a rarity. The €200 and €500 bills are only ever really used by the kind of people who wear dark glasses at night and carry their money in anonymous black briefcases.

If you don't want to have to break too many large bills, it's best to avoid taking money out of the ATM in multiples of 50. Most restaurants, stores, and cafés will have no problem with €50 and €100 bills, however. Euro bills aren't localized like the coins, so they'll be the same whether you change your money in Austria or before you leave.

Banks

On Mondays, Tuesdays, Wednesdays, and Fridays, banks typically open at 8 a.m. and close at 3 p.m. Some close for lunch between 12:30 and 1:30 p.m. On Thursdays many branches stay open until 5:30 p.m. Most banks are closed on Saturdays, Sundays, and public holidays, but exchange offices at airport and city rail terminals are open seven days a week.

Vienna has a plentiful supply of ATMs (known locally as *bankomats*) so you'll rarely have to walk far to find one.

Credit & Debit Cards

While most hotels and stores, and many restaurants, accept credit and debit cards, many of Vienna's smaller stores, cafés, and all market stalls accept only cash. If in doubt, ask before you order or try to make a purchase. Some levy a small fee for the use of credit cards or have a minimum transaction amount. If you're going to be using your credit or debit card abroad, it's a good idea to inform your bank before you leave; otherwise you might be shut out by an automatic fraud prevention system.

Opening Hours

The opening hours of shops and businesses in Vienna are subject to various city ordinances and federal regulations. As workplace laws ban most shops from opening for more than 72 hours a week, 24-hour stores are unheard of in Vienna. From Monday to Friday, shops in Vienna are not allowed to open before 6 a.m., nor stay open after 9 p.m. In practice most shops open at 9 a.m. and close at around 6 p.m.

On Saturdays the legally regulated hours are extended to 6 a.m.–6 p.m., but most shops stay open only from 9 a.m. to 1 p.m. at the latest. On the first Saturday of every month shops stay open until around 5 p.m. Vienna's commercial districts are legally required to completely shut down on Sundays. The only stores that are exempt from these rules are pharmacies and stores in airports and rail terminals.

Mercifully, the rules for restaurants, cafés, and bars are much more relaxed, with many staying open until the small hours of the morning. Traditional *kaffeehauser* (coffeehouses) typically open as early as 7 a.m. and close at around 11 p.m., while bars and trendy cafés stay open until 2 or 3 a.m.

Public Holidays

Austrians enjoy a large number of national holidays. On these days Vienna will be noticeably quieter, although, if the weather is good, places like the Alte Donau and the Prater will be packed with families. Museums tend to either shut down completely or open for free, seemingly at random—so it's worth checking before you head out.

January 1—Neues Jahr (New Year's Day)
January 6—Dreikönigstag (Feast of the Epiphany)
March or April—Ostermontag (Easter Monday)
May 1—Tag des Arbeit (Labor Day)
Sixth Thursday after Easter—Christi Himmelfahrt (Ascension Day)
Sixth Monday after Easter—Pfingstmontag (Whit Monday)
Ninth Thursday after Easter—Fronleichnam (Corpus Christi)
August 15—Maria Himmelfahrt (Feast of the Assumption)
October 26—Nationalfeiertag (National Day)
November 1—Allerheiligen (All Saints' Day)
December 8—Maria Empfängis (Feast of the Immaculate Conception)
December 25—Weihnachstag (Christmas Day)
December 26—Zweite Weihnachtsfeiertag (St. Stephen's Day)

Religion

The Austrian constitution guarantees freedom of religion, and most of the world's major faiths and denominations are represented somewhere in this multicultural city.

The most numerous places of worship are Catholic churches. Information on services held in different languages can be found on the website of the Archdiocese of Vienna (*www.erzdioezese-wien.at*). There are a few Protestant churches (known as *evangelische kirchen*) in every district, mostly belonging to either the Lutheran (*www.evang-wien.at*) or Reformed (*www.reformierkirche.at*) traditions. Greek Orthodox Christians worship at the Grecienkirche on the Fleischmarkt, and there is a weekly Russian Othodox service at the Russiche Kirche in the diplomatic quarter. In addition to the famous Stadttempe in Innere Stadt's old Jewish district, there are several more recently built synagogues in Vienna—you can find them listed on the Israelitische Kultusgemeinde Wien website (*www.ikg-wien.at*). The city's largest mosque is housed in the Islamic Center near the UNO City, and there are several others (*see www.derislam.at*).

Restrooms

Vienna has more than 400 public restrooms, which are usually clean and watched over by a full-time attendant. Many of the fancier facilities charge a small fee of between 10 and 50 euro cents, so it's wise to keep some change handy.

Smoking

Vienna is a notoriously smoky city, but it has recently been trying to improve its image in this regard. Smoking was banned on public transit in 2007, and a partial public smoking ban was introduced in 2009. This partial ban requires all restaurants, cafés, and bars over a certain size to provide a nonsmoking area. Smaller establishments, however, can choose whether they want to allow smoking or not, and most prefer to allow it. Similarly, whether smoking is allowed in hotels is decided at each proprietor's discretion.

Restaurants typically display a green smoking sticker on the door if they are entirely nonsmoking, a red one if they allow smoking throughout the restaurant, and both if they have smoking and nonsmoking areas.

Time Differences

Vienna, like the rest of Austria, is on Central European Time (GMT+1), which is 6 hours ahead of Eastern Standard Time.

Tipping

Service staff in Vienna typically have a significantly higher rate of basic pay than workers performing similar roles in the United States or Canada. As a result, tips are appreciated but don't usually represent the majority of anyone's income. In restaurants, where tipping culture is most firmly established, diners are expected to leave a tip of between 10 and 15 percent (more if it seems deserved)—which is sometimes included in the bill. In cafés, where the bills are not usually so high, tipping is less tightly regulated by social convention; most Viennese simply round up to the nearest euro (so if the bill is €8.50, they'll leave €9) as a friendly gesture, leaving

more if they feel the service was very good. A similar convention applies to tipping taxi drivers. In cafés and restaurants you should always pay the bill at the table with the waiter or waitress who served you. Leaving your tip on the table when you leave is considered rude. When handing over cash, you can use the phrase *stimmt so* (keep the change) but simply saying *danke* when handing over the cash is often taken to mean the same thing. If you don't have the right money, say the amount you would like to pay when you hand over the notes—for example, if the bill is €14 and you want to leave a €2 tip, but have only a €20 bill, say *sechszehn* (sixteen) and you should get €4 in change. In bars the situation is more varied, but generally if you get table service you will be expected to tip.

Travelers With Disabilities

With its cobbled streets and baroque staircases, Vienna is not a naturally disabled-accessible city. In recent years, however, the city government has made great strides in improving access to Vienna's great landmarks.

Public buildings are required by law to be wheelchair accessible, although in some historic buildings the accessibility adaptations can be a little convoluted. In many of these historic structures disabled access is provided by portable ramps, so visitors in wheelchairs should call ahead so the staff are prepared.

Several of the city's major cultural institutions have made a special effort to include people with disabilities. The Kunsthistorisches Museum, for example, has recently had many of its most famous works scanned and made into tactile bas-reliefs that can be appreciated by the blind or visually

impaired. Similar tactile copies have been made of some of the museum's sculptures.

Regulations require all new hotels, cafés, and restaurants to be disabled accessible, but this doesn't apply to older establishments. The situation is improving, however, with an increasing number of private establishments making their premises and facilities accessible.

Vienna's public transport system is generally very good when it comes to disabled access. Almost all of the city's bus and streetcar routes are plied by modern "kneeling" buses and trams with retractable ramps that make them wheelchair accessible. At Strassenbahn stops there is a display that shows how many minutes you'll have to wait before the next wheelchair-accessible vehicle arrives. All U-Bahn and S-Bahn stations have elevators and special guidelines for the visually impaired.

The Vienna tourist board has a series of downloadable guides (*www.wien.info/en/travel-info/accessible-vienna*) to the city's disabled-accessible museums, restaurants, hotels, cafés, bars, and other buildings, as well as detailed information about access to the city's public transport.

Unit Conversions

Austria, like most of Europe, uses the metric system. Weights are calculated in grams and kilograms (1 kg = 2.2 pounds), while liquids are usually given in liters (1 l = 0.2 gallon) or fractions of liters. It helps to remember that half a liter (500 ml) is equal to a little more than one pint. Distances are given in meters (1 m = 3.3 feet) and kilometers (1 km = 0.62 mile), while speed limits are given in kilometers per hour. Temperatures are given in degrees Celsius, a scale with a different zero point to Fahrenheit (0°C = 32°F). A quick way to convert one to the other is to double the figure in Celsius and add 30, so that, for example, 15°C converts to 60°F. This method is accurate to within a few degrees when converting the kinds of temperatures you're likely to encounter in Vienna.

Visitor Information
The Vienna Tourist Board (www .wien.info) operates a number of information offices around the city. Most are located in or near major U-Bahn interchanges, although there is also one in the airport. Information offered to visitors by the offices of the Austrian National Tourist Board includes a very good, well-detailed map, available at no cost from outlets across the city. Every office is well stocked with leaflets, brochures, and discount coupons for major attractions as well as lesser known sites. They also offer information on tour operators, bike rental companies, accommodations, and transport.

EMERGENCIES
Crime & Police
Austria has some of the lowest crime rates in Europe, and Vienna is a strikingly safe and law-abiding city. That said, however, it is still a large city, and like any large city it has its bad areas. Large stretches of the Gürtel ring road have a seedy reputation, particularly near the Westbahnhof, a notorious red-light district. The same is true of the area near the Stadion, northeast of the Prater. Karlsplatz, particularly its pedestrian underpasses, can be intimidating at night, as can some parts of the Stadtpark. Even at their worst they aren't no-go areas for travelers, but take the usual precautions. The police (who wear navy-blue uniforms and white caps) are generally friendly.

Lost & Stolen Property
All thefts and losses should be reported to the Viennese police within 24 hours; otherwise insurance claims will almost certainly not be valid. In the event of a lost or stolen passport, contact your embassy or consulate.

Foreign Embassies and Consulates in Vienna
Embassy of the United States
Boltzmanngasse 16, Alsergrund
(1) 313 39-0
http://austria.usembassy.gov

United States Consulate
Parkring 12a, Innere Stadt
(1) 512 58 35

Embassy of Canada
Laurenzerberg 2, Innere Stadt
(1) 531 38-3000
www.canadainternational
.gc.ca/austria-autriche/

British Embassy Vienna
Jauresgasse 12, Landstrasse
(1) 716 13-0
http://ukinaustria.fco.gov.uk

Medical Emergencies
If you're injured in an accident or suffer some other medical emergency, you'll likely end up in the Allgemeines Krankenhaus (AKH) hospital (Michelbeuern U-Bahn). The city's main pediatric hospital is Sankt Anna Kinderspital (Alserstrasse U-Bahn).

Emergency Phone Numbers
Fire: **122**
Police: **133**
Ambulance: **144**
In addition to these numbers, the European-wide emergency number, **112**, will connect you to an emergency services operator. You will then have to state whether you need the Fire Department (Feuerwehr), the police (Polizei), or the ambulance service (Rettung).

FURTHER READING
Fiction
Auto-da-Fé by Elias Canetti (1935)
Death in Vienna by Frank
   Tallis (2007)
The Man Without Qualities
   by Robert Musil (1941)
The Third Man by Graham
   Greene (1948)
The Radetzky March
   by Joseph Roth (1932)
A German Requiem by
   Phillip Kerr (1991)

History & Society
Hitler's Vienna: A Dictator's
   Apprenticeship by Brigitte
   Hamann (2010)
The Austrians: A Thousand-Year
   Odyssey by Gordon Brooke-
   Shepherd (2003)
A Nervous Splendor: Vienna
   1888–1889 by Frederick
   Morton (1980)
Last Waltz in Vienna by
   George Clare (1982)
The Enemy at the Gate: Habsburgs,
   Ottomans, and the Battle for
   Europe by Andrew Wheatcroft
   (2009)
The World of Yesterday by
   Stefan Zweig (1964)
Fin de Siecle Vienna by Carl E.
   Schorske (1980)

Music & the Arts
Vienna 1900: Klimt, Schiele,
   and Their Times (2010)
Gustav Klimt: Art Nouveau Visionary
   by Eva di Stefano (2008)
Wolfgang Amadeus Mozart:
   A Biography by Piero
   Melograni (2008)
Beethoven: The Universal Composer
   by Edmund Morris (2010)

Food & Drink
Austrian Cooking and Baking by
   Gretel Beer (1975)
Kaffeehaus: Exquisite Desserts From
   the Classic Cafés of Vienna,
   Budapest, and Prague by Rick
   Rodgers (2002)

Hotels & Restaurants

As one would expect from this glamorous baroque city, Vienna has some of the grandest, most sumptuous hotels in Europe, including several converted palaces, where the rooms look like they've come straight from the Schönbrunn. Luckily, Vienna also boasts a wide range of accommodation options, from funky modern hotels to friendly family-run pensions. The restaurant scene in Vienna is similarly varied, with high-class nouvelle cuisine competing with trendy young restaurants and the ever present Wiener schnitzel.

Hotels

Guesthouses in Vienna come in various different forms, the most common of which are hotels and pensions. Hotels are, as you'd expect, large businesses with plenty of carefully kept, standardized rooms. Pensions, on the other hand, are typically small, family-run establishments where the rooms come in all different sizes and arrangements. Pensions also usually consist of a few floors of a residential building, rather than a stand-alone property. These two different types of accommodation each has its own rating system—one to five stars for hotels, one to four stars for pensions—which are based more on the available facilities than on the general quality of the establishment. Hotels are not automatically better than pensions, despite what many hotel owners will say.

Bedrooms generally have en-suite bathrooms. Air-conditioning is something of a rarity in Vienna, where most of the guesthouses are in historic buildings that don't appreciate alterations. Many pensions are located in historic apartment buildings where you'll have to take a beautiful, but alarmingly crude, century-old elevator up to your floor.

Unsurprisingly, the Innere Stadt is the district with the most accommodation options. Guesthouses in this area, however, tend to be rather overpriced and usually have a bland, internationalized atmosphere. If you go just a few yards outside the Ringstrasse you'll find that the prices drop considerably, and the charm rises. The best places to stay for those on a budget are the nicer parts of the vorstädte, such as Mariahilf, Neubau, and Josefstadt, although there is a growing number of interesting options in Alsergrund and Leopoldstadt. Breakfast is usually included in the price of the room.

Restaurants

For many years, Vienna was known as something of a culinary backwater, with little innovation or change from the stodgy fare of traditional Austrian cooking. Since the 1990s, however, Vienna's restaurant scene has greatly broadened. The fashions of European haute cuisine have swept through the city's more expensive restaurants, while the mid- and low-priced establishments have benefited from an influx of new ideas from eastern Europe and beyond. Despite the city's reputation for opulence, restaurants in Vienna are actually surprisingly reasonably priced.

The cornerstone of Viennese restaurant culture has always been the *biesl*, a kind of traditional inn (*gasthaus*) that serves good beer and unpretentious food. In recent years these have been joined by so-called *neo-biesln*, which offer a wider variety of dishes and have a generally lighter atmosphere. Other uniquely Viennese eating establishments include the *heurigen* wine gardens and the traditional cafés or kaffeehauser (coffeehouses), where light meals, pastries, and sandwiches are served. Conventional restaurants come in just about every conceivable type, from simple backstreet pizzerias to high-class purveyors of nouvelle cuisine and fine wines.

Many restaurants close for a few hours between lunch (typically served between 11:30 a.m. and 2 p.m.) and dinner (usually served from 6–10 p.m.) Credit cards are still not widely accepted in Viennese restaurants, so it's a good idea to take out plenty of cash. As the cost of a main course varies considerably depending on what you order, these prices should be treated only as an approximation.

Organization & Abbreviations

Hotels and restaurants are listed by chapter, then by price, and finally by alphabetical order. Hotels are listed before restaurants within each section. The number of rooms listed includes both rooms and suites.

The no-smoking symbol can mean either that the hotel has nonsmoking rooms, which is common, or that it is entirely nonsmoking, which is currently rare. In restaurants it means that the restaurant is either entirely smoke free or has a nonsmoking area. The abbreviations used for credit and debit cards are AE (American Express), DC (Diner's Club), MC (MasterCard), V (Visa).

PRICES

HOTELS

The cost of a double room with en-suite bathroom is given by **$** signs. In the low season rates can be considerably lower.

$$$$$	Over €210
$$$$	€141–€210
$$$	€101–€140
$$	€55–€100
$	Under €55

RESTAURANTS

The average cost of a two-course meal for one person, excluding a tip or drinks, is given by **$** signs.

$$$$$	Over €30
$$$$	€26–€30
$$$	€18–€25
$$	€10–€17
$	Under €10

■ STEPHANSDOM QUARTER

HOTELS

⊞ HOTEL KÖNIG VON UNGARN
$$$$$
1, SCHULERSTRASSE 10
TEL (1) 515 84
FAX (1) 515 84-8
www.kvu.at
This hotel has been taking bookings since 1746, making it the oldest continuously operated hotel in Vienna. The interiors are an expertly designed mixture of Biedermeier coziness and modern style.
[] 33 P ⊟ ⊚ ⊛ ⊛ All major cards

⊞ KAISERIN ELISABETH
$$$$$
1, WEIHBURGGASSE 3
TEL (1) 515 26
FAX (1) 515 26-7

www.kaiserinelisabeth.at
Positioned on a quiet street just off Kärntner Strasse, this hotel has existed in various forms for hundreds of years. Each room is simply decorated with pleasingly solid, often antique furniture and tasteful old-fashioned ornamental features. One of the best places to stay if you want a taste of imperial Vienna.
[] 63 P ⊟ ⊚ ⊛ ⊛ All major cards

SOMETHING SPECIAL

⊞ PALAIS COBURG RESIDENZ
$$$$$
1, COBURGBASTEI 4
TEL (1) 518 18-0
FAX (1) 518 18-100
www.palais-coburg.com
This is Vienna's most opulent hotel. The suites are all massive, with their own terraces, antique furniture, and mezzanine floors. Most of the rooftop-level space is occupied by a spectacular spa, complete with large swimming pool. Even the cheapest suites in the Palais are about twice the price of a room in one of the city's other upscale hotels, and a few nights in one of the "Imperial" suites will cost you more than a new car.
[] 35 P ⊟ ⊚ ⊛ ⊛ ⊠ ⊠ All major cards

⊞ ALMA BOUTIQUE HOTEL
$$$$
1, HAFNERSTEIG 7
TEL (1) 533 29 61
FAX (1) 533 29 61-81
www.hotel-alma.com
Formerly the Pension Christina, this hotel has recently undergone a total renovation. The rooms are wonderfully chic with a warming color scheme and art-nouveau illustrations on the walls.

[] 26 ⊟ ⊚ ⊛ ⊛ MC, V

⊞ HOTEL AM STEPHANSPLATZ
$$$$
1, STEPHANSPLATZ 9
TEL (1) 534 05-0
FAX (1) 534 05-710
www.hotelamstephansplatz.at
While its biggest selling point is its amazing location—a stone's throw from St. Stephen's Cathedral—this welcoming and stylish hotel is a good choice even if you ignore the view of the cathedral (which is difficult). The rooms are clean and uncluttered, with comfortable beds, modern bathrooms, and good sound insulation (which you'll be grateful for when the *Pummerin* bell strikes).
[] 56 ⊟ ⊚ ⊛ ⊛ ⊠ All major cards

⊞ HOTEL KARNTNERHOF
$$$
1, GRASHOFGASSE 4
TEL (1) 512 19 23
FAX (1) 513 22 28-33
www.karntnerhof.com
This attractive hotel, housed in a *Jugendstil* residential building, is hidden down a narrow side street close to the Fleischmarkt. The rooms are a good size, and still have their original parquet floors. Some of the rooms can get very hot in the summer months.
[] 44 P ⊟ ⊚ ⊛ All major cards

⊞ PENSION AVIANO
$$$
1, MARCO-D'AVIANO-GASSE 1
TEL (1) 512 83 30
FAX (1) 512 83 30-6
www.secrethomes.at
This top-floor pension is just off the Neuer Markt, opposite the Kapuzinergruft. The rooms are decorated in a frilly, Biedermeier style, with chandeliers and ornate mirrors, but have

---

⊚ Nonsmoking ⊛ Air-conditioning ⊠ Indoor Pool ⊠ Outdoor Pool ⊠ Health Club ⊛ Credit Cards

a decent range of modern conveniences.

ⓘ 17 ⊜ 🕸 V

🏨 HOTEL WANDL
$$$

1, PETERSPLATZ 9
TEL (1) 534 55-0
FAX (1) 534 55-77
www.hotel-wandl.com
This traditional, family-run hotel is just 200 yards (180 m) from St. Stephen's Cathedral. It was built in 1700 and converted to a hotel in 1851. Each of the large, high-ceilinged rooms has recently been refurbished, and many have small balconies with great views of Stephansplatz. The interior rooms, which face onto a roofed courtyard, can get very hot in the summer.

ⓘ 138 ⊜ Ⓢ 🕸 All major cards

🏨 MARC AUREL HOTEL
$$–$$$

1, MARC-AUREL STRASSE 8
TEL (1) 533 36 40
FAX (1) 533 00 78
www.hotel-marcaurel.at
This relatively inexpensive hotel is a good place to stay if you're going to be in town for only a few days and want to be close to the sights. The rooms are a little on the small side but are generally well maintained and comfortable.

ⓘ 30 🅿 ⊜ 🕸 MC, V

🏨 PENSION CITY
$$

1, BAUERNMARKT 10
TEL (1) 533 95 21
FAX (1) 533 52 16
www.citypension.at
A simple, no-frills guesthouse that provides clean rooms only 3 minutes' walk from Stephansplatz. Before it became a hotel, this is where the 19th-century poet Franz Grillparzer was born. The rooms are comfortable but lack air-conditioning, which

can make them stuffy in the summer months.

ⓘ 19 ⊜ Ⓢ 🕸 MC, V

RESTAURANTS

🍴 GRAND CAFÉ IM GRAND
$$$

HOTEL WIEN
1, KÄRNTNER RING 9
TEL (1) 515 80-9120
www.grandhotelwien.com
This elegant bastion of stylish good taste is on the second floor of the Grand Hotel, with fine views along the Ringstrasse. The restaurant's own breakfast sponge is made from a secret recipe.

🍴 92 🕸 All major cards

🍴 HIMMELPFORTE
$$$

1, HIMMELPFORTGASSE 24
TEL (1) 513 64 13
www.himmelpforte.at
Open from 11 a.m. to midnight, this fine-dining venue specializes in the highest standard of Viennese cuisine, including fondue creations and a selection of fine local wines.

🍴 140 🕸 MC, V

🍴 CAFÉ OPER WIEN
$$

1, HERBERT-VON-KARAJAN-PLATZ, 1
TEL (1) 513 39 57
www.cafeoperwien.at
Enjoy morning coffee, light lunches, snacks, and afternoon pastries in the grand historic setting of the Vienna Opera House building.

Ⓢ 🕸 MC, V

🍴 GASTHAUS ZUR STEI-RISCHEN JAGASTUB'N
$$

1, LANDESGERICHTSSTRASSE 12
TEL (1) 405 61 33
www.jagastubn.at
For rustic homemade Vien-

nese fare in a traditional tavern setting, this is just the place. Expect cold beer on tap, a decent range of Austrian wines, and big plates of food cooked to age-old recipes.

🍴 60 🕒 Closed Sat. & Sun.
🕸 V, MC

🍴 HERRENHOF
$$

1, HERRENGASSE 10
TEL (1) 534 04-0
www.herrenhof-wien
.steigenberger.at
A popular place for business lunches, the Herrenhof's pleasant atmosphere and fine food are so much more than corporate fodder, with excellent Viennese classics imaginatively served at breakfast, lunch, and dinner.

Ⓢ 🕸 V, MC

🍴 KANZLERAMT
$$

1, SCHAUFLERGASSE 6
TEL (1) 533 13 09
www.restaurant-kanzleramt
.at
Located next to the Hofburg, this wood-paneled restaurant offers diners a cozy experience amid a mixed clientele of politicians, media types, and ladies who lunch. Choose from a menu of exquisitely prepared Austrian specialties, from goose to schnitzel.

🕒 Closed Sun. 🕸 MC, V

🍴 KORSO
$$

1, MAHLERSTRASSE 2
TEL (1) 515 16-546
www.restaurantkorso.at
A popular dinner venue due to its mellow but classy ambience, the Korso also serves breakfast, lunch, and afternoon tea with specialties that include *tafelspitz*, veal liver; and Wiener schnitzel as well as scallop, pike perch, and creamed lobster soup.

🕸 MC, V

🍴 LISTAURANT
$$
1, WEIHBURGGASSE 3–5
TEL (1) 513 81 59
With some bold versions of olden Austrian classics on its pleasing menu, this well-run traditional restaurant boasts a charming interior decor of polished wood, Viennese prints, and spotless tiles.
🕐 Closed Sun. 💳 MC, V

🍴 LUBELLA
$$
1, KÄRNTNER STRASSE 32
TEL (1) 512 62 55
www.lubella.at
Located close to Kärntner Strasse just 2 minutes' walk from the Vienna Opera House, this stalwart of traditional Viennese cuisine also serves Italian and Russian cuisine with a variety of set menu options.
💳 AE, MC, V

🍴 MOTTO AM FLUSS
$$
1, SCHWEDENPLATZ 2
TEL (1) 25 255-11
www.motto.at/mottoamfluss
This bar, café, and restaurant caters for breakfasts from 8 a.m. through to drinks well past midnight when the last cocktail guzzler calls it a night. Lunch and dinner are recommended—the fish is particularly good.
💳 MC, V

🍴 OFENLOCH
$$
1, KURRENTGASSE 8
TEL (1) 533 88 44
www.ofenloch.at
At dinnertime the Ofenloch's wooden dining room is illuminated by candles lending a bygone charm to its character-packed period decor of stained glass, old prints, and high ceilings. In summer, terrace tables are popular—so

reserve ahead.
🕐 Closed Sun. 💳 MC, V

🍴 SOWIESO
$$
1, FLEISCHMARKT 19
TEL (1) 532 21 12
www.restaurantsowieso.com
This family-run Viennese eatery offers a highly tempting special menu that combines the best local produce and ingredients with some time-trusted recipes and considerable panache—the fillet steak is particularly good.
🕐 Closed Sun. 💳 MC, V

🍴 CAFÉ BRÄUNERHOF
$
1, STALLBURGGASSE 2
TEL (1) 512 38 93
Open only for breakfast, coffee, snacks, and lunch with a fine line of pastries, cakes, and desserts, as well as hot and cold light bites. An impressive range of coffees, soft drinks, beers, and wine.
💳 V

🍴 CAFÉ FRAUENHUBER
$
1, HIMMELPFORTGASSE 6-8
TEL (1) 512 53 53
www.cafefrauenhuber.at
Cozy hangout of resting shoppers and chatting office workers, with a good little menu packed with cakes, breads, and pastries, plus a first-rate range of coffees.
🔲 108 💳 MC, V

🍴 EINSTEIN
$
1, RATHAUSPLATZ 4
TEL (1) 405 26 26
www.einstein.at
Choose from croissants and freshly made sandwiches and baguettes to fresh juices, a wide variety of coffee options, and sodas. Opens at 7 a.m. weekdays for breakfast.
💳 AE, MC, V

🍴 EISSALON ZANONI
$
1, LUGECK 7
TEL (1) 512 79 79
www.zanoni.co.at
Pop in for crepes, freshly churned ice cream, desserts, and pastries in this popular pavement café where drinks and breakfast are served from 8 a.m. and light lunch snacks until 3 p.m.
💳 MC, V

■ THE HOFBURG QUARTER

HOTELS

SOMETHING SPECIAL

🏨 HOTEL BRISTOL
$$$$$
1, KÄRNTNER RING 1
TEL (1) 515 16-0
FAX (1) 515 16-550
www.starwoodhotels.com
Compared to its Ringstrasse neighbors, this 117-year-old hotel doesn't look that remarkable. Once you're inside, however, you can see why this place has developed a reputation as Vienna's finest luxury hotel. The public spaces are decorated with enough marble, gold leaf, and colossal paintings to make a Habsburg emperor jealous. The spacious rooms have been updated with the latest stylish features.
ⓘ 138 P 🔲 🅢 🅢 🌀 💳 All major cards

🏨 HOTEL SACHER
$$$$$
1, PHILHARMONIKERSTRASSE 4
TEL (1) 514 56-0
FAX (1) 514 56-810
www.sacher.com
This hotel is one of Vienna's finest. It was built in 1876, and some sections of the hotel maintain the opulent velvet and wood-paneling decor of

the original design. Opposite the Opera House and only a few minutes' walk from St. Stephen's Cathedral, the Hofburg Palace, and Karlsplatz.

🛈 152 🅿 ⬍ 🅂 🅂 📺
🖾 All major cards

🏨 HOTEL GRABEN
$$$$
1, DOROTHEERGASSE 3
TEL (1) 512 15 31-0
FAX (1) 512 15 31-20
www.kremslehnerhotels.at
The rooms are light and clean, with white walls and hardwood floors. The restaurant and public areas have retained the elegant period interiors that date from the time when the Hotel Graben was a popular hangout for the city's café intellectuals.

🛈 52 🅿 ⬍ 🅂 🖾 All major cards

🏨 A UND A
$$$–$$$$
1, HABSBURGERGASSE 3/14–16
TEL (1) 890 51 28
FAX (1) 890 51 28-28
www.aunda.at
Behind its fin-de-siècle facade, this small, family-run pension boasts striking modern decor and light, and uncluttered rooms. All the rooms have air-conditioning, flat-screen TVs, and high-speed Internet. With its stellar reputation and only eight rooms, it pays to reserve a long way in advance.

🛈 8 ⬍ 🅂 🅂 🖾 MC, V

🏨 HOTEL MAILBERGER HOF
$$$–$$$$
1, ANNAGASSE 7
TEL (1) 512 06 41
FAX (1) 512 06 41-10
www.mailbergerhof.at
This family-owned palais hotel was once the home of the crusading Knights Hospitaller, hence the Maltese cross over the entrance. The large rooms

are decorated in an ornate, but not overwhelming, neo-baroque style. The staff are helpful, the location excellent.

🛈 40 🅿 ⬍ 🅂 🅂 🖾 All major cards

🏨 HOTEL PERTSCHY
$$$–$$$$
1, HABSBURGERGASSE 5
TEL (1) 534 49-0
FAX (1) 534 49-49
www.pertschy.com
With its richly patterned wallpaper, marble staircases, and intricate stucco decoration, this converted palais is the best place to go if you want to immerse yourself in baroque Vienna. The bathrooms tend to be smallish, but the facilities are otherwise excellent.

🛈 55 ⬍ 🅂 🖾 All major cards

🏨 ZUR WIENER STAATSOPER
$$$
1, KRUGERSTRASSE 11
TEL (1) 513 12 74
FAX (1) 513 12 74-15
www.zurwienerstaatsoper.at
Housed in a grand baroque building just off the Ring-strasse, this charming hotel is a good option for those who want a central location without breaking the bank. Some of the rooms are cramped, but they have all the usual facilities, including tiny but well-maintained bathrooms.

🛈 22 ⬍ 🅂 🖾 MC, V

🏨 PENSION NEUER MARKT
$–$$
1, SEILERGASSE 9
TEL (1) 512 23 16
FAX (1) 513 91 054
www.hotelpension.at
Probably the most affordable option in the Innere Stadt, offering uncluttered, clean rooms at very low prices.

🛈 37 ⬍ 🖾 MC, V

PRICES

HOTELS
The cost of a double room with en-suite bathroom is given by $ signs. In the low season rates can be considerably lower.

$$$$$	Over €210
$$$$	€141–€210
$$$	€101–€140
$$	€55–€100
$	Under €55

RESTAURANTS
The average cost of a two-course meal for one person, excluding a tip or drinks, is given by $ signs.

$$$$$	Over €30
$$$$	€26–€30
$$$	€18–€25
$$	€10–€17
$	Under €10

RESTAURANTS

🍴 AT EIGHT
$$$
1, KÄRNTNER RING 8
TEL (1) 221 22-38 30
www.ateight-restaurant.at
This light, roomy bistro prides itself on gourmet food that combines different spices and sauces with fresh local and exotic herbs. With 50 seats plus an outside terrace (spring and summer only), At Eight is famous for its irresistible, reasonably priced lunch menu.

🍴 50 🖾 MC, V

🍴 LE CIEL
$$$
1, GRAND HOTEL WIEN KÄRNTNER RING 9
TEL (1) 515 80-9100
www.leciel.at
Mixing French cooking technique with Austrian traditions, the menu at Le Ciel is accented by the heavenly

---

views from the restaurant windows. Housed on the seventh floor of the Grand Hotel Wien, Le Ciel provides good food, creatively presented.

🕐 Closed Sun. 🅢 🅒 MC, V

🍴 MARTINJAK
$$
1, OPERNRING 11
TEL (1) 535 69 69
www.martinjak.com
This modern, light, and airy bistro-style diner is a favorite for its menu of small portions of Austrian classics.

🅒 🅒 MC, V

🍴 WEINBOTSCHAFT
$$
1, ANNAGASSE 12
TEL (1) 512 85 10
www.weinbotschaft.at
Combines organic food and excellent local wines with a touch of an Italian *osteria* and a Spanish *taperia*. Plenty of Viennese charm in a comfortable setting where conviviality reigns supreme.

🕐 Closed Sun. 🅒 MC, V

■ ALSERGRUND

HOTELS

🏨 ARKADENHOF HOTEL
$$$-$$$$
9, VIRIOTGASSE 5
TEL (1) 310 08 37
FAX (1) 310 76 68
www.arkadenhof.com
While it looks to be a long way from the city center, the nearby U-Bahn and Strassenbahn stations mean that you're rarely more than 20 minutes from any of Vienna's sights. The rooms are spacious and comfortable.

🛈 45 🖃 🅢 🅒 🅒 MC, V

🏨 HOTEL DEUTSCHMEISTER
$$-$$$

9, GRÜNENTORGASSE 30
TEL (1) 310 34 04
FAX (1) 310 04 80
www.city-hotels.at
A reliable, old-fashioned hotel at a reasonable price. Located just off the Donaukanal waterfront, it provides decent-size, if rather gloomy, rooms and comfortable beds.

🛈 52 🖃 🅢 🅒 🅒 MC, V

🏨 HOTEL BLECKMANN
$$
9, WÄHRINGER STRASSE 15
TEL (1) 408 08 99
FAX (1) 402 20 24
www.hotelbleckmann.at
Simple, comfortable accommodation in a convenient spot. You won't get much in the way of frills or luxuries, but it is a good option for those on a tight budget.

🛈 27 🅿 🖃 🅒 MC, V

🏨 HOTEL-PENSION FRANZ
$$
9, WÄHRINGER STRASSE 12
TEL (1) 310 40 40-0
FAX (1) 310 40 40-23
www.hotelpensionfranz.at
The overall impression given by this budget pension is one of faded grandeur. The hallways and public rooms are spectacular, with dark oak paneling, carved wooden staircases, and heavy-framed oil paintings. The rooms, however, are rather mixed, with curiously mismatched furniture and faded decor. Try to get a room with a view of the nearby Votivkirche.

🛈 24 🅿 🖃 🅒 Cash only

🏨 PENSION ANI-FALSTAFF
$$
9, MÜLLNERGASSE 5
TEL (1) 317 91 27
FAX (1) 317 91 27-10
www.freerooms.at
This family-run pension is a block away from the restaurants of Servitengasse. The Ani-Falstaff doesn't have many

modern luxuries, but it does have spacious, clean rooms, friendly staff, and very reasonable prices. Only 15 minutes' walk to the Innere Stadt.

🛈 15 🅒 MC, V

🏨 BENEDIKTUSHAUS
$-$$
1, FREYUNG 6A
TEL (1) 534 98-900
FAX (1) 534 98-905
www.benediktushaus.at
One of Vienna's more unusual hotels, the Benediktushaus is within the Schottenstift—an active Benedictine monastery. The rooms are scrupulously neat and clean, with rather narrow beds (which can be put together for married couples), and simple, modern furniture. Guests will have to respect the wishes of the monks who run the establishment, so it's probably not a place to go for a romantic weekend getaway.

🛈 21 🖃 🅢 🅒 MC, V

RESTAURANTS

🍴 STOMACH
$$$
9, SEEGASSE 26
TEL (1) 310 20 99
Unpretentious and cozy, Stomach offers a mix of traditional Austrian fare and zany specialties. Excellent quality, filling portions, and a good choice of wine. If you visit in winter don't opt for the two seats next to the traditional tiled stove: They are reserved for the cats. Service is friendly and the owner will probably drop by your table for a chat.

🪑 30 🕐 Closed Mon. & Tues. 🅒 MC, V

🍴 FLEIN
$
9, BOLTZMANNGASSE 2
TEL (1) 319 76 89
Flein offers tasty local dishes

at budget prices. This popular organic café, alongside the grounds of the French lycée, has outdoor seating in good weather. The menu changes daily. Flein can get crowded at lunchtime, so be sure to reserve a table.
🪑 60 🕐 Closed Sat. & Sun. 🃏 All major cards

■ EASTERN VIENNA

LEOPOLDSTADT

HOTELS

🏨 **SOFITEL VIENNA STEPHANSDOM**
$$$$–$$$$$
2, PRATERSTRASSE 1
TEL (1) 906 16-0
FAX (1) 906 16-2000
www.sofitel.com
This spectacular addition to the Vienna skyline was designed by the renowned French architect Jean Nouvel. The architect's radical design extends to the interior spaces as well as the landmark exterior, with all the rooms boasting custom-designed furniture and a bold monochromatic color scheme. Most of the rooms offer jaw-dropping views, and those facing the Innere Stadt cost more.
ⓘ 182 🅿 🖃 🚫 🎇 🛗 🃏 All major cards

🏨 **HOTEL IMLAUER**
$$$$
2, ROTENSTERNGASSE 10
TEL (1) 211 40-0
FAX (1) 211 40-7
www.imlauer.com /imlauerwien
Close to Augarten, this hotel features air-conditioned, soundproofed rooms with Wi-Fi, as does its neighbor and sister hotel, Hotel Nestroy.
ⓘ 60 🅿 🖃 🚫 🎇 🛗 🃏 All major cards

🏨 **HOTEL STEFANIE**
$$$$
2, TABORSTRASSE 12
TEL (1) 211 50-0
FAX (1) 211 50-160
www.schick-hotels.com
This traditional hotel has been run by the Schick family (who now run several hotels around the city) since it opened its doors in 1870. It is a characterful old building with fin-de-siècle decor in the public spaces and simply furnished but comfortable rooms. The courtyard restaurant is also excellent. The hotel offers a quieter location and more spacious accommodation than similar hotels around the Ringstrasse.
ⓘ 131 🖃 🚫 🎇 🃏 All major cards

🏨 **DER WILHELMSHOF**
$$$
2, KLEINE STADTGUTGASSE 4
TEL (1) 214 55 210
FAX (1) 214 55 212-33
www.derwilhelmshof.com
No other hotel captures Leopoldstadt's youthful character as well as the Wilhelmshof. The rooms are uncluttered and modern, with stylish decoration designed by local artists, and are fitted with luxury features like under-floor heating in the bathrooms. Convenient for Praterstern Station and the city center.
ⓘ 58 🅿 🖃 🚫 🎇 🃏 All major cards

🏨 **HOTEL CAPRI**
$$$
2, PRATERSTRASSE 44–46
TEL (1) 214 84 04
FAX (1) 214 27 85
www.hotelcapri.at
The standard of accommodation here is of a much higher quality than many of its upscale rivals. The rooms are spacious, light, and well maintained, with some offering views over the Prater. Nestroyplatz subway station is only a few yards from the entrance.
ⓘ 70 🅿 🖃 🃏 MC, V

🏨 **HOTEL RESONANZ**
$$–$$$
2, TABORSTRASSE 47
TEL (1) 955 32 52
FAX (1) 955 32 52-35
www.adler-hotels-wien.at
Recently refurbished, this conveniently located hotel offers decent, if rather small, rooms close to the Augarten.
ⓘ 37 🖃 🃏 MC, V

🏨 **HOTEL FRANZENSHOF**
$$
2, GROSSE STADTGUTGASSE 19
TEL (1) 216 62 82
FAX (1) 216 84 61
www.hotel-franzenshof.at
Just a 5-minute walk from the Prater, and 10 minutes by U-Bahn from the city center, this popular hotel boasts bold, bright decor and modern amenities, plus a restaurant and bar.
ⓘ 38 🅿 🖃 🚫 🃏 DC, MC, V

RESTAURANTS

🍴 **SOFRA**
$$$
2, KAFKASTEG 9
TEL (1) 890 04 24
www.sofra-restaurant.at
With gorgeous waterside views and expansive outside seating, this charming restaurant has a strong Austro-international menu.
🃏 MC, V

🍴 **STADTGASTHAUS EISVOGEL**
$$$
2, RIESENRADPLATZ 5
TEL (1) 908 11 87
www.stadtgasthaus-eis vogel.at
This highly regarded Viennese eatery first opened its doors in the early 19th century.

🏨 Hotel 🍴 Restaurant ⓘ No. of Guest Rooms 🪑 No. of Seats 🅿 Parking 🕐 Closed 🖃 Elevator

Today, its loyal clientele adores a menu of traditional home-cooked favorites at the foot of Vienna's giant Ferris wheel—a truly iconic setting.

⬛ MC, V

FLORIDSDORF & DONAUSTADT

HOTELS

⊞ ARCOTEL KAISERWASSER
$$–$$$$
22, WAGRAMER STRASSE 8
TEL (1) 224 24-0
FAX (1) 224 24-710
www.arcotel.at/en
/kaiserwasser_hotel_vienna
A spectacular waterfront position differentiates this attractive modern hotel from the clutch of other international chain hotels nearby. Its location—close to the Alte Donau's swimming beaches and U-Bahn station—makes it a good choice. The rooms are spacious, clean, and artfully decorated.

ⓘ 282 🅿 ⬛ ⬛ ⬛ ⬛ ⬛
⬛ All major cards

⊞ STRANDHOTEL ALTE DONAU
$$$
22, WAGRAMER STRASSE 51
TEL (1) 204 40 40
FAX (1) 204 40 40-40
www.strandhotel-alte
-donau.at
From its position on the north bank of the Alte Donau, this small family-run hotel combines an outside-of-town atmosphere with inner-city convenience (the nearby U-Bahn station will get you to Stephansplatz in about 10 minutes).The rooms feature vibrant, modern decor, and many have spectacular views over the Alte Donau to the glittering towers of the UNO City beyond. The hotel has a private deck on the waterfront

for those who want to go swimming or out on the hotel's rowboat.

ⓘ 29 🅿 ⬛ ⬛ ⬛ DC, MC, V

⊞ HOTEL WIENER KINDL
$–$$
22, STADLAUERSTRASSE 31
TEL (1) 280 57 72
FAX (1) 282 14 68-8
www.hotelwienerkindl.at
This small family hotel is far out in the suburbs of Donaustadt, but still close enough to the U-Bahn (about a 5-minute walk to Aspernstrasse Station and a 20-minute ride to the Innere Stadt) to make it accessible. The rooms are clean and cozy.

ⓘ 26 🅿 ⬛ ⬛ ⬛ MC, V

RESTAURANT

🍴 DONAUTURM
$$–$$$
22, DONAUTURMSTRASSE 4
TEL (1) 263 35 72
www.donauturm.at
For a meal with a view, the restaurant high on the Donauturm tower is unforgettable. You must book for a 2-hour table reservation, during which time the restaurant rotates, giving diners a slowly changing panorama of the city below. Favorite dishes include roast beef and Viennese grilled chicken. Expect to pay a little more than you would for similar dining at ground level.

⬛ ⬛ MC, V

◼ SOUTHERN VIENNA

KARLSPLATZ

HOTELS

⊞ HOTEL JOHANN STRAUSS
$$$$
4, FAVORITENSTRASSE 12

TEL (1) 505 76 24
FAX (1) 505 76 28
www.hotel-johann-strauss.at
Traditional Viennese charm meets international modernity at this popular mid-size hotel. Close to Karlsplatz and most city sights.

ⓘ 75 🅿 ⬛ ⬛ ⬛ ⬛ All major cards

SOMETHING SPECIAL

⊞ HOTEL KAISERHOF
$$$$
4, FRANKENBERGGASSE 10
TEL (1) 505 17 01
FAX (1) 505 88 75-88
www.hotel-kaiserhof.at
After a recent refurbishment, this hotel is one of the most elegant establishments in the vorstädte. Although the decor and furnishings are traditional, the hotel's facilities are well maintained and up to date. Each room has air-conditioning, free Wi-Fi, and unique adjustable beds that can be tailored to individual tastes.Visitors can relax in the luxury spa or enjoy a snack in the hotel's lounge bar area surrounded by historic prints, maps, and shelves of Viennese literature.

ⓘ 76 🅿 ⬛ ⬛ ⬛ ⬛ ⬛ All major cards

⊞ ART HOTEL VIENNA
$$–$$$
5, BRANDMAYERGASSE 7–9
TEL (1) 544 51 08
FAX (1) 544 51 08-10
www.thearthotelvienna.at
This unique hotel is ideal for those who have come to Vienna for its galleries and art museums. Paintings by local artists are displayed throughout. Try upgrading to the "studio" rooms. These aren't much more expensive than the regular doubles but have more space and character—some even have balconies.

ⓘ 48 🅿 ⬛ ⬛ ⬛ MC, V

CARLTON OPERA HOTEL
$$–$$$

4, SCHIKANEDERGASSE 4
TEL (1) 587 53 02
FAX (1) 581 25 11
www.carlton.at

Set on a peaceful one-way street, this elegant art nouveau hotel is wedged between the Naschmarkt and Karlsplatz. It is the perfect base for anyone keen to do some serious shopping along Mariahilf and Kärntner Strasse.

ⓘ 52 🅿 ⇕ Ⓢ Ⓒ 📺
AE, MC, V

HOTEL DREI KRONEN
$$–$$$

4, SCHLEIFMÜHLGASSE 25
TEL (1) 587 32 89
FAX (1) 587 32 89-11
www.hotel3kronen.at

This listed historic building was built in 1897 by Jugendstil architect Ignaz Drapala and painstakingly renovated in 2008. It is near the Naschmarkt's fascinating cafés and bars, and a 5-minute walk from the Botanical Garden at Belvedere Palace.

ⓘ 75 🅿 ⇕ MC, V

HOTEL PAPAGENO
$$–$$$

4, WIEDNER HAUPTSTRASSE 23–25
TEL (1) 504 67 44
FAX (1) 504 67 44-22
www.hotelpapageno.at

Modern, arty decor and well-appointed rooms combine to make this a first-rate option close to Karlsplatz. It's not traditional Viennese style or sumptuous luxury, but it's good value for the location.

ⓘ 50 🅿 ⇕ Ⓢ MC, V

RESTAURANTS

KUNSTHALLE-CAFÉ AM KARLSPLATZ

$–$$

4, TREITLSTRASSE 2
TEL (1) 587 00 73
www.kunsthallencafe.at

This popular central café is a favorite meeting place for the young creative set. In the same building as the Kunsthalle Art Project Space, it has an outdoor terrace feturing a DJ on summer evenings. Try the generous hamburgers.

AE, MC, V

ART CORNER, GRIECHISCHES CAFÉ & SPEZIALITÄTEN

$

4, PRINZ-EUGEN-STRASSE 56
TEL (1) 505 18 21
www.art-corner.at

Another fine Viennese culinary institution where an inexpensive menu covers all the favorites together with a surprisingly long list of cocktails and an impressive specials board that changes every day.

🎟 60 MC, V

LANDSTRASSE

HOTELS

IMPERIAL RIDING SCHOOL
$$–$$$$$

3, UNGARGASSE 60
TEL (1) 711 75-0
FAX (1) 711 75-8145
www.imperialrenaissance.com

A luxurious hotel on the edge of the diplomatic quarter. The rooms are nicely decorated and spacious. Few hotels in Vienna can match the Riding School for facilities. However, the hotel is not necessarily as good a deal as it appears—watch out for the additional charges.

ⓘ 369 🅿 ⇕ Ⓢ Ⓒ 🅱
🅰 📺 All major cards

GARTENHOTEL GABRIEL

$$–$$$

3, LANDSTRASSER HAUPTSTRASSE 165
TEL (1) 712 32 05
FAX (1) 712 67 54-10
www.adler-hotels-wien.at

As the name would suggest, this hotel is far enough from the city center to have its own leafy garden—where breakfast is served in summer. The rooms have been refurbished and are well maintained, if not particularly distinctive.

ⓘ 55 🅿 Ⓢ All major cards

MERCURE GRAND HOTEL BIEDERMEIER WIEN
$$–$$$

3, LANDSTRASSER HAUPTSTRASSE 28
TEL (1) 716 71-0
FAX (1) 716 71-503
www.mercure.com

The cozy style of the Biedermeier era has been used

throughout this modern hotel, giving it a distinctive and comfortable atmosphere. The rooms are spacious and clean, although some might find the bathrooms a little cramped.

ⓘ 198 P ⊟ Ⓢ Ⓢ Ⓥ
Ⓢ All major cards

RESTAURANTS

⅋ BIERAMT
$$

3, AM HEUMARKT 3
TEL (1) 712 47 19
www.bieramt.at
A trusted bastion of Viennese fare, from roasted game to pan-fried river fish and dumplings, Bieramt is popular with romantic hand-holding couples, small family groups, and business groups alike.

⊞ 70 Ⓢ MC, V

⅋ STADTPARKBRÄU
$$

3, AM HEUMARKT 5
TEL (1) 713 71 02
www.stadtparkbraeu.at
Expect big jugs of Austrian beer, wines from the country, and old-fashioned hospitality at this traditional Vien-nese food joint. Fabulous vintage architecture and rustic furnishings combine in a cozy ambience.

⊞ 200 Ⓢ MC, V

⅋ PETRUS UND PAULUS STUBEN
$–$$

3, PAULUSGASSE 2
TEL (1) 967 37 98
www.petrus-paulus.at
With its wood-paneled dining rooms, thick floor tiles, and old-fashioned fixtures and fittings, this traditional eatery offers a quintessential Vien-nese culinary splurge. Expect man-size portions of home-cooked classics and a selection of robust Austrian beers.

Ⓢ MC, V

⅋ ROCHUS
$–$$

3, LANDSTRASSER HAUPT-
STRASSE 55–57
TEL (1) 710 10 60
www.rochus.at
Offering a myriad of local dishes, from dumplings and schnitzel to braised game, roasted pork, and hearty des-serts, this stalwart of Austrian cuisine hosts numerous calendar events and has put a modern spin on old-style cooking.

Ⓢ Ⓢ MC, V

⅋ SILBERWIRT
$

5, SCHLOSSGASSE 21
TEL (1) 544 49 07
www.schlossquadr.at
Order tasty Austro-Italian fare from the restaurant, or fast food, snacks, and cocktails from the diner at this simple family-run eatery—grab an outside table in summer.

Ⓢ Cash only

⅋ STEGERS
$

3, UNTERE VIADUKTGASSE 3
TEL (1) 713 54 71
www.stegersgasthaus.at
Visitors looking for an authen-tic neighborhood kitchen will enjoy mingling with the locals at this no-frills food and drink hangout. Tables spill out onto the street, and the menu runs from early morning until late at night.

⊞ 30 ⏱ Closed Sat.
Ⓢ MC, V

◼ WESTERN VIENNA

HOTELS

⌂ K+K HOTEL MARIA THERESIA
$$$$$

7, KIRCHBERGGASSE 6
TEL (1) 521 23

FAX (1) 521 23-70
www.kkhotels.at
This friendly medium-size hotel is in the heart of Spittelberg, just behind the MuseumsQuartier. The rooms are spacious and modern.

ⓘ 123 P ⊟ Ⓢ Ⓢ Ⓥ
Ⓢ All major cards

⌂ BOUTIQUE-HOTEL STADTHALLE
$$$$

15, HACKENGASSE 20
TEL (1) 982 42 72
FAX (1) 982 42 72-56
www.hotelstadthalle.at
This eco-friendly boutique hotel, 5 minutes from the Westbahnhof U-Bahn Station, is the world's first city hotel with a zero energy-balance. The rooms are sleek and modern, and guests can enjoy breakfast in the quiet garden.

ⓘ 81 P ⊟ Ⓢ Ⓢ All major cards

⌂ HOTEL RATHAUS
$$$$

7, LANGE GASSE 13
TEL (1) 400 11 22
FAX (1) 400 11 22-88
www.hotel-rathaus-wien.at
Although it doesn't look like much from the outside, this boutique hotel is widely regarded as one of the finest in Vienna. The rooms are beauti-fully decorated and furnished in a minimalist, modern style. The staff are enthusiastic, with plenty of insider information. Convenient for the Museums-Quartier.

ⓘ 40 ⊟ Ⓢ Ⓢ Ⓥ
Ⓢ All major cards

SOMETHING SPECIAL

⌂ HOTEL ALTSTADT
$$$–$$$$

7, KIRCHENGASSE 41
TEL (1) 522 66 66
FAX (1) 523 49 01
www.altstadt.at

This achingly stylish modern hotel is the work of Otto Wiesenthal, a designer and art collector. Each of the playfully decorated modern rooms and suites has been designed around the work of a particular local artist, whose paintings adorn the walls. This is one of Vienna's coolest places to stay.

[I] 42 [P] [⇄] [⊗]
[⬦] All major cards

🏨 HOTEL DAS PRESIDENT
$$$–$$$$

6, WALLGASSE 23
TEL (1) 599 90
FAX (1) 599 90-904
www.daspresident.at
Housed in a rather brutal modern building opposite the famous Raimund Theater, the Hotel Das President is much nicer on the inside, with comfortable rooms and well-appointed public areas. It is close to Gumpendorfer Strasse U-Bahn and Mariahilfer Strasse's shops.

[I] 77 [P] [⇄] [⊗] [⬦] MC, V

🏨 HOTEL AM BRILLANTENGRUND
$$$

7, BANDGASSE 4
TEL (1) 523 36 62
FAX (1) 523 36 62-83
www.brillantengrund.at
The Brillantengrund prides itself on home comforts and makes a superb alternative to a large, impersonal city hotel. Built in the Biedermeier style, it is a protected national landmark, and the rooms, while not original, match the general style. It is conveniently located just 350 yards (320 m) from the shopping district of Mariahilfer Strasse.

[I] 77 [P] [⇄] [⊗] [⬦] MC, V

🏨 HOTEL ZIPSER
$$–$$$$

8, LANGE GASSE 49

TEL (1) 404 54-0
FAX (1) 404 54-13
www.zipser.at
This hotel, housed in a fine Ringstrasse-era building, has been run by the Austerer family for three generations. Although its old-fashioned exterior hasn't changed much in that time, the rooms inside have been extensively modernized, and now boast stylish modern decor, spacious bathrooms, and comfortable beds.

[I] 55 [P] [⇄] [⊗] [⬦] MC, V

🏨 HAYDN HOTEL
$$–$$$

6, MARIAHILFERSTRASSE 57–59
TEL (1) 587 44 14-0
FAX (1) 586 19 50
www.haydn-hotel.at
Despite being right in the center of Vienna's main shopping district and close to Neubaugasse U-Bahn, the Haydn offers surprisingly quiet and comfortable accommodation.

[I] 50 [P] [⇄] [⊗] [⬦] MC, V

🏨 HOTEL KOROTAN
$$

8, ALBERTGASSE 48
TEL (1) 403 41 93
FAX (1) 403 41 93-99
www.korotan.com
Behind its striking glass-and-steel facade, this is a fairly conventional no-frills hotel, with simple, plain rooms and very reasonable rates. The hotel often seems a little short-staffed, so it's worth calling ahead to make sure someone will be there to check you in on arrival.

[I] 61 [P] [⇄] [⊗] [⬦] MC, V

RESTAURANTS

🍴 GÜRTELBRÄU
$$

8, LERCHENFELDER GÜRTEL 24
TEL (1) 402 41 95

www.guertelbraeu.com
This lively old brew-house eatery hosts a happy hour every day at 6 p.m. It offers a daily menu of ever changing special dishes, together with a standard menu that runs Mon.–Fri., plus regular themed nights.

[🪑] 80 [⬦] MC, V

🍴 SALONICA
$$

7, ZIEGLERGASSE 29
TEL (1) 524 98 11
www.salonica.at
Inexpensive family-run Greek taverna with a menu straight from the backstreets of Athens, from grilled squid and octopus to skewered pork and lamb stews. Be sure to try the *skordalia* (mashed potatoes with garlic)—it's truly divine.

[⊘] Closed Sun. [⬦] V

🍴 SELINA
$$

8, LAUDONGASSE 13
TEL (1) 405 64 04
www.selina.at
With the look and feel of an Austrian living room, the Selina is a welcoming place to enjoy a pretheater dinner or post-performance supper at well-dressed tables groaning under heavy cutlery and flower-filled jugs.

[🪑] 70 [⬦] MC, V

🍴 G'SCHAMSTER DIENER
$

6, STUMPERGASSE 19
TEL (1) 597 25 28
www.gschamsterdiener.com
This family-owned Austrian café serves up big bowls of soup and goulash, as well as great-tasting sausages, potato pasta, and pancakes—all at shoestring prices.

[⬦] DC, MC, V

🏨 Hotel 🍴 Restaurant [I] No. of Guest Rooms 🪑 No. of Seats [P] Parking [⊘] Closed [⇄] Elevator

■ DAY TRIPS

EAST OF THE CITY

⌂ ALTES KLOSTER
$$$–$$$$
FABRIKSPLATZ 1A
HAINBURG AN DER DONAU
TEL 2165 64020
www.alteskloster.at
This hotel is housed in a
converted monastery. The
hotel's interior walls have been
left white and unadorned
to show off the elegance of
the old barrel-vaulted rooms.
Many rooms have views of
the river and others look on to
the quiet, tree-filled courtyard.
The restaurant is excellent.
ⓘ 52 🅿 🅂 🅂 Cash only

⌂ HOTEL DANUBIUS
$–$$
AM MARKT 6
ORTH-AN-DER-DONAU
TEL 2212 24 00-0
FAX 2212 24 00-82
www.hotel-danubius.at
Located in the picturesque
town of Orth-an-der-Donau,
on the edge of the Donau-
Auen National Park, this
small family-run hotel and
restaurant is distinguished by
its bright yellow exterior.
ⓘ 25 🅿 🅂 🅂 All major cards

⌂ PENSION SCHLOSSBLICK
$–$$
HANFGARTENWEG 10
ORTH-AN-DER-DONAU
TEL 2212 27 72
www.pension-schlossblick
.com
A lovely modern bed-and-
breakfast surrounded by a
lovely garden on the outskirts
of Orth. The Schlossblick
(castle view) offers light, comfortable rooms, all with
en suite bathrooms.
ⓘ 5 🅿 🅂 🅂 Cash only

SOMETHING SPECIAL

▥ UFERHAUS
$$–$$$
UFERSTRASSE 20
ORTH-AN-DER-DONAU
TEL 0664 1800 322
www.uferhaus.at
A friendly, family-run restaurant in a beautiful riverside
location just outside Orth.
The restaurant specializes in
traditional fish dishes, using
pike, trout, and carp from
local rivers.
🄴 90 🅿 🅂 🄴 Closed Tues.
& Wed., Oct.–April 🅂 Cash
only

SOUTH OF VIENNA

⌂ HOTEL SCHLOSS WEIKERSDORF
$$$$$
SCHLOSSGASSE 9–11, BADEN
TEL 2252 48301-0
FAX 2252 48301-150
www.austria-hotels.at/
hotel-schloss-weikersdorf
One of Baden's most luxurious spa hotels, the Schloss
Weikersdorf is located just
outside the center of town.
This converted palace houses
a well-equipped spa as well
as a spacious hotel.
ⓘ 100 🅿 🄴 🅆 🅂 All
major cards

WEST OF VIENNA

⌂ HOTEL SCHLOSS DÜRNSTEIN
$$$$$
SCHLOSS DÜRNSTEIN
DÜRNSTEIN
TEL 2711 212
FAX 2711 212-30
www.schloss.at
A room in this converted
castle is certainly not cheap,
but with its sumptuous
baroque rooms and spec-
tacular views over the river
and the town of Dürnstein it
has no equal in the area.

ⓘ 41 🅿 🄴 Closed Nov.–
April 🄴 🄴 🅂 🅆
🅂 All major cards

⌂ HOTEL STADT MELK
$$$
HAUPTPLATZ 1, MELK
TEL 2165 64020
www.tiscover.com
This delightful little hotel,
with its flower-covered
facade and old-fashioned
atmosphere, is right in the
center of Melk. You may be
woken by the bells of nearby
Melk Abbey.
ⓘ 14 🅿 🅂 🅂 All major
cards

⌂ SÄNGER BLONDEL
$$$
DÜRNSTEIN 64, DÜRNSTEIN
TEL (0) 2711 253
FAX (0) 2711 253-7
www.saengerblondel.at
Named after the legendry
minstrel who searched the
Donau Valley for his master,
Richard the Lion-Hearted (see
p. 24), this charming guesthouse combines comfortable
accommodation with an
excellent restaurant.
ⓘ 15 🅿 🅂 🅂 MC, V

Shopping

When it comes to shopping, Vienna is invariably associated with the luxuries of a bygone age. Visitors tend to expect a city of dark old-fashioned stores where expensive jewelry and fine crystal are sold with the same earnest formality you'd expect from an undertaker. In reality, however, Vienna offers vibrant and varied opportunities, where a broad spectrum of international brands compete with quirky independent stores and local craftspeople.

Vienna has two main shopping districts: Mariahilfer Strasse (see pp. 208–209) and the Golden U (see p. 124). The former is where the Viennese go when they want to do some serious shopping—it is a long avenue lined with big-brand clothing stores, consumer electronics shops, and large department stores. In the side streets off the main avenue you'll find clusters of independent stores and trendy boutiques. The Golden U is a considerably more upscale shopping area formed by the intersecting streets of Kohlmarkt, Graben, and Kärntner Strasse. On the Kohlmarkt you'll find Vienna's most upscale stores, where few will ever be able to do more than window-shop, while on the Graben and Kärntner Strasse things are a little cheaper. Just off the Graben is Dorotheergasse, where most of the city's antiques stores are to be found.

In addition to these two main shopping areas there are numerous smaller clusters of independent shops scattered around the city. It's worth remembering that many of the city's smaller stores don't take credit cards, or take them only for large purchases, so make sure you've got a reasonable amount of cash.

Antiques

Whether you're looking for an elegant Jugendstil lamp or a brightly colored piece of 1970s kitsch, Vienna has a store for you. Between the two poles of the high-class Dorotheum and the weird knickknacks of the

Flohmarkt (see p. 204) there's no shortage of interesting stores to investigate.

Bel Etage
1, Mahlerstrasee 15
Tel (1) 512 23 79
www.beletage.com
This store specializes in furniture, art, clocks, and other decorative items from the Jugendstil era. The stock on display is simply stunning, but it's not cheap.

Carla
5, Mittersteig 10
Tel (1) 505 96 37
www.carla.at
A massive vintage store in Wieden, owned and operated by the international charity Caritas. Best described as a kind of indoor Flohmarkt. Not a place to find high-quality antiques, but good for vintage clothing and curios.

Dorotheum
1, Dorotheergasse 17
Tel (1) 515 60-0
www.dorotheum.com
Vienna's premier auction house. There are daily auctions as well as a wide range of antiques and collectibles available to buy. You probably won't find any bargains here, but it's worth visiting to view the mesmerizingly pretty items on display.

Glasfabrik
16, Lorenz Mandlgasse 25
Tel (1) 494 34 90
www.glasfabrik.at
Named for the huge old glassworks in which it is located, this sprawling antiques store in

Ottakring sells items from as recently as the 1970s and as far back as the 1670s. You'll find everything from antique furniture to off-the-wall 1960s kitsch.

Books

Vienna has more than its fair share of bookshops, ranging from dusty antiquarian stores to colossal bookshops that cover several floors and have works in almost every language. Of course, most of these shops are of little interest to people who don't speak German, but there are a few stores worth a look—whether you want a souvenir, or just something to read on the plane home.

Babettes
4, Schleifmühlgasse 17
Tel (1) 585 51 65
www.babettes.at
Not many bookshops have a large open kitchen in the middle of the store, but that's all part of the hands-on approach at this cookery bookshop. Many of the books are in German, but the recipes aren't usually that hard to follow. Good if you're hooked on Viennese cuisine. Near Karlsplatz.

Shakespeare & Co.
1, Sterngasse 2
Tel (1) 535 50 53
www.shakespeare.co.at
A well-stocked English-language bookshop hidden down a charming side street in the Jewish Quarter.

Walther König Books
1, MuseumsQuartier

Tel (1) 512 85-880
Occupying a high vaulted room in
the MuseumsQuartier, this large
store specializes in big glossy
books on art and architecture.

Fashion

In addition to all the usual
designer brands, Vienna has a
lively fashion scene, with a vast
number of small independent
boutiques, each selling its own
unique creations, often at very
reasonable prices.

Fräuleinwunder
7, Neubaugasse 6
Tel (1) 535 40 34
www.fraeuleinwunder.info
A women's clothing store in Neubau that stocks dresses by many
young Austrian designers.

Freistil
1, Judengasse 4
Tel (1) 535 94 77
www.freistil.at
A cavernous vintage store with
a fine selection of old hats and
formal wear.

Gloom
7, Neubaugasse 75
Tel (1) 523 86 57
www.gloom.at
This oddly named store (it's
actually painted in a psychedelic
rainbow color scheme) sells
quirky summer dresses and bright
casual wear. In Neubau.

Göttin des Glücks
4, Operngasse 32
Tel (0) 676 358 74 15
www.goettindesgluecks.com
All the stylish outfits in this
great store near Karlsplatz are
designed and made in a fair-trade
collaboration with a company in
Mauritius.

Handschuh Peter
3, Landstrasser Hauptstrasse
83–85

Tel (1) 715 97 31
www.handschuhpeter.at
Handschuh Peter has been making fine gloves for more than 150
years. Its products range from
sturdy leather driving gloves to
delicate satin evening gloves. In
Landstrasse.

Herzilein Wien
1, Wollzeile 17
Tel (0) 676 657 71 06
www.herzilein-wien.at
Vienna's finest children's fashion
boutique, selling handmade clothing for girls and boys. All its lines
are designed and made in the city.

Kabine
2, Karmelitergasse 6
Tel (1) 236 02 88
Located at the heart of Leopoldstadt's hip Karmeliterviertel
neighborhood, this store sells
clothes, accessories, and offbeat
gifts made from recycled objects
like bike tires and plastic bottles.

Mühlbauer
1, Seilergasse 10
Tel (1) 512 22 41
www.muehlbauer.at
Lovingly handcrafted men's and
women's hats. Very expensive,
but they are really nice hats.

Polyklamott
6, Hofmühlgasse 6
Tel (1) 969 03 37
www.polyklamott.at
The emphasis in this trendy
vintage store in Mariahilf is not
on fine couture but on everyday
clothes and quirky T-shirts from
times gone by.

Sisi Vienna
1, Annagasse 11
Tel (1) 513 05 18
www.sisi-vienna.at
This small boutique takes
Empress Sisi as its inspiration,
crafting outfits that are a unique
mixture of old and new.

Song
2., Praterstrasse 11–13
Tel (1) 532 28 58
www.song.at
Über-trendy fashion boutique
in the bohemian Leopoldstadt
district.

Tostmann
1, Schottengasse 3a
Tel (1) 533 53 31
www.tostmann.at
Vienna's biggest and best shop
for traditional Austrian clothing
(tracht). Come here if you feel
you need a dirndl dress or some
lederhosen.

Vintage Flo
4, Schleifmühlgasse 15a
Tel (1) 586 07 73
www.vintageflo.com
Vienna's best vintage clothing
store, where you'll find fine couture from as much as a century
ago. Situated in Wieden.

Food & Drink

The Viennese take their food
and drink very seriously. Here's a
selection of stores where you can
purchase goodies—or have them
shipped home.

Altmann & Kühne
1, Graben 30
Tel (1) 533 09 27
www.altmann-kuehne.at
With a store designed by Josef
Hoffmann (see p. 55) and Wiener
Werkstätte–designed packag-
ing, the confectioner Altmann &
Kühne is an atmospheric slice of
fin-de-siècle Vienna. The candies
and chocolates are good, too.

Böhle
1, Wollzeile 30
Tel (1) 512 31 55
www.boehle.at
Upscale delicatessen and wine
cellar that sells a wide variety of
Austrian beers and wines, as well
as local culinary specialties.

Demel
1, Kohlmarkt 14
Tel (1) 535 17 17-0
www.demel.at
The shop attached to this famous confectioner and café stocks a huge variety of hard candies and boxes of chocolates.

Gerstner
1, Kärntner Strasse 13–15
Tel (1) 743 44 22
www.gerstner.at
In addition to its endless shelves of cakes, this former imperial confectioner displays boxes filled with dozens of small handmade chocolates.

Julius Meinl
1, Graben 19
Tel (1) 532 33 34
www.meinlamgraben.at
This giant store is the home of Vienna's finest purveyor of luxury and specialty foods. In addition to everyday items, the shop retails a wide variety of products from all over the world, as well as the finest Viennese coffee blends, handmade chocolates, and wines from the Wachau Valley.

Manner
1, Stephansplatz 7
Tel (1) 513 70 18
www.manner.at
The flagship store of an Austrian confectioner whose business was established in the 1890s with the motto "Chocolate for everyone." More affordable than the city's upscale confectioners, Manner's wafer biscuit, the *Manner Schnitten,* is consumed in vast quantities by the Viennese.

Unger & Klein
1, Gölsdorfgasse 2
Tel (1) 532 13 23
www.ungerundklein.at
This upscale wine store sells more than a thousand different varieties of wine, many of which are from around Vienna.

Xocolat
1, Freyung 2
9, Servitengasse 5
Tel (1) 535 43 63
www.xocolat.at
Vienna's newest chocolatier has already established a reputation for its irresistibly rich chocolates. The branch in Servitengasse also offers courses in chocolate-making.

Jewelry & Crafts

Vienna has been a renowned home of art and design for centuries, and this is reflected in the many stores around the city that still sell their own handmade products. Examples of the city's design heritage, including many objects designed by the Wiener Werkstätte, can be bought in the city, often from their original manufacturers.

Augarten
1, Spiegelgasse 3
Tel (1) 512 14 94
www.augarten.at
The city-center flagship store of Vienna's venerable porcelain manufacturer. Although Augarten is often associated with chintzy Biedermeier ornaments, this store demonstrates a variety of designs, which range from baroque ornaments to minimalist Jugendstil designs and colorful modern pieces.

Backhausen
1, Schwarzenbergstrasse 10
Tel (1) 285 25 02
www.backhausen.at
During the early 20th century Backhausen was closely associated with the Wiener Werkstätte, and still sells textiles, jewelry, and accessories based on the designs of Koloman Moser and Josef Hoffmann.

Frey Wille
6, Gumpendorfer Strasse 81
Tel (1) 599 25
www.frey-wille.com
A sleek modern jewelry store in Mariahilf that sells its own beautiful, if expensive, designs. Famous for its jewelry based on the work of Viennese artists Friedensreich Hundertwasser and Gustav Klimt.

MAK Design Shop
Museum of Applied Arts
1, Stubenring 5
Tel (1) 711 36-308
www.makdesignshop.at
This shop sells all manner of quirkily designed household objects. Some are the work of local design students, others are reproductions of iconic pieces of Wiener Werkstätte design.

Wallmann Lederwaren
14, Schanzstrasse 55/2
Tel (0) 650 861 77 55
www.wallmann-lederwaren.at
Traditional Viennese leather-working techniques have been revived by this small company based in Vienna's southern suburbs, near Ottakring. Products include stylish handbags, shoulder bags, and briefcases.

Wiener Silber Manufactur
1, Spiegelgasse 14
Tel (1) 513 05 00
www.wienersilbermanufactur
.com
The flagship store of a newly reopened Viennese silversmiths' workshop. The product range includes jewelry, ornaments, and elegant Wiener Werkstätte silverware that is made using Josef Hoffmann's original molds.

Entertainment

It's hard to get bored while staying in Vienna. Unsurprisingly for the self-proclaimed musical capital of Europe, Vienna's nightlife is dominated by live music. Visitors have many choices, with orchestral concerts, choral performances, and opera together with modern jazz and rock. The city's theater scene, though largely inaccessible to visitors who don't speak German, is worth checking out, and the city has a healthy collection of art-house movie theaters.

Live Music

Today, the city of Haydn, Beethoven, Mozart, and Strauss has no shortage of orchestras. These range from major international organizations to small ensembles put together to play Strauss to tourists. Those who don't much care for classical music will also find plenty to listen to in the city, however, as it has a lively jazz and rock scene.

Arena

3, Baumgasse 80
Tel (1) 798 85 95
www.arena.co.at
One of Vienna's few dedicated rock venues, located in a converted slaughterhouse in the far south of Landstrasse. Hosts gigs by local bands, as well as touring acts from across Europe.

Elektro Gönner

6, Mariahilfer Strasse 101
Tel (1) 208 66 79
www.elektro-g.at
Aptly located in a converted electrician's shop, this sleek modern venue has become one of Vienna's biggest venues for electronic music.

Fluc

2, Praterstern 5
www.fluc.at
This live-music venue and club is housed in a former pedestrian underpass close to Praterstern Station. Its location in a concrete-walled underground chamber means that acts don't have to worry about breaching noise regulations. The venue attracts touring pop and rock bands from across Europe and the United States, as well as plenty of local bands.

Jazzland

1, Franz-Josefs-Kai 29
Tel (1) 533 25 75
www.jazzland.at
Vienna's oldest and best jazz club, located in the cellars under the Ruprechtskirche, Jazzland regularly attracts international stars, as well as a constant stream of local musicians.

Konzerthaus

3, Lothringerstrasse 20
Tel (1) 242 00-2
www.konzerthaus.at
Founded in the early 20th century, this classical concert venue has several halls of various sizes, each named for a famous Viennese composer. The music here tends to be a little more varied than in the Musikverein.

Musikverein

1, Bösendorferstrasse 12
Tel (1) 505 81 90
www.musikverein.at
The Musikverein is Vienna's oldest concert hall. It has two performance spaces, one for large orchestral pieces, the other for chamber music.

Orangery, Schönbrunn

Schlosskonzerte
13, Orangery, Schönbrunn Palace
Tel (1) 812 50 04-0
www.imagevienna.at
The small Schönbrunner Schlosskonzerte orchestra performs here. Concerts tend to be pretty light, mostly featuring music by Mozart and Johann Strauss.

Porgy & Bess

1, Riemergasse 11
Tel (1) 512 88 11
www.porgy.at
Housed in an attractive 19th-century theater, Porgy & Bess has been a fixture of the Viennese jazz scene since it first opened its doors in 1993.

Rhiz

8, Stadtbahnbogen 37
Tel (1) 409 25 05
www.rhiz.org
The home of avant-garde electronic music in Vienna. Events here tend to be more sedate than at Elektro Gönner.

Vienna Residence Orchestra

8, Auerspergstrasse 1
Tel (1) 817 21 78
www.wro.at
This orchestra is based in the grand baroque Palais Auersperg, located just behind the Parliament Building. They usually perform in full 18th-century costume, and stick to a repertoire of Mozart and Strauss. A bit touristy, but the impressive setting outweighs the cheesy presentation.

Movie Theaters

Vienna has plenty of movie theaters, including numerous large multiplexes dotted around the city. The listings pages of local newspapers and the local listings weekly *Falter* (*www.falter.at*) give a full explanation of what's playing where, and what language it's in. The following are some of the city's more notable venues.

Burg Kino

1, Opernring 19
Tel (1) 587 84 06
www.burgkino.at
This Viennese institution is set just across the Ringstrasse from the Burggarten. It is best known for its weekly showing of the Vienna-set classic film noir *The Third Man* (1949).

Filmcasino

5, Margaretenstrasse 78
Tel (1) 587 90 62
www.filmcasino.at
The opulent 1950s interior of this large movie theater makes it worth visiting, even if you don't really want to see a film.

Filmmuseum

1, Augustinerstrasse 1
Tel (1) 533 70 54
www.filmmuseum.at
Located in the basement of the Albertina (see pp. 113–114) the Filmmuseum is Vienna's most prestigious art-house cinema. The program is varied and unpredictable, with films shown in dozens of different languages (often without subtitles), but it's worth checking the listings in case there's something interesting showing.

Gartenbaukino

1, Parkring 12
Tel (1) 512 23 54
www.gartenbaukino.at
This sumptuously decorated 1960s movie theater shows a mixture of new releases and old favorites, often in their original language.

Opera

Vienna is probably the finest city in Europe for opera lovers, with four top-class opera houses and numerous one-off summer performances.

Staatsoper

1, Opernring 2
Tel (1) 513 15 13
www.wiener-staatsoper.at
Despite being one of the most prestigious opera houses in Europe, tickets for the Staatsoper are surprisingly cheap. The opera's repertoire cycles between several different productions each week, so you always have plenty of choice.

Theater-an-der-Wien

6, Linke Wienzeile 6
Tel (1) 588 85
www.theater-wien.at
The recently rejuvenated birthplace of Mozart's *The Magic Flute* hosts a year-round program of opera performances, including frequent premieres of new works.

Volksoper

9, Währinger Strasse 78
Tel (1) 514 44-3670
www.volksoper.at
Founded in the late 19th century as a relatively cheap alternative to the aristocratic Staatsoper, the Volksoper is home to slightly more adventurous productions than its famous rival. It has even been known to stage the occasional musical.

Wiener Kammeroper

1, Fleischmarkt 24
Tel (1) 512 01 00-77
www.kammeroper.at
Vienna's smallest opera house, the Kammeroper (Chamber Opera), is known for staging new operatic works and for searching out more obscure and little-performed gems from the baroque era.

Theater

For most visitors who do not speak fluent German, much of Vienna's theater scene will have only a very limited appeal. There are a few venues, however, that either stage productions in English or that put on shows that don't require much, if any, knowledge of the German language.

International Theatre

9, Porzellangasse 8
Tel (1) 319 62 72
www.internationaltheatre.at
A small theater owned and operated by a group of American expats. The company stages several plays each season, mostly 20th-century British and American works.

Ronacher Theater

1, Seilerstätte 9
Tel (1) 588 85
www.musicalvienna.at
This fine late-19th-century theater stages lively musicals, including many German translations of Broadway standards (which can be a rather peculiar experience).

Tanzquartier Wien

1, Museumsplatz 1
Tel (1) 581 35 91
www.tqw.at
Set within the MuseumsQuartier, this modern performance space stages modern dance productions from all over the world.

Vienna's English Theatre

8, Josefsgasse 12
Tel (1) 402 12 60-21
www.englishtheatre.at
Founded in 1963, this medium-size professional theater company is a firm favorite with visitors and the city's large English-speaking community. It stages a mixture of productions imported from Britain and the U.S., 20th-century classics, and, occasionally, original works.

Activities

Vienna is a fairly sedate, stately city, not much given to extreme sports. Indeed, with its low-lying landscape and sluggish river, there aren't many opportunities for anything too active. That said, Vienna does offer some outdoor activities, especially in the summer when the Viennese flock to the city's green spaces and riverfronts.

Cycling

There are several bike rental companies in Vienna, offering well-maintained bikes for reasonable prices. Many of them are based in or around the Prater. If you don't feel you'll be using a bike that much, however, it might be worth looking into the Vienna Citybike program (see pp. 242–243).

Enzovelo
9, Spittelauer Lände 11
Tel (1) 310 05 45
www.enzovelo.at
Also rents electric bikes.

Fahrradverleih Prater
2, Prater Hauptallee, Parzelle 94
Tel (0) 676 635 73 88
www.fahrradverleih-prater.at

Pedal Power
2, Ausstellungsstrasse 3
Tel (1) 729 72 34
www.pedalpower.at

Radverleih Hochschaubahn
2, Prater 113
Tel (0) 676 635 73 88
www.radverleih-hochschaubahn.com

Vienna Explorer
12, Haidmanngasse 8
Tel (1) 890 96 82
www.viennaexplorer.com

Rock Climbing

Vienna makes up for its general lack of mountains with a large number of indoor and outdoor artificial climbing walls. The most prominent of these runs up the side of the *flakturm* (see p. 205) in Esterházypark.

Kletterhalle Wien
22, Erzherzog-Karl-Strasse 108
Tel (1) 890 46 66-0
www.kletterhallewien.at
Austria's largest indoor climbing wall, with carefully designed routes for everyone from absolute beginners to seasoned pros.

Kletterzentrum Flakturm
6, Fritz-Grünbaum-Platz 1
Tel (1) 585 47 48
www.oeav-events.at/flakturm
Reasonably experienced climbers will appreciate this unusual climbing wall, which rises 112 feet (34 m) above the streets of Mariahilf up the side of a Second World War antiaircraft tower. It provides a challenging climb as well as excellent views of the city.

Sailing

There are two sailing schools based on the calm waters of the Alte Donau.

Segelschule Hofbauer
22, An der Oberen Alten
Donau 191
Tel (1) 204 34 35
www.hofbauer.at

Segelschule Irzl
22, An der Unteren Alten
Donau 29
Tel (1) 203 67 43
www.irzl.at

Swimming Pools

Outdoor swimming pools have been an important part of summer in Vienna for more than a century. Today these pools range from family-friendly water parks to stylish hangouts that double as nightclubs.

Badeschiff
On the Donaukanal between Schwedenplatz and Urania,
Innere Stadt
www.badschiff.at
The Badschiff (pool-boat) swimming pool is in a barge moored on the Donaukanal. The floating leisure complex is also home to a restaurant and bar.

Krapfenwaldbad
19, Krapfenwaldgasse 65–73
Tel (1) 320 15 01
This large pool is located in the foothills of the Wienerwald at the northern end of Döbling. It is positioned on a hilltop terrace that offers spectacular panoramic views of Vienna.

Schönbrunner Bad
12, Schlosspark 1
Tel (1) 817 53 53
www.schoenbrunnerbad.at
The former swimming pool of the Habsburg royal family now provides a unique setting for swimming and sunbathing, with a great view of the Schönbrunn Palace and its gardens.

Strandbad Gänsehäufel
22, Moissigasse 21
Tel (1) 269 90 16
www.gaensehaeufel.at
Located on its own private island in the Alte Donau, the Strandbad Gänsehäufel is the biggest of the Alte Donau's many swimming pools (see p. 168).

INDEX

ILLUSTRATIONS CREDITS